Word and Story
in C. S. Lewis

Edited by Peter J. Schakel
and Charles A. Huttar

University of Missouri Press
COLUMBIA AND LONDON

Library of Congress Cataloging-in-Publication Data

Word and story in C. S. Lewis / edited by Peter J. Schakel and
   Charles A. Huttar.
        p.   cm.
      ISBN 0-8262-0760-X (alk. paper)
      1. Lewis, C. S. (Clive Staples), 1898–1963—Fictional works.
   I. Schakel, Peter J. II. Huttar, Charles A. (Charles Adolph),
   1920–   .
     PR6023.E926Z98   1991
     823'.912—dc20   90-48193
                                                          CIP

Designer: Liz Fett
Typesetter: Connell-Zeko Type & Graphics
Printer: Thomson-Shore, Inc.
Binder: Thomson-Shore, Inc.
Typeface: Elante

Contents

II. *Narrative*

Acknowledgments

We are grateful to the editors of *Word and World* and *VII: An Anglo-American Literary Review* for permission to reprint the essays by Gilbert Meilaender and Michael Murrin. We are grateful also to the Executors of the Estate of C. S. Lewis for permission to quote from unpublished letters of Lewis and to the Marion E. Wade Center at Wheaton College, Wheaton, Illinois, and the Bodleian Library, Oxford—each of which has a collection of Lewis manuscripts and copies of originals held by the other—for approval to publish the quotations.

Assistance in preparing the manuscript was provided by Hope College. We acknowledge with thanks the help and support of Provost Jacob Nyenhuis and Dean Bobby Fong. And we are deeply grateful to Myra Kohsel for her excellent typing of the entire manuscript and for retyping, without complaint, major sections of it.

P.J.S.
C.A.H.

Abbreviations

Books by C. S. Lewis are cited from the first editions; essays, in most cases, from modern reprints (with the date of original publication given in parentheses). The following abbreviations of titles are used for those works by C. S. Lewis referred to most frequently in this book. For works by other authors which are available in many editions, an edition is specified in the notes only when pagination is significant.

Abol	*The Abolition of Man: or, Reflections on Education with Special Reference to the Teaching of English in the Upper Forms of Schools.* London: Oxford University Press, 1943.
"Blu"	"Bluspels and Flalansferes: A Semantic Nightmare" (1939). In *Selected Literary Essays,* edited by Walter Hooper, 251–65. Cambridge: Cambridge University Press, 1969.
Experiment	*An Experiment in Criticism.* Cambridge: Cambridge University Press, 1961.
HB	*The Horse and His Boy.* London: Geoffrey Bles, 1954.
"Lang"	"The Language of Religion." In *Christian Reflections,* edited by Walter Hooper, 129–41. London: Geoffrey Bles, 1967.
LB	*The Last Battle.* London: Bodley Head, 1956.
Letters	*Letters of C. S. Lewis,* edited by W. H. Lewis. London: Geoffrey Bles, 1966.
LWW	*The Lion, the Witch and the Wardrobe.* London: Geoffrey Bles, 1950.
Malcolm	*Letters to Malcolm: Chiefly on Prayer.* London: Geoffrey Bles, 1964.
MC	*Mere Christianity.* London: Geoffrey Bles, 1952.

Mir	*Miracles: A Preliminary Study.* London: Geoffrey Bles, 1947.
MN	*The Magician's Nephew.* London: Bodley Head, 1955.
NP	*Narrative Poems,* edited by Walter Hooper. London: Geoffrey Bles, 1969.
"OnS"	"On Stories." In *Essays Presented to Charles Williams,* edited by C. S. Lewis, 90–105. London: Oxford University Press, 1947.
OSP	*Out of the Silent Planet.* London: Bodley Head, 1938.
PC	*Prince Caspian.* London: Geoffrey Bles, 1951.
Per	*Perelandra.* London: Bodley Head, 1943.
PH	(With E. M. W. Tillyard) *The Personal Heresy: A Controversy.* London: Oxford University Press, 1939.
Poems	*Poems,* edited by Walter Hooper. London: Geoffrey Bles, 1964.
PR	*The Pilgrim's Regress: An Allegorical Apology for Christianity, Reason and Romanticism.* London: J. M. Dent, 1933.
Preface	*A Preface to Paradise Lost.* London: Oxford University Press, 1942.
SC	*The Silver Chair.* London: Geoffrey Bles, 1953.
SJ	*Surprised by Joy: The Shape of My Early Life.* London: Geoffrey Bles, 1955.
SW	*Studies in Words.* Cambridge: Cambridge University Press, 1960.
THS	*That Hideous Strength.* London: Bodley Head, 1945.
TWHF	*Till We Have Faces: A Myth Retold.* London: Geoffrey Bles, 1956.
VDT	*The Voyage of the "Dawn Treader."* London: Geoffrey Bles, 1952.

Word and Story
in C. S. Lewis

Introduction

Peter J. Schakel

Words and stories fascinated C. S. Lewis from his earliest years. He grew up in a home and environment which created and fed that fascination. It was nourished particularly by his father, who had the Irishman's legendary volubility and effervescence. Lewis describes in the second paragraph of his autobiography his father's love of eloquence and anecdote:

> He was fond of oratory and had himself spoken on political platforms in England as a young man. . . . He was fond of poetry provided it had elements of rhetoric or pathos, or both. . . . [He was], almost without rival, the best *raconteur* I have ever heard; the best, that is, of his own type, the type that acts all the characters in turn with a free use of grimace, gesture, and pantomime. He was never happier than when closeted for an hour or so with one or two of my uncles exchanging "wheezes" (as anecdotes were oddly called in our family). (SJ, 12)

Lewis resisted, and built defenses against, his father's influence in several areas (his own emotional reserve was probably a reaction against his father's excessive emotionalism, for example). But in his passion for language and story, he was clearly his father's son. His love of "good talk"—of eloquent argument, witty repartee, and humorous tale—is proverbial.

His interest in language and story goes beyond talk, however; he gave much thought to both and developed theories regarding their importance. He considered the nature of word and story in themselves and the connection between word and the Word, between story and Story. The thesis of this book is that an awareness of Lewis's ideas about language and narrative is essential to a full understanding and appreciation of his thought and works, and that this awareness is essential for all readers of Lewis, for those interested in his religious thought as well as his literary theory, for those who love his stories and those who prefer his essays, for highly educated readers as well as "general" readers. Most of the book deals with familiar parts of the Lewis canon: his fairy tales, adult fiction, religious writings, and works of literary criticism; but it also examines works which have not received much (or adequate) attention elsewhere: his poetry, *The Dark Tower, After Ten Years,* and *Studies in Words,* for example.

For the sake of order and unity, the book focuses on two crucial essays by Lewis, one on language, "Bluspels and Flalansferes," published in 1939, and one written in 1940 and published seven years later under the title "On Stories." Thus, within a year or perhaps two, Lewis wrote an essay theorizing about language and a closely related essay theorizing about story; both deal with the imaginative experience of literature, both emphasize the achievement of "meaning" in art, both seek to show the influence of art upon life. The significance of the essays—written during two rich, productive years when Lewis's dominant ideas were still being shaped—deserves to be explored. This book conducts such an exploration from a number of approaches and viewpoints, all unified by an effort to relate and clarify two key passages from these essays.

The first half of the book focuses on the final paragraph of "Bluspels and Flalansferes," a passage near the heart of Lewis's theories regarding language:

> It will have escaped no one that in such a scale of writers the poets will take the highest place; and among the poets those who have at once the tenderest care for old words and the surest instinct for the creation of new metaphors. It must not be supposed that I am in any sense putting forward the imagination as the organ of truth. We are not talking of truth, but of meaning: meaning which is the antecedent condition both of truth and falsehood, whose antithesis is not error but nonsense. I am a rationalist. For me, reason is the natural organ of truth; but imagination is the organ of meaning. Imagination, producing new metaphors or revivifying old, is not the cause of truth, but its condition. . . . If those original equations, between good and light, or evil and dark, between breath and soul and all the others, were from the beginning arbitrary and fanciful—if there is not, in fact, a kind of psycho-physical parallelism (or more) in the universe, then all our thinking is nonsensical. But we cannot, without contradiction, believe it to be nonsensical. ("Blu," 265)

In the first essay of this collection, Lyle Smith clarifies the theory of metaphor the passage builds on and locates Lewis within the present-day "world" of metaphorical theorists. Lewis was drawn toward the "collusion" or "resemblance" approach to metaphor—that metaphor makes us aware of previously unnoticed similarities between things (consistent with his adherence to Platonism)—in contrast to I. A. Richards and other more recent theorists who deny referentiality and hold that metaphor creates its own meaning. Lewis's formal treatments of metaphor can be considered under three related categories: semantic (where the influence of Owen Barfield is evident), predicative, and referential (in both of which he anticipates the ideas of Paul Ricoeur). He also anticipates Max Black through development of his own "tensive" theory of the way metaphor works, recognizing the necessity of keeping both the metaphorical and the literal meaning of the terms of a metaphor in view simultaneously.

The influence of Barfield and disagreement with Richards appear equally in *Studies in Words,* which reveals further Lewis's interest in meaning. It traces the history of changes in a number of words and phrases in order to keep readers from misunderstanding older literature, particularly from misunderstandings created by the then-current methodology of New Criticism, popularized by I. A. Richards. In his study of the book, Michael Covington argues that although Barfield's influence is evident, there are significant differences between his ideas and Lewis's: whereas Lewis uses culture to explain meaning-changes, Barfield uses meaning-changes to reconstruct culture. Lewis ends up midway between Barfield's theory of all-pervasive metaphor and the scientific literalism of Richards and C. K. Ogden.

The next two essays in this volume trace the influence of Barfield's ideas on Lewis's handling of language in the Ransom trilogy. Verlyn Flieger explains how Lewis's invented language, Old Solar, and his invented fictive world, Malacandra, dramatically illustrate Barfield's concepts of original participation and semantic unity (the "original equations . . . between breath and soul and all the others" in the passage quoted above). In *Out of the Silent Planet,* Lewis adapts Barfield's ideas and links them with the mythos of Christianity so that each validates the other. Suggesting that Lewis grappled with linguistic issues primarily in his poetry and fiction rather than theorizing extensively about them, Gregory Wolfe posits that language is the predominant metaphor unifying all three of the Ransom novels. Lewis blends Barfield's ideas about the "evolution of consciousness" with a form of Christian Platonism. Language reveals our moral condition and can help us grow imaginatively, becoming more attuned to our relationship to the world, integrating soul and body (as modeled in the Incarnation). The trilogy, Lewis's attempt to revive the reader's mythopathic capacity, conveys his concern about the decay of language through abstraction and the failure of imagination. Wolfe believes, however, that Lewis's Platonism prevents him from developing a clear answer to the problem of recovering incarnational language and imagination.

Thomas Werge disagrees. He argues that at the heart of Lewis's reasoned apologies for Christianity in *Miracles* are images—invariably literal, ultimately sacred. Contrary to the gnostic, Platonic, and demythologizing traditions that severed faith from material imagery, Lewis posits the necessity and inevitability of image and metaphor. The Incarnation provides the ontological ground for the integrity of the literal, in life as in metaphor; only through image and the imagination—the methods central to Lewis's apologetics—can the salvific mystery be directly apprehended. Charles Huttar's study of Lewis's poetry has two themes in common with Werge's examination of the apologetics, the critique of modernism and the emphasis on the need for concrete experience rather than abstraction. Lewis's love of playing with the sensory qualities of poetry is one way of providing for this need. But the poetry also uses semantics as a tool in the critique of modernism; here Huttar's analysis supplements Smith's and Covington's accounts of the Lewis-Richards controversy. And Lewis's poetry examines the fundamental role of language as a human attribute, one that reveals both our greatness and our limitations. Central to our limitations, in Lewis's view, is that language—even the language of poetry—is too abstract to capture reality completely. How Lewis conceived of narrative as a way of getting beyond this limitation becomes a dominant theme in the second section of this book.

The final essay of the first half, by Stephen Medcalf, deals with the relation between Lewis's personae—the series of selves he projects in his various works—and his style in those works. Lewis simultaneously employs a mask and desires strongly to shatter that mask. Medcalf analyzes how struggles with personae affect Lewis's prose, especially its diction, syntax, rhythm, and tone, in three fairly distinct periods of Lewis's career. He finds Lewis moving from the "New Look" of the twenties and early thirties, antiromantic and anti-introspective, to the classical-idealist Christian persona of the mid-thirties through the mid-fifties, with its classic English prose style evoking familiar, "stock" responses. Finally, after 1955, Lewis accepts consciousness of consciousness and achieves a more immediate style, less classical and polished, able (as in *Till We Have Faces* and *After Ten Years*) to enter and convey an alien consciousness and expression, not limited (as in the Ransom trilogy) to mirroring his own.

The second half of the book focuses on a passage near the end of "On Stories" that is central to Lewis's ideas about story:

To be stories at all they must be series of events: but it must be understood that this series—the *plot*, as we call it—is only really a net whereby to catch something else. The real theme may be, and perhaps usually is, something that has no sequence in it, something other than a process and much more like a state or quality. . . . In life and art both, as it seems to me, we are always trying to catch in our net of successive moments something that is not successive. ("OnS," 103, 105)

Gilbert Meilaender shows that ideas stemming from this passage anticipated theological trends of the past two decades by affirming, in theory as well as practice, the importance of story for communicating Christian belief. As "net" and "narrative," story involves a tension between the timeless and the temporal, just as life is a succession of attempts in time to catch something outside time. Story can convey, as abstract theology cannot, the *quality* of the tension in human experience of being able to touch the Eternal but not (within history) to rest in it. Abstraction, though it has its place and importance, involves a loss of immediacy; Lewis's writings appeal in part because of their immediacy, because they convey the quality, the feel, of living in a world which unifies plot and theme, knowledge of God and experience of what it is to be human.

The issues of abstraction and temporality, explored by Meilaender, are applied by Mara Donaldson to *Till We Have Faces*, Lewis's finest fictional work. To attempt to transcend the limitation of temporality, Lewis gives three "retellings" of the central story. These become less and less linear, shifting from a "profane" (temporal) telling to an increasingly "sacred" (timeless) telling, from plot (narrative) to theme (the power of narrative to transform a life). Going beyond Meilaender, Donaldson argues that Lewis's theory of "net" (or Logos) and "narrative" (or Poiema) is inadequate to account for what he achieves in practice; it needs to be supplemented by the ideas of "episode" (linear temporality) and "configuration" (eliciting a pattern from succession) from another twentieth-century theorist, Paul Ricoeur, whose theories regarding story are having a major influence on contemporary theology.

Donaldson's analysis of the way Lewis's story *Till We Have Faces* is about the nature of and importance of story is followed by Donald Glover's discussion of Lewis's exploration of fictionality—and the pitfalls posed by it—in *Perelandra*. Through theory and example Lewis raises questions about truth in fiction: Why do we believe what we read in a story? How do we know what is truth? At the heart of the Unman-Lady-Ransom debate is the nature of story, its potential for glory and its vulnerability to distortion. What is elsewhere an aspect of the theory of story Lewis accepted, here becomes a threat to the Lady's soul: the ability of story to release us from one reality into countless possibilities of others becomes a temptation to choose Story over Life. As Ransom gains an understanding of his own role in the debate and in the actions on Malacandra, he learns also how to discern "bent" fiction and use of language from the true.

One of the means Glover notes for discerning fictional truth is literary tradition. The writer must stay "focused on the models which have carried truth through the ages." The next group of essays in the book examines the models to which Lewis gave most attention in his theory and practice. John D. Haigh believes that the most important such model for Lewis was the medieval and later prose romance, growing out of the epic poem. Lewis, in theory and practice, turned from the modern novel and the "realistic" criticism that dominated literary study during most of his lifetime and offered in their place a unified clarification and defense of the romance. While fiction employing "realism of content" might at first seem "immediate" and the romance "abstract," removed from experience, Haigh shows that for Lewis the opposite is true: realistic fiction comes across as a sort of isolated analysis of life, while through the imagination romance gets at truth, the deeper and universal aspects of human experience that can be touched only through myth and archetype.

Paul Piehler examines a second literary model by which truth is focused in Lewis's fiction, the medieval allegory, subject of Lewis's most extensive theoretical studies. Piehler shows that Lewis's statements about allegory are generally inadequate because they fail to distinguish between the "allegory of demystification" (exemplified in Lewis's failed allegory, *The Pilgrim's Regress*) and the "allegory of vision" (present in the great medieval allegories Lewis loved). In practice, however, Lewis's later fiction revives and incorporates features of the finest medieval allegory, particularly through employment of archetypal patterns. Here Piehler carries farther Haigh's examination of archetypes in the romance. Like the "visionary romance," "visionary allegory" can speak to depths of human experience "realistic fiction" cannot reach.

Jared Lobdell, bringing forth a third model, argues that Lewis's Ransom trilogy is a product of eighteenth-century as well as medieval influences. He holds that in these stories Lewis combines medieval pageantry (detailed description, gilding, "realism of presentation") with the didactic emphasis of the eighteenth-century "novel of ideas." The "narrative" of detailed accounts of daily life creates a "net" of moral pageantry in a unique combination that reminds one not so much of H. G. Wells or David Lindsay, as of Defoe, Swift, Fielding, or Johnson. Lobdell's essay includes extended assessment of *The Dark Tower*, the authenticity of which has been the subject of recent controversy; this is not only one of the few critical studies to give extended attention to *The Dark Tower*, but also is timely in its demonstration that such concern is worthwhile.

In addition to literary traditions as a means of focusing the truth of fiction, Glover points also to structural means, particularly the juxtaposition of story against story in *Perelandra*. Michael Murrin's essay extends that point, showing that narrative throughout the Narnian Chronicles is grounded in an interactive juxtaposition, or dialectic, between worlds—usually our universe and Narnia, sometimes with parallel worlds or a mirrored higher world added. The dialectic of multiple worlds reflects the tension between Lewis's main sources (the dialogues of Plato and the tradition of the German romantic art fairy tale). This dialectic draws one (through a longing aroused by ideal scenes irresistibly desired) to journey out of oneself, it helps establish traditional morality, and it creates a sense of discrimination between the true and the false, the evil and the good.

Colin Manlove describes other patterns by which such discrimination is made possible. Juxtaposed dialectically in Lewis are linear and circular patterns of movement. Through patterns of dislocation, escape from enclosures, and journeys out of the self, the reader is led to see events in terms of an ever-widening pattern of interrelationships: fiction and reality, accident and design, are closely entwined. The narrative structure imitates the character of divine reality. But simultaneously there is a pattern of circularity, of return or "regress," in Lewis's works and in his career, as his last book comes back to the concerns and structures of the first. Each pattern needs the other, and together they help us discern Lewis's vision of truth.

In the final essay of the collection, word and story—though they have overlapped throughout the collection—come together in a more complete way. Allegory is a narrative form, but one which employs words in a particularly dynamic, fluid way. It is a radically linguistic procedure, one which has come to be highly valued and emphasized in modern critical theory. Marius Buning applies such theory to *Perelandra*. It is a story deeply concerned with language; its exploration of the relation of language and myth to truth and essence can be illuminated and clarified by examining it through the categories supplied by a modern allegorical model.

Buning's essay and several others are necessarily rather theoretical. Despite that, the editors intend the collection for all serious readers of Lewis, partly because most of it is applied rather than abstract, partly because of the importance of the subjects to Lewis as fiction writer, poet, critic, and apologist. The book does not exhaust word and story in Lewis—because of their breadth and importance, much more can and will be said about them. It aims, rather, to explore an area previously neglected in Lewis studies and thus to stimulate further study and debate that will lead to a fuller, more accurate grasp of Lewis's thought, work, and influence.

I. Language

IT WILL HAVE ESCAPED no one that in such a scale of writers the poets will take the highest place; and among the poets those who have at once the tenderest care for old words and the surest instinct for the creation of new metaphors. It must not be supposed that I am in any sense putting forward the imagination as the organ of truth. We are not talking of truth, but of meaning: meaning which is the antecedent condition both of truth and falsehood, whose antithesis is not error but nonsense. I am a rationalist. For me, reason is the natural organ of truth; but imagination is the organ of meaning. Imagination, producing new metaphors or revivifying old, is not the cause of truth, but its condition. It is, I confess, undeniable that such a view indirectly implies a kind of truth or rightness in the imagination itself. I said at the outset that the truth we won by metaphor could not be greater than the truth of the metaphor itself; and we have seen since that all our truth, or all but a few fragments, is won by metaphor. And thence, I confess, it does follow that if our thinking is ever true, then the metaphors by which we think must have been good metaphors. It does follow that if those original equations, between good and light, or evil and dark, between breath and soul and all the others, were from the beginning arbitrary and fanciful—if there is not, in fact, a kind of psycho-physical parallelism (or more) in the universe, then all our thinking is nonsensical. But we cannot, without contradiction, believe it to be nonsensical.

"Bluspels and Flalansferes"

C. S. Lewis and the Making of Metaphor

Lyle H. Smith, Jr.

C. S. Lewis, himself a skillful user of metaphor, wrote about metaphor occasionally. His thoughts on the subject are always provocative, but also almost always "by the way"—he needs to talk about metaphor for a moment so that he can talk about something else more clearly. When he does talk about metaphor, he is concerned with what it does, rather than with how it works. If we read Lewis for a clearly articulated theory of metaphor, such as those of I. A. Richards, Max Black, Monroe Beardsley, Douglas Berggren, Marcus Hester, Philip Wheelwright or Paul Ricoeur, we shall not find it. It would be surprising if we did, for Lewis was a literary historian, Christian apologist, and writer of fiction, not a linguist or a rhetorician.

However, it can be demonstrated that, like many postwar theorists of metaphor, Lewis rejected the old assumption of post-Aristotelian classical rhetoric that metaphor is simply a disposable verbal decoration or, at its worst, a deviant substitute for a more literal term. He readily saw that metaphors could be used in those ways. But he championed the idea that metaphor could also function cognitively and heuristically. Modern theories about metaphor generally support Lewis's conclusions about what it does and how it performs its cognitive and heuristic tasks.

Metaphoric theory has become a glamour item in literary, philosophic, and linguistic circles in the last several years, as Mark Johnson explains:

> We are in the midst of a metaphormania. Only three decades ago the situation was just the opposite: poets created metaphors, everybody used them, and philosophers (linguists, psychologists, etc.) ignored them. Today we seem possessed by metaphor. As Wayne Booth has mused, judging from the jump in interest in metaphor between 1940 and the present, if we extrapolate to the year 2039, there will then be more students of metaphor than there are people.[1]

1. Johnson, Preface to *Philosophical Perspectives on Metaphor,* ed. Mark Johnson (Minneapolis: University of Minnesota Press, 1981), ix.

Although Johnson emphasizes the increase in attention to metaphor in the postwar era, the major shift in thinking about metaphor dates to the 1920s, when I. A. Richards, in *Principles of Literary Criticism* (1924), challenged the conventional designation of metaphor as an essentially decorative figure of speech, one of the "flowers of rhetoric," which if pruned would reveal an unadorned but "proper" and literal meaning. Classical rhetoric had for centuries classified the metaphor as a trope. As a result, metaphor was historically regarded as something extra laid onto literal meaning, which would be clearer without it. Philosophy regarded the metaphor as a nuisance. Hobbes attacked metaphor as a form of deception. The late seventeenth-century founders of the Royal Society strove for a plain, unadorned style of writing. Scientists prided themselves on their avoidance of figurative speech, and in our century logical positivists such as Gilbert Ryle have dismissed the metaphor as a logical aberration, designating it a "category mistake."

Richards challenged the assumption of a "proper," literal meaning behind the metaphor, suggesting strongly that the metaphor created its own meaning. Although Richards, too, ended up trivializing metaphor, reducing it to merely an indicator of emotive response, he nevertheless granted it more than a decorative function. Lewis's friend Owen Barfield challenged the claim of philosophy and science to metaphor-free language by demonstrating that all language is radically metaphorical. Ernst Cassirer, like Barfield, posited the radically metaphorical nature of language, asserting that as language itself first developed, it was not only metaphorical in nature, but inextricably intertwined with mental processes that produced myth.[2]

Once the importance of metaphor to language was firmly reestablished, interest turned to increasing the precision with which this importance was to be defined. The relation of metaphor to meaning was approached in two different and not altogether compatible ways. Karsten Harries distinguishes these two schools of thought as the "collision" and "collusion" theories. Paul Ricoeur, employing a different vocabulary and emphasizing somewhat different aspects of the two theories, refers to "resemblance" and "interaction." The "collusion" or "resemblance" theory stresses the comparative function of metaphor, emphasizing that metaphor brings to our attention the previously unapprehended similarities between things. The "colli-

---

2. Barfield, *Poetic Diction: A Study in Meaning* (London: Faber and Gwyer, 1928); Cassirer, *The Philosophy of Symbolic Forms* (1923–1929), trans. R. Mannheim, 3 vols. (New Haven: Yale University Press, 1953).

sion" or "interaction" theory (referred to by Max Black and Douglas Berggren as the "tensive" theory of metaphor) argues that metaphor, by displacing familiar meanings, actually creates new meanings.[3]

Not only is there some disagreement about how metaphor creates meaning, there is also disagreement about the kind of meaning metaphor can create. Structuralist criticism resembles the practice of the old Formalist school in denying the referentiality of metaphor, just as Formalism denied the referentiality of the poem to anything outside itself. On the other hand, there is a sizable body of theorists that champion the referentiality, hence the cognitive function, of metaphor. Some of the better-known figures in this latter group are Nelson Goodman, Philip Wheelwright, and Paul Ricoeur.[4]

Modern metaphorical theory, then, agrees in assigning metaphor a semantic function. Disagreement arises over (1) how this semantic function is carried out, and (2) whether or not this semantic function may also be considered a cognitive function—whether the fact that metaphor contributes to the meaning of a sentence makes metaphor a source of knowledge about reality as a whole, outside the structures of language. Obviously, this question is part of the larger question of whether language in general tells us about anything other than itself. (That it does, or even can, is strongly questioned by Deconstructionism.) The relevance of the foregoing discussion to C. S. Lewis's use of language should by this point be apparent. If language in general and metaphor in particular are nonreferential, this is a double blow to the work of Lewis as Christian apologist and myth-creator, since all he writes in these two roles is taken by his readers as referring not only to reality, but to an aspect of reality that is currently strongly challenged.

Lewis was primarily a literary historian. He paid relatively little formal attention to literary theory; his debate with E. M. W. Tillyard, *The Personal Heresy*, is one of his most extensive forays into that arena. He paid even less formal attention to linguistics, although, as he shows in *The Abolition of Man*, he was fully aware of some of the potentially harmful aspects of I. A. Richards's handling of the relation between truth and meaning in language. However, the student

3. Harries, "The Many Uses of Metaphor," in *On Metaphor*, ed. Sheldon Sacks (Chicago: University of Chicago Press, 1978), 71; Ricoeur, *The Rule of Metaphor* (1975), trans. Robert Czerny (Toronto: University of Toronto Press, 1977), 171; Black, "Metaphor" (1955), in Johnson, *Philosophical Perspectives*, 63–104; Berggren, "The Use and Abuse of Metaphor, I," *Review of Metaphysics* 16 (1962): 237–58.

4. Goodman, *Languages of Art: An Approach to a Theory of Symbols* (Indianapolis: Bobbs-Merrill, 1968); Wheelwright, *The Burning Fountain* (Bloomington: Indiana University Press, 1968); Ricoeur, *Rule of Metaphor*.

of Lewis can easily find, scattered throughout the corpus of his writings, enough evidence to show that Lewis indeed thought about metaphor a good deal. It is possible as well to determine Lewis's orientation on the subject of metaphor in relation to the current critical approaches that are briefly sketched above. Lewis strongly defended the cognitive function, hence the referentiality, of metaphor. And though there may be some evidence that Lewis charted his own path between the "resemblance" theorists on the one hand and the "interaction" or "tension" theorists on the other, he was ultimately committed to the theory that the human mind found preexisting meaning.

Lewis's view of metaphor is, not surprisingly, consistent with his adherence to Platonism. Far from thinking of metaphor as a creator of "new truth" or even new categories that create new insights, he held that metaphor does its work by showing resemblances—revealing categories that have been there all the time, but that human minds must uncover discursively. In keeping therefore with the conservative "resemblance" school of metaphoric theory, his formal treatments of metaphor concentrate on substitution metaphors, metonymy, and catachresis. Imagination, producer of new metaphors and revivifier of old ones, is for Lewis the "organ of meaning," as he puts it in the passage from "Bluspels and Flalansferes" that focuses our concerns in the first half of this volume. Imagination manifests the "psycho-physical parallelism (or more)" that must exist between our thoughts and reality if our thoughts are to make any sense at all. Metaphor in particular and language in general, then, enable us to get at the meanings of things. "All our truth, or all but a few fragments, is won by metaphor," Lewis says, and thus metaphor cannot be considered "arbitrary" or "fanciful" ("Blu," 265). Lewis's interest in metaphor, then, is overwhelmingly an interest in its ability to reveal, rather than create, meaning. Lewis's theory of metaphor, culled from the handful of pieces in which he wrote specifically on the subject, displays a primary concern with meaning and can be schematized into three related categories: semantic, predication, and reference.[5]

Semantic

Lewis's semantic of metaphor is based on his oft-repeated assertion that language itself is metaphorical in nature. In "Bluspels and

5. I should emphasize that the schematization created is mine, not Lewis's, and that it is not the only way Lewis's thinking on metaphor can be presented; unavoidably, it highlights some aspects of his thinking and obscures others.

Flalansferes" Lewis argues that language, even so-called literal language, is a tissue of metaphors, living and dead. Anyone who claims to speak literally forgets the dead metaphors buried in the "literal" words used. One who thinks to avoid metaphoric speech by defining or describing his ideas in nonmetaphoric language is only "changing the metaphors in rapid succession."

> Either literalness, or else metaphor understood: one or other of these we must have; the third alternative is nonsense. But literalness we cannot have. The man who does not consciously use metaphors talks without meaning. We might even formulate a rule: the meaning in any given composition is in inverse ratio to the author's belief in his own literalness. . . . Not all our words are equally metaphorical, not all our metaphors are equally forgotten. And even where the old metaphor is lost there is often a hope that we may still restore meaning by pointing to some sensible object, some sensation, or some concrete memory. But no man can or will confine his cognitive efforts to this narrow field. At the very humblest we must speak of things in the plural; we must point not only to isolated sensations, but to groups and classes of sensations; and the universal latent in every group and every plural inflection cannot be thought without metaphor. ("Blu," 262, 264)

The chapter "Horrid Red Things" in *Miracles* similarly argues the metaphorical nature of language and goes on from there to develop the implications for any sort of discussion of supersensible reality:

> The truth is that if we are going to talk at all about things which are not perceived by the senses, we are forced to use language metaphorically. Books on psychology or economics or politics are as continuously metaphorical as books of poetry or devotion. There is no other way of talking, as every philologist is aware. . . . All speech about supersensibles is, and must be, metaphorical in the highest degree. (*Mir*, 88)

Lewis's confidence in the radically metaphorical nature of language is consistent with a body of thought on metaphor that has been growing slowly since the late eighteenth century. In his own case, it stemmed largely from his agreement with Barfield, who argues on linguistic and anthropological grounds in *Poetic Diction* that the distinction between metaphorical and literal meanings of words is a relatively recent analytical distinction that had nothing to do with the way language originally developed. Rather, contends Barfield, these "*apparently* 'metaphorical' values were latent in meaning from the beginning." One may imply, he continues, that "the earliest words in use were 'the names of sensible, material objects' *and nothing more—* only, in that case, you must suppose the 'sensible objects' themselves to have been something more; you must suppose that they were not, as they appear to be at present, isolated, or detached, from thinking and feeling." Barfield concludes that

> men do not *invent* those mysterious relations between separate external objects, and between objects and feelings or ideas, which it is the function of poetry to reveal. These relations exist independently, not indeed of Thought, but of any individual thinker. . . . The language of primitive men reports them as direct perceptual experience. The speaker has observed a unity, and is not therefore himself conscious of *relation*. But we, in the development of consciousness, have lost the power to see this one as one.[6]

Lewis views imagination as the "organ of meaning" because it, not discursive reason, is the maker of metaphors. In "Bluspels and Flalansferes" Lewis calls Plato one of the "great creators of metaphor, and therefore among the masters of meaning" ("Blu," 265). Some of the wittiest passages in Lewis's apologetics occur where he challenges those who attack metaphoric utterance as "pseudo-statements" that create only the illusion of meaning and not its substance. Sometimes people who reject biblical concepts that are highly metaphorical in favor of more up-to-date and advanced theological descriptions generate genuine nonsense. He tells in *Miracles* of a girl "brought up by 'higher thinking' parents to regard God as a perfect 'substance'; in later life she realised that this had actually led her to think of Him as something like a vast tapioca pudding" (*Mir*, 90). The fatherhood of God is, to be sure, a metaphor. But it is a less misleading metaphor than "perfect substance" or "ground of being," largely because it is so manifestly a metaphor; the tension between our knowledge that God is a spirit and the concept of God as a father—a bodied creature fulfilling a biological function—is so great that we cannot forget that tension is present, that we are in fact dealing with a metaphor. A Galilean peasant, writes Lewis, might conceivably have thought that Christ had literally and physically "sat down at the right hand of the Father." If he then went to Alexandria and got a philosophical education, he would have learned to regard all that about throne rooms and painted chairs as being in fact metaphorical. But that realization would have made no difference in his belief; it was not the physical details he cared about. "What mattered must have been the belief that a person whom he had known as a man in Palestine had, as a person, survived death and was now operating as the supreme agent of the supernatural Being who governed and maintained the whole

6. Barfield, *Poetic Diction*, 85, 86–87.

field of reality" (*Mir*, 91). The belief could be detached from the image without suffering harm. And, Lewis notes, Church councils in the first centuries of the Christian era developed a series of definitions and creedal statements clearly demonstrating their understanding of the metaphorical nature of theological language. Meaning, at first expressed metaphorically and grasped with the imagination, was clarified and tested by reason.

Much modern debunking of poetic language and value statements in general turns upon the refusal of contemporary positivistic thought to recognize metaphor's cognitive value and upon positivism's reference to all metaphoric language and all predication of value (Lewis gave metaphor a significant predicative function) as "pseudo-statement." This position he takes to task in the first chapter of *The Abolition of Man*. He criticizes an unnamed elementary English textbook not only for belaboring the obvious—that the metaphorical statements are not literal statements—but also for going on to draw the conclusion that "all emotions aroused by local association are in themselves contrary to reason and contemptible" (*Abol*, 6). This conclusion is extended to all predicates of value, with the result that, although such statements "*appear* to be saying something very important," they are in reality "*only* saying something about our own feelings" (*Abol*, 4–5). Predications of value thus cannot be regarded as making valid truth claims.

Lewis begins *The Abolition of Man*, however, by contending that "Gaius and Titius" simply do not understand the relation of metaphor to meaning. They comment on an anecdote about Coleridge at a waterfall in the company of two others, one person calling the waterfall "sublime," the other calling it "pretty." Coleridge approved the first judgment but not the second. Gaius and Titius take the opposite tack, rejecting the first because, although the man who called the waterfall sublime "appeared to be making a remark about the waterfall . . . , actually . . . he was not making a remark about the waterfall, but a remark about his own feelings. What he was saying was really *I have feelings associated in my mind with the word 'Sublime,'* or shortly, *I have sublime feelings*" (*Abol*, 3). Lewis's rejoinder is worth quoting in full:

> Even if it were granted that such qualities as sublimity were simply and solely projected into things from our own emotions, yet the emotions which prompt the projection are the correlatives, and therefore almost the opposites, of the qualities projected. The feelings which make a man call an object sublime are not sublime feelings but feelings of veneration. If *This is sublime* is to be reduced at all to a statement about the

speaker's feelings, the proper translation would be *I have humble feelings*. If the view held by Gaius and Titius were consistently applied it would lead to obvious absurdities. It would force them to maintain that *You are contemptible* means *I have contemptible feelings*: in fact that *Your feelings are contemptible* means *My feelings are contemptible*.
(*Abol*, 4)

Lewis held that, far from producing meaningless pseudo-statements, metaphors—rightly understood for what they are—keep us equally from meaningless tautologies on the one hand and self-contradiction on the other. In addition, metaphor freely granted its predicative function enables us to make statements that are at once meaningful and true. He argues in the remainder of the chapter that "our approvals and disapprovals are thus recognitions of objective value or responses to an objective order" (*Abol*, 11), an order he finds in the very history of the world's philosophies and religions, in cultures advanced and primitive alike.

Thus Lewis was able to maintain that metaphor is cognitive—it gives us knowledge of reality. It is heuristic, giving us the foundation of meanings upon which serious philosophy may be built. It describes supersensibles, to which category ideas and predications of value surely belong. And metaphor involves the reader's emotions cognitively, making them participants in the process of knowing. Our feelings, though nonrational, are not for that reason contemptible. As Lewis affirms, "I had sooner play cards against a man who was quite sceptical about ethics, but bred to believe that 'a gentleman does not cheat,' than against an irreproachable moral philosopher who had been brought up among sharpers" (*Abol*, 13). Like the man who called the waterfall sublime, the noncheating card player experiences the validity of a connection between his behavior (whether verbal or card-playing) and a total order of reality, a context that in itself can only be spoken of in terms of metaphor, whether *ordo amoris*, the *Rta*, the Good, Nature, the Law, the Way, the Road, or the *Tao*—the Chinese term Lewis himself selects to refer to this order throughout the remainder of the book.

Predication

We have seen that Lewis, in his discussion of practical uses of metaphor, takes into consideration the entire utterance of which the metaphor is a part. In light of his interest in the relation between metaphor and meaning, this is hardly surprising. In doing so, he draws attention to metaphor's way of expressing not only value—as it does in the sentence "This waterfall is sublime"—but also the quality of a thing. In "The Language of Religion," Lewis goes into this matter at some length. Although he is primarily interested in distinguishing between the language of science and the language of religion, he points out that the language of religion and that of poetry are more alike than either is like the language of science.

Lewis must not be understood as equating poetic language solely with metaphor; indeed, he is careful throughout "The Language of Religion" to avoid suggesting any such oversimplification. Nonetheless, much of what he says about poetic language might be equally said of metaphor. Like metaphor, for instance, poetic language does a better job than scientific language of giving us an idea of the quality of an object. Whereas ordinary, conversational language might say of St. Agnes' Eve, "It was a very cold night," and scientific might say, "On such and such a night there were thirteen degrees of frost," poetic language says "Ah, bitter chill it was!" ("Lang," 129). (Lewis himself draws attention to the catachresis "bitter" without belaboring the issue of metaphoric language in Keats's poem.)

Poetic language is capable of arousing emotional responses without itself being emotional. Lewis writes that "poetry contains a great many more adjectives" than does prose. "Poets are always telling us that grass is green, or thunder loud, or lips red. It is not, except in bad poets, always telling us that things are shocking or delightful. . . . It seems anxious to bombard us with masses of factual information which we might, on a prose view, regard as irrelevant or platitudinous" ("Lang," 131). Poetic language, although it might also express emotion, does not evoke emotion for its own sake but "in order to inform us about the object which aroused the emotion" ("Lang," 132). Though inevitably triggering an affective response in the hearer or reader of the line "This waterfall is sublime," the metaphor is similarly a means of telling us something about the waterfall through our emotional response, which is in fact a recognition of the kinship between itself and the waterfall on the basis of shared membership within the larger reality.

Poetic language functions heuristically and cognitively. One of the more remarkable powers of poetic language, Lewis suggests, is its ability "to convey to us the quality of experiences which we have not had, or perhaps can never have, to use factors within our experience so that they become pointers to something outside our experience— as two or more roads on a map show us where a town that is off the map must lie" ("Lang," 133). An example of heuristic metaphor in poetry occurs in Shelley's *Prometheus Unbound* when Asia says, "My soul is an enchanted boat." Lewis says of this line, "If anyone thinks this is only a more musical and graceful way of saying 'Gee! this is fine,' I disagree with him. . . . Effortless and unimpeded movement to a goal desired but not yet seen is the point. If we were experiencing Asia's apotheosis we should feel like that. In fact we have never experienced apotheosis. Nor, probably, has Shelley. But to communicate the emotion which would accompany it is to make us know more fully than before what we meant by apotheosis" ("Lang," 133). Lewis concludes that such instances of poetic language are "by no means merely an expression, nor a stimulant, of emotion, but a real medium of information" ("Lang," 134).

Poetic language, then, including metaphor, tells about the quality of an object. That is its predicative function. In so doing it may also imply judgments of value, which we recognize by way of our emotional responses to them. By informing us of the quality, the "what kindness," of the object, moreover, poetic language leads us off the map of experience, suggesting associations with a larger order of reality than that presented explicitly in the poetic utterance. The English romantics, of course, are notorious for doing just this sort of thing, so Lewis's choice of Keats and Shelley as examples is an apt one.

Metaphor is a way of talking about inner states as well as values, as we have observed in Asia's metaphor describing her apotheosis. This function of metaphor is also very much the point of Lewis's description of allegory in *The Allegory of Love*. The personifications of the passions in Prudentius's *Psychomachia*, for instance, suggest an entire epic battle as a natural extension of the metaphors "internal conflict" and "warring passions." Metaphor is thus clearly capable of reference to a number of different things: to inner states, to the qualities of objects, to values, and to large ethical or philosophical frames of reference.

Reference

We have seen that as early as 1943, when *The Abolition of Man* was first published, the idea that metaphor referred only to the emotions of the speaker or writer and not to "objective reality" had already gained some currency. It was imported into literary criticism from the philosophical school of logical positivism, which stated that "all language that is not *descriptive,* in the sense of giving information about *facts,* must be *emotional.* Furthermore, the suggestion [was] that what is 'emotional' is sensed purely 'within' the subject and is not related in any way whatsoever to anything outside the subject."[7] The effect of this thinking made itself felt in the Formalist insistence that the literary work of art as a whole is self-contained, independent of any external structures, a "verbal icon." Deconstructionism has extended this notion to the level of words, so that the issue of poetic or even verbal referentiality is, if anything, even more pointed than it was in Lewis's time.

Lewis argues strongly for the referentiality of metaphor on much the same grounds that he argues for the validity of reason: if there is to be any thinking at all, reason must be valid. Otherwise, the statement "Reasoning is invalid," insofar as it is a reasoned statement, is itself invalid. Similarly, as Lewis argues in "Bluspels and Flalansferes," since all but a few fragments of our truth are won by metaphors (language being both necessary to thought and itself inescapably metaphorical in nature), if our thinking is true, our metaphors must have been valid; for unless there is "a kind of psycho-physical parallelism (or more) in the universe," "all our thinking is nonsensical" ("Blu," 265). That is to say, if our metaphors tell us nothing about the already-out-there-now real universe, then all our thinking about it that moves beyond simple descriptions to causes, relations, and meanings is about nothing at all. Both reason, the "organ of truth," and imagination, the "organ of meaning," must be allowed validity and reference respectively. Without either, meaningful thought is not possible.

For those who maintain that metaphor has reference, part of the difficulty has been the insistence of positivist philosophers and positivist-influenced linguists and literary critics on dividing all language between nonemotive and emotive, scientific and poetic—speech that is verifiable and speech that lies beyond the possibility either of verification or falsification. This division went on long before positivism and probably goes back to Plato's strictures in *The Republic* against the language of poets.

Plato's objection to poetic language (despite the fact that he was himself a poet and a formidable employer of metaphor) was that, when abused, it referred to reality merely at second hand, to the derivative reality of the phenomenal rather than the ultimate reality of the ideal world. The objection of the positivist critics of poetic language was quite the reverse, that it refers to no aspect of reality that is verifiable or falsifiable—that is, subject to scientific or quantitative operations—but to predicates of quality that lie wholly within

7. Ricoeur, *Rule of Metaphor*, 226–27.

the realm of mental or emotional events, themselves unobservable from outside. The standard line of defense against either the Platonic or the positivist attacks on poetic language has been to attempt to remove it entirely from the realm of truth. "The *Poet*, he nothing affirmeth," wrote Sidney in his *Defence of Poesie*.[8] In our own time, Valéry saw dance, movement without destination, as the paradigm of the poetic act.[9] In the modern English tradition, the catchword has been that the poem must not mean, but be.

Thus, poetry is saved from the clutches of the Platonist and the positivist critic by removing it entirely from the realm of meaning. But the cost of saving poetry thus is its destruction as significant discourse—a price Lewis was unwilling to pay. Lewis constantly maintains that language itself is metaphorical in nature, and that unless we wish to give over any pretense whatever to the meaningful use of language, we must accept that metaphorical quality. Language, moreover, is the only means we have of making truth claims. Likewise, it is the only means we have of debating the veracity of such claims. Unless we wish to give over the entire business of making and challenging claims to truth, we must accept the referentiality of language, metaphoricity and all. Otherwise, we must be ready to admit that statements such as "Metaphor is nonreferential" do not refer to anything except themselves. Such would probably be the starting point of any defense Lewis might make of the referentiality of metaphor.

In support of this assertion, we might recall the way in which Lewis dealt with Gaius and Titius in *The Abolition of Man*. In response to their argument that value judgments, being nonliteral, are not about their purported objects but merely about the speaker's emotions, Lewis demonstrated that by this reasoning their own judgments of value would have to refer only to their emotional states. The same point is applied directly to the referentiality of metaphor in the sermon "Transposition." Lewis is not talking here specifically about metaphor or even about language; he is talking about why many sorts of human experiences that are superficially similar are nevertheless qualitatively different. How, for instance, are we to know that glossolalia is not simply hysteria, love simply lust, justice simply revenge? By extension, we might similarly ask how it is that value judgments are not simply projections of emotion, and metaphors no more than

8. *The Prose Works of Sir Philip Sidney*, ed. Albert Feuillerat, 4 vols. (1912; reprint, Cambridge: Cambridge University Press, 1962–1965), 3:29.
    9. Ricoeur, *Rule of Metaphor*, 224.

expressions of feeling. How can we say that "My soul is an enchanted boat" is not to be literally rendered as "Gee! this is fine"? Gaius and Titius (and by extension Richards and others who reduce metaphor to the expression of emotion) might be collectively represented as an individual capable of perceiving only two dimensions in space. At first, he might be willing to take our word that three dimensions actually exist. But, if we pointed to a drawing of a road on a sheet of paper, he would probably reply that the shape we pointed to as evidence of the perspective of distance was the very same shape we freely confessed at other times to be a triangle. Soon, Lewis writes, he would say,

> You keep on telling me of this other world and its unimaginable shapes which you call solid. But isn't it very suspicious that all the shapes which you offer me as images or reflections of the solid ones turn out on inspection to be simply the old two-dimensional shapes of my own world as I have always known it? Is it not obvious that your vaunted other world, so far from being the archetype, is a dream which borrows all its elements from this one?[10]

Lewis's point, of course, is that one cannot understand what a two-dimensional drawing is about unless one understands three-dimensional reality. Similarly, language itself cannot properly be understood apart from a preexisting concept of meaning. The richer medium, reality, will always be represented in a poorer medium, whether picture or language, by elements that appear to be similar but actually mean very different things. Lewis's theory, as we noted at the outset, holds that metaphor functions in terms of resemblance, showing how things may be like one another without actually being identical. In fact, it is the very tension between the literal and figurative meanings of the metaphor that enables it to work at all, just as the tension between the two-dimensional representation and our knowledge of three-dimensional reality enables us to understand and appreciate a drawing—or, for that matter, a blueprint or a map. If metaphor lacked reference, it would cease to exist as metaphor.

Lewis and Postwar Theories of Metaphor

A comparison of Lewis's views with those of postwar linguistic theorists suggests not only that Lewis was an astute thinker on meta-

---

10. Lewis, "Transposition," in *Transposition and Other Addresses* (London: Geoffrey Bles, 1949), 15.

phor and very much in the subject's avant-garde, it also establishes, in
my opinion, the basic soundness of a theory of metaphor one finds
corroborated and developed by a variety of independent thinkers in
the United States and on the Continent.

Lewis started with the essentially metaphorical nature of language, a conviction influenced by the theories of Owen Barfield and
enunciated in "Bluspels and Flalansferes." Although this idea did not
originate with Barfield, it is not a very old one. It is romantic, going
back to Rousseau's *Essay on the Origin of Languages,* in which he
argued that "figurative language was the first to be born." Nietzsche,
writing "On Truth and Falsity in Their Ultramoral Sense," agrees
with Rousseau on the primacy of figurative language, going on to
claim that our experience and our very thought processes themselves
come to us metaphorically.[11] Shelley claimed that the language of
poets is "vitally metaphorical; that is, it marks the before unapprehended relations of things and perpetuates their apprehension,
until the words which represent them become, through time, signs
for portions or classes of thoughts instead of pictures of integral
thoughts,"[12] a process remarkably like that described by Lewis in the
formation of the imaginary metaphors "bluspels" and "flalansferes."
Less than a decade after the appearance of Barfield's *Poetic Diction,*
Richards was claiming in the fifth chapter of *The Philosophy of
Rhetoric* that not only language but the very mechanisms of thought
are metaphoric; "metaphor," Richards stated, "is the omnipresent
principle of language." Today it is widely accepted that language and
metaphor are inseparable. As Johnson notes, "Metaphor is no longer
confined to the realm of aesthetics narrowly conceived—it is now
coming to be recognized as central to any adequate account of language and has been seen by some to play a central role in epistemology and even metaphysics."[13]

The notion of the metaphorical nature of language, then, is widely
shared among modern theorists and is the starting point for any
discussion of what role metaphor plays in language. This role is
widely held to be that of catalyst, or even creator, of meaning, not
simply on the level of the single word, but on that of the sentence or
even of the entire verbal/conceptual context of which the metaphor

11. For Rousseau and Nietzsche, see Johnson, *Philosophical Perspectives,* 15.

12. Percy Bysshe Shelley, "A Defence of Poetry," in *Shelley's Critical Prose,* ed.
Bruce R. McElderry, Jr. (Lincoln: University of Nebraska Press, 1967), 6.

13. I. A. Richards, *The Philosophy of Rhetoric* (New York: Oxford University Press,
1936), 92; Johnson, *Philosophical Perspectives,* 3.

is a part. Lewis saw the imagination, the "organ of meaning," as the creator of new metaphors and the revivifier of dead ones. It is on this aspect of metaphor, its semantic function or the work it does as a conveyer of meaning, that Lewis's interest centers.

To convey meaning is in fact to predicate. The predicative function of metaphor encompasses its importance on the level both of the word and of the entire sentence. Classical rhetoric treated metaphor as a trope, an emphasis that limited the focus of investigation to the word. That limitation resulted in the relegation of metaphor to either verbal decoration or catachresis. Lewis argued forcefully for the importance of the metaphor on the level of discourse, of the statement as a whole. In this insistence he anticipates Ricoeur, who points out in *The Rule of Metaphor* the inadequacy of the merely tropological status of metaphor in traditional or classical rhetoric and argues that metaphor can be understood in semantic as well as semiotic terms— both as meaning and as sign. On the level of sign, the metaphor is considered as a word. On the level of meaning, it is considered as a part of discourse. In "Study Two" and "Study Three" of his book, Ricoeur argues that it is the sentence, not the word, that is the "primary unit of meaning" and that failure to recognize this function of the sentence is to stop language on the level of naming, merely pointing to things. As a consequence of this failure, metaphor would never be considered as more than a way of naming things. Berggren, similarly, stresses the importance of the context in which the metaphor is embedded.[14]

Such attention to context implies referentiality. Lewis would have opposed the view that metaphor, like poetry and like language in general, is "opaque," iconic, and without reference to fields of meaning outside the limits of its own conventions. Such a "verbal icon" view has found many proponents, not only within Formalism, but among linguists still heavily influenced by logical positivism. One such is Marcus B. Hester, who argues that metaphor generates images to be "contemplated as ends in themselves which do not necessarily correspond with either the physical world or 'reality.'"[15]

This position is strongly countered by Ricoeur, who devotes an entire chapter, "Study Seven," of *The Rule of Metaphor* to the issue of reference. We have already seen that Ricoeur carefully separates semiotic and semantic in his consideration of metaphor, a step that enables him to argue the ability of metaphor to refer to reality outside

14. See Berggren, "The Use and Abuse," 237.
15. Hester, *The Meaning of Poetic Metaphor* (The Hague: Mouton, 1967), 169.

itself: "The distinction between sense and reference is a necessary and pervasive characteristic of discourse, and collides head-on with the axiom of the immanence of language. There is no reference problem in language: signs refer to other signs *within* the same system. In the phenomenon of the sentence, language passes outside itself; reference is the mark of the self-transcendence of language." The distinction between sense and reference is equivalent to the distinction between semiotic and semantic. Ricoeur, building upon this distinction, admits that "the possibility that metaphorical discourse says something about reality collides with the apparent constitution of poetic discourse, which seems to be essentially nonreferential and centred on itself." Ricoeur avoids this collision by describing poetic discourse differently: "The suspension of literal reference [which is what happens when a metaphor is used] is the condition for the release of a power of second-degree reference, which is properly poetic reference. Thus, to use an expression borrowed from Jakobson, one must not speak only of split sense but of 'split reference' as well."[16] Ricoeur, in short, counters the idea of the nonreferentiality of metaphor by demonstrating that it is too simple. Lewis, in turning the language of Gaius and Titius back on itself, points implicitly to this idea of split reference—the simultaneous existence of literal and poetic reference in the metaphor when it is recognized as a metaphor.

The progress of the discussion to this point makes it appropriate to end by returning to the relation between Lewis's thinking about metaphor and the notion of metaphoric tensiveness. Although Lewis saw metaphor as revealing meaning by revealing resemblances between things or between ideas and aspects of nature, he did not fully agree that the meaning it reveals is already inherent in the resemblances. Instead, he charted a path of his own between that theory and the theory that metaphor creates new meanings—a notion first presented by Max Black and developed as the tensive theory of metaphor, which he also calls an "interaction view of metaphor." Black takes as his starting point this statement by Richards: "In the simplest formulation, when we use a metaphor we have *two thoughts of different things active together* and supported by a single word, or phrase, whose meaning is a resultant of their interaction" (my italics).[17] Lewis more than once anticipates the tensive theory in arguments he develops about the way in which metaphor works. In *Mira-*

16. Ricoeur, *Rule of Metaphor*, 74, 6.
17. Richards, *Philosophy of Rhetoric*, 93; quoted by Black, "Metaphor," 285.

cles he points out that modern metaphors about God, such as "force" or "perfect substance," are far less satisfactory than biblical metaphors, partly because, in the attempt to narrow the gap between the word and the thing itself, they encourage us to forget that metaphors are nevertheless still in use. A metaphor such as "father" applied to God, however, retains its obviously nonliteral character, enabling us to talk about God in metaphorical terms without forgetting that we are using metaphors. The tension between the biological metaphor "father" and the nonphysical nature of God is so strong that it cannot be neglected. The resulting cognitive dissonance, sustained throughout the history of theological discourse, makes for a far more sophisticated understanding of the complex and ultimately mysterious nature of God than does any attempt at metaphor revision (or demythologizing) that seeks to narrow the gap between the word and the thing.

Similarly, in "Transposition" Lewis develops a position that has certain affinities with the tensive theory of metaphor, when he points out that metaphoric resemblance—whether in the realm of emotions, physical sensations, or artistic representations of reality—presents not *only* resemblance but implicitly an understanding that resemblance is not identity; a thing can resemble another thing only if it is not that thing, and only if the difference between the two is apparent. Hence a two-dimensional picture may resemble three-dimensional reality, but it cannot do so effectively unless the viewer clearly understands the difference between the reality and the picture, and unless the viewer understands the conventions by means of which the picture represents its subject.

Lewis of course is not presenting a theory of metaphoric interaction as such in these passages, though he knew about Richards, whose hint Black developed into a full-fledged theory. However, he is implicitly presenting one of the correlatives of the tensive theory: the necessity of keeping both the metaphorical and the literal meanings of the terms of a metaphor in view simultaneously. This act is referred to by Berggren (following W. B. Stanford) as "stereoscopic vision"; Ricoeur and Jakobson, as we have seen, use the term "split reference."[18] Lewis's view of the double nature of metaphor is further borne out by later developments in the notion of metaphorical tensiveness by Berggren in 1962 and Ricoeur in 1975.

Much more could be said on the subject of Lewis's understanding and use of metaphor. The relationship between metaphor and myth

18. Berggren, "Use and Abuse," 243; Ricoeur, *Rule of Metaphor*, 6.

in Lewis, for instance, has not been touched upon, but the subject repays study and leads to some provocative ideas about the cognitive function of metaphor, implying strongly that metaphor makes possible an understanding not only of insensible reality, but of specifically spiritual aspects of reality. Such, at any rate, are the conclusions set forth by Dabney Adams Hart and Francis J. Morris.[19] Another subject that has not been touched upon here is the way in which Lewis employs metaphor in his own writing—his criticism and apologetics as well as his fiction.

As he is on any subject he takes up, Lewis is an engaging and stimulating writer when he considers the subject of metaphor. Indeed, his manner is so easy, the point of his discussion so immediate and practical, that the reader may often take as obvious common sense a statement on the meaning of figurative language that cost the writer years of experience and thought. But lifelong fans of Lewis— among whom I count myself—have found from the beginning that reading Lewis is always this way. We are led by the delights of a witty and transparent style to levels of insight often lying beyond what we, by our own powers, can reach unaided, but we arrive there with a sense of somehow having done it ourselves. For me, this is the essential mystery of Lewis's power as a user of words and a master of metaphor.

19. Hart, *Through the Open Door: A New Look at C. S. Lewis* (University, Ala.: University of Alabama Press, 1984), 15–16; Morris, "Metaphor and Myth: Shaping Forces in C. S. Lewis's Critical Assessment of Medieval and Renaissance Literature" (Ph.D. diss., University of Pennsylvania, 1977), 26, 43–44, 69.

C. S. Lewis as a Student of Words

Michael A. Covington

The place and importance of C. S. Lewis's *Studies in Words* have not been widely recognized. Based on a series of lectures Lewis gave to Cambridge undergraduates about English words that have changed meaning, its purpose is to warn readers of the danger of misreading older literature by taking a word in a newer sense when the author meant it in an older one. Lewis wants to develop his readers' instinct for recognizing possible changes in meaning until "the slightest semantic discomfort in one's reading rouses one, like a terrier, to the game" (SW, 1–2). He does not claim to be contributing to semantic theory or even presenting new data. Nonetheless, *Studies in Words* has become, and should be better known as, one of three or four standard works on change of meaning.[1] It also deserves to be better known as an important theoretical challenge to the then still influential methodology of New Criticism.

Studies in Words was published in 1960, late in Lewis's career, and the public received it with enthusiasm. An indication of Lewis's popularity is the fact that the book got four separate reviews, all favorable, in the *Times*, the *Sunday Times*, the *Times Literary Supplement*, and the *Times Educational Supplement*. Other favorable reviews appeared in periodicals ranging from the *Guardian* to the *Archives of Internal Medicine*.[2] Reviews in philological journals were

1. I know of only three good treatments of meaning change: Michel Bréal, *Semantics: Studies in the Science of Meaning* (1897), trans. Mrs. Henry Cust (1900; reprint, New York: Dover Publications, 1964) and Gustaf Stern, *Meaning and Change of Meaning* (1931; reprint, Bloomington: Indiana University Press, 1964), neither of which Lewis cites; and perhaps Stephen Ullmann, *Semantics: An Introduction to the Science of Meaning* (Oxford: Basil Blackwell, 1962).

2. Joe R. Christopher and Joan K. Ostling cite and annotate thirty-six reviews of *Studies in Words* (*C. S. Lewis: An Annotated Checklist of Writings about Him and His Works* [Kent, Ohio: Kent State University Press, 1973], 299–304); that in the *Guardian*, 9 September 1960, 6, is cited by *Book Review Digest*, 1961. See especially the comment

more varied. No scholarly reviewer found substantial errors in Lewis's data.[3] The noted linguist William G. Moulton gave Lewis good marks as a teacher and popularizer while noting his failure to connect his work with that of others: "Though he makes a reference or two to I. A. Richards, L[ewis] seems otherwise quite unaware of the fact that scholars before him have dealt with semantics, including semantic change. The book therefore has little to offer the professional beyond a delightful style and many well-chosen examples." Other reviewers dealt with this "amateurishness" more harshly.[4]

Lewis in fact makes very limited claims for *Studies in Words*. He describes the work as "at first my necessity and later my hobby" (*SW*, 1) and makes it clear that "it is not an essay in the higher linguistics" (*SW*, vii). It is simply a collection of practical advice for readers of literature who want to stay out of semantic traps. Worse, Lewis does something that no linguist would ever do: he expresses value judgments about how English ought to be used. Twentieth-century linguists insist on describing languages in a completely nonjudgmental way. This is a reaction against earlier pedagogical grammarians who often produced erroneous descriptions by letting their sense of "good grammar" or "good style" cloud their objectivity. So Lewis's exhortations against "verbicide" (the weakening of a word's meaning to near uselessness) grate on some scholars' nerves.[5] The answer, of course, is that scientific neutrality is merely a methodological tool, not a moral virtue. Lewis is studying Western language and culture, not as a visiting anthropologist, but as an active

---

of Paul Christophersen (*English Studies* 45 [1964]: 256–59), quoted by Christopher and Ostling (300).

3. Begislav von Lindheim (*Anglia* 74 [1961]: 62–64) offers a few minor corrections. *Geboren*, "born," cannot mean *hochgeboren*, "of noble birth," in German (contra Lewis, 31). And Lewis commits two German solecisms: he should have said *Völkerwanderung* instead of *Volkwanderung* (84) and *das Erlebte* instead of "the *erlebt*" (148).

4. Moulton, review of *Studies in Words, Romance Philology* 16 (1962): 217. According to Jackson J. Campbell's review, the book is "learned, based on apparently sound old-line philology, but riddled with ideas which linguistically are either truisms or errors" (*Journal of English and Germanic Philology* 61 [1962]: 144). W. K. Wimsatt, Jr., wrote that "there is not a little about this book that suggests a *Spirit of St. Louis* making its flight in 1960" (review in *Philological Quarterly* 40 [1961]: 355).

5. "It is curious to find him [Lewis], in the midst of a book in which he many times over demonstrates 'natural' principles of language, actively protesting against one principle that he particularly abhors" (Campbell, review in *JEGP*, 145). Von Lindheim is more willing to take Lewis on his own terms. He observes, "As always with C. S. Lewis, this work too is strongly inspired by moralistic impulses" (review in *Anglia* 74:62; my translation of the German).

participant. He cares how English is used because he has to use it himself.

Lewis's work should first be placed within its field. The main areas of linguistics are phonology, the study of the use of sound in language; morphology, the study of word formation; syntax, the study of sentence structure; and semantics, the study of meaning. Each of these can be studied from either a synchronic or a diachronic standpoint; that is, one can study either the characteristics of a language at a particular date, or else the changes the language has undergone over time.

Semantic theory is much less developed than the theory of phonology or even syntax. Speech sounds are obviously physical phenomena, and words and sentences can be treated as strings of sounds. Hence phonology, morphology, and syntax deal with clearly observable entities. Semantics, on the other hand, links language with the whole of human thought and its boundaries are therefore much less clearly defined. Diachronic semantics is particularly difficult. Historical linguists determine the ancestry of languages by finding systematic relationships between their sound systems. This method succeeds because it sticks close to the phonological ground; phonological changes are rarely influenced by nonphonological factors. Semantic change, on the other hand, can be precipitated by anything that affects thought and therefore cannot be studied apart from the entire culture of the people speaking the language. If the meaning changes are well known, they can reveal the culture; if the culture is well understood, it can illuminate and explain the meaning changes. In *Studies in Words* Lewis chose to work with a language and culture whose history he knew extremely well.

After the first, introductory chapter of *Studies in Words*, each subsequent chapter treats a group of related words: first *nature, kind,* and Greek *physis;* then *sad* and *gravis;* then, in succession, *wit, free, sense, simple;* and finally *conscience* and *conscious.* The final chapter, "At the Fringe of Language," deals with emotive meaning, of which more later. Chapters on *world, life,* and the phrase *I dare say* were inserted before the last chapter in the posthumous second edition.

In the introduction Lewis points out seven recurrent principles of meaning change. His list is not meant to be exhaustive, nor are all seven on the same level. They are:

(1) *The effects of ramification.* Lewis takes the meaning of a word to be a treelike structure in which each transfer or extension of meaning constitutes a branch. The word *sense,* for example, branches

into two basic meanings, "good sense" and "sense-perception," each of which then throws out a number of specialized branches. Most changes of meaning are carried out by adding branches to the tree.

This tree structure is uncontroversial and, in fact, implicit in the outline structure of definitions in the *Oxford English Dictionary*. Lewis mentions it in order to make a distinction that some etymologists neglect. The tree that exists in speakers' minds at a particular time need not match the tree that shows the growth of the word's meaning throughout history. Over time, two meanings of a single word can separate so widely that speakers eventually take them as wholly separate, especially if a crucial link has been forgotten. Is *sentence* (in grammar) the same word as *sentence* (of imprisonment)? Historically, yes, but the connecting link—"thought" or "opinion"— has been completely lost.

Speakers can also join words that were originally separate. We nowadays treat *sorrow* and *sorry* as the noun and adjective forms of the same word, though they are historically unconnected. Many of us think that *schools* of fish are named by analogy to *schools* of the educational type, but in reality the first word is originally Germanic, the second Greek. The practical consequence is that the earlier history of a word's meanings does not reveal the relations among the meanings in any given speaker's mind, and is therefore of doubtful value for determining the word's associations or poetic effect.

(2) *The insulating power of the context.* Human language tolerates an amazing amount of ambiguity as long as the different senses of a word occur in different contexts. Indeed, speakers are usually unconscious of the ambiguity. We laugh at the story of the ghost who materialized in a pub and asked, "Do you serve spirits?" because it forces us to consider at once two senses of *spirit* that are normally well separated. This is a profoundly important principle. There is good psycholinguistic evidence that, upon hearing a word, the hearer does not, even subconsciously, call up all its possible senses and search through them for the right one; he or she retrieves only enough information to interpret the word in that particular context.[6]

This principle strongly influences language change. In general, speakers of a language would rather give a new sense to an existing word than coin a new word; apart from a few modern trademarks, no words are known to have been invented *ex nihilo* since prehistoric

---

6. P. N. Johnson-Laird, "Mental Models of Meaning," in *Elements of Discourse Understanding*, ed. Aravind K. Joshi, Bonnie L. Webber, and Ivan A. Sag (Cambridge: Cambridge University Press, 1981), 122–23.

times. Idioms are formed very readily; if a phrase begins to be associated with a stock meaning, speakers attribute that meaning to it without analyzing it further. Few of us now know what *bucket* means in "kick the bucket," and we have all known people who repeat distorted or incomplete clichés such as "you can't judge a cover" without realizing that they do not quite make sense.

(3) *The "dangerous sense."* This is the sense of a word that is most likely to intrude, inappropriately, into a modern reader's interpretation of an older author. In most cases the dangerous sense is a relatively new sense that has largely displaced all the earlier senses. For example, the dangerous sense of *philosophy* is "metaphysics, epistemology, logic, etc. as distinct from the natural sciences" (*SW*, 13); in older times the word encompassed a wider range of studies.

In some cases the dangerous sense is obviously anachronistic (a *supply train* in the American Revolution could not have run on rails), but sometimes the dangerous sense already existed, as a minor sense, in the author's time, as was the case with *wit* in Pope's *An Essay on Criticism*:

> Some have at first for *Wits*, then *Poets* past,
> Turn'd *Criticks* next, and prov'd plain *Fools* at last.[7]

Here we are tempted to take *wit* as indicating a quick sense of humor, but Lewis argues convincingly that in Pope's time the word still meant "genius," and for that matter, *poet* could still include writers of prose fiction as well as verse. In this case, the modern reader must shift the balance of preferences between the various senses in his own mind; this is much harder than simply discarding one of the newer senses outright.

(4) *The word's meaning and the speaker's meaning.* Here Lewis makes, informally, a distinction between sense and reference. The meaning (sense) of a word determines the range of things to which it can refer, together with its connotations; the referent is the thing to which it refers on a particular occasion. *Book* means "bound sheaf of papers" but usually refers, in this essay, to *Studies in Words*.

The reference of a word is easy to determine by observing its use; the sense, however, must be guessed. If one reference is overwhelmingly more common than others, hearers will hypothesize a sense that corresponds closely to that reference. Lewis's example is Berkeley's

7. Alexander Pope, *Pastoral Poetry and An Essay on Criticism*, ed. E. Audra and Aubrey Williams, vol. 1 of *The Twickenham Edition of the Poems of Alexander Pope* (London: Methuen, 1961), p. 243, lines 36–37.

phrase "all the choir of heaven and furniture of earth" (SW, 15). For Berkeley, *furniture* means "contents"; for modern readers it means chairs, tables, and the like. The change occurred because *furniture* was used to refer to the contents of a house more often than the contents of anything else. An even clearer example is the use of *premises* to mean "piece of real estate." The word originally meant *aforementioned* (the Latin *praemissa*), as in "the *premises* of a logical argument," i.e., the other arguments stated earlier. In legal documents *premises* referred to "the aforementioned property," and soon enough, the element "aforementioned" was lost. So now we can tell someone to "get off the premises" without having given a legal description of the property. Closer to home, *immorality* now means "unchastity" so often that some people are bound to misunderstand it if it is used in any other sense.[8]

This kind of semantic change corresponds most closely to ordinary phonological change: without realizing it, new generations of speakers learn a language subtly different from that of their parents because, although they are hearing the same references, they are hypothesizing different senses to account for them.[9] But the principle has a practical implication. Evidence about past word meanings almost always tells us the reference but not the sense. If we find *furniture* referring to chairs and tables in, say, 1650, this does not prove that it had its modern sense, only that its most common modern referent was already somewhere within its range of possible referents.

(5) *Tactical definitions.* An author's statement that a word means such-and-such is good evidence that the word actually meant something slightly different. After all, a meaning that is widely understood does not need explaining. "Tactical definitions" serve either to preserve a sense that is falling out of use, or to adjust the meanings of terms for the sake of an argument.

> We tell our pupils that *deprecate* does not mean *depreciate* or that *immorality* does not mean simply *lechery* because these words are beginning to mean just those things. We are in fact resisting the growth of a new sense. We may be quite right to do so, for it may be one that will make English a less useful means of communication. But we should not

8. See C. S. Lewis, "Christian Apologetics," in *God in the Dock: Essays on Theology and Ethics,* ed. Walter Hooper (Grand Rapids: Eerdmans, 1970), 96–98.

9. See Rulon S. Wells, "Metonymy and Misunderstanding: An Aspect of Language Change," in *Current Issues in Linguistic Theory,* ed. Roger W. Cole (Bloomington: Indiana University Press, 1977), 195–214.

be resisting it unless it had already appeared. We do not warn our pupils that *coalbox* does not mean a hippopotamus. (SW, 18)

Teachers of grammar are known for their opposition to language change. Though often taken for simple recalcitrance, this opposition has practical grounds. A grammarian's job is to teach a style that all educated people will understand and accept. An incipient change is by nature unfamiliar to some speakers of the language. Moreover, speakers adopting a change typically sacrifice one advantage to gain another; *immorality* is losing versatility in order to provide a name for one type of immorality that otherwise lacks a concise designation, at least for speakers who do not know the obsolescent words *lechery* and *unchastity*. Grammarians, who have larger vocabularies and a more philosophical turn of mind, often weigh such factors differently than the common people.

(6) *The methodological idiom.* "Freud's psychology" can refer either to Freud's theories about the mind, or to the characteristics of Freud's mind. In general, the name of a study or art can refer also to the things contemplated or produced by that study or art. This is the classical rhetorical figure of metonymy: things that co-occur in a regular way can be interchanged. Metonymy is sometimes intentional and sometimes almost unconscious; the speaker simply gropes for an appropriate word and uses the nearest one he can find, whereupon that word sprouts a new sense. For Lewis, the methodological idiom is important because failure to recognize it can produce muddled interpretations of words like *art* and *history*. The latter can mean the past events themselves, the study of past events, or various trends or principles reflected in past events.

(7) *The moralization of status words.* All words that connote high status or widespread approval tend to weaken their meanings until they mean simply "good." *Noble* now means something like "of exemplary character" rather than "descended from aristocrats." The transition was easy; aristocrats were expected to display good character, and a metaphorical use of the word, referring to character rather than ancestry, was used so often that it ceased to be taken as a metaphor. In the preface to *Mere Christianity*, Lewis notes that *Christian* nowadays sometimes denotes high moral character rather than adherence to the teachings of Christ (MC, 9–11). The motive is quite charitable—surely the word should apply to people who exemplify Christ's virtues rather than those who merely mouth His doctrines. The difficulty, as Lewis points out, is that this makes the word much less useful. Christians in the old sense are easy to identify, and we often

need to talk about them as a group; Christians in the new sense are vaguely defined, and we have little practical need for a concise way to refer to them. Thus Lewis insists on using *Christian* only in the old sense.

Likewise, words indicating low status come to mean simply "bad." A *villain* was originally a hanger-on of a Roman villa, and hence, later, an untrustworthy rustic. More recently, *fundamentalist* meant someone who adhered to the Five Fundamentals, a statement of biblical orthodoxy. The word became associated with unsophisticated extremists to the point that the news media can now talk of "fundamentalist Moslems," and fundamentalists in the old sense have to call themselves "conservatives" or "evangelicals."

Why doesn't this process empty a language's semantic coffers, so that eventually no precise status words are left? There are two answers. First, people's values change, and status words become weakened only when people lose interest in the status to which they originally referred. We use *noble* to mean *valiant* because we no longer care whether people are descended from aristocrats; we no longer need the word's original meaning in everyday discourse. The same thing can happen when a technical term with a precise sense is taken up by people who do not care about technicalities and use it only for its vaguer associations. Important status words, such as *president,* are in no danger of weakening. Second, there is a steady supply of new status words to meet the needs of newer value systems. Modern society values success against competition—especially in business—and is creating an abundance of words to describe or explain it. Consider for instance *go-getter, up-and-coming, multi-talented, winner,* and *loser,* and notice how many are athletic metaphors.

(8) An eighth principle, implicit in the organization of the book, is *the parallel development of similar words in different languages.* Lewis attributes such parallelism to the versatility of the human mind, which "can produce the same results under very different conditions" (*SW,* 6), and uses it to contest Benjamin Lee Whorf's hypothesis in *Language, Thought, and Reality* that thought is entirely shaped by language.[10] If Whorf's hypothesis were true in its most extreme form, there would be no semantic change at all; no one could ever think anything not already provided by his language. Linguists now agree that although language influences thought, it does not control it completely. Even a milder form of Whorf's hypothesis would dic-

10. Whorf, *Language, Thought, and Reality: Selected Writings,* ed. John B. Carroll (Cambridge, Mass.: MIT Press, 1956).

tate that similar changes could happen only in languages that had similar semantic systems.

The parallelism that Lewis notes, however, can often be explained much more easily: the words are standard translation equivalents, and the constant interaction of the two languages causes them to change together. Latin *liberalis* mirrors the senses of Greek *eleutherios* because the Romans were constantly exposed to Greek language and culture. In other cases the parallel developments appear to be independent: Latin *liberalis* and English *free* both, at quite different times, came to mean "generous." Even then, however, as Paul Christophersen has pointed out, the cultures are not quite separate. Some trend in Western culture may have affected Latin at an early stage and English at a much later stage; or English may even have borrowed the new senses, in succession, from Latin (*SW*, 258).

One would expect these principles, and *Studies in Words* generally, to reflect the influence of Lewis's lifelong friend Owen Barfield. After all, Barfield had published a similar book, *History in English Words*, in 1926, as well as discussing semantic change in *Poetic Diction* (1928, dedicated to Lewis) and *Speaker's Meaning* (1967). Barfield's work, however, differs from Lewis's in important ways. Whereas Lewis uses culture to explain meaning changes, Barfield's *History in English Words* uses them to reconstruct culture; that is, Barfield uses etymological evidence to infer otherwise unrecorded facts about earlier cultures, often going all the way back to Indo-European. Moreover, though he says little about it in this book, his ideas about the evolution of culture are derived from Rudolf Steiner's Anthroposophy, a metaphysical system with which Lewis disagreed strongly.[11]

In *Poetic Diction*, Barfield makes an important claim about meaning change—that words ordinarily develop, not by adding new senses, but by introducing distinctions. From the fact that Greek *pneuma* means both "breath" and "spirit," one should not infer that the Greeks took their word for "breath" and applied it *metaphorically* to the intangible soul. The point is that no conscious metaphor was involved; *pneuma* originally designated an undifferentiated range of intangible forces, and the distinction into wind, breath, and spirit came later. Lewis recognizes this point: glossing a passage from Varro, he asks whether *divina natura* means "the divine nature" (God), or the divine species (the gods), or nature in the modern sense (trees, flow-

11. See Lionel Adey, *C. S. Lewis's "Great War" with Owen Barfield*, E.L.S. Monograph Series, 14 (Victoria, B.C.: University of Victoria Press, 1978), especially 47–55.

ers, etc., with their goddess)—"or could Varro have told us?" Presumably not, since to his mind they were not distinct (*SW*, 73, note 1).

Indeed, Barfield appears to have arrived independently at the fundamental insight of structural linguistics: a language is a system of relationships and distinctions, not a collection of physical objects.[12] This is clearest in phonology because each language divides the continuum of possible sounds into a set of discrete phonemes, but it also applies to meanings. Literary Welsh, for instance, designates the colors blue and green with a single word where English has two. The split of *pneuma* into two distinct senses is, then, an instance of a familiar phenomenon. Its senses are related metaphorically because they were once a single sense.

In other cases, of course, a word has multiple senses because it has been used in consciously created metaphors. C. K. Ogden and I. A. Richards had criticized Michel Bréal for his excessive and unscientific use of metaphor. Nonsense, says Barfield—all words are metaphorical in one way or another. Metaphor is the stuff of which scientific as well as poetic creativity is made. We cannot speak of a *point of view* without, at least subconsciously, using a visual metaphor where another language might have chosen a tactile, auditory, or geographical one. One is never more the slave of metaphor than when denying that the metaphor exists.

Lewis answered *Poetic Diction* in his 1939 essay "Bluspels and Flalansferes" by sketching a position midway between Ogden and Richards's scientific literalism and Barfield's theory of all-pervasive metaphor. Lewis distinguishes between a metaphor created by a teacher to explain a point and the same metaphor understood, half-understood, or misunderstood by a pupil. The teacher is not enslaved by metaphor; he chooses one of many possible metaphors in order to express a truth that he understands clearly. If the pupil understands the metaphor and goes on to grasp the truth behind it, he is in the same position. The metaphor becomes a source of enslavement if the pupil merely parrots the metaphor without quite understanding it— as often happens in scientific and philosophical discourse.

Lewis's concern with proper understanding and handling of the multiple senses of words throughout *Studies in Words* comes to focus on his disagreement with the New Criticism and especially with two of its proponents, I. A. Richards and William Empson. The New

12. See Ferdinand de Saussure, *Course in General Linguistics* (1915), ed. Charles Bally and Albert Sechehaye, trans. Wade Baskin (New York: McGraw-Hill, 1966), 102–7.

Critics held that a poem should be appreciated in itself, not as an extension of the personality of the author, that poetry conveys a fundamentally different type of meaning than prose, and that all the senses and associations of a word enter at once into its effect in a poem. Lewis agreed with the first of these claims (see *PH*). He was at least mildly opposed to the second, as evidenced by his advocacy of narrative poems, which bridge the gap between poetry and prose. Against the third claim he directs, at least implicitly, most of *Studies in Words.*

His main target is Empson's analysis of *wit* in Pope's *Essay on Criticism.* Empson claims that the modern sense "jokester" played a central role in Pope's use of the word, and that the other senses formed an elaborate system around this: "There is not a single use of the word in the whole poem in which the idea of a joke is quite out of sight." The word already had that sense in Shakespeare, says Empson, and when Pope uses it in such a way as to make one of the other senses more prominent, "the other meaning . . . then appears as the subject of the equation, the thing 'meant by the word,' but the idea of the joke or the smart joker will still crop up as a predicate of it."[13]

Lewis's chapter on *wit,* the centerpiece of *Studies in Words* illustrating nearly all the semantic principles noted in the introduction, is shaped as a direct reply to Empson. Lewis picks up *gewit* in Anglo-Saxon and follows it to modern English, pausing along the way to note parallels in the development of Latin *ingenium.* After describing Empson as "a critic to whose *ingenium* we all owe a willing debt" (*SW,* 93), Lewis argues that when Pope says, "Great Wits sometimes may *gloriously offend,*"[14] he cannot be talking about humor. Pope goes on to describe "brave disorder" that obtains "grace beyond the reach of Art" and produces an effect like that produced in a landscape by "the shapeless rock, or hanging precipice." The poetic effect to which he refers is breathtaking or inspiring, but certainly not jocular. This poses serious difficulties for Empson's analysis, but not for Lewis's own, which relies on the insulating power of the context.

The New Criticism stressed the sharp distinction between referential and emotive meaning made by Ogden and Richards in *The Meaning of Meaning.* Referential or "symbolic" meaning determines the thing or set of things to which the word refers; emotive meaning comprises all its other effects in conveying attitudes and feelings.

13. William Empson, *The Structure of Complex Words* (London: Chatto and Windus, 1951), 87, 88.
14. Pope, *An Essay on Criticism,* in *Pastoral Poetry,* p. 257, line 152.

Ogden and Richards hold that scientific discourse, whose only purpose is to inform, should be wholly referential. Conversely, poetry, whose function is to convey feelings, need not aspire to referential truthfulness at all. In *Principles of Literary Criticism,* Richards ties his literary theory explicitly to stimulus-response psychology and even diagrams a network of neurons.[15]

Ogden and Richards's referential-emotive distinction belongs to the same philosophical movement as the logical positivism of A. J. Ayer and the emotive ethics of C. L. Stevenson.[16] The goal of the movement was to distinguish statements of fact, testable by observation, from untestable ("emotive") statements such as "My soul is an enchanted boat," "Murder is wrong," and "Ouch!" Difficulties have arisen on both logical and linguistic grounds. The definition of "testable" is highly problematic, and, perhaps more importantly, it is not clear that the various kinds of "emotive" statements form a single class.[17]

Lewis tackles emotive meaning in the last chapter of *Studies in Words,* "At the Fringe of Language," and confines himself to the second of the two difficulties. He applauds Empson's efforts to narrow and subdivide the vast range of "emotive" utterances, noting that language serves many functions—"to propitiate and pardon, to rebuke, console, intercede, and arouse." In this he anticipates modern speech-act theory, which studies the logical properties of declarations, questions, commands, promises, and many other uses of language.

His next step is to sweep away some clutter. A statement is not "emotional" (as opposed to factual) merely because it arouses or reflects emotion. "The Germans have surrendered" is a statement of fact, regardless of the feelings with which one greets it. Nor are metaphors emotive: "I am washed in the blood of the Lamb," though false in its literal sense, is an attempt to state a fact on a higher level. And—contra Stevenson, who says that "X is good" is emotive because it means "I approve of X"—Lewis observes that "approval and disapproval do not seem to me to be emotions. If we felt at all times about the things we judge good the emotion which is appropriate, our lives would be easier" (*SW,* 315).

15. Ogden and Richards, *The Meaning of Meaning* (London: Routledge and Kegan Paul, 1923); Richards (1924; reprint, New York: Harcourt Brace, 1958), 116.

16. Ayer, *Language, Truth and Logic* (London: V. Gollancz, 1936); Stevenson, *Ethics and Language* (New Haven: Yale University Press, 1944).

17. See William P. Alston, "Emotive Meaning," in *The Encyclopedia of Philosophy,* ed. Paul Edwards (New York: Macmillan, 1967), 2:486–93.

Finally Lewis makes his main point: poetic language achieves emotional effects, not simply through "associations," but by creating mental images, which is as much of a cognitive process as reasoning about facts. "My soul is an enchanted boat" does not *merely* call up emotive associations; it first creates a mental image of a boat that moves by magic, and further associations arise from the image, not just the words.

This acknowledgement of the power of images is one of the strengths of Lewis's work. He recognizes, as others do not, that informing someone means equipping him with appropriate mental images. *Studies in Words* undertakes this task for obsolete vocabulary; *The Discarded Image* does it for medieval culture; *Beyond Personality* does it for the Holy Trinity; and one of the main purposes of *Surprised by Joy* is to present a seldom-described mental image—a longing for the infinitely remote—and show how it is fulfilled in Christianity. While most twentieth-century expository writers think it desirable to communicate in "facts" alone, Lewis communicates in images that withstand analytic thought as well as express feelings. In so doing, he conveys a complete view of humanity that bridges the gap between reason and intuition.

The Sound of Silence: Language and Experience in *Out of the Silent Planet*

Verlyn Flieger

For adventure in perception, vividly and forcefully conveyed through what I shall call the language of experience, C. S. Lewis's space novels have few rivals in the field of fantasy. Only David Lindsay's *A Voyage to Arcturus* comes near *Out of the Silent Planet* and *Perelandra* in offering the reader not just new experience, but *newness* of experience—the sensory apprehension of strangeness. The necessary paradox inherent in the use of the known (language) to express the unknown was not lost on Lewis, all of whose work exhibits a more than usual awareness of the power of the word. But in the space novels this continuing awareness converts to deliberate purpose: Lewis used his invented worlds of Malacandra and Perelandra to explore and illustrate the interdependence of language and experience, as well as to validate the mythos of Christianity. Indeed, we might substitute "in order to" for "as well as" because Lewis has put words in the service of the Word, not dialectically or hortatorily, but imaginatively, through speculative invention. His novels use the language of experience and the experience of language to explore the shifting tensions of man's relationship with God.

Let us begin with the language of experience. Consider two visual impressions, each on a different planet, as seen through the eyes of Lewis's hero, Ransom. First, Perelandra:

> His first impression was of nothing more definite than of something slanted—as though he were looking at a photograph which had been taken when the camera was not held level. And even this lasted only for an instant. The slant was replaced by a different slant; then two slants rushed together and made a peak, and the peak flattened suddenly into a horizontal line, and the horizontal line tilted and became the edge of a vast gleaming slope which rushed furiously towards him. (*Per,* 37)

This is Ransom's first experience of the water-world, and he is so new to this situation that he is as yet unaware of being in water. Like a child emergent from the womb, he cannot yet separate himself from his surroundings enough to identify them, to recognize the "slants" as waves. Here is his equally bewildering first impression of Malacandra:

> He saw nothing but colours—colours that refused to form themselves into things. Moreover, he knew nothing yet well enough to see it: you cannot see things till you know roughly what they are. His first impression was of a bright, pale world—a watercolour world out of a child's paint-box; a moment later he recognised the flat belt of light blue as a sheet of water. (*OSP*, 46)

I know of no writer who does this sort of thing better than Lewis. Ransom's experience of the unfamiliar is a familiar one, an experience we have all had at one time or another, waking up suddenly, or returning out of a reverie: shapes and colors ride meaninglessly on the eyeball, but the mind does not at once translate. Then, in a moment, everything shifts just slightly, and we know where we are. Such is Lewis's skill that the reader feels with Ransom first the dissociation and then the recognition. The point here is that this conversion of meaningless sensations into meaningful things is engineered largely through language. The "flat belt of light blue" becomes a "sheet of water," and Ransom both sees and names it. The simultaneity of the two processes is important, for as Lewis says of Ransom, "you cannot see things till you know roughly what they are," that is, when you know their names.

This process of naming and of knowing things in terms of their names is central to the way in which Lewis treats language in his space novels and is the key to his major theme, loss of the immediate experience of God consonant with the loss of words to convey that experience. This approach to language, the recognition that it is agent as well as medium, derives in large measure from the work of Owen Barfield in the joint areas of language and consciousness, and I suggest that it is in the context of Barfield's work that Lewis's novels can best be understood.

Barfield's major statement on language is also his best-known work, *Poetic Diction*, which is dedicated to Lewis with the comment "Opposition is true friendship." This recognition not just of the friendship but of its special quality acknowledges the energetic intellectual collision which was its hallmark, for by both their accounts, the two men argued vigorously and disagreed often. The dedicatory phrase, it is well to note, puts friendship and opposition on equal footing, as poles defining common ground. You cannot argue where you do not understand. For Lewis and Barfield the common ground included sensitivity to the power of words, shared enjoyment of poetry, and appreciation of myth as a valid expression of human experience.

Myth was for both men an avenue to God. For Lewis it led to orthodox, doctrinaire Christianity; for Barfield it led to Anthroposophy, a system of belief based on the teachings of Rudolph Steiner which, while it goes beyond Christianity, does not contradict it. It was Barfield who showed Lewis that, as Humphrey Carpenter puts it, "myth has a central place in the whole of language and literature."[1] Through understanding the interconnection of myth and language, Lewis linked his experience of God with his lifelong fascination with word and story, thus animating his vision of Christianity and enabling him to bring it to life in his space romances. The treatment of myth and language in Lewis's invented worlds draws directly on two interlocking Barfieldian concepts: original participation and semantic unity. It was Lewis's creative gift to be able to marry these two concepts to his view of Christianity and to use both to make a world and—even more important—to make a point.

In an association as long and deep as that of Lewis and Barfield, no one work can be singled out as a primary influence. The friendship itself is the influence. Barfield has said of his work that, like most authors, he is "always really saying the same thing over and over again."[2] And readers acquainted with Lewis's work find the same to be true of him. One cannot, however, footnote a friendship, so for specific reference I have selected two books representative of Barfield's work that seem to me to have the most direct bearing on Lewis's theme: *Poetic Diction,* which deals with the concept of semantic unity, and *Saving the Appearances,* which describes Barfield's theory of original participation. The two books complement each other, though with different emphases, in their exploration of language, myth, and consciousness as parts of a reciprocal system whereby a culture's myth and language shape one another and both shape the cultural consciousness out of which they arise.

Barfield's thesis is that this spiral process had its beginning at the

1. Carpenter, *The Inklings: C. S. Lewis, J. R. R. Tolkien, Charles Williams, and Their Friends* (London: George Allen and Unwin, 1978), 41.

2. Barfield, *The Rediscovery of Meaning, and Other Essays* (Middletown, Conn.: Wesleyan University Press, 1977), 3.

dawn of our development, in the earliest levels of human awareness. This awareness he calls "original participation." (It should be noted here that his complete theory takes humanity from a state of "original participation" through a progressive process of separation from the natural and supernatural worlds to a final reunification in full awareness, a "final participation" of mankind in the universe. Lewis's imaginative re-creation in the space romances dramatizes the first two aspects.) The original awareness, or participation, was the hallmark of a distinct difference in perception between primitive humanity and modern man, a difference which is both the agent and the product of evolving consciousness. Whereas we now observe a world wholly external to us, primitive humanity—like Ransom in the waters of the mother planet—felt itself a part of that which carried it. The perception of surroundings was immediate and intuitive rather than conceptual. Thus Ransom could see a "slant," but could not yet apply the concept "wave" to it. Language for him at that moment, as for primitive man always, was grounded in experience, and that experience was the immediate genesis of the language which described it. "Participation," says Barfield, "is the extra-sensory relation between man and the phenomena."[3]

This felt unity between man and his world gave to his language a similar "ancient semantic unity," a fusion of related meanings within one word. Every word had an "outside" and an "inside," the concrete referent with related meanings that have since been abstracted from it, meanings we now call metaphors, as the "old, single, living meanings" became split up and killed.[4] Barfield's example is Greek *pneuma*: at one time it conveyed a single idea, which is now split up into "wind," "breath," and "spirit" and translated according to context. The old, single, living meaning is lost. Wind and breath are still perceptible realities, still "outside," but spirit, which once was in and of them, has been abstracted, turned from a percept into a concept, useful still as a metaphor, but no longer a phenomenon.

Early language, describing a world perceptibly more alive and immediate than the one we know, was by its nature rich in what we would now call figures of speech, poetic diction. We mean by that words consciously used as metaphors to enhance meaning, but for the original speakers this was the only language available. All diction

3. Barfield, *Saving the Appearances: A Study in Idolatry* (London: Faber and Faber, 1957), 40.

4. Barfield, *Poetic Diction: A Study in Meaning* (London: Faber and Gwyer, 1928), 106.

was poetic. Further, and perhaps more important, such a language would have been for its speakers, as ours is for us, the agent as well as the medium of perception, creating reality as it described it. And that reality must have been, by the very nature of the words used, a different reality from the one we know. The development away from the concrete toward the abstract, "from homogeneity towards dissociation and multiplicity,"[5] has affected not only language, but thought and perceived reality as well, cutting humanity off from its original participation in the natural and supernatural worlds, isolating us and our concepts from the living universe, eroding belief. That Lewis was aware of this as a historical actuality as well as a theory is evident from his scholarly writing. Appropriately entitled "New Learning and New Ignorance," the introduction to his *Oxford History of English Literature* volume *English Literature in the Sixteenth Century* talks about the effect of the new science on human perception and the Renaissance:

> By reducing Nature to her mathematical elements it substituted a mechanical for a genial or animistic conception of the universe. The world was emptied, first of her indwelling spirits, then of her occult sympathies and antipathies, finally of her colours, smells, and tastes. . . . The mind, on whose ideal constructions the whole method depended, stood over against its object in ever sharper dissimilarity. Man with his new powers became rich like Midas but all that he touched had gone dead and cold. This process, slowly working, ensured during the next century the loss of the old mythical imagination: the conceit, and later the personified abstraction, takes its place.

He is quick to recognize the effect of this perception on language. He talks of "the Elizabethan or Henrican [*sic*] universe; tingling with anthropomorphic life, dancing, ceremonial, a festival not a machine. It is very important to grasp this at the outset. If we do not, we shall constantly misread our poets by taking for highly conceited metaphor expressions which are still hardly metaphorical at all."[6] While words such as "animistic" and "anthropomorphic" suggest that Lewis stopped short of total acceptance of Barfield's idea of participation, the general sense of these passages makes clear his understanding of the concept. It is no great leap to go from his discussion of it in scholarly writing to his dramatization of it in fiction. His imagination

5. Barfield, *Poetic Diction*, 81.
6. Lewis, *English Literature in the Sixteenth Century, Excluding Drama*, vol. 3 of *Oxford History of English Literature*, ed. F. P. Wilson and Bonamy Dobrée (Oxford: Clarendon Press, 1954), 3–4, 4.

grasped the essential link between Barfield's ideas on language and the *mythos* of Christianity, finding in his fictive world a way for each to validate the other. The science fiction format freed his invention, allowing him to recreate myth, not simply retell it, and to explore by way of Ransom the ramifications of its deep connections with language and perception.

It is, of course, no accident that Ransom is a philologist, thus ideally suited to correlate language, thought, and reality, and more than ordinarily sensitive to how they affect one another. He is, after all, the creation of the man who wrote books such as *Studies in Words* and who was an academic as well as a writer of fantasy. While the character of Ransom clearly owes much to Lewis's own persona of scholar, Christian, and college don, he has other sources as well. On the purely philological side he certainly derives from Lewis's friend, colleague, and fellow-fantasist, J. R. R. Tolkien, who said that he recognized some of his opinions and ideas "Lewisified" in Ransom.[7] But beyond these parallels, Ransom stands as the medium for and chief exponent of Barfield's theory of language and consciousness.

A few preliminary examples will show Ransom at work and illustrate his philological function. Kidnapped and on his way to Malacandra in the spaceship, Ransom discovers beyond its metal walls a reality so different from the abstraction he has been taught to call "space" that he finds himself reaching back to the much older notion of "the heavens" to describe what he sees and feels: "He had read of 'Space': at the back of his thinking for years had lurked the dismal fancy of the black, cold vacuity, the utter deadness, which was supposed to separate the worlds. He had not known how much it affected him till now—now that the very name 'Space,' seemed a blasphemous libel for this empyrean ocean of radiance in which they swam" (*OSP*, 36). Note that the older, more concrete word is also the more mythic; note also that the term *space* is not just inaccurate, it "seem[s] blasphemous." It has not just removed the idea of "the heavens" from man's thinking, but has broken his sense of connection with those heavens. Ransom's musings on the subject lead him to think of and to quote Milton, the major English mythmaker, whose great epic was a vehicle for the poetic reconnection of man with myth.

Ransom's arrival on Malacandra provides another example. Here, he has the almost preprimitive experience of being unable to see because he does not know—does not have words for—what he is looking at. Recall his sensation of color unseparated into form, the

7. Carpenter, *Inklings*, 182.

"flat belt of light blue" which becomes a "sheet of water." In *Saving the Appearances,* Barfield introduces the term "figuration" to describe this construction of sensations "by the percipient mind into the recognizable and *nameable* objects we call 'things.'"[8] This is the earliest process of language, and still the chief one by which we identify things in relation to ourselves, and by extension, ourselves in relation to things.

A more extended example of this process of figuration occurs with Ransom's progressive changes of attitude toward, and concomitant changes of nomenclature for, the *sorns,* inhabitants of Malacandra. On his first hearing of them and while they are still unseen and unknown, Ransom has no percept on which to fix his imagination, which consequently runs uncontrolled through a list of possible horrors: "Insect-like, . . . twitching feelers, . . . slimy coils, . . . bulbous eyes, grinning jaws, horns, stings, mandibles." He finally gives up for lack of material, deciding that "it would be an extra-terrestrial Otherness—something one had never thought of, never could have thought of" (*OSP,* 40). Something so utterly outside the known, outside all previous experience, will be unrecognizable, therefore unnameable. Ransom's first close look at a *sorn* produces a concrete change in his awareness. "A new conception of the *sorns* began to arise in his mind: the ideas of 'giant' and 'ghost' [which occurred when he first saw them at a distance] receded behind those of 'goblin' and 'gawk'" (*OSP,* 104). And Ransom's final judgment, the product of yet closer observation and acquaintance, is a shift from pejoration to awe for the mythic. "'Ogres' he had called them when they first met his eyes as he struggled in the grip of Weston and Devine; 'Titans' or 'Angels' he now thought would have been a better word." The change in attitude leads to a change in diction, which leads in turn to a further change in attitude. This last change includes Ransom's attitude toward himself: "His first human reaction . . . now appeared to him not so much cowardly as vulgar" (*OSP,* 114).

It is noteworthy that the changes wrought by Ransom's successive impressions send him back in time to find the proper words: "heavens" instead of "space," "Titans" instead of "insect-like creatures." The older words are better suited to an older world, one more archaic and more mythic than the one he has come from. Lewis is at some pains to emphasize this. Time and again he reminds us that Malacandra is an *old* world, not just in its senescence, but because it exists at a stage that predates our own world; it embodies a reality no longer

8. Barfield, *Saving the Appearances,* 24.

accessible to outside myth. Thus Ransom, leaving Malacandra, reflects from a distance on its mythic quality, its history "before human history began . . . before animal history began," and he wonders, "Or was that only mythology? He knew it would seem like mythology when he got back to Earth" (*OSP*, 164). Through his experience on Malacandra he has come to learn that what is "only mythology" has a reality that transcends history to verify its own truth. The archaic society, primitive life, and poetic language of Malacandra are not "only mythology" or, as Ransom more historically mislabels them, "old stone age" (*OSP*, 74). They are the living remnants of the mythic childhood of creation, the emblems of original participation. They are of the universe before the Fall.

As Ransom discovers this new old world, he rediscovers his own and sees its empty modernity through new perceptions brought about by his acquisition of a new "old" language. He learns that his Earth is Thulcandra, the silent planet, cut off by its own will from the music of the spheres, their song, their language. He discards his picture of Satan as "fallen," an image altered by time to metaphor and finally to cliché, in favor of Satan as "bent" (*OSP*, 136–37). So simple an adjective is not, as it at first seems, childish and therefore inadequate. Rather, it is childlike, consonant with the innocence of the world which produced it and perfectly expressing that world's immediacy of perception. For the modern reader—no longer, alas, childlike—the word has unexpected metaphoric value, embodying within it concomitant images of "crooked," "twisted," no longer "straight," and effectively illustrating Barfield's concept of ancient semantic unity. Such sensitivity to the twists and turns of language is a thread in the fabric of Lewis's text, often so densely interwoven with other threads that it is not immediately apparent. One of its earliest appearances, a first clue to the importance of the shifting relationship between language and experience, comes not on the new planet, but on a road in England, in an unmythic, unlinguistic, everyday conversation. Barely three pages into *Out of the Silent Planet*, Ransom, benighted on a walking tour, meets a woman who mistakes his approaching figure for that of her missing son. The woman—uneducated, stereotypically lower-class—is obviously beside herself with worry, though she cannot say so. She is fearful for the safety of her son—with good reason, as we later learn—yet "I don't like him coming home so late" is the most she can say about it. Clearly, words are not her long suit. But she is talking to a philologist, a man alert to language, to a speaker's meaning, to what words do and do not say. "The monotonous voice and the limited range of the woman's vocabulary," we are told, "did not express much emotion, but Ransom was standing sufficiently near to perceive that she was trembling and nearly crying" (*OSP*, 9).

The key phrase is "the limited range of the woman's vocabulary," information of little importance to plot or character, for she shortly disappears, not to be seen or mentioned again. The significance here is not that the woman is worried but that she does not know how to say so. Her language is out of touch with her feelings. In this case her physical reality, the tears and the trembling, translate for her, and her body says what her words cannot. But her inability with words, common phenomenon as it is, foreshadows Ransom's later inability to translate Weston in the climactic scene at Meldilorn. It is a dramatization of the great divorce of words from the reality to which they once belonged.

So far we have focused primarily on the language of experience. Experience of language becomes the dominant motif when the spaceship lands on Malacandra and Ransom escapes from his captors, Weston and Devine. Midway in the second day on the planet, Lewis gets to that scene so much a part of the formula and so dear to the readers of science fiction, the encounter with the alien. But because this is "Lewisified" myth only thinly disguised as science fiction, the encounter plays hob with the formula. The alien, one of three species on the planet, is a *hross*, a sort of giant, rational otter, endowed with speech. Faced with a potentially hostile creature a foot or so taller than he is, who may portend danger or even death, Ransom's initial reaction is typical of his profession, not of the fiction in which he appears. He wants to take notes. The habit of research overrides natural fear when Ransom jumps at the linguistic possibilities of the situation, prompting Lewis, as narrator, to remark, "The love of knowledge is a kind of madness." He is certainly talking as much about himself as about Ransom. And for Lewis, as for Ransom, knowledge is also one avenue to belief, access to the reverification of the mythos of Christianity. So his mind, rather than his instinct, goes into action:

> In the fraction of a second which it took Ransom to decide that the creature was really talking . . . his imagination had leaped over every fear and hope and probability of his situation to follow the dazzling project of making a Malacandrian grammar. *An Introduction to the Malacandrian language—The Lunar verb—A concise Martian-English Dictionary* . . . the titles flitted through his mind. And what might one not discover from the speech of a non-human race? The very form of language itself, the principle behind all possible languages, might fall into his hands. (*OSP*, 61–62)

Fortified with the knowledge of Barfield's theory of the beginning of language, we have no difficulty charting Ransom's philological course from here on. Never mind that writing a grammar or compiling a dictionary is not the standard response to meeting a Martian. Lewis is not H. G. Wells. Far from it. Although he yields to none in his admiration for Wells, his object in writing science fiction is almost at the other extreme. He intends to use the primacy of language, announced in this encounter, to shine light on man and God, not man and society.

Ransom's subsequent reactions to the *hross* and its to him are a predictable mixture of fear and friendliness. Each is wary of the other; each tries to communicate, babbling in a language unknown to the other. Acquaintance advances through gesture and body language at first. This is not altogether a happy expedient, for Ransom, at least, misunderstands the other's physiology as well as its speech. When the *hross* pours liquid into a shell from a spout at its middle and offers it, Ransom, who mistakes the spout for genitals, is understandably hesitant to accept. This rather repellant detail makes a necessary point: experience is as fragile a basis for understanding as words are. Apparent commonalities cannot be assumed in gesture any more than in word.

But when friendship has been established by the primitive and civilized ritual of one standing the other a drink (which is what the *hross* was pouring—"plainly alcoholic; [Ransom] had never enjoyed a drink so much" [*OSP* 63]), they get immediately to the business of exchanging introductions and thus to language. *Hross* and *man* are easy enough, though the *hross* pronounces it *hman*; but when it names a handful of dirt as *handra*, Ransom makes his first linguistic note. "Malacandra?" he inquires. Answered in the affirmative, he begins at once on his Malacandrian grammar:

> Ransom was getting on well. *Handra* was earth the element; *Malac-andra* the "earth" or planet as a whole. Soon he would find out what *Malac* meant. In the meantime "H disappears after C" he noted, and made his first step in Malacandrian phonetics. The *hross* was now trying to teach him the meaning of *Handramit*. He recognised the root *handra*- again (and noted "They have suffixes as well as prefixes"). (*OSP*, 64)

This, with the addition of some proper names, plural forms, a few more words—*sorn, pfifltrigg* (the other species), *hnau, hnakra, crah, arbol, -punt, hru, wondelone, hluntheline*—is pretty much the extent of invented language given by Lewis. But neither the function nor the effect resides in mere vocabulary. Verifying and extending Ransom's perceptions, the language invests the world with the texture of reality and, even more important, with strangeness, that re-presentation of the familiar as the new which Barfield has called the "moonlight of our experience"[9] and which resides in figuration and metaphor.

One of the chief purposes of the language is to characterize and differentiate the three species of Malacandra. As in the real world, in Lewis's invented one speech reflects and expresses social reality, cultural psychology, and world view. Thus the *sorns*—ogres turned Titans—the philosophers and speculative thinkers of the planet, have portentous, ponderous sounding names: Augray, Arkal, Falmay. The *hrossa*, the most primitive and also—or rather, therefore—the most poetic of the races, have animal-like, whinnying, "furry" names, such as Hyoi, Hnoh, Whin, Hnihi, Hleri. The *pfifltriggi*, the artisans and craftsmen of Malacandra, have busy, polysyllabic, technical-sounding names like Kanakaberaka, Parakataru, Tafalakeruf (*OSP*, 130). The names of these last two species are borrowed from real, though obsolete, earth language, *hross* being Old Icelandic *hross*, "horse," and *pfifltrigg* a compound of Old Icelandic *fifil*, "monster," and *tryggr*, "safe," which certainly fits the giant froglike species Lewis describes. I am unable to find an equally clear source for *sorn*, but a possible candidate is Old Icelandic *sonr*, "son" (the plural meaning "descendants" or "race"). *Sorn* would be a metathesized form of *sonr* and, since they are the species most human in shape and behavior, this seems a likely choice.

Inevitably, Lewis's Malacandrian invites comparison with Quenya and Sindarin, the invented languages of Tolkien's Middle-earth. But while there is a surface resemblance between the two men's work and in their mythopoeic approach to fantasy, the differences are as important as the similarities. For Tolkien, languages were the primary invention and the world was created as their context. As such, they are the genesis and underpinning of his myth and indivisible from it. For Lewis, the language is in the service of a somewhat different goal, the revalidation and revaluation of Christianity. Lewis, like Ransom, wants to find "the very form of language itself, the principle behind all possible languages," and to find in that form evidence of man's relationship to God. Lewis is after "language itself," not languages. His work approaches language as a cultural and mythological artifact in the Barfieldian sense.

Endowing Malacandra with three disparate but rational species affords Lewis ample room to enlarge his treatment of language and to

9. Barfield, *Poetic Diction*, 178.

realize Barfield's theory and his imaginary world in terms of one another. Near the end of his sojourn on Malacandra, Ransom learns that what he has taken to be the only language of the planet, since he has spoken it to all three species, is in actuality the language of the *hrossa* only. The *sorns* and the *pfifltriggi* each have their own speech, which they use among their own kind. *Hrossan* is the lingua franca of the planet. A *pfifltrigg* informs Ransom, "Once we all had different speeches and we still have at home. But everyone has learned the speech of the *hrossa*." When Ransom inquires why, the *pfifltrigg* explains:

> They [the *hrossa*] are our great speakers and singers. They have more words and better. No one learns the speech of my people, for what we have to say is said in stone and suns' blood and stars' milk and all can see them. No one learns the *sorns*' speech, for you can change their knowledge into any words and it is still the same. You cannot do that with the songs of the *hrossa*. [Anyone who has tried to translate poetry will understand immediately.] Their tongue goes all over Malacandra. I speak it to you because you are a stranger. I would speak it to a *sorn*. But we have our old tongues at home. (*OSP*, 129–30)

A gap in the coherence of Lewis's invention arises here. The *pfifltrigg* clearly states that at one time they "all had different speeches" and that they "still have at home," but that they have "learned the speech of the *hrossa*," implying that it is a second language for the other two species, acquired as an addition to their "old tongues." However, when Lewis came to write the sequel, *Perelandra*, some four years later, he altered this detail in such a way as to bring it more in line with Barfield's theory. At the opening of *Perelandra*, Ransom, now on his way to another planet, tells Lewis, the narrator:

> "It appears we were quite mistaken in thinking *Hressa-Hlab* the peculiar speech of Mars. It is really what may be called Old Solar, *Hlab-Eribol-ef-Cordi*."
> "What on earth do you mean?"
> "I mean that there was originally a common speech for all rational creatures inhabiting the planets of our system: those that were ever inhabited, I mean—what the eldils call the Low Worlds. . . . That original speech was lost on Thulcandra, our own world, when our whole tragedy took place. No human language now known in the world is descended from it." (*Per*, 26)

This is a change of some significance to the shape of Lewis's theme. Although it contradicts what appears in *Out of the Silent Planet*, the change brings the treatment of language into more complete agreement with Barfield, for it emphasizes the movement away from semantic unity toward dissociation and multiplicity. If there has been any doubt up to now of Lewis's purpose, the phrase "when our whole tragedy took place" removes it. The loss of original language is seated firmly in the context of the crucial events in Judeo-Christian history, and Lewis unites at one stroke the Fall, the Tower of Babel, and Barfield's theory. That the *hrossa* are the poets of the planet makes the change a simple one. Their poetic speech is the mother tongue of all three species, not a second language for the other two. It has been retained, not adopted, while other, more differentiated languages have evolved to accommodate the technological and scientific thinking of the *pfifltriggi* and *sorns*.

There is an elegance and simplicity to this new account which more than makes up for any inconsistency in continuity. The ancient semantic unity of Malacandra was an outward manifestation of ancient spiritual unity, a unity partially fragmented on Malacandra, but wholly lost on our world. Here we may safely substitute *communion* for *participation*—oneness of creature and Creator both in spirit and speech. The language of the *hrossa* is not just primitive. It is primal. It is the language Adam spoke to God, the original language of participation, of poetry, and of myth. On Thulcandra, the silent planet, the break is complete. The Word is lost, and silence echoes in the gulf between God and man. The break and the consequent loss and silence are dramatically illustrated in the scene toward which Lewis has been pointing, the climactic scene at Meldilorn, in which Weston confronts Oyarsa and makes the case for his ideology. And here knowledge of Lewis's use of Barfield is crucial to a proper understanding, for without it the scene is open to criticism for showing Lewis at his most dialectically manipulative, setting up straw opponents in order to knock them over. On the surface and with Barfield omitted, this is arguably the case. The cards are stacked against Weston from the beginning, as he blunders between baby talk and bombast while Ransom and Oyarsa are never less than serious and courteous. His misunderstanding of his audience goes beyond patronizing to be downright ridiculous; it is the broadest kind of lampoon of the White Man talking down to the Natives, dangling cheap beads and babbling inanities in pidgin. Thus Weston to a dozing *hross* whom he mistakes for the "witch-doctor": "Why you take our puff-bangs away? We very angry with you. We not afraid"; and "Great big head-man in sky he sends us. You no do what I say, he come, blow you all up—Pouff! Bang!"; and "Everyone who no do all we say—pouff! bang! . . . You do all we say and we give you much pretty things. See!

See!" (*OSP*, 143–44). For such a style, the narrator's apology that "his knowledge of the language was elementary" (*OSP*, 143) is scarcely an excuse. Tonto would be embarrassed. One is inclined to agree with Humphrey Carpenter that "the serious themes of *Out of the Silent Planet* come dangerously near to being lost in farce when Weston and Devine behave like a cartoon-strip caricature of the Englishman among the natives."[10] And when Weston shifts into English because he cannot speak the Malacandrian's "accursed language" (*OSP*, 152) the tone simply goes from low nonsense to high nonsense as he harangues his audience on manifest destiny and the Life Force.

But it is precisely here that knowledge of Barfield's theory makes all the difference. Weston's inability with the language is not simply a satiric device, it is a part of Lewis's theme. Moreover, that language, far from being "accursed," is blessed. Weston's own language is the one we come to see as accursed, and his choice of adjective has unconsciously ironic overtones. The Malacandrian language, with its direct perception, its unfallen innocence, is no longer fitted to Weston's mentality. He cannot speak it. He stands on the other side of a great divide, fallen, and (in his intellectual arrogance) unredeemed.

Weston ceases to be a real character in this scene; rather, he is Lewis's instrument. He is given no kind of real argument, for the point of the scene is not to be fair to Weston, or to present both sides equally. The point is to show, through Weston, what has befallen humanity and how this is manifest in language. Lewis's device for this, a running translation by Ransom of Weston's English into *hrossan*, is a field demonstration of Barfield's hypothesis. As Ransom tries to mediate between modern and archaic modes of thought and speech, we experience with an immediacy which no amount of paraphrase could convey the dissociation and abstraction that separate man from his surroundings, dissociation typical not just of the language, but of the spiritually arid society it represents. Every windy phrase, every rhetorical abstraction, appears absurd and inflated when translated into primal, concrete poetic diction. The concepts are empty and the argument barren:

Weston	Ransom
"vulgar robber"	"a kind of *hnau* who will take other *hnaus'* food and—and things, when they are not looking"

10. Carpenter, *Inklings*, 220.

"tribal life"	"one kindred all live together"
"elementary social structure"	"only one ruler"
"medicine"	"when the body of a living creature feels pains and becomes weak . . . we sometimes know how to stop it"
"law"	"many bent people and we kill them or shut them in huts and . . . have people for settling quarrels between the bent *hnau* about their huts and mates and things" (*OSP*, 152–53)

In every instance, in order to put it into *hrossan*, Ransom must replace the concept with the thing. The holding fast to experience, to the actual, is the hallmark of the difference. Inevitably, the scene recalls Gulliver among the Houyhnhnms, but there is this difference: Swift's is a moral point, Lewis's a theological one. When Weston makes the major statement of his philosophical manifesto, "Life is greater than any system of morality; her claims are absolute. It is not by tribal taboos and copybook maxims that she has pursued her relentless march from the amoeba to man and from man to civilisation" (*OSP*, 154), Ransom does his best to translate, but the attempt almost immediately breaks down. Not only can he not remember who "she" is, but the language he is using simply will not accommodate such abstract thinking: "He says . . . that living creatures are stronger than the question whether an act is bent or good—no, that cannot be right—he says it is better to be alive and bent than to be dead—no— he says, he says—I cannot say what he says, Oyarsa, in your language" (*OSP*, 154). Of course he can't; the concepts do not exist in the primal figuration that marks speech before the Fall. Ransom, as tongue-tied as the worried mother on the road back in England, cannot bend his language to Weston's ideas. And the fact that those ideas are not only familiar but acceptable to modern science, to modern philosophy, and to anyone who can read a newspaper or a textbook, that they are easily expressible in modern English, says much about how far Lewis feels we have come, and in what direction. The medium is the message.

Weston's actual defeat is anticlimactic; indeed the debate is not really resolved. It is broken off by Oyarsa, and this is just as well, for it could never be resolved. Communication between two such different speakers of two such different languages is sadly impossible. They do not merely have different words, they inhabit different worlds, morally, psychologically, and spiritually. Argument, if it is to progress, must start from common ground. It comes from difference of opinion, not disjunction of outlook. Here there is neither opposition nor true friendship, only silence speaking louder than words.

Essential Speech:
Language and Myth
in the Ransom Trilogy

Gregory Wolfe

*He found himself sitting within the very heart of language, in
the white-hot furnace of essential speech. All fact was broken,
splashed into cataracts, caught, turned inside out, kneaded, slain,
and reborn as meaning. For the lord of Meaning himself, the
herald, the messenger . . . was with them.* (THS, 398)

In the Preface to *Studies in Words,* C. S. Lewis says of the book
that "it is not an essay in the higher linguistics. The ultimate nature of
language and the theory of meaning are not here my concern" (*SW,*
vii). In its context, this comment is straightforward and functional:
Studies in Words is a merely "lexical and historical" book. But it also
reflects Lewis's habitual self-deprecation in his scholarly and polemi-
cal writings, his reluctance to claim as much expertise as his gener-
alizing capacity would appear to imply. Indeed, with the exception of
a few essays and poems, Lewis did not directly write about "the
ultimate nature of language and the theory of meaning." But anyone
familiar with Lewis's intellectual and literary preoccupations as manifested in his reading, correspondence, and scholarly studies knows
that he must have meditated deeply on the nature of language and
meaning.

It is my contention that despite Lewis's willingness to write discursively about myth and story, he chose to grapple with linguistic
problems primarily in the concrete, imaginative world of his poetry
and fiction. Above all, it is in the Ransom trilogy that Lewis elaborates
his ideas about language and its relation to perception and the spiritual life of the individual. In this essay I hope to reveal how the
scattered references to language in Lewis's writings are brought
together in the Ransom trilogy, where language itself becomes the
predominant metaphor linking all three novels.

I

In order to understand the role of language in the trilogy, it is necessary to recall that the earliest and most enduring influence on Lewis's thinking about language was that of his friend Owen Barfield, whose books *Poetic Diction* and *History in English Words* had appeared in the mid-1920s. In these and subsequent works, Barfield has developed his theory of the "evolution of consciousness," which traces the movement from the dense, mythic vision of ancient man to the rationalized, scientistic worldview of twentieth-century man. When a modern man looks at the stars, Barfield says, he is aware of space, distance, theories of the origin of the universe, etc.; but to ancient man the night sky was a living continuum of meaning, peopled by gods and spirits. Ancient man also thought about the origin of the cosmos, but in terms of divine activity, not of the Big Bang. In the course of human history, the discovery of the mind (to use a phrase of Bruno Snell) in the Greek experience of philosophy, the advent of Christianity, and the post-Renaissance development of the scientific method all involved major leaps in the evolution of consciousness. That evolution has consisted of a rationalizing process that differentiates the mind from the world it perceives. The ancient man was supremely unselfconscious; his consciousness was continuous with the world. Over time, man's awareness of himself as a perceiving individual has grown to the point that he has questioned his ability to know reality at all.

Barfield's theory does not see human history as one long decline, as it might at first appear—there is loss and gain. The immediate, intuitive consciousness of reality is differentiated into discrete concepts which are capable of "meaning." Meaning, however, is grounded in a yoking together of separate concepts into a new unity. This, according to Barfield, is the burden of metaphor. For the making of metaphor is an activity of the mind whereby the "ancient unity" is regained or approximated through poetic intuition. Even the most abstract and philosophical language is shot through with metaphor. Such words as "right," "cause," "stimulus," and "organism" originated in a figurative meaning.[1] To take a well-known example, "spirit" originally meant something like "breath." Only after a succession of differentiations could it evolve from that origin to mean something like the animating principle of the human consciousness.

1. Barfield, *Poetic Diction: A Study in Meaning* (London: Faber and Gwyer, 1928), 134.

In a poem entitled "The Birth of Language" (1946; *Poems*, 10–11), Lewis reveals his own blend of Barfield's ideas with a form of Christian Platonism. The poem combines Mercury as the messenger of the gods (therefore the lord of language) with the planet closest to the sun. In the heat of the sun's region, Mercury flings off "intelligible virtues," which dance with power and subtlety. Lewis pictures these pure essences (reminiscent of Plato's Ideas) descending (or moving outward) into the cold and empty realm which surrounds the Earth:

> They ache and freeze through vacant seas
> Of night. Their nimbleness and youth
> Turns lean and frore; their meaning more,
> Their being less. Fact shrinks to truth.
>   (lines 29–32)

In our world the essence experiences an incarnation—a "word made breath"—but it is "dry like death" (lines 34, 36). The gain in "meaning" is paralleled by a loss of "being." Lewis's Platonism is evident in the way he pictures the transcendent "virtues" (line 8) suffering diminution as they become "incarnate" (lines 33–34). Barfield, on the other hand, is less dualistic, more confident that matter and spirit are intimately related.

Barfield's theory places the process of linguistic change in an historical setting. Though Barfield does not rank one historical period over another (because over time there is gain as well as loss), he does hold that meaning itself can be destroyed. In his opinion, the rise of rationalism with Descartes in the seventeenth century put knowledge and consciousness on a purely abstract basis, in which the mind constructs the world *de novo*, starting from a premise of radical doubt. Only empirically verifiable facts are admitted to the status of the knowable. Consequently, words become increasingly emptied of meaning; nature is drained of its transcendent, metaphysical dimension and is conceived of as inert, subject to the manipulations of science. This is a thesis that Lewis endorsed and encapsulated in *The Abolition of Man,* a book he called in its preface the nonfictional companion volume to the Ransom trilogy.

Given this state of affairs, in which meaning itself is threatened by abstraction and rigidity, the role of the poet takes on a kind of redemptive mission. For the poet is the metaphor-maker, the imaginative consciousness in search of a union of the mind with the universe. As he put it in "Bluspels and Flalansferes," "It will have escaped no one that in such a scale of writers the poets will take the highest place; and among the poets those who have at once the tenderest care for old words and the surest instinct for the creation of new metaphors" (265). Lewis, whatever his internal conflicts over the relationship between reason and imagination, had by the time of writing the Ransom trilogy become convinced that the imagination must play a central role in restoring a whole vision of reality: "For me, reason is the natural organ of truth; but imagination is the organ of meaning. . . . Such a view indirectly implies a kind of truth or right-ness in the imagination itself" ("Blu," 265). In *That Hideous Strength* Ransom is preeminently an imaginative man, while his friend Mac-Phee, a rationalist and logician, sees only a fragment of reality, and is reduced to the role of jester and fool.

With characteristic audacity, Lewis divided language into three basic categories: Ordinary, Scientific, and Poetic ("Lang," 129). Both science and poetry are skills, and as such they take ordinary language and place it in the service of a specific mode of thought. Ideally, these three types of language should exist in harmony. But Lewis and Barfield were convinced that the language of science was claiming for itself an ability to account for human nature that only art, philosophy, and theology could provide. Empirical science cannot convey most of the deepest human experiences, Lewis argued. "To be incommunica-ble by Scientific language is, so far as I can judge, the normal state of experience" ("Lang," 138). In *Out of the Silent Planet* Lewis popu-lates the planet of Malacandra with three races, each representing different characteristics. The *sorns* are the scientists, the *pfifltriggi* artisans and craftsmen, and the *hrossa* hunter-gatherers who are also poets and chroniclers. Both the *sorns* and the *pfifltriggi* speak lan-guages dominated by their specialized functions, but the common language of the planet is that of the *hrossa*.[2] In a sense, the *hrossa* are representatives of Ordinary language, who build on their sensuous and moral experience to evolve both poetry and history.

But Lewis does not exalt poetry at the expense of science. Con-trary to the critics who accuse Lewis of being opposed to science, he shows, in the *sorns* and especially in the character of Hingest in *That Hideous Strength*, that science also builds from the common-sense world of ordinary experience. In the midst of the vacuous and unreal abstractions being spouted in the halls of Belbury by the members of the N.I.C.E., Hingest's marvelously colloquial language breaks in like a blast of fresh air: "And there's nothing extraordinary in the fact that the N.I.C.E. should wish, if possible, to hand over to Bracton the

---

2. For an extended discussion of the different languages on Malacandra, see Ver-lyn Flieger's essay in this volume.

odium of turning the heart of England into a cross between an abortive American hotel and a glorified gas-works" (*THS*, 66). He then warns Mark Studdock that the N.I.C.E. "could play the devil with *you*" (*THS*, 67). Like all earthy people, Hingest speaks more truly than he knows. Hingest's death signifies the death of true science and the triumph of scientism. Lewis held that both poetry and science must be grounded in a clear perception of concrete reality. Indeed, Lewis's belief that language and perception are intimately related underlies the unfolding of the trilogy's action. However, it would be more precise to use Barfield's term "consciousness" rather than "perception" in the context of Lewis's ideas about language and imagination. According to Barfield, consciousness "embraces all my awareness of my surroundings at any given moment, and 'surroundings' includes my own feelings."[3] It is widely thought that Lewis was unwilling to allow into his definition of consciousness the subjective element which is a central feature of Barfield's conception. Without attempting to delve into the philosophical issues related to Lewis's "Great War" with Barfield, I think that it can be shown that Lewis did hold to an idea of consciousness that stands between the poles of absolute subjectivism and objectivism. Lewis takes Barfield's notion and links it to a moral and even ontological ground. The nature of consciousness, whether the individual recognizes the fact or not, is inextricably tied to the ground of being. According to Lewis, "All our joys and sorrows, religious, aesthetic, or natural . . . are *about* something. They are a by-product of the (logically) prior act of *attending to* or *looking towards* something. . . . The very essence of our life as conscious beings . . . consists of something which cannot be communicated except by hints, similes, metaphors, and the use of those emotions . . . which are pointers to it" ("Lang," 139–40).

Lewis rarely wrote or spoke in the language of the philosopher, but it would do no injustice to him to say that along with the great classical and Christian philosophers (and here Lewis would think of Plato, Aristotle, Augustine, and Aquinas), he believed that the openness of the soul to the transcendent ground of being was the beginning of all wisdom. Philosophy, like art, begins in wonder. Or, to return to technical terms, when we sense the contingency of the created order, we experience an intuition of being. In sensing our creatureliness we become aware of the existence of the Creator. Moreover, the experience of the world as a created order involves an

---

3. Barfield, *Poetic Diction*, 48.

awareness of teleology—that creation is full of purpose and meaning, tending toward a destined end.

Both the philosopher and the poet must cultivate the virtues of openness to the transcendent. Lewis would undoubtedly agree that a philosopher or poet could go about his business without believing in God, but in doing so he would be diminishing himself. Language, as a register of consciousness, reflects our level of sensitivity to meaning. Thus language not only reveals our moral condition, but can become a means of grace. In and through language, man may grow imaginatively, become more attuned to his relationship to the world. The Ransom trilogy is largely the story of Ransom's "education"; his development is offered as a paradigm of the moral imagination. Ransom is an ordinary, pious scholar who is described on the first page of the trilogy as the "Pedestrian." Here Lewis not only manages to pun on Ransom's status as Everyman, but he also places him in a Dantean Dark Wood, at the beginning of a long journey. Ransom does have certain advantages: as a philologist he is aware of the way words have come to accrete meaning. In *That Hideous Strength*, we learn that he is the author of *Dialect and Semantics* (*THS*, 231), a subject that is thoroughly immersed in the earthy particularity of traditional speech. But whatever his advantages, he shares many of the prejudices of his age, prejudices which must be shed if he is to live up to the divine demands that are being made on him.

Out of the Silent Planet and *Perelandra*, which trace the larger part of Ransom's education, both begin with extended descriptions of his adjustment to the topography and language of Mars and Venus. These passages might have been written as a literal illustration of certain sections of Barfield's *Poetic Diction*. Barfield calls the faculty that enables one to perceive analogies and resemblances "knowledge," and the effort by which knowledge is acquired and imparted he calls "wisdom." To illustrate his point, he asks the reader to imagine a man stripped entirely of these faculties. For such a man, "all sounds would fuse into one meaningless roar, all sights into one chaotic panorama, amid which no individual objects—not even colour itself—would be distinguishable."[4] In *Reason and Imagination in C. S. Lewis*, Peter Schakel argues that at the time the Ransom trilogy was written, Lewis was still a convinced rationalist, suspicious of Barfield's apparent subjectivism: "Ransom's becoming able to see strange objects on Malacandra was only like the automatically adjusting lens on a projector coming into

4. Barfield, *Poetic Diction*, 55, 56.

focus."[5] But in fact Lewis is carrying out in these scenes his own variation of Barfield's theory. When he comes to in the spaceship, Ransom is described as being "poised on a sort of emotional watershed from which, he felt, he might at any moment pass either into delirious terror or into an ecstasy of joy" (*OSP*, 26). As he looks at the Earth, he tries to convince himself that he is only looking at the moon. But the familiar "man in the moon" is not visible in what Ransom perceives as a "megalomaniac disk" and a "monstrous orb" (*OSP*, 27). Lewis undoubtedly had fun in having Weston deflate Ransom's hysterics by flatly telling him that he is looking at the Earth. But throughout the trilogy Lewis will show that both the modern rationalist worldview and our own petty fears blind us to the glory of creation.[6] We perceive what is larger and prior to our being as a threat; hence our hostility to other races and our desire to subdue and tame nature. The same is true for the famous passage in which Ransom discovers that space is not empty and cold, but awash with light and life. One could point to Ransom's growing sensitivity to the spiritual meaning of the waves and floating islands in *Perelandra* as images of grace, as well as many other examples of this technique.

In another of his poems, "The Country of the Blind" (1951; *Poems*, 33–34), Lewis distilled his understanding of how the relationship between language and consciousness has decayed. Stimulated by H. G. Wells's short story with the same title, Lewis pictures a race of men whose sight had so atrophied that they began to use words inherited from the past (such as "see" and "dark" and "light") in a manner utterly devoid of metaphoric insight. To these blind men, to *see* came to mean merely to *understand*; in short, they emptied words of their primary meaning and transmuted the remaining image into an object, into what Barfield calls an "idol."[7] But in the transition period before all had become blind, there remained those who had not yet "achieved snug / Darkness, safe from the guns of heav'n" (lines 7–8)—archaic men continued to use the language of visual experience literally. The blind, Lewis says, far from condemning the man who spoke of literal seeing, claimed that they felt the same way. Without the proper vision, however, they could not possibly *experi-*

---

5. Schakel, *Reason and Imagination in C. S. Lewis: A Study of "Till We Have Faces"* (Grand Rapids, Mich.: Eerdmans, 1984), 41.

6. One of the themes that Lewis found running throughout the fiction of George MacDonald was the way in which we fail to perceive the goodness that is all around us.

7. This is the argument of Barfield's *Saving the Appearances: A Study in Idolatry* (London: Faber and Faber, 1957); see especially 110–11.

ence reality in the same way. The archaic man was helpless to explain this because "he / Knew too much to be clear" (lines 20–21). And the blind glibly went about the business of showing "how tricks of the phrase, sheer metaphors could set / Fools concocting a myth, taking the words for things" (lines 25–26). Lewis then addresses the reader and challenges him to deny that his portrait of a blind race is not an accurate account of contemporary experience. The leading men of the West no longer can understand the "truths that once,/ Opaque, carved in divine forms, irremovable,/ Dread but dear as a mountain-/ Mass, stood plain to the inward eye" (lines 29–32).

As "The Country of the Blind" indicates, the decay of language takes two forms in Lewis's thought. On the one hand, words are cut off from their metaphoric roots and become abstract, uniform, drained of meaning and fit for the primitive chant-words that modern politicians use to pacify and dominate the masses. On the other hand, language becomes subject to a false sensuality, a hollow "trickery" that concocts pleasing myths that satisfy an appetite for the sensationalistic. Both errors might be seen as failures to integrate soul and body; indeed, they are opposite sides of the same coin. Abstraction is the result of attempting to live like the angels, who apprehend essences without the mediation of the senses. But men who succumb to this temptation become radically alienated from experience and prone to inhuman ideologies. False sensuality—men imitating beasts—consists of the illusion that a diet of clever and appealing images is something that men can live on. But this form of materialism ends in the same hollowness and brutality as abstraction. The true balance of soul and body implies an acceptance of the limitations of the human condition. It is an integration that is modeled after the Incarnation itself, the union of heaven and earth in the *Logos*. For Lewis, the Incarnation stands between the extremes of mythic and rationalistic consciousness; our dilemma is that we have lost the incarnational imagination that once suffused Western culture.

Lewis once wrote: "If God chooses to be mythopoeic—and is not the sky itself a myth—shall we refuse to be *mythopathic*?"[8] The Ransom trilogy is Lewis's attempt to revive the reader's mythopathic capacity—to resensitize a secular, modern world to the spiritual realm. His special imaginative gift, it can be argued, was an ability to breathe new life into ancient myths and religious dogmas by taking

8. Lewis, "Myth Became Fact" (1944), in *God in the Dock: Essays on Theology and Ethics*, ed. Walter Hooper (Grand Rapids: Eerdmans, 1970), 67.

their symbolic patterns and placing them in a different context.[9] By combining science fiction, with its affinity to mythic romance, and the Wellsian novel of ideas, Lewis may have created a hybrid objectionable to the critics, but he also made the two levels of meaning reinforce each other in a dynamic and complex manner.[10] The imaginative challenge, as he saw it, was to reawaken the modern imagination to spiritual reality by bringing two visions of the world into opposition. Lewis sets a realm of mystery, plenitude, variety, and hierarchy against the dominant strain of post-Renaissance scientism, which permeates modern culture and is obsessed by power, abstraction, and uniformity.[11] For Lewis, life was more than a frenetic attempt to get and spend or to conquer nature and "improve" the human race through social engineering, the twin errors represented by Devine and Weston. "Real life is meeting," Lewis thought (title of chapter 14, *THS*)—meeting other persons and ultimately meeting the personal God. But meeting implies communication, a willingness to know and be known by the Other. Without self-knowledge, sacrifice, and love—without an abandonment of self—no communication of any value can take place. In the Ransom trilogy, language itself acts as the "objective correlative" that discloses the presence (or absence) of true exchange.

Now we will turn to the novels to see how Lewis gives imaginative life to his fundamental ideas about language and consciousness.

9. See Gregory Wolfe, "C. S. Lewis's Debt to George MacDonald," *CSL: The Bulletin of the New York C. S. Lewis Society* 15.2 (1983): 5. The myth of Cupid and Psyche in *Till We Have Faces* and the Garden of Eden in *Perelandra* are two obvious examples of this technique, and in *That Hideous Strength* the novel concludes with a version of Pentecost set against a modern Tower of Babel. A perfect example of Lewis's ability to breathe new life into ancient myths is the fragment from a projected novel, "After Ten Years," which begins inside the Trojan horse (*Of Other Worlds: Essays and Stories,* ed. Walter Hooper [London: Geoffrey Bles, 1966], 127–45). Lewis plunges the reader *in medias res* with a vengeance here!

10. Critics of the Ransom trilogy have tended to classify it as a rather schematized version of the Wellsian science fiction novel of ideas popular in Lewis's youth. These critics point to the "Note" in *OSP*, 6 alluding to Wells and to Lewis's own comment in a letter (apropos of this novel) that "any amount of theology can now be smuggled into people's minds under cover of romance without their knowing it" (*Letters*, 167). There can be little doubt that Lewis had a "purpose" in writing the trilogy, but balanced against this must be his statement that most of his stories began with mental "pictures," often originating in dreams. In the science fiction novel, Lewis found a medium sufficiently close to romance to enable him to achieve a certain level of mythic density.

11. See Michael D. Aeschliman, *The Restitution of Man: C. S. Lewis and the Case Against Scientism* (Grand Rapids: Eerdmans, 1983).

II

Within the first ten pages of *Out of the Silent Planet,* Lewis not only establishes the centrality of language as theme and controlling metaphor, but also shows that language is not an absolute value in the spiritual life of man. Ransom comes upon a poor woman who is fearful that her son, a retarded or "simple" lad, is being mistreated by Weston and Devine. "The monotonous voice and the limited range of the woman's vocabulary did not express much emotion" (*OSP,* 9). Neither the woman nor her son can express themselves through language, yet their dignity and moral worth do not depend on words. A few pages later, Devine, who went to the same public school as Ransom, is described as having learned as a schoolboy "that kind of humour which consists in a perpetual parody of the sentimental or idealistic clichés of one's elders." Later in life, Ransom is said to have found Devine "flashy . . . and ready made" (*OSP,* 17). Devine's cynicism and superficiality are in fact a form of ossified schoolboy humor. Without making the contrast explicit, Lewis sets the infantile language of Devine beside the condition of the idiot boy, who is incapable of falseness or alienation. In *That Hideous Strength* Lewis depicts a wino whose knowing looks, gestures, and leers contain more *meaning* than all of the abstractions of the N.I.C.E. put together. Language, in short, is not an absolute value; communication and moral integrity, however achieved or expressed, are the crucial things in our hope for salvation.

On Malacandra, Ransom soon encounters a form of language that appears infantile, or primitive, but which he discovers to be far richer and more subtle than his own. The language spoken by the *hrossa* is characterized by Barfield's "ancient semantic unity." The word the Malacandrians use for evil, "bent," is figurative. In a single term, Lewis embodies the traditional Christian concept of human nature: originally created in God's image, damaged by the Fall, but not utterly degraded. Another example of a Barfieldian "ancient unity" would be the word *hnakra.* The *hnakra* is the shark-like creature hunted by the *hrossa*; the name means both "enemy" and "beloved." More than the elimination of a dangerous predator, the hunt for the *hnakra* is ritual or drama in which the glory of the kill is matched by a love for the power and grace of the *hnakra.*

Not all Malacandrian words fit Barfield's pattern. For instance, there are two words for "yearn," one which expresses true Eros or disinterested love (*wondelone*) and one which implies lust (*hlunthe-line*) (*OSP,* 83). This differentiation, however, is not an exercise in abstraction; rather, it represents a more accurate observation of reality. Lewis, with his constant emphasis on the relationship between language and perception, is suggesting that the Malacandrians have a more incisive psychology than the inhabitants of Earth.

Ransom's moral education stems both from his growing sensitivity to Malacandrian speech and from his increased awareness of the inadequacy both of the language and of the mental habits of the inhabitants of Earth. The modern prejudice against the past, which sees history as one long ascent from darkness and savagery to enlightenment and democracy, is embodied in the character of Weston (Devine is nothing more than a pirate). With all the moral superiority of a Victorian missionary, Weston preaches his faith in the evolutionary will to power of the human race. By the end of the novel, when Ransom must translate Weston's evolutionary rhetoric for the Oyarsa, it is evident that Weston's abstractions simply cannot fit into the concrete, figurative language of Malacandra. Weston's language is quite literally nonsense.

Perelandra is structured around the insight, which Ransom eventually achieves, that "the triple distinction of truth from myth and of both from fact was purely terrestrial—was part and parcel of that unhappy division between soul and body which resulted from the Fall" (*Per,* 163). Ransom's education has led him to see that it is not merely the idyllic worlds of Malacandra and Perelandra which are "mythological," but that reality itself, when perceived truly, is as dense with meaning as myth. Throughout *Perelandra* a series of allusions links the action not simply to the Garden of Eden, but to other archetypal events and experiences as well. The Green Lady, who is compared to the Madonna, utters a Magnificat (*Per,* 236–37); Ransom rejects the mission Maleldil prompts him to undertake three times, echoing the denials of St. Peter (*Per,* 167); the Un-man utters numerous blasphemies, such as the wish that the inhabitants of Perelandra may have "Death in abundance" (*Per,* 130). Later, during a respite in his combat with the Un-man, Ransom succumbs to a fear of the vast, dead emptiness of space (*Per,* 187–88)—the fear that Pascal articulated for modern man as early as the seventeenth century.

In addition to this technique of multiple allusions, Lewis portrays the temptation of the Green Lady in terms of the deadly conflict between mythopoeia and materialism. The Green Lady "translates" the words of Ransom and the Un-man into a form not unlike Christ's parables: her metaphors are of trees without fruit and fruit without taste (*Per,* 118–19). As a perfect creature, she is at one with her Creator. Thus, to use the philosophical terms discussed earlier in this essay, the Green Lady has a perfect "intuition of being." That is why she can even take the evil thoughts of the Un-man and find in them something that bespeaks the goodness of Maleldil. She is able to revel in the created order because she understands it to be contingent on the will of Maleldil. Diametrically opposed to this is the gnosticism of the Un-man, who is always trying to "see through" things.

But the Green Lady is not impervious to temptation. The deadliest and most effective phase of the temptation begins with the Un-man's introduction of the notion of the "alongside": "We put words together to mean things that have never happened and places that never were: beautiful words, well put together. And then tell them to one another. We call it stories or poetry" (Per, 117). As the Un-man's ploy develops, it becomes clear that he is putting forward a false, Promethean form of romanticism, in which the individual is pitted against a cruel fate and can only survive by asserting his will against his environment through an act of rebellion. This is confirmed when he begins to teach her new words: "Creative and Intuition and Spiritual" (Per, 150).[12] The Un-man begins to turn the Green Lady into a late-Romantic heroine; among his several variations on this theme is a tale of feminist rebellion against male domination (Per, 142–43) (intended to undermine the masculinity and authority of the King and of Maleldil himself).

The "alongside" imagination, rather than being a window onto reality, becomes a substitute reality—a mock creation. The Un-man not only writes a "play" for the Green Lady to act in, he dresses her up and tries to teach her vanity. But this "play" is itself a blasphemous usurpation of divine providence: the Un-man, acting like a God, sets the Green Lady in his own story, thus controlling her like a character in a work of fiction (Per, 153–54). For Lewis, the Romantic worship of "creativity" is ultimately a dangerous arrogation of God's creative power. In short, Lewis is suggesting that the Romantic writer's rejection of mimesis in favor of "originality" stems from a profound alienation from the created order.

The Un-man's corruption of the imagination is directly related to his gnostic revulsion from the material world: he sees the world as a thin rind over an abyss of nothingness (Per, 192–95). It is Ransom's recognition that myth, fact, and truth are one in the Incarnation and present in the sacraments of the church that enables him to accept

12. For Lewis's critique of the Romantic notions of "creativity," see his essay "Christianity and Literature" (1939), reprinted in Christian Reflections, ed. Walter Hooper (London: Geoffrey Bles, 1967), 1–11.

his vocation and destroy the Un-man. But so powerful is the Un-man's nihilism that Ransom gives way to it after killing him. Only through his slow recovery, in which he is "breast-fed by the planet Venus herself" (*Per*, 213)—restored by contact with the goodness of created being—can he attain the end of his education. At the end of the novel, the Green Lady tries to express the joy she shares with Ransom and the King: "It is like a fruit with a very thick shell. . . . The joy of our meeting when we meet again in the Great Dance is the sweet of it. But the rind is thick—more years thick than I can count" (*Per*, 255). The Un-man's image is reversed and becomes a mythopoeic affirmation of the goodness of being.

In *That Hideous Strength* Lewis pursues more explicitly the way in which the Incarnation, when properly understood and accepted, can heal the divisions brought about by modern dislocations of consciousness. The overarching metaphor of the novel is that of the body—its relation to the "head" and to gender and sexuality. Lewis elaborates his theme through the fictional technique known as "polyphony."[13] On each side of the conflict—represented by Belbury and St. Anne's—a large cast of characters reflect different personalities and approaches to the mind/body problem. What Lewis hoped to show was that those who accepted an incarnational belief experienced the infinite variety of goodness, whereas the apparent differences of the abstractionists ultimately express a uniform alienation toward life itself.[14] Thus, in terms of human love and sexuality, Grace Ironwood represents the unswerving loyalty and devotion of a celibate, the Dennistons Eros, and Mrs. Dimble domesticity and spiritual maternity. At Belbury, on the other hand, there is only Fairy Hardcastle's sadistic lust, the implied homosexuality of Frost and Wither, and the other characters' utter asexuality.

Parallel to the metaphor of the body is that of the Word. Lewis held that a word—a union of form and meaning—is analogous to the way a soul is incarnate in a body. At the beginning of *That Hideous Strength*, Jane Studdock tries to concentrate on her doctoral thesis, which is on John Donne's "triumphant vindication of the body" (*THS*, 10). For Lewis, however, Donne's "love" poetry exemplifies a

13. Two novelists who employ the "polyphonic" technique are Fyodor Dostoevsky and Aleksandr Solzhenitsyn. In Dostoevsky's *The Possessed* and Solzhenitsyn's *First Circle*, large casts of characters are used to weave a series of variations on the central problem of the story. It is a form well suited to the novel of ideas, since it allows the novelist to play out the implications of different intellectual positions.

14. It must be admitted that, as usual, evil characters manage to exert a special fascination—in spite of the author's best intentions.

shallow sensualism, the "sheer metaphor" he derides in "The Country of the Blind."[15] Jane reads the lines:

> Hope not for minde in women; at their best
> Sweetnesse and wit, they are but *Mummy* possest.
>
> (*THS*, 13)

Donne's false sensuality is but another aspect of the separation of soul and body. A "Mummy possest" is at two removes from being: it is a dead body possessed by an alien spirit. Jane does have a mind, but it will require an openness to the glories and purposes of the body before she achieves a reintegration within herself and with her husband. Soon after she reads Donne's lines, Jane dreams of the criminal Alcasan, whose head is separated from his body in the hideous experiment of the N.I.C.E.

If it is true that many of the characters in *That Hideous Strength* are little more than sketches or types, it is also true that Lewis had an uncanny ability to absorb and reproduce the linguistic styles he derived from a wide range of literary and personal sources.[16] The "caricatures" in the novel, thus, often have a deadly accuracy and relevance; their language mimics the varieties of modern, dislocated consciousness. Frost, for example, is typical of the Freudian, behaviorist social scientist as he enumerates ways to get Mark to bring Jane to Belbury: "Either by supplying him with some motive on the instinctive level, such as fear of us or desire for her; or else by conditioning him to identify himself so completely with the Cause that he will understand the real motive for securing her person and act on it" (*THS*, 294). Then there is the clergyman, Straik, who has responded to the tragic death of his daughter and the poor conditions of the working class with a millenarian cry for political revolution: "That is precisely the subterfuge by which the World, the organisation and body of Death, has sidetracked and emasculated the teach-

---

15. Lewis's ideas about Donne are crystalized in "Donne and Love Poetry in the Seventeenth Century" (1938), in *Selected Literary Essays*, ed. Walter Hooper (Cambridge: Cambridge University Press, 1969), 106–25. In my opinion, Lewis's essay is moralistic and blind to Donne's passion and inventiveness, but this does not affect Lewis's use of Donne in *That Hideous Strength*.

16. When Lewis wrote "roofers," thank-you notes to the hostess of a home where he had stayed, he effortlessly imitated the styles of such writers as Sir Thomas Browne, Sir Philip Sidney, Jane Austen, and Samuel Johnson. Some of his roofers were parodies and others were original verses. See George Sayer, "Jack On Holiday," in *C. S. Lewis at the Breakfast Table and Other Reminiscences*, ed. James T. Como (New York: Macmillan, 1979), 209.

ing of Jesus, and turned into priestcraft and mysticism the plain demand of the Lord for righteousness and judgement here and now" (*THS*, 92). And later: "The Son of Man—that is, Man himself, full grown—has power to judge the world—to distribute life without end, and punishment without end" (*THS*, 155). In Straik's rhetoric, Lewis, with uncanny foresight, caught the tone of political apocalyptic that characterizes the movement known as "Liberation Theology."

Mark Studdock, like Jane, is a character perched between the two worlds represented by Belbury and St. Anne's. His conscience, however, is more easily deadened by the ideology of the social sciences. Mark's education, it is said, "had the curious effect of making things that he read and wrote more real to him than things he saw" (*THS*, 104). In a sense, scientism creates an "alongside" world that separates man from reality; thus language can be the means whereby consciousness is closed. The two chief moments of moral decision for Mark involve writing. First, in order to preserve his position at Belbury, Mark has to write a deliberately vague and flattering letter to Curry (*THS*, 129–30). Soon after, he is asked to write manipulative leaders (editorials) justifying, before the fact, violence perpetrated by the N.I.C.E. Mark's leaders—one for the masses and one for the educated reader, who is said to be more "gullible"—are Lewis's biting satire on the "media." Here again caricature is averted by the sting of recognition the reader experiences in the rhetoric of the op-ed page.

Early in the novel, the Bursar of Bracton College rather innocently remarks, "We all have our different languages; but we all really mean the same thing" (*THS*, 40). But this is precisely what Lewis considered to be the opposite of the truth. Only through particularity of language that has slowly accreted meaning can anything universal be known. It is Merlin in *That Hideous Strength* who reintroduces the existence of earlier cultures possessed of Barfield's "ancient unities." Merlin, lying beneath Bragdon Wood, embodies an ancient British wholeness. The Puritans who walled off Bragdon Wood because of its associations with earthy, primitive celebrations of fertility (such as May Day) thought that the Word could stand alone and disembodied, without the physical elements of a sacrament. Merlin, with his preternatural and pre-Christian intimacy with and manipulation of the natural world, presents a problem for the Christian. Ransom (now the Director) says that "Merlin represents what we've got to get back to in some different way" (*THS*, 353). Unlike the inhabitants of Malacandra and Perelandra, our "primitive" cultures "confused . . . matter and spirit," due to the Fall. Their proper relationship can only be reestablished with the Incarnation and the sacraments.

The denouement of the novel takes its shape from the two biblical events representing the loss and recovery of communication through languages. Merlin submits to the Director and causes Belbury to collapse into the chaos of Babel, while the descent of the Planets brings a new Pentecost to St. Anne's. Mark, after suffering and ultimately rejecting evil, reads a children's story, and he reawakens to wonder. And Jane, ready at last to accept the burdens and joys of her femininity, will go beyond the artificial metaphors of a Donne, receive the Word, and bear new life within her womb.

III

In the course of the trilogy, Lewis has created a series of variations on the theme of the decay of language and perception. But the ending of *That Hideous Strength*, though satisfying to our sense of justice and even to a certain extent on the symbolic level, does not provide any clear answer to the problem of recovering incarnational language and imagination.[17] On one level, of course, it is always easier to reveal the inadequacy of a decadent order than it is to propose a way out. But I suggest that the problematic ending of *That Hideous Strength* raises the fundamental problem which dogs all of Lewis's theories about the imagination: namely, his Platonism.

As an orthodox Christian with a vivid sense of man's fallen state, Lewis is less willing than Barfield to allow the imagination a wholly positive function. Especially in *Perelandra*, Lewis characterized the ways the imagination can be twisted and distorted into serving the ends of carnality and egotism. For if Lewis has a powerful vision of the redemptive act of the Incarnation ("There is nothing now between us and Him"), he also, in a particularly Platonic and ultra-Protestant way, sees a tremendous gap between God and man opened by the Fall. Just as he visualizes words as coming from the heat of the sun and freezing as they descend to Earth (becoming "dry like death") in "The Birth of Language," he says that the ancient myths are

---

17. Owen Barfield's objections to the endings of *Out of the Silent Planet* and *That Hideous Strength*—that they revealed a strange kind of "undergraduate humour"—are pertinent to the problem of Platonism; see his Introduction to *Light on C. S. Lewis*, ed. Jocelyn Gibb (London: Geoffrey Bles, 1965), xvi-xvii. The theatricality of these endings suggests that Lewis found it difficult to resolve the thematic conflicts raised within the novels.

"gleams of celestial strength and beauty falling on a jungle of filth and imbecility" (*Per*, 232). The tension between his Platonism and sacramentalism is a source of some confusion and uncertainty in the trilogy as Lewis searches for a reconciling vision that will heal our psychic and spiritual wounds.

In the context of an essay on Lewis as a Christian apologist, the Anglican theologian Austin Farrer wrote: "Lewis was raised in the tradition of an idealist philosophy which hoped to establish the reality of the mental subject independently of, or anyhow in priority to, that of the bodily world. Though he moved some way from such positions he was still able to overlook the full involvement of the reasonable soul in a random and perishable system."[18] To be sure, Lewis did increasingly move away from a cruder form of Platonic idealism: he affirmed the Incarnation and the sacraments as living and efficacious unions of matter and spirit. Ransom, in *Perelandra*, has the courage to act when he links his "mythic" experiences on the unfallen worlds with the incarnate Logos and the church's sacraments. So, too, in his essay "Transposition," Lewis claims that a sign which actually becomes what it signifies is more properly called "sacramental" rather than "symbolical."[19]

But Platonism was a persistent mental habit with Lewis, and it characterizes much of his thought about language and the imagination—at least as that thought is present in the Ransom trilogy. In "The Birth of the Language" we have seen how Lewis imagines "intelligible virtues" being thrown off by Mercury and descending through cold space to become incarnate on Earth, though they are "dry like death." When Ransom beholds Tor and Tinidril, King and Queen of Venus, at the end of *Perelandra*, he is told by them that our mythology is based on the truth of supernatural beings. "Our mythology is based on a solider reality than we dream: but it is also at an almost infinite distance from that base. And when they told him this, Ransom at last understood why mythology was what it was—gleams of celestial strength and beauty falling on a jungle of filth and imbecility" (*Per*, 231–32). Aside from being an example of Lewis's passion for rationalizing things, this passage appears to echo the extreme Protestant notion of a totally fallen and corrupted nature—a notion that Lewis elsewhere repudiates. However, this is not a mere lapse. In Ransom's explanation of Old Solar, the language of the *hrossa* and

18. Farrer, "The Christian Apologist," in *Light on C. S. Lewis*, 41.

19. Lewis, "Transposition," in *Transposition and Other Addresses* (London: Geoffrey Bles, 1949), p. 15.

once the common language of the sentient races, he says: "That original speech was lost on Thulcandra, our own world, when our whole tragedy took place. *No human language now known in the world is descended from it*" (*Per*, 26; my italics). According to this view, human language is not a "bent" form of a language that was once in contact with spiritual reality; it has no intrinsic relationship with the transcendent.

The ending of *That Hideous Strength* discloses the same dichotomy. The Descent of the Gods on St. Anne's, though it is intended to echo Pentecost, is less a moment of grace in which the Good News is affirmed than a kind of possession. The characters, under the "influence" of the planets, behave more like puppets than apostles. In this scene and others, when the supernatural simply irrupts into the fallen world, Lewis fails to find the balance between grace and nature. When the gods descend on St. Anne's, grace does not perfect or complete nature, but dominates and supplants it.

In short, there is nothing in the natural order to which Lewis can turn in resolving this dualism between the realm of ideal essences and the fallen, contingent order. Or, as Farrer put it, Lewis could not see the "full involvement of the reasonable soul in a random and perishable system." Merlin, with his ambiguous pagan and Christian aspects, is the only model of a premodern man given in *That Hideous Strength*. Lewis does not offer a way to get back to what Merlin represents because he cannot see in the natural order any stay against the corruption of language. Of course, Lewis was far from alone in this anxiety; most thinkers about language have at one time hoped to find an ideal order of language. But if Lewis had attended more closely to Barfield's more historical understanding of language and to the philosophy of Aristotle and Aquinas, he might have seen in human nature and history more evidence of how meaning can be lost and recovered. Unfortunately, Lewis was unable to appreciate the efforts of modernists such as Joyce, Eliot, and Pound, who sought to cleanse and restore language.

Despite the Platonic contradictions about language in the trilogy, the fact remains that Lewis's sense of the modern crisis is remarkably acute. Lewis not only raises the issues entailed by the decay of meaning, but also gives those issues a vivid dramatic enactment. The Ransom trilogy represents a more profound and more complex achievement than it is usually credited with.

Sanctifying the Literal:
Images and Incarnation
in *Miracles*

Thomas Werge

Common bread, miraculous bread, sacramental bread—these
three are distinct, but not to be separated. . . . Our featureless
pantheistic unities and glib rationalist distinctions are alike
defeated by the seamless, yet ever-varying texture of reality.

C. S. Lewis, "Miracles"

God's imagination has in His own creative act cut through all
the lies of impossibility, penetrated into the last bit of mud
at the hidden bottom of the sea, to illuminate the lines of
possibility and reality. *Infulsit* is His word.

William Lynch, *Christ and Apollo*

In *Miracles* (1947) C. S. Lewis provides an orthodox apologia for
the traditional Christian belief in miracles that had been badly eroded
by modern skepticism. Yet his argument relies not so much on formal
logic and analysis as on an affirmation of images, imagery, and the
imagination as ways of knowing ("Blu," 265).[1] For Lewis the literalism
of imagery and metaphor is not a curse, but a blessing in its anthropomorphic power and in its reflection of the "Grand Miracle" of the
Incarnation. Further, the intensity of Lewis's emphasis and his own
use of image, anecdote, and story in *Miracles* seeks to counter the
"demythologizing" theological climate in which *Miracles* was written.
The great enemy of faith and miracle for Lewis is not a crude materialism or anthropomorphism—indeed, each of these may in fact
point toward truth—but the abstract and amorphous intellectualism

---

1. Cf. John Beversluis, *C. S. Lewis and the Search for Rational Religion* (Grand
Rapids: Eerdmans, 1985), 58–83. Lewis's book *Miracles* was preceded by an essay "Mir-
acles" (1942), in *God in the Dock: Essays on Theology and Ethics*, ed. Walter Hooper
(Grand Rapids: Eerdmans, 1970), 25–37.

that rejects the literal, and hence the divine, dimension of ordinary experience and images. It is precisely this literal dimension of reality that constitutes the heart of Lewis's celebration of the *analogia entis,* and the Incarnation that makes both real analogy and real being possible.

To be sure, skepticism toward miracles is rooted in traditions other than demythologizing and gnosticism. Eighteenth-century Deism often held that God was bound by nature's order and could not manifest his power supernaturally in anomalous forms. Hume opposed the miraculous on materialist and rationalist grounds, and Emerson later, in his Divinity School Address, set off supernatural miracles against nature's inherent and redemptive goodness: "[Christ] spoke of miracles; for he felt that man's life was a miracle, and that all man doth. . . . But the word Miracle, as pronounced by Christian churches, gives a false impression; it is Monster. It is not one with the blowing clover and the falling rain."[2] Yet despite the power and influence of materialist and pantheist rejections of miracles, whether in the biblical tradition or in the form of "special providences," it is the rise of angelism in modernity—with its gnostic origins, its contempt for sensory experience as well as for the literal imagery of myth and story, and its exaltation of pure intellect and reason—that accounts for the tone and substance of Lewis's argument and vision. For if Rudolf Bultmann's demythologizing forms of biblical interpretation provide the most immediate context for the argument (and narrative) of *Miracles,* his orientation is but one expression of an older gnostic tradition that severed faith from material imagery.

The visual and literal imagery of miracles in the Old and New Testaments is striking: water turned to wine; the blind made to see, the deaf to hear; the sun held still. Yet Origen and other Platonic commentators and exegetes mistrusted precisely such images in their literal rather than purely spiritual resonance, so agitating Tertullian that he denounced the separating of the literal and spiritual by proclaiming in *On the Resurrection of the Flesh* that the Virgin Mary bore Christ in her womb, not in a figure of speech, and insisting that word and reality, metaphor and literal experience, must never be severed. Word, image, and meaning were coalescing dimensions rather than exclusive properties. Later, however, a Reformation confession of faith quoted with approval the ancient writer Lactantius, who

2. Emerson, "The Divinity School Address" (1838), in *Selections from Ralph Waldo Emerson,* ed. Stephen E. Whicher (Boston: Houghton Mifflin, 1957), 105.

states, "Undoubtedly no religion exists where there is an image."[3] In our own time, Daniel J. Boorstin in *The Image* decries the dominance of the image in manipulating the political faith of Americans, and Jacques Ellul, in *The Humiliation of the Word*, maintains that the distinction between word and image is sharp and telling: "The word belongs to the order of the *question of truth*. An individual can *ask* the question of truth and attempt to *answer* it *only through language*." But the domain of reality in which the image participates exists, for Ellul, apart from truth: "It can in no way convey anything at all about the order of truth. It never grasps anything but an appearance or outward behavior. It is unable to convey a spiritual experience, a requirement of justice, a testimony to the deepest feelings of a person, or to bear witness to the truth. In all these areas the image will rely on a form."[4]

Whether this split between form and substance, image and reality, icon and real object of faith is specifically gnostic, Platonic, post-Kantian—as in Feuerbach, for example, in whom the distinction between outward image and inward essence becomes absolute—or takes a more contemporary shape, it often results in a radical skepticism toward the concrete, definite images of ordinary experience and the narratives and myths in and by which the believing imagination and traditional faith are shaped. Bultmann argues that the myth of the New Testament sharply differs from "its imagery with its apparent claim to objective validity." This imagery demands criticism, he insists, for while "the real purpose of myth is to speak of a transcendent power which controls the world and man," this purpose "is impeded and obscured by the terms in which it is expressed." The importance of New Testament mythology, then, "lies not in its imagery but in the understanding of existence which it enshrines. The real question is whether this understanding of existence is true. Faith claims that it is, and faith ought not to be tied down to the imagery of New Testament mythology."[5] Austin Farrer, in "An English Appreciation" of the questions of demythologizing Bultmann poses, notes in 1948, one year after the publication of *Miracles*, that faith makes images necessary. But he quickly adds that we must acknowledge

3. Arthur C. Cochrane, ed., *Reformed Confessions of the Sixteenth Century* (Philadelphia: Westminster, 1966), 230.
4. Boorstin, *The Image* (New York: Atheneum, 1962); Ellul, *The Humiliation of the Word* (1981), trans. Joyce Main Hanks (Grand Rapids: Eerdmans, 1985), 29.
5. Rudolf Bultmann, "New Testament and Mythology," in *Kerygma and Myth: A Theological Debate* (1948), ed. Hans Werner Bartsch, trans. Reginald H. Fuller (London: S.P.C.K., 1953), 11.

their inadequacy in order "to adhere nakedly to the imageless truth of God." He concludes:

> The promise of God's dealing with us through grace can be set before us in nothing but images, for we have not yet experienced the reality. When we proceed to live the promises out, the images are crucified by the reality, slowly and progressively, never completely, and not always without pain: yet the reality is better than the images. Jesus Christ clothed himself in all the images of messianic promise, and in living them out, crucified them: but the crucified reality is better than the figures of prophecy. This is very God and life eternal, whereby the children of God are delivered from idols.[6]

This mistrust of image and imagination, with its corresponding exaltation of "the imageless truth of God," constitutes the overly spiritualizing and potentially gnostic vision against which Lewis relentlessly argues in *Miracles*. To be sure, Lewis addresses the claims of naturalistic reductionism and Hume's skepticism as well as the flight from the world and concrete experience he locates as the center of gnosticism. But it is the vagueness and abstraction associated with the demythologizing imagination that most outrages Lewis, whether he describes its effects on our vision of ordinary experience or on our eschatological vision:

> We desire, like St. Paul, not to be un-clothed but to be re-clothed: to find not the formless Everywhere-and-Nowhere but the promised land, that Nature which will be always and perfectly . . . the instrument for that music which will then arise between Christ and us. . . . I suspect that our conception of Heaven as *merely* a state of mind is not unconnected with the fact that the specifically Christian virtue of Hope has in our time grown so languid. Where our fathers, peering into the future, saw gleams of gold, we see only the mist, white, featureless, cold and never moving. (*Mir*, 193–94)

When the end of faith is imageless, Lewis argues, its essence may not be an ineffable transcendence but emptiness and the void. If anthropomorphism and the images of faith are often crude, they also may be compelling, vibrant, and even the most telling expression of our nature as imagining as well as rational beings.

Berdyaev has said that the overpowering curse of the twentieth-century mind is its incessant desire to make abstract everything that is concrete. Throughout his arguments in *Miracles*, Lewis reflects

---

6. Farrer, "An English Appreciation," in *Kerygma and Myth*, 222–23.

precisely this position. To the claim that the language of faith is replete with metaphor and imagery, Lewis argues first that all language, whether political, economic, or scientific, is metaphorical, and second that finally such images are not only necessary but good. To argue that a "pure" and even mathematical language might be able to exclude images entirely is for Lewis a patent absurdity:

> The people who recommend it have not noticed that when they try to get rid of man-like, or as they are called, "anthropomorphic," images they merely succeed in substituting images of some other kind. "I don't believe in a personal God," says one, "but I do believe in a great spiritual force." What he has not noticed is that the word "force" has let in all sorts of images about winds and tides and electricity and gravitation. "I don't believe in a personal God," says another, "but I do believe we are all parts of one great Being which moves and works through us all"—not noticing that he has merely exchanged the image of a fatherly and royal-looking man for the image of some widely extended gas or fluid. A girl I knew was brought up by "higher thinking" parents to regard God as a perfect "substance"; in later life she realised that this had actually led her to think of Him as something like a vast tapioca pudding. (To make matters worse, she disliked tapioca.) (*Mir*, 90)

For Lewis, images inhere both in language and in our nature as experiencing, imagining beings. Further, a key to this argument and anecdote, with its imagined statements, humor, and insistence on the pervasiveness of images is the "low"—rather than "higher"—image of tapioca pudding and the analogy to the "substance" of this amorphous God. Just as images inhere, so they emerge from and point to the *analogia entis* inherent in mind, imagination, and world. Lewis surely had his quarrels with the theology of Paul Tillich and its existential and at times abstruse tenor. But *Miracles* makes clear that Lewis assents to Tillich's analysis of the analogy of being and the place of concrete language within it. It is evident, writes Tillich, that "any concrete assertion about God must be symbolic, for a concrete assertion is one which uses a segment of finite experience in order to say something about him."

> It transcends the content of this segment, although it also includes it. . . . The crucial question must now be faced. Can a segment of finite reality become the basis for an assertion about that which is infinite? The answer is that it can, because that which is infinite is being-itself and because everything participates in being-itself. The *analogia entis* is not the property of a questionable natural theology which attempts to gain knowledge of God by drawing conclusions about the infinite from

the finite. The *analogia entis* gives us our only justification of speaking at all about God.[7]

In a more literary and dramatic context but one equally persistent in stressing the presence of image and analogy in language and human nature, Graham Greene describes a priest observing the smashed and desecrated images of angels and crosses in a cemetery:

> One image of the Mother of God had lost ears and arms and stood like a pagan Venus over the grave of some rich forgotten timber merchant. It was odd—this fury to deface, because, of course, you could never deface enough. If God had been like a toad, you could have rid the globe of toads, but when God was like yourself, it was no good being content with stone figures—you had to kill yourself among the graves.[8]

It is telling that Greene's emphasis on the inexorable and, here, haunting power of the *analogia entis* utilizes these concrete images of divinity. Telling as well is Greene's still deeper delineation of this analogy between humanity and divinity, finiteness and infinity, image and reality. For Greene, as for Lewis, the *imago Dei*, with its sometimes hidden, sometimes nascent, sometimes revealed and paradoxical sacramentalism, embodies the ground for all true images of faith. As Greene's priest reflects:

> Sometimes, instructing children in the old days, he had been asked by some black lozenge-eyed Indian child: "What is God like?" and he would answer facilely with references to the father and the mother, or perhaps more ambitiously he would include brother and sister and try to give some idea of all loves and relationships combined in an immense and yet personal passion. . . . But at the centre of his own faith there always stood the convincing mystery—that we were made in God's image— God was the parent, but He was also the policeman, the criminal, the priest, the maniac and the judge.[9]

Religious images, argues Tillich, are double-edged because they are directed at once toward the finite and infinite, the human and divine. His commentary serves to point the way toward the dynamism of faith and imagination in *Miracles* and the ultimate ground of Lewis's "sanctified literalism," the Incarnation through which world and image are consecrated: "If God is symbolized as 'Father,' he is brought down to the human relationship of father and child. But at the same time this human relationship is consecrated into a pattern of the

7. Tillich, "The Actuality of God" (1951), in *Four Existentialist Theologians*, ed. Will Herberg (New York: Doubleday, 1958), 261.

8. Greene, *The Power and the Glory* (London: Heinemann, 1940), 126.

9. Greene, *Power*, 125; ellipsis in the original text.

divine-human relationship. If 'Father' is employed as a symbol for God, fatherhood is seen in its theonomous, sacramental depth."[10]

Whatever the form of our ultimate vision of reality, writes William Lynch, "whether that be beauty, or insight, or peace, or tranquillity, or God —the heart, substance, and center of the human imagination, as of human life, must lie in the particular and limited image or thing." Further, he insists,

> the images are in themselves the path to whatever the self is seeking: to insight, or beauty, or, for that matter, to God. . . . This path is both narrow and direct; it leads . . . straight through our human realities, through our labor, our disappointments, our friends, our game legs, our harvests, our subjection to time. There are no shortcuts to beauty or to insight. We must go *through* the finite, the limited, the definite, omitting none of it lest we omit some of the potencies of being-in-the-flesh.[11]

Lynch's affirmation of the centrality of the image and his insistence, in contrast to Bultmann and Ellul, that images participate not only in the order of truth but in the *ordo salutis,* the order of salvation, illuminate the persistent, even incantatory dynamism and concreteness of the imagery of *Miracles.*

While this imagery, as we have seen, often embodies the dynamism of human seeking and the human imagination, it also embodies the dynamism of God's search for humanity. Nothing so sharply differentiates for Lewis the gnostic or pantheist divinity from the biblical and personal God as their respective motions of grace. The pantheist's God, says Lewis, "does nothing, demands nothing. He is there if you wish for Him, like a book on a shelf. He will not pursue you" (*Mir,* 113). Yet in describing the living God, Lewis finds that stasis will not serve. On the contrary, even such apparently archaic images as God's "kingship" become not only useful but indispensable, for they speak to the reality of God's own dynamism—and, indeed, God's literal and imaginative search for his children. Here Lewis's images and concluding analogy take on an incantatory tone, and his argument becomes dramatized through a kind of narrative vision in which imagery is an absolute necessity:

> An "impersonal God"—well and good. A subjective God of beauty, truth and goodness, inside our own heads—better still. A formless life-force surging through us, a vast power which we can tap—best of all. But God

10. Tillich, "Actuality of God," 262.
11. Lynch, *Christ and Apollo* (1960; reprint, New York: New American Library, 1963), 20, 23.

Himself, alive, pulling at the other end of the cord, perhaps approaching at an infinite speed, the hunter, king, husband—that is quite another matter. There comes a moment when the children who have been playing at burglars hush suddenly: was that a *real* footstep in the hall? There comes a moment when people who have been dabbling in religion ("Man's search for God"!) suddenly draw back. Supposing we really found Him? We never meant it to come to *that*! Worse still, supposing He had found us? (*Mir*, 114)

Lewis's rejection of the gnostic and amorphous simultaneously constitutes a rejection of solipsism. God's "real footstep" reveals itself to and intrudes upon the self-contained mind. God's descent, approach, and discovery are indispensably dramatic and anthropomorphic, and the studied yet gentle irony of Lewis's concluding question addresses the ultimate justification for his images of faith.

For Lewis, as for the Christian tradition, "The Grand Miracle" (title of a seminal chapter in *Miracles*) can be none other than the mystery and paradox of the Incarnation. If, as Lynch argues, "the first and basic image of the literary imagination is the definite or the finite, and not the infinite, the endless, the dream," the most definite and finite image and reality of the Christian claim and story is the incarnating of divinity in Christ. For Augustine, the paradox demands images: "He lies in the manger, but contains the world; He sucks at the breasts, but feeds the Angels; He is wrapped in swaddling clothes, but vests us with immortality; He is suckled, but adored; He found no place in the inn, but makes for Himself a temple in the hearts of believers."[12] For Chesterton, the paradoxes are as striking as they were for Augustine, Aquinas, and the Reformers:

Any agnostic or atheist whose childhood has known a real Christmas has ever afterwards, whether he likes it or not, an association in his mind between two ideas that most of mankind must regard as remote from each other; the idea of a baby and the idea of unknown strength that sustains the stars. His instincts and imagination can still connect them, when his reason can no longer see the need of the connection. In more general terms, "a mass of legend and literature, which increases and will never end, has repeated and rung the changes on that single paradox; that the hands that had made the sun and stars were too small to reach the huge heads of the cattle. Upon this paradox . . . all the literature of our faith is founded."[13]

12. Lynch, *Christ and Apollo*, 19; Augustine, *An Augustine Synthesis*, ed. Erich Przywara (New York: Harper, 1958), 182.

13. G. K. Chesterton, *The Everlasting Man* (London: Hodder and Stoughton, 1925), 192–93, 191.

The God of believers, writes Lewis in *Miracles*, is "the God of corn and oil and wine. He is the glad Creator. He has become Himself incarnate" (*Mir*, 194).

While reason and logic may approximate the paradox of the Incarnation, only faith and imagination can directly apprehend its salvific mystery and be moved by the dramatic images from which that mystery cannot be separated. Imagination makes the connection, as Chesterton argues, when reason cannot see the need of the connection. Three years before the publication of *Miracles*, Lewis conjoined myth and fact in this way in light of the Christian story, and *Miracles* in part may be interpreted as a fleshing out of the position he takes there: "Now as myth transcends thought, Incarnation transcends myth. The heart of Christianity is a myth which is also a fact. The old myth of the Dying God, *without ceasing to be myth*, comes down from the heaven of legend and imagination to the earth of history . . . . By becoming fact it does not cease to be myth: that is the miracle."[14] Christ sanctifies the literal and makes literal the sacred, and for Lewis the events of the Incarnation, Crucifixion, and Resurrection—as well as the images of ordinary, limited, and earthly experience—manifest a coalescing of the concrete and the spiritual. Life is concretely sacramental rather than a gnostic dream. As Greene's Sarah Miles ponders a crucifix, she attempts the gnostic flight but is brought back to an incarnate God: "I hated the . . . crucifix, all the emphasis on the human body. I was trying to escape from the human body and all it needed. I thought I could believe in some kind of a God that bore no relation to ourselves, something vague, amorphous, cosmic. . . . [But] to-day I looked at that material body on that material cross, and I wondered, how could the world have nailed a vapour there?"[15]

For Lewis, the reascent of Christ and the entire story of the Christian faith reconciles the old polarities of flesh and spirit, nature and grace, reason and imagination. The gnostic story and vision, as Hans Jonas points out, speaks only of eternally conflicting polarities. Opposed to the divine light, he writes, is "the world of darkness, utterly full of evil . . . full of falsehood and deceit." He describes this world as chaos: "A world of turbulence without steadfastness, a world of darkness without light . . . a world of death . . . in which the good things perish and plans come to naught. . . . Indeed, we shall find that in gnostic thought the world takes the place of the traditional under-

14. Lewis, "Myth Became Fact" (1944), in *God in the Dock: Essays on Theology and Ethics*, ed. Walter Hooper (Grand Rapids: Eerdmans, 1970), 66–67.
15. Graham Greene, *The End of the Affair* (London: Heinemann, 1951), 130, 133.

world."[16] For the gnostic imagination, Christ was a phantom who could never have become an actual human being in such a dark and evil world. Mind and spirit alone are real; the body, in its concreteness and in the images and analogies of being that it at once incorporates and informs, is as malign as the world in which it is trapped; and the longing for transcendence and escape—not the idea of incarnation, itself a nightmare—defines our human identity.

As a kind of narrative rather than an entirely logical series of formal arguments (though, to be sure, Lewis's arguments appeal throughout to logic as well as imagination), *Miracles* tells a very different story. The Incarnation reconciles the ancient gnostic dualism between spirit and matter, nature and transcendence. The concrete, not the amorphous, is most real. Images, like the imagination, do in fact participate as fully as do the literal world and our literal bodies in the order of truth. Ultimately, the resurrection of the body constitutes a sanctification of the literal; it exists beyond yet remains linked to the imagination, like the ending (and beginning) of the narrative and reality of Christ's own life. By teaching this doctrine, writes Lewis in *Miracles*, Christianity

> teaches that Heaven is not merely a state of the spirit but a state of the body as well: and therefore a state of Nature as a whole. Christ, it is true, told His hearers that the Kingdom of Heaven was "within" or "among" them. But His hearers were not *merely* in "a state of mind." The planet He had created was beneath their feet, His sun above their heads; blood and lungs and guts were working in the bodies He had invented, photons and sound waves of His devising were blessing them with the sight of His human face and the sound of His voice. (*Mir*, 192–93)

In the order and narrative of salvation, the Incarnation provides the ontological ground for the integrity of the literal, in life as in metaphor. Just as the allegorical interpretation of Scripture sought to remain anchored to its most basic dimension, the literal, so Lewis's celebration of the Incarnation as the "Grand Miracle" points to a resurrection in which "the dry bones [will be] clothed again with flesh, the fact and the myth re-married, the literal and the metaphorical rushing together" (*Mir*, 192). For Lewis, the ultimate miracle of the Christian vision is the concreteness and definiteness infusing that vision and realizing—indeed, incarnating—its reality and its story.

16. Jonas, *The Gnostic Religion* (Boston: Beacon Press, 1958), 57, 68.

A Lifelong Love Affair
with Language:
C. S. Lewis's Poetry

Charles A. Huttar

Early in his career, Lewis wanted to be remembered, above all, as a poet. He had a recognized facility in versing and was on familiar terms with the Muse all his life. His early verse includes several mythopoeic works, most of them on a grand scale. Two of these have been published: *Dymer*, a romantic tale of rebellion, quest, and apotheosis; and the poem his editor entitled *The Nameless Isle*, a retelling of *The Magic Flute* with his own variations (*NP*, 7–91, 105–27). Significantly, one of his early poetic narratives, a retelling of the Eros and Psyche myth, was never completed and eventually was recast in prose to become his finest work of fiction, *Till We Have Faces* (see Walter Hooper, Preface to *NP*, xi). For by age thirty, it appears, Lewis had committed his main energies to other forms of writing, fiction and nonfiction prose, and had settled for the rank, in poetry, of a minor figure. Barring a major revolution in taste, he will never be accorded a higher position.

Despite the romantic themes in Lewis's poetry, which are especially pronounced in the early work,[1] one is tempted to say that he would have gained more recognition as a poet had he lived in the eighteenth century. The fact that Lewis has often been compared in other respects with Samuel Johnson is not irrelevant to this point. There is a quality of neoclassic wit about Lewis's best later poems, a fondness for epigram and satire, and a preference for incisive direct statement over richness of symbolic suggestion that make them very good works of their kind but reduce their appeal to modern sensibilities. His friend Ruth Pitter, herself a poet of note, has called him

---

1. See, in addition to the longer poems already mentioned, those collected in *Spirits in Bondage*—a title, appropriately enough, that alludes to the Satanic portions of *Paradise Lost*.

"a very good poet-craftsman," "a great word master." She adds, "He could do anything with words except, perhaps, the true poetic magic."[2]

Yet for all the reservations with which a modern reader might approach Lewis as a poet, it must be granted that his poetry is an important source for anyone who would study his ideas about language. For one thing, some of his keenest insights on language are given expression there. For another, his practice as a poet reveals his attitudes toward language, including a respect for its illusive and elusive nature and at the same time an overflowing enjoyment of it.

I

Most immediately striking is the enjoyment—Lewis's sheer love of the sounds of words and the "sport that mingles / Sound with senses, in subtle pattern, / Words in wedlock" (*Poems*, 12). "I am enamoured of metrical subtleties," he wrote.[3] This love is revealed especially in his virtuoso deployment in poem after poem of intricate patterns of exact or slant rhyme, both final and internal.[4] Well over one-fourth of the poems in his posthumously collected *Poems* exemplify his fascination with the most unlikely ways in which words may echo one another. The one poem self-consciously subtitled "Metrical Experiment" ("On the Atomic Bomb," *Poems*, 64–65)[5] is far from exhibiting the most intricate of such arrangements, but it is a good starting point for a cursory view of Lewis at play. The pattern is slant feminine rhyme at all four line-endings of a stanza, echoed internally at the first stress of line 2, with the further requirement that the

2. Pitter, "Poet to Poet," in *In Search of C. S. Lewis*, ed. Stephen Schofield (South Plainfield, N. J.: Bridge, 1983), 112.

3. Letter to Ruth Pitter, 10 August 1946; microfilm copy of MS in the Marion E. Wade Center, Wheaton, Ill., transcript 5-T; original MS in the Bodleian Library (MS Eng. lett. c. 220/3, fol. 24–25). The quotation is worth continuing: "not as a game: the truth is I often lust after a metre as a man might lust after a woman. The effect I want, even if attained, wd. not be of the elusive kind—more like heraldry or enamel—a blaze." Permission to quote from Lewis's unpublished letters was granted by Curtis Brown for the C. S. Lewis Estate, copyright holder, and by the owners of the manuscripts: the Bodleian Library (for the letters to Ruth Pitter) and the Marion E. Wade Center (for the others).

4. "Young King Cole" (*Poems*, 19–21), "Vitrea Circe" (25–26), "The Ecstasy" (36–37), "On the Atomic Bomb" (64–65), "Vowels and Sirens" (76–77), and "Pattern" (79) all exhibit patterns of slant final rhyme.

5. That is, the one poem apart from "Pattern" (*Poems*, 79), which was entitled "Experiment" when first published in 1938.

rhyming syllables always close on a blend of two or more consonant sounds. Thus: *engine, injur*(y), *angels, plunges, danger; gadget, dodge the, logic, tragic, trudge it.* Since an entire stanza contains only thirty-two syllables, the often surprising rhymes bombard us with great frequency—doubly so in the second line of each stanza, where the internal rhyme catches us on the first rebound. That the unstressed syllable concluding such a rhyme may sometimes belong to a separate word is no defect in the scheme, but perhaps even an enhancement of its audacious inventiveness. Nor is such light-hearted play misplaced, as it might seem, in a poem whose content is so heavily somber, for the fun we can have with language is Lewis's means for going beyond abstraction to show us concretely in our experience of the poem, alongside the "wretched" road ahead for humanity, "a glimpse of . . . the happy orchards" (lines 26, 28).

In "Solomon" (*Poems*, 46–47) an even greater richness of ornament reinforces the description of the king's exotic palace. Here the end-rhyming is in traditional couplets, but every line also contains internal rhyme in which the echoes may last as long as three syllables and into a fourth. They are never quite so short as a single syllable, though we have pairs like *aloft/soft* (line 3) and *wrong/longer* (line 25). In a pair such as *flame-like/came late* (line 24) the echo continues into the initial *l* of the weaker syllable. In *popinjays/stopping praised* (line 5) the echo covers three syllables, even though unlike consonants intervene. In the preceding line we have the same pattern, the trisyllabic *emerald* rhyming (in all except the final *d*) with *tremor of light*, where the parallels extend across the schwa in *of* and on to the beginning of the next syllable. Lewis's absorption in maintaining such an intricate pattern over twenty-eight lines may indeed be one reason he is accounted minor, but more germane to our present theme, there is something infectious about his enjoyment of language as here displayed, something in itself praiseworthy.

Some of the principles behind such practice are articulated in a letter Lewis wrote to a poet, Laurence Whistler, who had sent him works to criticize. "I spotted your 'fore-rhymes' at once," he told Whistler, "but I bet half your readers won't. I think this technique has possibilities. Perhaps, for weak ears, the rhymes shd. be louder, supported by plenty of consonance. I mean *nuptial* rhyming with something like *upshot* or *language* with *anguish* or *rang with*. Obviously what immediately follows the rhyming syllable is going to have great importance once rhymes cease to be terminal."[6]

6. Letter to Laurence Whistler, 30 October 1961, Wade Center.

Part of the game for Lewis apparently was the invention of ever new patterns of sound repetition. The five-line stanzas of "Two Kinds of Memory" (*Poems*, 100–101) each have internal rhyme in the first and last stressed syllables of lines 1, 2, and 4, while line 3 rhymes with line 5 on the last major stress, which is the third-from-last syllable. My italics emphasize the effect in the opening stanza:

> Oh *still* vacation, *silver*
> *Pause* and relaxing of severer *laws*,
> Oh Memory the com*passio*nate,
> For*ever* in dim labyrinths of *reverie*
> The cruel past disarming and re*fashion*ing!

Another variation is to establish a strict pattern of double internal rhymes in some of a poem's lines. "The Birth of Language" (*Poems*, 10–11) is an example; I quote the first and last of its ten stanzas:

> How *near* his *sire's* careering *fires*
> Must Mercury the planet *run*;
> What *wave* of *heat* must *lave* and *beat*
> That shining suburb of the *Sun*
> . . . .
> So *dim below* those *symbols show*[7]
> Bony and abstract every *one*.
> Yet *if* true *verse* but *lift* the *curse*,
> They feel in dreams their native *Sun*.[8]

Much of this tends to be sheer play; rarely, here or in the eighteen poems with patterned internal rhyme that I have not mentioned, are the rhymes functional in terms of the explicit content of the poems. "Narnian Suite" (*Poems*, 6–7) is an exception. As the title, subtitles, and musical terms in the work itself indicate, this is conceived as a quasi-musical composition, the music being that of word sounds. Thus, there is less in the way of "content" and no thesis except whatever may be implied in the antihuman stance of both sections. Still, the two movements of the suite are marches by dwarfs and giants respectively, and both the rhythms and the phonemes chosen for rhyming and consonance reflect the great difference between the

7. In this line the first *l* belongs to both rhyming pairs.
8. See "On the Text of 'The Birth of Language'" at the end of this chapter. Other poems with regular double internal rhyme in some lines are "Pan's Purge" (*Poems*, 5–6), "Le Roi s'Amuse" (23–24), "The Small Man Orders His Wedding" (31–33), and "The Turn of the Tide" (49–51).

two species. The dwarfs march double-quick to a Paeonic rhythm (modified every fifth line by replacing two normally four-syllabled feet with monosyllables), and they favor voiceless stops, often followed by unaccented *l* (*prattle/battle* in lines 1–2) or *r* (*clatter* of ac*coutre*ment in line 2). Here, for example, is the second stanza:

> The chuckle-headed humans think we're only petty poppetry
> And all our battle-tackle nothing more than pretty bric-a-brac;
> But a little shrub has prickles, and they'll soon be in a pickle if
> A scud of dwarfish archery has crippled all their cavalry—
> (Whizz! Twang! The quarrel and the javelin).

The giants, in contrast, march much more heavily in iambic tetrameter to a music of nasal/stop blends (*stumping, pomp, thump, bump, lumpish* and so on to *trumpet*), whose relentless weight is not even affected by the *l* endings that sounded so trippingly in the dwarf movement:

> Ho! tremble town and tumble down
> And crumble shield and sabre!
> Your kings will mumble and look pale,
> Your horses stumble or turn tail,
> Your skimble-scamble counsels fail,
> So *rumble drum bel*aboured—
> Oh rumble, rumble, rumble, rumble, rumble drum belaboured!

In "Narnian Suite" Lewis is doing more than playing with rhyme patterns; he is, clearly, fascinated by the onomatopoeic possibilities of language.

A rather different sort of phonetic patterning caught Lewis's attention as a medieval scholar and spurred his imagination as a poet. I refer, of course, to alliterative verse in the Old English style. Part of his job as a teacher was to explain the principles of this form, and what better way than by supplementing his account of the possible permutations of scansion with an illustrative modern example written for the purpose?

> We were talking of dragons, Tolkien and I,
> In a Berkshire bar. The big workman
> Who had sat silent and sucked his pipe
> All the evening, from his empty mug
> With gleaming eye glanced towards us:
> "I seen 'em myself," he said fiercely.[9]

9. Lewis, "The Alliterative Metre" (1935), in *Selected Literary Essays,* ed. Walter Hooper (Cambridge: Cambridge University Press, 1969), 18.

Those six made-to-order lines Lewis inserted in the middle of his essay on "The Alliterative Metre." At the end of the essay, he published a much more substantial invention, a poem entitled "The Planets," which has been reprinted in *Poems* (12–15). In the original setting, he also provided a metrical analysis for each alliterative line. Still more ambitiously, he used the alliterative meter for *The Nameless Isle,* which has been collected in *Narrative Poems.* To it, dated 1930 in the manuscript, he appended a brief instructive note on the scansion of alliterative meter (*NP*, 176–77), a forerunner of the much longer account in "The Alliterative Metre."[10]

In this activity there is much more than just pedagogical enthusiasm at work and more than an exhibitionist antiquarianism or an overflowing playfulness, though the latter is certainly present.[11] But Lewis is seriously promoting the alliterative line as a reasonable vehicle for modern expression (and is pleased to find support in the work of W. H. Auden).[12] It is on linguistic grounds that he holds this view. In "our ancient alliterative poetry," he writes, "I find a prosody based on the same speech rhythms that I hear in conversation to-day. I find a sense of language so native to us all that the phrases which hit the eighth-century audience hard hit me hard too as soon as I have learned to understand them; I see at once that words like *gold* and *wolf* and *heart* and *blood* and *winter* and *earth,* had the same overtones for them as for me. Everything is already unmistakably English."[13] Given Lewis's feeling for the modern potential of the Old English form, we may well ask whether the alliterative line, with its great flexibility as to location of the key syllables within the half-line, might have contributed to his experiments with internal rhyme, which, though distinct from allitera-

10. James Pursell thinks that the meter of *Launcelot* (*NP*, 95–103) may be connected in similar fashion to another of Lewis's scholarly essays of the 1930s, "The Fifteenth-Century Heroic Line," in *Selected Literary Essays*, ed. Walter Hooper (Cambridge: Cambridge University Press, 1969), 45–57. He calls it "an innovative student's model of late Middle English prosody" ("*Narrative Poems,*" *CSL: The Bulletin of the New York C. S. Lewis Society* 4.1 [1972]: 3).

11. He would use Chaucerian verse in writing the minutes of a meeting (Margaret Patterson Hannay, *C. S. Lewis* [New York: Frederick Ungar, 1981], 179) or begin a bread-and-butter letter with a parody of Milton (George Sayer, "Jack on Holiday," in *C. S. Lewis at the Breakfast Table and Other Reminiscences,* ed. James T. Como [New York: Macmillan, 1979], 209).

12. Lewis, "Alliterative Metre," 15.

13. Lewis, "The Idea of an 'English School,'" in *Rehabilitations and Other Essays* (London: Oxford University Press, 1939), 72.

tion, is akin to it.[14] We know from his diary that, in verses no longer extant, he tried yet a different variation, the "rhythm of O.E. verse, but riming" (*NP*, xii).

"Mingl[ing] sound with senses" was a vital part of Lewis's poem-making. Poetry he defined as "'the art of utilizing the informal or irrational values of words to express that which can only be symbolized by their formal or conventional meanings.' These values include chiefly sound & association: also of course their 'group'-sound or rhythms which are above and beyond their individual sounds: here is the meaning & justification of metre."[15] As to "association," like any poet Lewis paid close attention to the connotations of words, but his linguistic bent gave him a canny sensitivity to the process of their gaining associations in the course of their history. One illustration is this comment on the "patina" of archaic language: "No Old French poet got that peculiar Old-Frenchness wh. to us is part of the charm. Half the beauties of the Old Testament did not exist for the writers."[16]

II

Surprisingly, for all his love of phonological wordplay and his keen interest in the meanings of words, we find in Lewis's poetry few instances of semantic wordplay. He is not fond of exploiting *double entendres*. What does interest him, however, as subject matter for a few poems, is semantic change, specifically the alteration of meaning which may disrupt communication between members of a speech community. In the poem *Launcelot* he describes such a situation, when the Grail knights return to Arthur's court:

> Ladies of Britain mourned the losing of their joys:
> "What have they eaten? or in what forgetful land
> Were their adventures? Now they do not understand
> Our speech. They talk to one another in a tongue
> We do not know. Strange sorrows and new jests, among
> Themselves, they have. . . ."
>
> (*NP*, 96)

14. John Kirkpatrick mentions "The Saboteuse" (*Poems*, 38–40) in particular as an example of such adaptation of the Old English line: "Fresh Views of Humankind in Lewis's Poems," *CSL: The Bulletin of the New York C. S. Lewis Society* 10.11 (1979): 5.

15. Letter to Leo Kingsley Baker, September 1920, Wade Center.

16. Letter to Ruth Pitter, 10 August 1946, Bodleian Library; Wade transcript 4-T, pp. 2–3.

Estrangement has occurred because, through experiences not shared by those who stayed at home, the adventurers have gained new language. But more often it is the opposite situation that occupies Lewis's attention: the experience of loss when a speaker finds that his fellows are using a certain word but no longer fully appreciate what it means. The meaning is outside their narrowed experience. They do not acknowledge this, of course; instead, they redefine the word according to their limited idea of what it can mean. This reductionism was no mere theoretical possibility: Lewis could see it happening again and again in contemporary writing and speech.[17]

Semantics thus proved to be a tool for Lewis to use in the critique of contemporary culture. In "Re-adjustment" (*Poems*, 102) the speaker laments that "Between the new *Hominidae* and us who are dying, already / There rises a barrier across which no voice can ever carry, / For devils are unmaking language."[18] One kind of "unmaking" is the reduction of a word's range of meaning, an example of which Lewis offers us in the word *paganism*. To the speaker in "A Cliché Came Out of Its Cage" (*Poems*, 3-4), *paganism* connotes the highest of ethical ideals, whether the *pietas*, moderation, self-control, and self-sacrifice of Greco-Roman civilization at its best or the Norse ideal of loyalty to right in the struggle against evil, albeit doomed. But the persons he is addressing can no longer even apprehend such concepts. Their reduction of the meaning of *paganism* only signals how severely they themselves have been diminished: "Are these [whether Roman or Norse] the Pagans you spoke of? Know your betters and crouch, dogs."

"Unmeaning" is seen more intensely in the frustration that arises from being unable to communicate, as presented succinctly in "Re-adjustment" (*Poems*, 102) in the speaker's realization that there would be no one in the new society "who could pick up our signal, who could understand a story." The idea is developed more fully in a poem written in classical Asclepiads, "The Country of the Blind" (*Poems*, 33-34), which would have us imagine a society "of eyeless men, / Dark bipeds not aware how they were maimed" (lines 1-2). Words having a literal referent in the visible world (*light*, for example) such people would naturally assume were nothing but a fanciful way of "symbol[izing] / Abstract thoughts" (lines 12-13). Suppose, then, "a

17. See, for example, the 1935 letter quoted by Leo Baker, "Near the Beginning," in *C. S. Lewis at the Breakfast Table*, 10.
18. This quasi-sonnet condenses the situation which is presented narratively at greater length in "The Last of the Wine" (*Poems*, 40-41).

luckless few" (line 5) who had not yet reached the same stage of evolution, who could still see. Their accounts of visual experience would be interpreted by the rest as metaphors. Never having experienced the visible, society would deny its reality, patronizing those who could see and thereby frustrating their wish to communicate a broader range of experience. As the poem's close makes plain, it is a parable for the spiritual blindness of contemporary culture. "Truths that once ... stood plain to the inward eye" are now no longer acceptable, perhaps not even imaginable, as valid matters of discourse.

A slightly more elaborate prose version of the same parable appears in Lewis's essay "The Language of Religion," and the context makes the cultural criticism more explicit. For himself, Lewis writes, "the very essence of ... life ... consists of something which cannot be communicated except by hints, similes, metaphors, and the use of those emotions (themselves not very important) which are pointers to it." Yet he wonders whether the human species may not be losing awareness of this "something":

> There seem to be people about to whom imagination means only the presence of mental images (not to mention those like Professor Ryle who deny even that); to whom thought means only unuttered speech; and to whom emotions are final, as distinct from the things they are about. If this is so, and if they increase, then all real communications between them and the earlier type of man will finally be impossible. ("Lang," 140)

Lewis's deep concern over this threat provides a context for considering one of his least appreciated poems, "A Confession" (*Poems*, 1), which begins:

> I am so coarse, the things the poets see
> Are obstinately invisible to me.
> For twenty years I've stared my level best
> To see if evening—any evening—would suggest
> A patient etherized upon a table;
> In vain. I simply wasn't able.

One reason this poem is underrated is that the reading of it is always in danger of getting mixed up with the biographical question of Lewis's relationship with and attitude toward T. S. Eliot. There are, to be sure, biographical facts that may not simply be set aside. Lewis did strongly oppose the poetic program of Eliot and his followers and at one time had an angry scheme of publishing "mock Eliotic" parodies. His antipathy to free verse and his own efforts to revive traditional metrical forms for contemporary poetic expression bespeak a lack of sympathy with the metrical dogmas (if such they be) of modernism.[19] On the matter of imagery and content, which more immediately concerns us, the following scene is recorded in his brother's diary: "Some enjoyable talk arising out of T. S. Eliot, one of whose poems J[ack] read superbly, but broke off in the middle, declaring it to be bilge: Hugo defended it, J[ack] and Sayer attacked. I thought that though unintelligible, it did convey a feeling of frustration and despair. J[ack] thought he had nothing to say worth saying in any case."[20]

We are not told which poem of Eliot's was read on this occasion in 1947, but in 1954, a few months before "A Confession" appeared in *Punch,* we find Lewis referring explicitly to the image from "Prufrock" with which his poem commences, as he writes to Kathryn Farrer concerning

a widespread tendency in modern literature which strikes me as horrid: I mean, the readiness to admit extreme uses of the pathetic fallacy in contexts where there is nothing to justify them and always of a kind that belittles or "sordidises" ("sordidifies") nature. Eliot's evening "like a patient etherised upon a table" is the *locus classicus.* I don't believe one

19. For the parody scheme, see Walter Hooper, Preface to *Selected Literary Essays* (Cambridge: Cambridge University Press, 1969), xv–xvi. For Lewis's dislike of free verse, see *Letters,* 51–52 (1920); letter to Ruth Pitter, 24 July 1946 ("dull or sordid facts in subpoetical rhythms"); and letter to Robert Longacre, 19 June 1952, Wade Center, in which Lewis declares himself "insensitive" to "Rhapsodical" poetry like that of Whitman: "the more vast and supersensible a poem's subject is, the more it needs to be fixed, focussed, incarnated in regular metre and concrete images." In these citations the rejection of free verse is always joined with a criticism of other aspects of the poems. In addition to the alliterative meter discussed above, examples of traditional forms used by Lewis include the sonnet (fourteen examples in *Poems,* three of them in hexameters), limerick (*Poems,* 135; see J. R. Christopher "A Serious Limerick," *Chronicle of the Portland C. S. Lewis Society* 1.8 [1972]: 4–5), rhyme royal (*Dymer*), terza rima (*Queen of Drum* 1.1), monorhyme as in the *Song of Roland* (*Queen* 4.6; cf. his description of the effect on his ear of the Old French monorhyme, quoted in Roger Lancelyn Green and Walter Hooper, *C. S. Lewis: A Biography* [London: Collins, 1974], 95), various classical meters—Sapphics, Alcaics, Scazons, Asclepiads—and the Rubáiyát stanza (*Queen* 4.2). See Kenneth Ernest Matthews, "C. S. Lewis and the Modern World" (Ph.D. diss., UCLA, 1983), 123–24.

20. W. H. Lewis, *Brothers and Friends: The Diaries of Major Warren Hamilton Lewis,* ed. Clyde S. Kilby and Marjorie Lamp Mead (San Francisco: Harper and Row, 1982), 209. For a glimpse of Lewis's attitude more generally toward Eliot's "errors," see his remark to Dorothy L. Sayers quoted in James Brabazon, *Dorothy L. Sayers: A Biography* (New York: Charles Scribner's Sons, 1981), 235.

person in a million, under any emotional stress, wd. see evening like that. And even if they did, I believe that anything but the most sparing admission of such images is a v[ery] dangerous game. To invite them, to recur willingly to them, to come to regard them as normal, surely poisons us?[21]

Well, *if* Lewis believed that Eliot considered "a patient etherised upon a table" to be a suitable figure for the sunset, or that Eliot advocated or even tolerated our regarding such an image as normal, then, I think, he seriously misread "Prufrock." The famous simile tells us nothing about sunsets, nor is it meant to; it tells us a great deal about the abnormal state of J. Alfred. Perhaps Lewis is right that in real life that particular likeness would not occur to one in a million, yet Eliot's art persuades us that it is precisely what his fictional Prufrock, who as a type is not *that* rare, would think of. It is an objective correlative for the way Prufrock feels about himself, and Prufrock is always, even in the presence of natural grandeur, thinking or feeling about himself. It is his malaise.

I am not prepared to concede that Lewis did so misread Eliot's poem. There is a difference between either table talk or personal correspondence and a published statement. In *A Preface to Paradise Lost*, Lewis calls Prufrock's simile "a striking picture of sensibility in decay," which suggests that he understood what Eliot was up to.[22] But he also knew what other contemporaries were making of it: "I have heard" this comparison, he writes, "praised, nay gloated over, not as a striking picture of sensibility in decay, but because it was so 'pleasantly unpleasant'" (*Preface*, 55). In other words, the Eliot passage may well have been just what Lewis calls it, a *locus classicus* for a widespread attitude which he finds objectionable, yet without itself, properly read in context, expressing that attitude. The misreading might be one perpetrated by other readers and noticed by Lewis, but not one of which he was guilty.

But even if Lewis did misread Eliot's poem, that is not particularly relevant to our reading of *his* poem, nor does it detract from his

21. Letter to Kathryn Farrer, 9 February 1954, Wade Center.
22. So also does the attention Lewis gave to the idea that "the right answer to a disintegrated civilisation is a disintegrated poem"; he underlined these words when he encountered them in a discussion of Eliot's deliberate use of "weak syntax" to reinforce the critique of culture in his poetry (in Lewis's copy of G. Rostrevor Hamilton, *The Tell-Tale Article: A Critical Approach to Modern Poetry* [London: William Heinemann, 1949; Wade Center], 57; Hamilton is quoting C. Day Lewis, *The Poetic Image* [London: Jonathan Cape, 1947], 117. In both sources, the context includes a disclaimer rejecting the idea as too extreme).

achievement in it. It would be naive anyhow to assume (as some critics appear to have done) that the persona of "A Confession" is a pure, unfictionalized representation of the author. From the title on down, the tone is too much that of the *poseur*, or if you will, the waggish don. The persona of this poem is a master of Socratic irony, repeatedly, exaggeratedly, yet strategically belittling himself, confident that the values he favors can win the field on their own and he has only to keep out of their way. Thus he presents himself as a failure (line 6), a "dunce" (line 25), "coarse" (line 1), and even as an inept reader of Eliot. He apologizes for his own perceptions—evening as a ship's final departure, the moon as a reminder of our precarious existence, "dull things" like peacocks, honey, and so on—giving the impression that he cannot appreciate them but accepts that they must be inferior. And this pretended failure drives *us* to affirm the value of those things, in a way that more direct, positive assertion would not do. The rhetoric is that of understatement, and Lewis is a master of it. He has, moreover, come out swinging and delivered not one punch but two: he has flaunted (safely, through a persona) a refusal to bow at the modern poetic shrines, and at the same time, in creating the fictional speaker of this poem, he has demonstrated how well he can match Old Possum at his own game.

It is, of course, more than a game. A serious point is being made about language, one that has moral implications as well. The phrase "stock responses" (line 26) is a plain clue: it was a current term in the criticism of poetic language. A few years before, Lewis had written a few pages in defense of the stock response (*Preface*, 53–57), seeking to counter the influence of I. A. Richards, whose writings on the subject continued to enjoy great popularity. This disagreement with Richards was rooted in a more basic one over the place of emotion in language and especially in the language of poetry. In the final chapters of his *Principles of Literary Criticism*, Richards distinguished two (and only two) uses of language, scientific and emotive. In the "scientific use of language"—or as he also calls it, more briefly but not without introducing a certain confusion, in "scientific language"—words are used "for the sake of . . . *reference*," and the value of what is said depends on the accuracy of the references, how well they correspond to the real world. In "emotive language" words are used "for the sake of the[ir] effects in emotion and attitude." Any references which they may make as well are merely instrumental for producing the emotions and attitudes desired, and the truth or falsity of such references is irrelevant. As for the emotional responses themselves, there is for Richards no question of any possible correspondence between them and the real world; thus, such criteria as their "internal necessity," whether they "have their own proper organisation, their own emotional interconnection," or their "success for the needs of the being" form the yardsticks for judging the value of the emotive statements that induce them. "There can be no doubt that originally all language was emotive," Richards thought, "and most language is still emotive," but "the supreme form" of emotive language is poetry.[23]

It is curious that no support should be offered for the idea that "most language" today serves only to evoke emotions or attitudes; the statement itself is offered in the "scientific" form (or so one conceives Richards's intent) and thus invites an attempt at verification or falsification, and it is not—when we think of all the daily legal and commercial and domestic and academic instances in which language misses its aim if it fails to inform—obviously true. The confusion arises in part, I think, from the odd use of "scientific" to embrace a much wider range of meaning than we are ordinarily prepared to conceive it as covering. If Richards had said that "most language [today] is not scientific [in the ordinary, narrower sense]," we should not question the statement.

Perhaps it was to avoid such confusion that Lewis, when he began a paper on "The Language of Religion" with a necessary preliminary consideration of language in general, distinguished not two kinds of language but three: "Ordinary," "Scientific," and "Poetic," the latter being "two different artificial perfections of Ordinary," and Scientific being "special[ized]" as well ("Lang," 129).[24] It is, by the way, important in the context of our overall theme to keep in mind that "Poetic language" is different from poetry, of which the language is only one ingredient ("Lang," 134). Lewis's approach differs from that of Richards in other ways, too. By keeping to "kinds" of language and not "uses" he avoids introducing the difficult and unnecessary issue of intent; and his three categories are not separated by absolute boundaries but there are gradations between them ("Lang," 129). The most important difference between Lewis's position and that of Richards, however, is not in the approach but in the outcome. For all three kinds of language, Lewis stresses their capacity to convey information: in pure Scientific language, quantitative and abstract infor-

---

23. Richards, *Principles of Literary Criticism* (1924; reprint, New York: Harcourt Brace, 1952), 267–69, 281, 273.

24. Lewis adumbrates this analysis in a short passage in *The Personal Heresy*, where the terms are: "conversation," "scientific or philosophical language," and "poetical language" (*PH*, 108).

mation only; in Ordinary or Poetic language, qualitative and concrete information. The concreteness—the conveying of a whole experience and not just portions abstracted from it (cf. *PH*, 109–11, 114)—includes, especially in Poetic language, the expression of emotions. Lewis makes a careful distinction here: the expression of emotions, as opposed to the arousal or discharge of emotions, is still a conveying of a kind of information. The reader's emotions may at the same time be aroused, but that effect is, or at least may be, incidental, not primary ("Lang," 130–32). "Often," says Lewis, the emotional content in Poetic language is there "*not for its own sake* but in order to inform us about the object which aroused the emotion" in author or fictional character ("Lang," 132; my italics). More of our experience, Lewis thinks, is communicable through Ordinary or Poetic language than is through Scientific ("Lang," 138). On the other hand, the information conveyed in Scientific language, while more attenuated, is more fully subject to verification than that conveyed in Poetic language, which also is "verifiable or falsifiable" ("Lang," 132–33) but "only to a limited degree and with a certain fringe of vagueness" ("Lang," 135). Richards, of course, would deny to Poetry or emotive language any significant verifiability at all, any possible correspondence to the real world that scientific language is concerned with.

Behind this difference is a yet more basic cleavage between Lewis and Richards, or more strictly (since, as we shall see, Richards is not wholly consistent on the matter), between Lewis and other modern critics who share Richards's views and follow out the implications of them in a more thoroughgoing fashion. This cleavage is more metaphysical than linguistic in nature, and there is correspondingly more than literary theory at stake. We have already heard Lewis lamenting the truncated sense of what is real, which threatens discourse about such concepts as imagination, thought, and emotions ("Lang," 140, quoted above). Lewis's view that to convey reality, the whole actual quality of events, requires "bringing in the observer's heart and the common emotional reaction of the species" ("Lang," 134) supposes a much more broadly inclusive conception of reality than that view which denies to emotive language any significant "reference." "The typical modern critic," Lewis says elsewhere, "thinks that everything except the buzzing electrons is subjective fancy; and he therefore believes that all poetry must come out of the poet's head" (*PH*, 28). From other passages by Richards we may conclude that he did not subscribe to this "modern" view, but neither is it far removed from his doctrine of emotive language. For Lewis, however, the "real world" includes "roses, onions, and love" together with the proper emotional responses to them, and it is from that real world, "trailing clouds of glory," that a rose comes into poetry as a symbol (*PH*, 97).

This moves us close to the subject of stock responses, but we need first to look at one possible weakness in Lewis's analysis. Intent as he is in "The Language of Religion" to show that all three kinds of language convey information, he says very little (unless in the missing pages of this paper, which was published posthumously) about the arousal of emotions and attitudes, though that is undeniably another of the functions of language. Poetry itself, surely, sometimes achieves powerful emotional effects. Whether Lewis would attribute these to some other aspect of the poetry than its language or call them indirect results of the "information" that is conveyed and therefore, however powerful, still not primary, I cannot say with certainty. But he does observe that "momentous matter . . . will arouse emotion whatever the language"—even if it is Scientific ("Lang," 136). His insistence that Poetic language is not "merely" emotional "but a real medium of information" ("Lang," 134), that to express and "thereby" arouse emotion is "not . . . *always* its sole, or even its chief function" ("Lang," 132; my italics), may seem to leave room for thinking that sometimes, at any rate, it fits Richards's description. In another critical work, however, Lewis in effect rules out this possibility and at the same time identifies yet a fourth kind of language, one in which emotional effect is primary. This might, following the pattern of nomenclature used for the other three, be called Rhetorical language. Carefully qualified with "very roughly" and "almost," the distinction Lewis puts forward is this: "In Rhetoric imagination is present for the sake of passion (and, therefore, in the long run, for the sake of action)" (*Preface*, 53). Poetry, however, "aims at producing something more like vision than it is like action" (*Preface*, 52)—that is, something close to what Lewis in "The Language of Religion" calls "information." Thus, contrasting with rhetoric, "in poetry passion is present for the sake of imagination, and therefore, in the long run, for the sake of wisdom or spiritual health—the rightness and richness of a man's total response to the world" (*Preface*, 53). Lewis himself notes "a point of contact" between this position and that of Richards, for whom, in Lewis's summary, "poetry . . . produces a wholesome equilibrium of our psychological attitudes" (*Preface*, 53).

If "the rightness and richness of [one's] total response to the world" is something that concerns both Lewis and Richards, why do they take opposite positions on the stock response? Richards considered stock responses a practical necessity, but dangerous because they may displace "a response more appropriate to the situation."[25] To rely on them too much is a mark of emotional immaturity. It is the poet's task, says Richards, to block the stock responses of readers, formed through their withdrawal "from actual experience," and to reopen readers instead to "the free direct play of experience."[26] (There is a strong hint of a behaviorist model in this line of thinking. Words are stimuli, and Richards wants the poet to provide stimuli that will keep us out of the accustomed grooves of response.) Lewis replied that "most people's responses are not 'stock' enough, . . . the play of experience is too free and too direct in most of us for safety or happiness or human dignity" (*Preface*, 54).

To understand this opposition we begin by noticing that Richards's starting point was a concern which practically everyone must share; where Lewis differed was only on the best way to solve the problem. The stock responses Richards disliked were those automatic reflexes that spring from private prejudices or obsessions and, still more, those widespread stereotypes fostered by bad popular art, best-selling films, books, and so on, which "are an influence of the first importance in fixing immature and actually inapplicable attitudes to most things."[27] As a solution, Richards thought that good poetry should encourage readers to set such habitual responses aside and expose themselves again directly to experience; this honest exposure could be counted on to produce more refined responses, better adjusted to the demands of reality. Lewis distrusted this solution for what he considered its unjustified faith in raw experience and innate human goodness (*Preface*, 54) and its overvaluing of novelty (*PH*, 102–3). What might come from such blind reliance on the free play of experience—exquisite perversity rather than refinement—was typified for him by Prufrock's way of seeing the evening sky. Lewis's solution, instead, would be to replace the inadequate stereotype with attitudes and emotional responses grounded in "such memories, associations, and values as are widely distributed among the human family in space and time" (*PH*, 147). We have seen how he exulted in the constancy of words like *gold* and *blood* in retaining their primitive connotations. Both Lewis and Richards wanted a greater "rightness

25. I. A. Richards, *Practical Criticism* (1929; reprint, New York: Harcourt Brace, 1952), 241. In the following account of Richards's views, I assemble ideas set forth in his chapters "Badness in Poetry," in *Principles*, 199–206, and "Irrelevant Associations and Stock Responses," in *Practical Criticism*, 235–54.

26. Richards, *Principles*, 202.

27. Richards, *Principles*, 203; see also 229–31, where he considers in more detail how this happens. On the role of prejudices, see *Practical Criticism*, 241–42.

and richness of . . . response," but Lewis did not think that increased subjectivity was the way to achieve it nor that inner coherence, or pragmatic adequacy for some need, was the best way to measure it. He would rely instead on moral tradition, what he labeled for ease of reference "the *Tao*" (*Abol*, 12). "Until quite modern times," Lewis wrote, "all . . . believed the universe to be such that certain emotional reactions on our part could be either congruous or incongruous to it—believed, in fact, that objects did not merely receive, but could *merit*, our approval or disapproval, our reverence, or our contempt" (*Abol*, 9). Though such a response could result only from training, to be sure, Lewis saw it not as a matter of behavioral conditioning but as involving endorsement of the underlying moral values. He went on to cite Shelley's exposition of the familiar Aeolian lyre analogy to underscore the role played by the person making the response.[28] But now the loss of that ancient tradition was already well under way—the moral side of the same coin which Lewis examined on the linguistic side in poems like "The Country of the Blind." "Those Stock responses which we need in order to be even human are already in danger," Lewis wrote (*Preface*, 55).

> The older poetry, by continually insisting on certain Stock themes—as that love is sweet, death bitter, virtue lovely, and children or gardens delightful—was performing a service not only of moral and civil, but even of biological, importance. Once again, the old critics were quite right when they said that poetry "instructed by delighting," for poetry was formerly one of the chief means whereby each new generation learned, not to copy, but by copying to make, the good Stock responses. Since poetry has abandoned that office the world has not bettered. While the moderns have been pressing forward to conquer new territories of consciousness, the old territory, in which alone man can live, has been left unguarded, and we are in danger of finding the enemy in our rear. We need most urgently to recover the lost poetic art of enriching a response without making it eccentric, and of being normal without being vulgar. Meanwhile—until that recovery is made—such poetry as Milton's is more than ever necessary to us. (*Preface*, 56)

Richards's criteria of "internal necessity" and "their own proper organisation" Lewis sees as an attempt to justify "new territories of consciousness" in place of the ancient verities. But even Richards is not always easy about the substitution. For a while in *Practical Criticism* he plays with an idea that is closer to Lewis's diagnosis and cure:

28. Percy Bysshe Shelley, "A Defence of Poetry," in *Shelley's Critical Prose*, ed. Bruce R. McElderry, Jr. (Lincoln: University of Nebraska Press, 1967), 4–5.

The man who, in reaction to the commoner naive forms of sentimentality, prides himself upon his hard-headedness and hard-heartedness, his hard-boiledness generally, and seeks out or invents aspects with a bitter or squalid character, for no better reason than this, is only displaying a more sophisticated form of sentimentality. Fashion, of course, is responsible for many of these secondary twists. Indeed the control of Society over our sentiments, over our publicly avowable sentiments, is remarkably efficient. Compare, for example, the attitudes to tears (especially to masculine tears) approved by the eighteenth and twentieth centuries. Very little reflection and inquiry will show conclusively that the eighteenth century in regarding a profuse discharge of the lachrymal glands as a proper and almost necessary accompaniment of tender and sorrowful emotion was much more *representative of humanity in all ages* than are our contemporary wooden-eyed stoics. . . .

A widespread general inhibition of all the simpler expansive developments of emotion (not only of its expression) has to be recognised among our educated population. It is *a new condition not easily paralleled in history,* and though it is propagated through social convention its deeper causes are not easy to divine. . . . *Possibly it is due to the increasing indefiniteness of our beliefs and disbeliefs, to the blurring of the moral background of our lives.* (268–69; my italics)

Richards then breaks off this line of thought, reluctant as he is to entertain notions of a transcendent reality: sentiments about "an illusory childhood heaven, for example," are to be considered "dream-infected" and cured by a dose of "actuality" such as one has already experienced (269–70). But Lewis, not hampered by what he called "the uneasy theophobia of . . . our contemporaries" (*PH*, 51), promoted the sympathetic reading of the older poets such as Milton, who could rely on readers to respond in a morally sound way when presented with such a spectacle as pride, treachery, or someone else's pain (*Preface*, 55) and with "archetypal" images (*Preface*, 46–47, 56). Granted that the moral response can be faked (*Preface*, 54), the risk of pretense is insufficient reason to abandon its cultivation.

With this considerable excursus, we are better able to appreciate the energy behind Lewis's poem "A Confession." He was seeking to counter a palpable and present threat of the eventual, perhaps imminent, abolition of Man.

III

Finally, there is a handful of poems in which Lewis examines language as a fundamental human attribute, one that reveals both our greatness and our limitations. In his wonderfully lighthearted creation poem, "Le Roi s'Amuse" (*Poems*, 23–24), the world comes into being as the product of Jove's glance, his bright laughter, his sighs. Finally, Jove's "thought" begets Athena, and

> Our sires at the fires of her lucid eyes began
> To speak in symbols, to seek out causes, to name the creatures; they
> became Man.

Here is the birth of language, of human reason and dominion (that is, of science and technology)—all inseparable. One more ingredient is also part of the package: freedom of the will. Thus, at the completion of creation

> Jove laughed to see
> The abyss empeopled, his bliss imparted, the throng that was his and no
> longer he.

But free will introduces a problem. The gift of language can be abused. Words can be "idle" (*Poems*, 135) and mere "trumpery" (*Poems*, 129). "The skill of concrete utterance can be used for almost any purpose," to utter folly or wisdom—or poison (*PH*, 114). Rhetoric, in itself a good thing, can be used mischievously (*Preface*, 52); the unity of language and reason can be destroyed, the once-unified concept *logos* bifurcated. Dymer, the hero of Lewis's longest poem, learns what happens "once the lying spirit of a cause / With maddening words dethrones the mind of men" (*NP*, 44). Even if we avoid these effects of human sin, human finitude imposes on language other limitations. Words, in fact, are inherently less than the realities they represent:

> This withering breath
> Of words is the beginning of decay
> In truth, when truth grows cold and pines away
> Among the ancestral images.
>
> (*NP*, 79)

The Queen of Drum learns from her Archbishop:

> Truths may be such
> That when they have cooled and hardened at the touch
> Of language, they turn errors. So our speech
> Fails us, and waking discourse cannot reach
> The thing we are in dreams.
>
> (*NP*, 148)

The Archbishop adds, a few speeches later,

> I yet believe (if such a word
> Of these soiled lips be not absurd)

That from the place beyond all ken
One only Word has come to men,
And was incarnate and had hands
And feet and walked in earthly lands
And died, and rose. And nothing more
Will come or ever came before
With certainty. And to obey
Is better than the hard assay
Of piercing anywhere besides
This mortal veil, which haply hides
Some insupportable abyss
Of bodiless light and burning bliss.
                              (NP, 152–53)

The imagery of these last lines is very much like that of "The Birth of Language" (*Poems*, 10–11), in which Lewis creates a myth of origins that expresses again the essentially Platonic doctrine we have just been noticing, that names are the merest shadows of the real. In the myth "intelligible virtues" begin as fragments from the sun itself; on the planet Mercury they each receive a sort of body, whose iconography is that of the god Mercury—each is "a god of speech."[29] Then, after receiving "their proper names," they start on the long journey to Earth, during which

                    their nimbleness and youth
Turns lean and frore; their meaning more,
Their being less. Fact shrinks to truth.

They reach this Earth. There each has birth
Miraculous, a word made breath,
Lucid and small for use in all
Man's daily needs; but dry like death.

Language, then, is merely "symbols" (line 37). That may seem to have a familiar sound, but there is a vast chasm between the Platonic notion conveyed by "symbol" here and the usual Structuralist connotations of the term. These verbal symbols are far from arbitrary conventions. Still, they have become fleshless, "bony and abstract" (line 38), representing the original concrete realities ("Fact") no longer so closely as they did on Mercury but at a farther remove, through the shrunk medium of mental constructs ("truth"; not to be confused with that word used in an opposite sense in the Archbishop passage). In a

29. Cf. the role of Mercury in *THS*, 397–98; in *The Discarded Image* (Cambridge: Cambridge University Press, 1964), 107–8; and in "The Planets" (*Poems*, 12).

letter Lewis lamented the inadequacy of language: "One can't put these experiences into words. . . . One can hardly put anything into words: only the simplest colours have names, and hardly any of the smells. The simple physical pains and (still more) the pleasures can't be expressed in language." To consider "what [is] wordless" to be "therefore vague and nebulous" is a mistake, and Lewis continues, in a very unplatonic vein: "It is just the clearest, the most concrete, and the most indubitable realities which escape language: not because *they* are vague but because language is. What goes easily into words is precisely the abstract—thought about 'matter' (not apples or snuff) about 'population' (not actual babies), and so on."[30]

Nowhere is the shortcoming of language more evident, Lewis believed, than in language directed to God, who is the most concrete reality of all ("Lang," 136; *SJ*, 237). To "attempt the ineffable Name," he wrote in the poem "Footnote to All Prayers" (*Poems*, 129), is to risk worshiping an "idol" shaped by one's "own unquiet thoughts"; the language of prayer references only "frail images" in the speaker's mind, "which cannot be the thing Thou art." For the perfecting of prayers, a divine initiative is required: "Take not, oh Lord, our literal sense. Lord, in Thy great, / Unbroken speech our limping metaphor translate."[31]

Can language ever be redeemed from its fall, enabled to recollect its original glory? Only partially, as if "in dreams," says the final stanza of "The Birth of Language," and then only by poetry, "true verse" (cf. "Blu," 265). The letter to Bodle quoted just above continues with this: "Poetry I take to be the continual effort to bring language back to the actual." Elsewhere Lewis defines poetry as "using all the extra-logical elements of language [note the oxymoronic play on *logos*]—rhythm, vowel-music, onomatopoeia, associations, and what not—to convey the concrete reality of experiences" (*PH*, 108).

But when it comes to apprehending the ultimate Reality, even poetry is not up to the task. In "No Beauty We Could Desire" (*Poems*, 124) the speaker, having vainly pursued the ineffable by the most delicate of human means—music, poetry, and "the winding stair of thought"—turns instead "to the appointed place where you [God]

30. Letter to Rhona M. Bodle, 24 June 1949, Wade Center.

31. There is a close relation between this line of thought and the process described by Stephen Medcalf toward the close of the next essay. It is worth noting, then, that this poem first appears in 1933 in *The Pilgrim's Regress* (PR, 183–84). Later revisions do not alter the essential idea.

pursue": to the Word become flesh, to a special wine, a special bread. When struggling fails, acceptance may be all that is left, and may succeed; when words and the thoughts behind them fail, silence.

> Thoughts are but coins. Let me not trust, instead
> Of Thee, their thin-worn image of Thy head.
> From all my thoughts, even from my thoughts of Thee,
> O thou fair Silence, fall, and set me free.
> ("The Apologist's Evening Prayer"; *Poems*, 129)

In the silence, new language may be born: words which at once are and are not one's own. So apposite here is what Paul says in Romans 8:26–27 that it must be quoted (I use the version in *The New English Bible*): "We do not even know how we ought to pray, but through our inarticulate groans the Spirit himself is pleading for us . . . in God's own way." This doctrine underlies the solution reached by the speaker of "Prayer" (*Poems*, 122). In the silence of having acknowledged that "the things I meant to say" are not to be found "in myself," there is space for the divine surrogate to act:

> seeing me empty, you forsake
> The Listener's rôle, and through
> My dead lips breathe and into utterance wake
> The thoughts I never knew.[32]

In their echoes of Shelley's "Ode to the West Wind" ("*my dead thoughts*"; "Be *through my lips* to unawakened earth"), these lines place before us the image of an Aeolian lyre, that instrument whose music arises passively from the operation of wind (breath, Spirit) upon it. Yet for both Lewis and Shelley, as Lewis himself noted in *The Abolition of Man* (9), the human instrument retains its own identity. The words which emerge from the self-silencing are not, after all, imposed from without but awakened from within. From our littleness and only thence, Lewis believes, all human greatness springs.

On the Text of "The Birth of Language"

Concerning "The Birth of Language," Owen Barfield has written me (12 January 1988), and I quote with his permission:

---

32. See Stephen Medcalf's further discussion of this poem on p. 142 below. Kirkpatrick ("Fresh Views," 7) points out the similarity to "Prayer" of lines 13–16 in "The Naked Seed" (*Poems*, 117).

When Lewis wrote *The Birth of Language,* he did not put it in 4-line stanzas of octosyllabics. It was in couplets of 8-foot lines. Whether he himself later altered the arrangement, I can't say. From the Appendix to the 1964 Collection [*Poems*] it looks as if he may have done. If so, it was a great mistake. Half the internal rhymes become end-rhymes and, with the chopping up, all the torrential rush of its richness is lost:

How near his sire's careering fires must Mercury the planet run . . .

I wonder if you will agree. I have a very vivid memory of receiving it by post. I was very busy at the time and quite immersed in a non-literary milieu. I seized a postcard, wrote the one word "Whew!" on it and dropped it in the letter-box! . . . I learnt [the poem] off by heart and later recited it to Jack (to his no small gratification) when we were out for a walk.

Barfield comments further that the speed of the lines as originally written, the "torrential rush," is "appropriate incidentally to Mercury as the most mobile of the planets."

By the time of its first publication in *Punch* (210 [1946]: 32), "The Birth of Language" already had been given its present arrangement in four-line stanzas. Whether that arrangement was the editor's or his own, Lewis retained it six months later when he sent to Ruth Pitter for criticism a fair autograph copy, somewhat revised (letter, 24 July 1946, Bodleian Library [MS Eng. lett. c. 220–23, fol. 20]; microfilm and transcript in the Wade Center).

These two extant earlier versions provide a possible emendation for the received text in line 16: they agree on the word "Beside" which seems an obviously more likely reading than "Besides" (1964 text).

Language and Self-Consciousness: The Making and Breaking of C. S. Lewis's Personae

Stephen Medcalf

I. The Special Nature of Lewis's Personae

The boy Eustace in C. S. Lewis's *The Voyage of the "Dawn Treader"* becomes, or at least everything about him except his mind becomes, a dragon. But he still has on his arm a golden ring, which he put on when he was a boy. Since dragons are bigger than boys, the ring hurts. The lion Aslan brings him to a well on a mountain, and he thinks it would ease his pain if he could bathe in it. But the lion tells him that he must first cast his skin. As he later recounts the story:

> I started scratching myself and my scales began coming off all over the place. And then I scratched a little deeper and, instead of just scales coming off here and there, my whole skin started peeling off beautifully, like it does after an illness, or as if I was a banana. In a minute or two I just stepped out of it . . . . But just as I was going to put my feet into the water I looked down and saw that they were all hard and rough and wrinkled and scaly just as they had been before. (*VDT*, 101)

Twice more he scratched off his skin, only to find another dragon's skin beneath. Finally he allowed Aslan to tear the skin off: "It hurt worse than anything I've ever felt. The only thing that made me able to bear it was just the pleasure of feeling the stuff peel off" (*VDT*, 102). Even now he remained a dragon, but "smooth and soft." Then

This essay is a companion to "The Coincidence of Myth and Fact" (in *Ways of Reading the Bible*, ed. M. Wadsworth [Brighton: Harvester, 1981]), an exercise in developing C. S. Lewis's thought on the Gospels, and to *An Anatomy of Consciousness*, a study of T. S. Eliot to be published shortly by Harvester Press. It originated from a suggestion by George Craig, was designed for the Conference of the Inklings Gesellschaft at Aachen in 1983, and was read there and in various forms at the Gladstone Memorial Library at Hawarden, Westham House at Barford, and Pusey House in Oxford.

Aslan threw him, tender as he was, into the water. It hurt, but he became a boy again.

The image is disconcertingly tactile, and so, remarkable in itself; but it also echoes something which Lewis wrote at about the same time (somewhere between 1948 and 1955—*The Voyage of the "Dawn Treader"* was written early in 1950) in his autobiography *Surprised by Joy*. He described an experience of his own on a bus going up Headington Hill in 1927 or 1928:

> Without words and (I think) almost without images, a fact about myself was somehow presented to me. I became aware that I was holding something at bay, or shutting something out. Or, if you like, that I was wearing some stiff clothing, like corsets, or even a suit of armour, as if I were a lobster. I felt myself being, there and then, given a free choice. I could open the door or keep it shut; I could unbuckle the armour or keep it on. Neither choice was presented as a duty; no threat or promise was attached to either, though I knew that to open the door or to take off the corslet meant the incalculable. . . . I chose to open, to unbuckle, to loosen the rein. (*SJ*, 211)

We could hardly come closer than the lobster's armor of the second image to the dragon's skin of the first, and even the alternative image of the suit of clothes in the second passage is paralleled in Eustace's story, for Aslan's actual word of command is to "undress."

Lewis makes it clear in the subtle though still tactile description of his autobiography that those images were supplied by him later to express a vivid but "almost" imageless memory. Eustace in contrast recounts an experience realized in clear images while it was still happening. This kind of image seems to have appealed to Lewis in the early 1950s: besides these instances, for example, he used something similar in the theme and title of what is probably his finest piece of writing, *Till We Have Faces*, composed in 1955–1956.

But it seems clear that in the story of Eustace, Lewis was drawing on his experience of 1927–1928, while using an image which seemed appropriate to him in 1950. And he seems to draw as well on the experiences that followed. In both story and autobiography, the removal of the skin or armor is followed by a change in what lay beneath. Eustace's now tender dragon's body becomes in the pool the boy's body he had lost, while in *Surprised by Joy*, "I felt as if I were a man of snow at long last beginning to melt. The melting was starting in my back . . ." (*SJ*, 212).

These experiences Lewis later came to see as preliminary to his acceptance of theism in 1929 and of Christ in 1931. The story of

Eustace seems to run all these together: throughout, Eustace is aware of the action of Aslan, who is Christ, and the images of the pool and of being thrown into it seem to suggest not only the melting of the snowman but the last stage of Lewis's transformation.

For if one turns to Lewis's letters written during the conversion to Christianity, one finds not the image of the skins, but the profounder image of dying into life and presently the image of diving. Yet the image of dying into life is developed in a way that resembles Eustace's successive castings of his skins. Thus on 15 June 1930, Lewis comments with admiration on George MacDonald's story in *The Princess and the Goblin* about Curdie, who

> in a dream, keeps on dreaming that he has waked up and then finding that he is still in bed. This means the same as the passage where Adam says to Lilith "Unless you unclose your hand you will never die & therefore never wake. *You may think you have died and even that you have risen again*: but both will be a dream."
>
> This has a terrible meaning, specially for imaginative people. . . . I am appalled to see how much of the change wh. I thought I had undergone lately was only imaginary. The real work seems still to be done.[1]

On July 8 he introduces a version of the second image in Eustace's story: "I learned to dive wh. is a great change in my life & has important (religious) connections."[2] What he meant by this is made clear in *The Pilgrim's Regress*, written in late 1932, in which Mother Kirk says to the pilgrim John, "The art of diving is not to do anything new but simply to cease doing something. You have only to let yourself go" (PR, 216). John, like Eustace with his scratching and like Lewis himself, half believes that he has dived and then finds he is still on the edge, and only after much temptation does he "let himself go" (PR, 218). Lewis's acceptance that it is Christ who opens salvation to us (which I take it he found was the crucial difference between the dream and the reality of the death of self) had happened on 28 September 1931, after his learning to dive: the reality following the image by fifteen months.

The means by which he was enabled to accept the agency of Christ involved a further image of the death of self. He had been held back from Christianity by a difficulty in knowing what it would mean to believe that "the life and death of Christ 'saved' or 'opened salva-

---

1. *They Stand Together: The Letters of C. S. Lewis to Arthur Greeves (1914–1963)*, ed. Walter Hooper (London: Collins, 1979), 361.
2. Lewis, *They Stand Together*, 369.

tion to' the world." A conversation with his friends Dyson and Tolkien enabled him to see the story of Christ as a myth of a god dying, sacrificed, himself to himself, and resurrected, which might be understood like the myths of Odin, Balder, and Adonis, as pregnant with meanings through, beyond, and under its surface, meanings which one's deepest self might accept and be changed by—but with this tremendous difference, that it really happened: "The 'doctrines' we get *out of* the true myth are . . . translations into our *concepts* and *ideas* of that wh. God has already expressed in a language more adequate, namely the actual incarnation, crucifixion, and resurrection."[3]

It seems likely that either Dyson or Tolkien advised him to read the epistle of St. Paul to the Romans. At any rate, between 22 September and 1 October, he was finding in it George MacDonald's understanding of death, as expressed in Adam's words to Lilith, here embodied in St. Paul's interpretation of Christ's death: "If we have been planted together in the likeness of his death, we shall be also in the likeness of his resurrection: knowing this, that our old man is crucified with him."[4]

The story of Eustace makes clear and the accounts in Lewis's letters and *Surprised by Joy* confirm that between 1927 and 1931 two different transformations took place in Lewis's self: one a continued attempt to shed a persona which he could not shed until he underwent the other transformation. He had to be transformed in that part of the self which "we cd. hope to take with us if there were another life," a transformation "incorporated into the unconscious depths," as he put it in a letter of 29 July 1930, a few weeks after he had reflected on diving and its significance.[5]

About the superficial change there is something very odd. The 1930 image of diving and the retrospective images in the 1950s of the dragon's skin and the pool imply a freeing both from a persona and from the effort of maintaining a persona. But it is about Lewis as he displayed himself in writing from about 1935, some four years after this freeing, that Owen Barfield, one of his most perceptive and most long-standing friends, delicately and exactly asks, "*Was* there something, at least in his impressive, indeed splendid, literary personality which was somehow—and with no taint of insincerity—*voulu?*"[6]

3. Lewis, *They Stand Together*, 427, 428.

4. Romans 6:5–6; cf. Lewis, *They Stand Together*, 425–26.

5. Lewis, *They Stand Together*, 370.

6. Barfield, Introduction to *Light on C. S. Lewis*, ed. Jocelyn Gibb (London: Geoffrey Bles, 1965), xi.

Barfield, who had already known Lewis for sixteen years, first observed the development of this quality at the conclusion of an essay in 1934, in the rhetoric of such sentences as: "We have both learnt our dialectic in the rough academic arena where knocks that would frighten the London literary coteries are given and taken in good part; and even where you may think me something too pert you will not suspect me of malice. If you honour me with a reply it will be in kind; and then, God defend the right!" (*PH*, 69). To my ear, the rhetoric is not unlike what Lewis already had used in 1932 in the article "What Chaucer Really Did to *Il Filostrato*." But the pattern in *The Personal Heresy* of combat with E. M. W. Tillyard impels Lewis to a new extreme of style, causing Barfield to shout, "I don't believe it! It's *pastiche!*" What Barfield felt then, he continued to feel: in the 1950s he remarked of a poem of Lewis's, "It left me with the impression, not of an 'I say this,' but of a 'This is the sort of thing a man might say.'" Lewis answered that "he was not at all sure that the distinction could really be maintained."[7] Indeed, in his first contribution to *The Personal Heresy* in 1934, Lewis had said that "the 'I' and 'me' of whom poets speak . . . are phases of human nature, detached from their historical context—οἷα ἂν γένοιτο" (*PH*, 10), which may be fairly translated almost in Barfield's words as "the sort of thing a man might be." And even in autobiography, Lewis says in the same essay, no one can describe himself "without making of himself, to some extent, a dramatic creation. The character whom I describe as myself leaves out, at least, this present act of description" (*PH*, 10).

This may be so, but Lewis carried self-dramatization far beyond the license this argument would give. Indeed he wonderfully mythicized his memory of his life. In *Surprised by Joy* (about 1955) he remembered the trip to Whipsnade Zoo—during which, nine days after his conversation with Dyson and Tolkien, he found that he believed that Jesus Christ is the Son of God—as happening in spring. "They have spoiled Whipsnade since then. Wallaby Wood, with the birds singing overhead and the bluebells underfoot and the Wallabies hopping all round one, was almost Eden come again" (*SJ*, 223). No doubt that lovely sentence expresses something true within Lewis. It was a kind of spring, it was almost Eden come again: there ought to have been bluebells. But there were not. Lewis came to believe in Christ on a visit to Whipsnade in the autumn, on 28 September

7. Lewis, "What Chaucer Really Did to *Il Filostrato*" (1932), in *Selected Literary Essays*, ed. Walter Hooper (Cambridge: Cambridge University Press, 1969), 27–44; Barfield, Introduction to *Light on C. S. Lewis*, x, xi.

1931.[8] The bluebells must belong to a later visit, perhaps that of 14 June 1932.

There is then evidence that Lewis's strongest appearance of persona manifested itself over a period well after his strongest sense of release from persona. I want in this essay to explore the manifestations of this later persona in language and awareness; to consider its foundations in theories of consciousness and personality which began during the period of the earlier persona; and to describe how violently these things changed in his last years and his late books, issuing finally in something mystical.

II. The Persona of Lewis's First "New Look"

Lewis himself describes what I mean by persona in his Cambridge lectures on *The Faerie Queene*, written at about the same time that he produced the images of armor and dragon, in the mid-fifties. Many of Spenser's images, he remarks, can be identified with Jung's archetypes, but the only one on which he enlarges is the persona: "The double role of Britomart as stern knight and lovesick girl is a symbol of the Persona. So is the illusory appearance of the False Florimell. And so, more obviously, is the brave facade of Braggadocchio the pseudo-knight."[9]

He interprets a similar, perhaps identical, perception in the language of metaphysics when he recalls being wounded on Mount Bernenchon on 15 April 1918:

> I found (or thought I found) that I was not breathing and concluded that this was death. I felt no fear and certainly no courage. . . . The proposition "Here is a man dying" stood before my mind as dry, as factual, as unemotional as something in a text-book. . . . When, some years later, I met Kant's distinction between the Noumenal and the Phenomenal self, it was more to me than an abstraction. I had tasted it; I had proved that there was a fully conscious "I" whose connections with the "me" of introspection were loose and transitory. (*SJ*, 187)

In both passages Lewis rightly implies that he is describing a normal aspect of the self; it is his perception and his handling of it that are abnormal. One might delve into his early life to find causes

---

8. See *SJ*, 223 and W. H. Lewis, *Brothers and Friends: The Diaries of Major Warren Hamilton Lewis*, ed. Clyde S. Kilby and Marjorie Lamp Mead (San Francisco: Harper and Row, 1982), 87 n. 114.

9. Lewis, *Spenser's Images of Life*, ed. Alastair Fowler (Cambridge: Cambridge University Press, 1967), 117.

for this, but for us the important cause is the extraordinary contrast in him of clear, aggressive intellect both with an immense receptiveness to literature and friendship and with an enormously active involuntary imagination: the imagination which gave him vivid dreams and those sharp, bright pictures that provided the starting points of his stories and at times, as we have seen, transformed even his memory.

The development of his special self-consciousness is chronicled in *Surprised by Joy* in that style, classic in balance and syntax, romantic in emotional color, at once detached and vivid, which is itself a product of the development. He describes wisely and clearly, with an introspection that is largely retrospection, his awareness of two urges—moral effort and the longing for an unknown something, which he calls "Joy," the longing that was roused in Keats by the song of a nightingale for what he images as "the foam / Of perilous seas, in faery lands forlorn." Lewis is sensitive to the doubling of self-consciousness in both Joy and moral effort, to the longing for longing, the effort towards effort in both urges, to the self-defeating act of standing "anxious sentinel at my own mind to watch whether the blessed moment was beginning and to endeavour to retain it if it did" (*SJ*, 160).

The style in which he expressed his reaction against this state while it was happening was very different. In March 1923 he had to be present while a friend, Dr. Askins, suffered extreme mental anguish ending in death. Lewis's response was violent, and violently expressed in crudely psychoanalytic terms:

> Never allow yourself to get a neurosis. You and I are both qualified for it, because we both were afraid of our fathers as children. The Doctor who came to see the poor Doc . . . said that every neurotic case went back to the childish fear of the father. But it can be avoided. Keep clear of introspection, of brooding, of spiritualism, of everything eccentric. Keep to work and sanity and open air—to the cheerful & the matter of fact side of things. We hold our mental health by a thread: & nothing is worth risking it for. Above all beware of excessive day dreaming, of seeing yourself in the centre of a drama, of self pity, and, as far as possible, of fears.[10]

Here is a clear and powerful program for a persona, what Lewis calls in *Surprised by Joy* his "New Look." He earnestly endeavored to carry it out for a time, and in it we can find, not indeed his first persona, for like all of us he tentatively constructed characters for himself as far

---

10. Lewis, *They Stand Together*, 292.

back as we can find written evidence, but the first persona of which we can trace the beginning and the shattering. It was constructed deliberately against his deepest feelings, against his former delight in romantic longing, in Joy, which he now identified with wish-fulfill-ment fantasy: it was constructed too against his urge, never quite to be escaped from, to introspection.

A little later he made a discovery in philosophy which was crucial to his thought for the rest of his life. This was Samuel Alexander's division of consciousness into two aspects, enjoyment and contem-plation.[11] As I read this book, I contemplate it; I enjoy my act of contemplation. If I turn to examining my consciousness of this book, then I cease to contemplate the book and cease therefore to enjoy that contemplation. Instead, I contemplate my consciousness and enjoy that different, second-order consciousness of consciousness. But in fact I have stopped reading. So, at least, Lewis thought, and he believed in consequence that to examine one's own consciousness is at best to examine an imperfect memory, and more commonly to indulge in a distorted fantasy: "The enjoyment and the contempla-tion of our inner activities are incompatible" (SJ, 206). He would admit no activity between the two aspects of consciousness, no look-ing, as he would regard it, out of the corner of one's eye to see what seeing is like. Introspection finds only "mental images and physical sensations" left behind by "the thought or the appreciation, when interrupted . . . like the swell at sea, working after the wind has dropped" (SJ, 207).

Moreover, introspection not only falsifies, it interferes with our inner life: "You cannot hope and also think about hoping at the same moment; for in hope we look to hope's object and we interrupt this by (so to speak) turning round to look at the hope itself." This he thought "could be verified in daily and hourly experience. The surest means of disarming an anger or a lust was to turn your attention from the girl or the insult and start examining the passion itself" (SJ, 206).

Now it seems to me that (as often with Lewis's beliefs) a partial, relative truth and a distinction of convenience are being treated as absolute. The incompatibility between enjoyment and contempla-tion of an inner activity depends on the degree to which we are involved in that activity, or if it is an emotion, on the strength or obsessiveness of that emotion. You will not disarm a powerful lust nor take the sting from a really wounding insult by turning to examine your response. You may find yourself more entangled in them. I once

11. Alexander, *Space, Time and Deity* (London: Macmillan, 1920).

stood near Dondra Head in Ceylon looking south, with palm trees on either side, a fisherman's catamaran drawn up on the beach behind me and the surf of the Indian Ocean breaking about my knees, and asked myself, "Am I happy?" A weaker happiness would have been weakened—a happiness which I inhabited less, or which was less exactly matched by the environment. The happiness of that day was increased.

As a fact of introspection, Lewis was without doubt always well aware of this—after all, he only says "the surest means of disarming," not "the sure means," and in a letter of 1949 puts the observation in the form, "In my experience only v. robust pleasures will stand the question, 'Am I really enjoying this?'" (*Letters*, 221). But as a philosophic presupposition, he treats the fact as if it were absolute.

There is a second objection with a similar consequence. The notion that introspection finds only what is left behind by thought when interrupted is clearly related to that other doctrine—which we have already associated with Lewis's tendency to freeze his personae—that "the 'I' and 'me' of whom poets speak . . . are phases of human nature, detached from their historical context." It was his intent, as he put it in March 1926, to use introspection only "as a necessary preliminary to being rid of" "the object Me."[12] But his gloss on Alexander seems to have produced a tendency to conform his living and acting self to that fossilized picture of it which was, he was determined to think, all that could be seen. It was associated with that state of the self which in the next couple of years became suddenly apparent to him on Headington Hill as wearing a suit of armor and holding something at bay.

In the late 1920s, to illustrate his interpretation of Alexander's dictum, Lewis wrote for Owen Barfield, who doubted its truth, a brilliant fable (printed in *The Dark Tower*) about a man born blind, who recovered his sight through an operation. "The result," as Barfield says, "was disastrous for the protagonist, because he insisted on trying to see the mysterious thing he had heard people calling 'light'; whereas you do not see light itself, but only the objects it illumines."[13] It would seem from the two objections we have raised that Barfield was justified in his doubts, that however hard it may be to state it introspection can report more responsively on a more moving and alive state of consciousness than Lewis in the middle part of his life

12. Lewis, *They Stand Together*, 384.

13. Barfield, Introduction to *Light on C. S. Lewis*, xviii. See Lewis, "The Man Born Blind," in *The Dark Tower and Other Stories*, ed. Walter Hooper (New York: Harcourt Brace Jovanovich, 1977), 99–103.

allowed. The remainder of this essay will suggest how in certain ways he came to modify his views.

Meanwhile, however, the Alexander-Lewis doctrine joined with a developing interest in idealist philosophy and a reading of a chorus in the *Hippolytus* (I suppose that which Gilbert Murray translates "To the strand of the Daughters of the Sunset, / The Apple-tree, the singing and the gold")[14] to enable Lewis to recover Joy for his mental life without too great a break with the New Look. For he no longer supposed that in this longing he was enjoying a merely subjective sensation, nor even contemplating a projected image of fantasy. Rather, he thought he was contemplating "something which, by refusing to identify itself with any object of the senses, or anything whereof we have biological or social need, or anything imagined, or any state of our own minds, proclaims itself sheerly objective" (*SJ*, 208–9). To begin with, he identified that "something" with the absolute mind of which we are appearances, and Joy with looking for "that self-contradictory waking which would reveal, not that we had had, but that we *were*, a dream" (*SJ*, 209).

Lewis graphically describes in *Surprised by Joy* how the endeavor to transcend self led to attempts to find help in the endeavor by recourse to the Absolute Self and how those attempts became prayer. In these attempts he must have allowed introspection in terms of clearly defined concepts of good and evil—of what in *The Abolition of Man* (1943) he was to describe as the tradition, the Way, the Tao. The Tao is like a Copernican system by which you can stand outside yourself and see your own world moving in relation to God, or like the word of God which the 119th Psalm describes as "a lantern unto my feet, and a light unto my paths" and which might therefore, if one could make sense of the double analogy with light, take the place of the light of individual consciousness in illuminating "the object Me."

In chapter 2 of *The Allegory of Love*, drafted in the summer of 1929 when he accepted "that God was God" (*SJ*, 215), Lewis describes what must be his own sense of a self divided in moral struggle— divided by the perhaps pathological activity of introspection and endeavoring to create a unitary persona—in an account of the development of a sense of these things during the late Roman Empire:

> To be thus conscious of the divided will is necessarily to turn the mind in upon itself. Whether it is the introspection which reveals the division,

---

14. Euripides, *Hippolytus*, trans. Gilbert Murray (London: George Allen and Unwin, 1902), 39.

or whether the division, having first revealed itself in the experience of actual moral failure, provokes the introspection, need not here be decided. Whatever the causal order may be, it is plain that to fight against "Temptation" is also to explore the inner world; and it is scarcely less plain that to do so is to be already on the verge of allegory. . . . It would be a misunderstanding to suggest that there is another and better way of representing that inner world, and that we have found it in the novel and the drama. The gaze turned inward with a moral purpose does not discover *character*. No man is a "character" to himself, and least of all while he thinks of good and evil. Character is what he has to produce; within he finds only the raw material, the passions and emotions which contend for mastery. That unitary "soul" or "personality" which interests the novelist is for him merely the arena in which the combatants meet.[15]

This self engaged through moral struggle and failure in producing character is plainly another picture of what is represented in Eustace, tearing off his skins, and John, dreaming again and again that he has let himself go; that is, of Lewis himself from a little before his conversion to theism until his conversion to Christianity. And it is very noteworthy that whereas the description of the struggle in the self is always in terms of what Lewis would call allegory, its actual resolution was achieved through what he calls the true myth, the death and resurrection of the soul consequent upon the death and resurrection of Christ. The true myth is operative at deeper levels of the self than the creation of personae, but his descriptions in both *The Allegory of Love* and *Spenser's Images of Life* of the struggle in the self and of the naturalness of its representation in allegory, suggest how natural it was also to Lewis, having shed one persona in the process of this radical alteration, immediately to begin building that second persona whose curious distancing from ordinary individuality struck the perceptive eye of Owen Barfield.

III. The Language and Nature of Lewis's Middle-Period Persona

It is by the persona of his middle life, his most *evident* persona, that Lewis is probably best known: as a moralist, as a Christian thinker, as a scholar and as a tale-teller, as the author of *The Problem of Pain*, of *Mere Christianity*, of *The Abolition of Man* and of *Miracles*; of *The Screwtape Letters* and *The Great Divorce*; of *Out of the Silent Planet*, *Perelandra*, and *That Hideous Strength*; of *A Preface to Paradise*

15. Lewis, *The Allegory of Love: A Study in Medieval Tradition* (Oxford: Clarendon Press, 1936), 60–61.

Lost and *English Literature in the Sixteenth Century.* The Narnia
books and *Surprised by Joy,* which he wrote between 1948 and 1955,
seem to carry symptoms of this persona's passing, but they still bear
most of the marks of its persistence. I am sorry he is best known for
this period because, superb as some of those books are and profoundly wise as much of the thought that they embody is, I do not
think they include his very best and am sure they do not include his
most original work.

But then it was at the heart of his beliefs during this period that he
did not value originality at all highly. It is no accident that Barfield
first had the sense of "the sort of thing a man might say" from *The
Personal Heresy,* which not only in style but in theme exalts the
objective work, the objective tradition, at the expense of the individual and the creative. Lewis valued tradition, the great tradition of
European thought as it subsumed Greco-Roman and Hebrew thought,
myth, and revelation in Christianity; he loved the medieval habit
which scarcely valued individual artist or author in comparison with
the continuing work or story to which he contributed. The two pairs
of books which form the core of his work at this time demonstrate
those loves: *A Preface to Paradise Lost,* which might rather be called
The Epic Tradition and How It Culminates in Paradise Lost, together
with *Perelandra,* Lewis's own version of *Paradise Lost;* and *The Abolition of Man,* which again might rather be called *The Moral Tradition
of Humanity and the Present-day Attack on It,* together with Lewis's
parable on this theme, *That Hideous Strength.*

Just as with his theory and practice regarding the individual self,
so in his theory about the classical, medieval, and renaissance system
of thought, Lewis tended to overstress its unity and stability, and for
reasons ultimately connected with the same cause, his theory of
consciousness. In *The Allegory of Love* he justifies this tendency on
the ground that unity *must* be a feature of the "essence" of an art,
even if that art is particularly subject, as he represents the art of the
Middle Ages as being, to the "disease" of irregularity. Most reveal-
ingly he says, "Unity in diversity if possible—failing that, mere unity,
as a second best—these are the norms for all human work, given, not
by the ancients, but by the nature of consciousness itself."[16]

It is not easy to give content to the idea of "mere unity" in human
work, but Lewis makes the drift of his ideas about aesthetics and
consciousness clear in his analysis of modernism in *A Preface to
Paradise Lost.* A work such as Joyce's *Ulysses* owes some of its popu-

16. Lewis, *Allegory of Love,* 141.

larity, he says, to the belief that "to organize elementary passions into sentiments is simply to tell lies about them." But the Lewis-Alexander doctrine of enjoyment and contemplation suggests that this belief is false:

> The disorganized consciousness . . . is discovered by introspection—that is, by artificially suspending all the normal and outgoing activities of the mind and then attending to what is left. In that residuum it discovers no concentrated will, no logical thought, no morals, no stable sentiments, and (in a word) no mental hierarchy. Of course not; for we have deliberately stopped all these things in order to introspect. The poet who finds by introspection that the soul is mere chaos is like a policeman who, having himself stopped all the traffic in a certain street, should then solemnly write down in his note-book "The stillness in this street is highly suspicious." (*Preface*, 135–36)

Consciousness "is, from the outset, selective, and ceases when selection ceases. Not to prefer any one datum before another, not to attend to one part of our experience at the expense of the rest, is to be asleep." To Joyce's style, or at least to the admiration of it as specially realistic in its representation of consciousness, he objects as being artificial: "You cannot make a true picture of that no-man's-land between the visible and the invisible which exists on the edges of our field of vision, because just in so far as you make a picture you are bringing it into the centre" (*Preface*, 136).

It is striking how much more formal and absolute Lewis's convictions about the consequences of the distinction between enjoyment and contemplation and the corrosive effect of introspection became after *The Allegory of Love* and before *A Preface to Paradise Lost*. His dislike of most modern writers and thinkers—not only Joyce, but Kierkegaard, Freud, D. H. Lawrence, T. S. Eliot, Sartre—is to be ascribed, I think, not to something automatically reactionary in him, but to the perfectly correct perception that they are all concerned with the attempt to catch consciousness in the act to which he refused assent.

His own use of words is necessarily affected. "As I write this book" is subject to the same laws as "As I read this book." His language cannot appear to be altering itself as he writes; it can only be corrected afterward. Charles Williams, whom he deeply admired, but who had a greater tincture of modernism in him, could write like this: "The famous saying 'God is love,' it is generally assumed, means that God is like our immediate emotional indulgence, and not that our meaning of love ought to have something of the 'otherness' and terror

of God."[17] It is a statement with which Lewis would not have quarreled, but in his middle period he would have eschewed the interactive form by which Williams reveals his awareness that, if you intend
to enlarge the meaning of *love* or any other word, you must not
confine yourself to multiplying existing models for its use, but show
how those models are themselves modified in the process. Lewis
himself takes the way of multiplying models, as in *The Problem of
Pain*:

> You asked for a loving God: you have one. The great spirit you so lightly
> invoked, the "lord of terrible aspect," is present: not a senile benev-
> olence that drowsily wishes you to be happy in your own way, not the
> cold philanthropy of a conscientious magistrate, nor the care of a host
> who feels responsible for the comfort of his guests, but the consuming
> fire Himself, the Love that made the worlds, persistent as the artist's
> love for his work and despotic as a man's love for a dog, provident and
> venerable as a father's love for a child, jealous, inexorable, exacting as
> love between the sexes.[18]

That is tremendous, yet it is a rhetoric based on an absolute assurance
that the meaning of words can be found with certainty in their past
uses in the tradition of Christian English writing and can only be
developed straightforwardly like boughs from that trunk. The style
rests in a certain assumed or chosen security about the relation of
consciousness to the world and of language to the objects it describes.
Lewis aggressively proclaimed his faith in "stock responses"; he was a
master of integrating scraps of language into his writing from writers
he loved, neither losing anything of their power, nor changing it, nor
increasing it. Take as one example among many—one which may be
contrasted with what Eliot does in *The Waste Land* or P. G. Wodehouse in his novels—the integration almost intact of William Morris's
pentameter line describing Christ into the prose description of the
King of Perelandra: "Whose face no man could say he did not know."[19]
It is not clear whether Lewis was even aware of what he was doing.

Another case which makes a revealing comparison with Charles
Williams is one of Lewis's masterpieces of this period, *The Screwtape
Letters*. The characteristic excellence of *The Screwtape Letters* is a
fresh and acute description of human consciousness seen objectively

17. Williams, *He Came Down from Heaven* (London: Heinemann, 1938), 11.
18. Lewis, *The Problem of Pain* (London: Geoffrey Bles, 1940), 35.
19. Morris, "Sir Galahad, A Christmas Mystery," *Prose and Poetry* (1856–1870)
(London: Oxford University Press, 1913), p. 209, line 86. Lewis has: ". . . that face
which no man can say he does not know" (*Per*, 236).

because seen from the viewpoint of the general moral law, the Tao. A wholly moral consciousness surveys human consciousness rigorously in terms of good and evil. That the moral consciousness is evil and that its interest in the Tao is to invert it gives the book its wit. Lewis imagines how a devil would think and feel, and he recorded in a later edition how disagreeable the task was of immersing himself in a devil's world, a world of grit, itch, and rancor.

But there is an important limitation on his imagining. Screwtape's consciousness is given only in relation to his function and to the objects of his labors, as befits someone imagined as a bureaucrat. In Alexander's terms it is given only as contemplative. It would distract the reader's attention from the moral wit to imagine the enjoyment of a consciousness which (one hopes) would appear to us insane. So it is an advantage that Lewis scarcely portrays such enjoyment even when he wants for the sake of moral insight into the human consciousness to contrast it with the diabolical. Thus Screwtape says, "Remember, he is not, like you, a pure spirit. Never having been a human (Oh that abominable advantage of the Enemy's!) you don't realize how enslaved they are to the pressure of the ordinary." He illustrates the dry, abstract, functional little phrase "the pressure of the ordinary" with the anecdote of an atheist who, while reading in the British Museum, began a train of thought going "the wrong way" and was cured by the distraction of "a newsboy shouting the midday paper, and a No. 73 bus going past."[20]

Charles Williams, reviewing the book for *Time and Tide*, could not resist imagining, even syntactically, the anguish and fragmentation of a devil's consciousness. He puts the same point about incarnation thus:

> Why, Scorpuscle, can't we get into their flesh? Not that one wants to; the vision revolts me; but it would be our duty. I should undertake it reluctantly, but I would undertake it. There —the lowest, the nastiest, the hatefullest gate into man's nature, and we cannot even find it! Yet he, he up there, did it. Our Father Below is said himself to have tried once or twice, but it is the one thing he never speaks of—when he does speak; coherently, I mean, of course; his breathless whispers go on all the time, drawing us in, drawing us.[21]

The effect of consciousness on style suggests a much larger comparison with William Golding's *The Inheritors*. In *The Problem of*

20. Lewis, *The Screwtape Letters* (London: Geoffrey Bles, 1942), 12–13.
21. Williams, "Letters in Hell," *Time and Tide*, 21 March 1942, 245–46.

Pain, Lewis outlines a myth of unfallen man which closely corresponds with Golding's in that novel, and since Golding read and admired *The Problem of Pain* when it came out, Lewis's picture may have influenced Golding's. Lewis suggests that "all that experience and practice can teach he had still to learn. . . . He may have been utterly incapable of expressing in conceptual form his paradisal experience."[22] The greater part of Golding's book is written in prose that expresses just this consciousness: that of a being who conceptualizes very little and knows nothing of chains of reasoning except that some imaginative pictures help in forming others and most of whose mental life is emotional, sensory, or imaginative—the consciousness of people as they feel it, in words such as they could never have conceived.

From both *Perelandra* and *The Problem of Pain,* it emerges that Lewis would make paradisal humanity in the image of his ideal hierarchical consciousness, having already a clear distinction of will, intellect, and appetite, although the unity conferred by the will is perfect, and makes man "all consciousness" and even sleep "willed and conscious repose." Golding in contrast conceives a humanity in whom intellect, intuition, will, and appetite are innocent and undivided, and sleep is a relaxation into a communal unconsciousness. He pushes fallenness back to the awareness of oneself over against everyone else, which for Lewis would be only a preliminary, still unfallen step to the wish to exist independently of God, "to be on their own, to take care for their own future," which, when embodied in action, would constitute the Fall.[23] One can compare, moreover, Golding's Fa as she approaches the fallen state through dim pictures of altering the state of the world by carrying water or transplanting shoots with Lewis's creation, the Lady of Perelandra, as she approaches the Fall through argument with the Un-man.

In this middle period, Lewis allowed, as he does in the description of the bear in *That Hideous Strength,* that there are "states below reason" and states above it which "have, by their common contrast to the life we know, a certain superficial resemblance. Sometimes there returns to us from infancy the memory of a nameless delight or terror, unattached to any delightful or dreadful thing, a potent adjective floating in a nounless void, a pure quality" (*THS,* 379). But it is clear from his remarks on Joyce that he would have thought it lost

22. Golding, *The Inheritors* (London: Faber and Faber, 1955); Lewis, *Problem of Pain,* 67.
23. Lewis, *Problem of Pain,* 65–66, 68.

labor to go further than this detached *contemplating* in describing the states "below reason" or to attempt to convey what it would be like to enjoy them. And although he certainly would have allowed that poetry can go further in this direction than prose, even his poem of 1949 "The Magician and the Dryad" (*Poems*, 8–9) goes in fact no further. And in his magnificent sermon "Transposition," in which he touches on the possibilities of expressing states "above reason," he makes no attempt to do so. Even in 1962, when he had made attempts (*Till We Have Faces* and "After Ten Years") which date and style might suggest emulated Golding, he still felt uneasily that the writing of *The Inheritors* was "so good that you couldn't find out what was happening. . . . All these little details you only notice in real life if you've got a high temperature."[24]

Yet in his middle period Lewis did not shrink from putting words into the mouth of a devil or an unfallen Lady. For satire that was the correct decision, and Lewis did not alter it when he added in 1960 a new piece by Screwtape to the edition whose introductory remarks on the unpleasantness of writing like Screwtape I have cited. In that introduction he added something which recognizes the difficulties of expressing an unfallen consciousness, but not without suggesting that they might be overcome. He would have liked, he says, to write a companion volume to Screwtape, "archangelical advice to the patient's guardian angel." However, "even if a man . . . could scale the spiritual heights required, what 'answerable style' could he use? For that style would really be part of the content. Mere advice would be no good: every sentence would have to smell of Heaven. And nowadays even if you could write a prose like Traherne's, you wouldn't be allowed to, for the canon of 'functionalism' has disabled literature for half its functions."[25]

How that consideration about style came to bulk more largely in Lewis's mind, as I think it does here, than it had in his middle period, and how in the end he did create a humbler version of that companion to Screwtape in *Letters to Malcolm* remains to be considered.

24. Lewis, "Unreal Estates," in *Of Other Worlds: Essays and Stories,* ed. Walter Hooper (London: Geoffrey Bles, 1966), 92. "After Ten Years" was first published in *Of Other Worlds*, 127–45.

25. Lewis, Preface to *The Screwtape Letters and Screwtape Proposes a Toast* (New York: Macmillan, 1961), 5–6.

IV. The Breaking of the Middle-Period Persona:
the Acquiring of Immediacy

The persona of this middle period seems to have been first seriously shaken by an assault on something only indirectly related to
Lewis's theory of consciousness: the belief that reason, held by each
person separately, but impersonal in itself, forms a bond between the
natural and supernatural kingdoms because reason could not be valid
if it were simply part of nature. He advanced this theory in *Miracles*,
and it was heavily attacked by G. E. M. Anscombe in a paper given to
the Socratic Club on 2 February 1948. With the logical success or
otherwise of her attack we are not here concerned. Anscombe has
since said that she did not think that Lewis's position need be entirely
abandoned, and it seems possible that it was the way in which the
then novel linguistic philosophy forced him back on a kind of self-
examination ("What *can* you mean by 'valid' beyond what would be
indicated by the explanation you would give for distinguishing between valid and invalid?") that Lewis found disconcerting and made
him speak of the debate in terms of "the fog of war, the retreat of
infantry thrown back under heavy attack." The effect on Lewis's
beliefs was described by Hugo Dyson a few days later: "now he had
lost everything and was come to the foot of the Cross."[26] I take it that
this, which might sound hyperbolic for even the most violent of
intellectual disturbances, signifies the abandonment of all supports
to faith except the Cross, such as Bonhoeffer had experienced in the
same decade.

In the month after that of Miss Anscombe's attack, in March 1948,
Lewis began to write his autobiography.[27] It was an enterprise that
might be regarded in two ways: as the exploration of how he had
found belief, i.e., a self-questioning; or as the rebuilding of his now
shaken persona in its old form. I think it was both. The seven years
which it took him to write the book form an intermediate period in
his life. During it, he played down somewhat his role of public apologist for Christianity. For example, whereas since 1942 he had nor-

26. Anscombe, "A Reply to Mr C. S. Lewis's Argument that 'Naturalism' is Self-
Refuting" (1947), in *Metaphysics and the Philosophy of Mind*, vol. 2 of *The Collected
Philosophical Papers of G. E. M. Anscombe* (Oxford: Basil Blackwell, 1981), 226; Lewis,
quoted in Roger Lancelyn Green and Walter Hooper, *C. S. Lewis: A Biography*
(London: Collins, 1974), 288; Dyson, quoted in Humphrey Carpenter, *The Inklings:
C. S. Lewis, J. R. R. Tolkien, Charles Williams, and Their Friends* (London: George
Allen and Unwin, 1978), 217.
27. Green and Hooper, *C. S. Lewis*, 257.

mally given the opening address at the Socratic Club twice each year, after Miss Anscombe's paper he never introduced a meeting at all except in April 1953, when he spoke on one of the fortifications of his persona, the proper conditions of "Obstinacy in Belief." The paper on this subject fits nicely the hypothesis I am developing as to what Lewis might be expected to write in the early 1950s. He is supporting his classical-idealist middle period's Christian persona, but not by what he calls in the paper (after Dante) the *fisici e metafisici argomenti*, by which in his apologetic books he would have supported that persona. He argues that maintaining Christian belief must operate by a quite different logic from that by which it is adopted: "the assent, of necessity, moves us from the logic of speculative thought into what might perhaps be called the logic of personal relations."[28] More strikingly still, "the logic of personal relations" bears a strong resemblance to what Aslan says to Eustace in *The Voyage of the "Dawn Treader"*—written three years before—to persuade him to allow his skin to be torn off.

Lewis further tried to consolidate his position by revising *Miracles* and the earlier books that became *Mere Christianity*, and he issued the already written sermons and papers of *Transposition and Other Addresses*. Other than these, he wrote no more works of dogmatic exposition. But his imagination was at its most active: all seven Narnia books were written between 1948 and 1954, and their characteristic form of creation would seem to have been like that of *Perelandra* and *That Hideous Strength*, the presentation of an involuntary picture (as of "a queen on a sledge") or of dreams (as of lions) and the development of these pictures by a kind of architectural intellectual effort which draws on the great structure of doctrines and images of the classic Lewis persona put into fabular form.[29]

In the first of these, *The Lion, the Witch and the Wardrobe*, it is very striking how much Lewis in developing his pictures relies on a myth in its most schematic form—that is, on a pattern beyond historic events, what Matthew Arnold called *aberglaube*. It is striking because Lewis removes the myth in question, the Anselmian or satisfaction theory of the atonement, from the facts which are its

28. Lewis, "On Obstinacy in Belief" (1955), in *The World's Last Night and Other Essays* (New York: Harcourt Brace, 1960), 17, 29, 30.

29. Green and Hooper, *C. S. Lewis*, 237–39. Lewis, "Sometimes Fairy Stories May Say Best What's to Be Said" (1956), in *Of Other Worlds: Essays and Stories*, ed. Walter Hooper (London: Geoffrey Bles, 1966), 36; Lewis, "It All Began with a Picture . . ." (1960), in *Of Other Worlds*, 42.

expression in history and provides it with new fabular expressions—a lion and a stone table, the emperor's magic, magic from before the dawn of time. It is a technique which he uses again in others of the Narnia books, as he does at the end of *The Voyage of the "Dawn Treader,"* for example, with the lamb who offers roast fish to the children and becomes the lion.

But the technique is oddest in *The Lion, the Witch and the Wardrobe* because the Anselmian theory of the atonement is not really part of the plot of the Gospels, but is an interpretation of them, and therefore especially a myth detached from event. An insistence that this theory is something beyond the essence of mere Christianity had been in 1941 one of only two points on which Lewis found himself so convinced as to maintain it against one of his theological advisers, Dom Bede Griffiths.[30] And in 1931 it had been the general doctrine of the atonement that had held Lewis back from Christianity, because he neither liked it as a story nor could understand its relevance to the actual sinful human condition for which it was presented as the answer. It was in relation to this doctrine that the idea of the true myth was most important to him, because it allowed the story of Christ's death and resurrection to be understandable as one understands myth and not as one understands abstract statements.

We find in the first of the Narnia books, then, the most striking case of a slight imbalance in Lewis's renderings of Christianity as compared with the Gospels: his tendency to remove the idea or myth of Christianity from its involvement in contingent fact, although of course he retained its embodiment in concrete image (the sacrifice of the actual death of the son of God). It is as if he were trying to short-circuit the relation between the deeper levels of the self and the deeper levels of objective reality by omitting the empirical self's relation to empirical fact (for example, his own native coolness to the story of the atonement, in relation to the historic facts of Christ's passion).

Austin Farrer describes this tendency as Lewis's overlooking "the full involvement of the reasonable soul in a random and perishable system" because as an idealist he stressed "the reality of the mental subject independently of, or anyhow in priority to, that of the bodily world."[31] I believe this tendency to be principally characteristic of Lewis's midlife persona, not of his last years, and it is plain that

30. Green and Hooper, *C. S. Lewis,* 209.

31. Farrer, "The Christian Apologist," in *Light on C. S. Lewis,* ed. Jocelyn Gibb (London: Geoffrey Bles, 1965), 41.

Farrer's description of it fits well with the odd relation of person and persona which we are exploring. Still more interestingly for our exploration, Barfield parallels the idea of a short-circuiting between self and meaning by quoting Coleridge's remarks on John Wesley: "The moment an idea presents itself to him, his understanding intervenes to eclipse it, and he substitutes a conception by some process of deduction. Nothing is *immediate* to him."[32] This seems to me a very good description in Coleridge's language of the style which Lewis produced for his midlife persona and which he retained in writing *Surprised by Joy* and the Narnia books: the classic English prose style we have described that relies on stock response in choice of words, easily and unironically employed allusion and quotation, architectonic syntax with a tendency to long sentences harmonious in stress and sound, and narrative and description implying one universal observer—adding up in Barfield's phrase to "the sort of thing a man might say." Coleridge's remark is also a good critique of Lewis's theory of consciousness, of his tendency to freeze its contents, and of his belief that organization and selection are coextensive with it.

The retention of this style seems to me good evidence that Lewis's prime intention during this intermediate period was the strengthening of his persona. His most notorious and I think rather silly expression of this persona came in 1954, when, in his inaugural lecture as Professor of Medieval and Renaissance English Literature at Cambridge, he most intelligently argued the case that a great gap divides man since the Industrial Revolution from the great European tradition, and then not so intelligently presented himself as the very embodiment of the subject he was to profess, as Old Western Man from before the gap. Yet he ended that lecture with an odd image for his persona: "There are not going to be many more dinosaurs."[33] I wonder if that dinosaur does not come from the same stable, so to speak, as the dragon and the lobster whose sheddings of skins he put into words in about the same year? And whether the image does not bespeak some awareness of a scaly hide to be shed, quite soon?

For in the year after this lecture, in 1955, Lewis did abruptly and significantly change the style I have described. It became and remained much more personal—he shed a skin. Some attribute the various changes which came upon him at this period to his acquaintance with, and double marriage to, Joy Gresham. No doubt this was

32. Barfield, Introduction to *Light on C. S. Lewis*, xvii.
33. Lewis, "De Descriptione Temporum" (1955), in *Selected Literary Essays*, ed. Walter Hooper (Cambridge: Cambridge University Press, 1969), 14.

important, but I think the beginnings of the change were spontaneous and internal. My reason is the nature of the book in which the change was manifest, *Till We Have Faces.*

Lewis had been experimenting for many years with retelling the myth of Cupid and Psyche, but it was only in the spring of 1955 that suddenly "the right form presented itself" (*TWHF,* 1). The myth had from its beginning an element of allegory about the human soul; this is much heightened, however, by the form of Lewis's version, which is the telling of her life by Psyche's sister, who is looking at her past and finding herself changed by the act of looking. I do not think it can be a coincidence that this form should present itself to Lewis so close on his completion of his own examination of his past in *Surprised by Joy,* of which the final typescript was ready for the publisher in March 1955. And I guess therefore that it was primarily the writing of that autobiography which changed him.

The new form of *Till We Have Faces* is bound up with a change in the way in which, in Lewis's practice, myth is related to embodiment, and so bound up also with a change of style. Because of the narrator's relation to her story, the myth, as compared with the myths of *Perelandra* and *The Lion, the Witch and the Wardrobe,* is more freely handled (in the original myth of Apuleius, Lewis's narrator is only one of a pair of sisters who play an equal and minor part in the story, and her relation of mixed jealousy, love, and coinherence with Psyche is scarcely even latent) and is much more immersed in the contingent, the puzzling, the (at least apparently) random—just as the Gospels are. And one meaning of Lewis's story is a theory of the atonement which transcends Anselm's. It is Charles Williams's doctrine that we all bear one another's burdens in virtue of Christ's doing so, coupled with a perception characteristic of Lewis, that it is only in so doing that we find our true faces. As in Donne's "Good Friday, 1613. Riding Westward" and in a manner in Lewis's chapter on the tin soldiers in *Mere Christianity* (Book 4, Chap. 5), this finding of our true selves is the ultimate effect of Christ's self-offering. The climax of the book presages the vision of the god's face: "The most dreadful, the most beautiful, the only dread and beauty there is, was coming. The pillars on the far side of the pool flushed with his approach. I cast down my eyes" (*TWHF,* 318–19). But within the text, all that Orual sees in the pool is Psyche and herself perfected as Psyche. A few moments before her own death, she ends her book reflecting: "I know now, Lord, why you utter no answer. You are yourself the answer. Before your face questions die away" (*TWHF,* 319); here her writing breaks off.

The style changes in a manner appropriate to a book in which the notion of persona has been transcended in the conviction that to find our true faces has something to do with meeting the gods face to face, and to a book whose form is bound up with a prolonged self-anatomizing. But the change extends itself to Lewis's later books. His syntax and rhythm become relatively abrupt, his choice of words surprises, he employs much less allusion to former literature, and he substitutes for the one diffused observer the evocation of feelings, physical and emotional, from within. It is hard to find a truly comparable pair of examples from Lewis's middle and late period. In the best I can find, the second passage is not from *Till We Have Faces*, but from Lewis's next essay in fiction, "After Ten Years," the first few pages of which seem to date from the summer of 1956.[34] The first passage is from 1940, from *Perelandra*, and describes Ransom's arrival on that world:

> His first impression was of nothing more definite than of something slanted—as though he were looking at a photograph which had been taken when the camera was not held level. And even this lasted only for an instant. The slant was replaced by a different slant; then two slants rushed together and made a peak, and the peak flattened suddenly into a horizontal line, and the horizontal line tilted and became the edge of a vast gleaming slope which rushed furiously towards him. At the same moment he felt that he was being lifted. Up and up he soared till it seemed as if he must reach the burning dome of gold that hung above him instead of a sky. Then he was at a summit; but almost before his glance had taken in a huge valley that yawned beneath him—shining green like glass and marbled with streaks of scummy white—he was rushing down into that valley at perhaps thirty miles an hour. And now he realised that there was a delicious coolness over every part of him except his head, that his feet rested on nothing, and that he had for some time been performing unconsciously the actions of a swimmer. (*Per*, 37)

This is the opening of "After Ten Years":

> For several minutes now Yellowhead had thought seriously of moving his right leg. Though the discomfort of his present position was almost unbearable, the move was not lightly to be undertaken. Not in this darkness, packed so close as they were. The man next to him (he could not remember who it was) might be asleep or might at least be tolerably comfortable, so that he would growl or even curse if you pressed or

<hr>

34. Green and Hooper, *C. S. Lewis*, 263–64; however, Green elsewhere suggests 1959 ("Notes to *After Ten Years*," in *Of Other Worlds*, 146).

pushed him. A quarrel would be fatal; and some of the company were hot-tempered and loud-voiced enough. There were other things to avoid too. The place stank vilely; they had been shut up for hours with all their natural necessities (fears included) upon them. Some of them—skeery young fools—had vomited. But that had been when the whole thing moved, so there was some excuse; they had been rolled to and fro in their prison, left, right, up and (endlessly, sickeningly) down; worse than a storm at sea.

That had been hours ago. He wondered how many hours. It must be evening by now. The light which, at first, had come down to them through the sloping shaft at one end of the accursed contraption, had long ago disappeared. They were in perfect blackness. The humming of insects had stopped. The stale air was beginning to be chilly. It must be well after sunset.[35]

Both passages describe surroundings whose form the reader cannot immediately make into a figure, and although the observer of "After Ten Years" does know (it turns out) what he is experiencing, the observer of *Perelandra* does not. With both it is the immediate perceptions of the observer that are focused on, but in Yellowhead's case this focus is not dictated by the fact that the observer knows no more of his environment than his immediate perceptions. The reason, rather, for the focus on Yellowhead's sensations is to make the reader see with his alien eyes and feel with his alien senses. Lewis in the earlier case is looking through the perceptions of someone like himself and his readers, at something strange, in the later case through those of someone from the ancient world, at something which is (it turns out) the subject of a familiar story but normally figurated somewhat differently. In the later case his object is to make the familiar strange, in the earlier to create something strange in familiar language. (One should note how good the earlier style is at expressing enjoyment in the ordinary sense, enjoyment of objects, as in the railway journey of *That Hideous Strength*.)

Between the earlier and the later, the harmony of syntax, of sound, and of phrases demanding familiar responses much diminishes. There is a movement toward more primitive responses—to description of the categories of time and space rather than sensations, among sensations to muscular responses rather than sight, within sight to shape rather than color. In the passage about Ransom, for all the intended immediacy, there is a certain framing ("His first impression was . . ."); in the passage about Yellowhead everything is sensa-

35. Lewis, "After Ten Years," 127.

tion happening. In the first, Lewis uses mechanical parallels for the strangeness of Ransom's sensations. Am I right in saying that as a result one moves alongside Ransom, held there by a universal observer, whereas one has nothing except Yellowhead's sensations to feel? The distortion of time and space in the second passage, the cramp, dark, and meaninglessness of day and night, remind me of the absolute tyranny to be exercised over his reader's sense of the cosmos by Samuel Beckett in the decades after Lewis wrote this.

In both "After Ten Years" and *Till We Have Faces,* part of the point is an attempt to describe the world through more or less Greek eyes. Perhaps the loveliest and most successful passage in this line is the vision of the palace of the god as Orual sees it in *Till We Have Faces,* written 1955–1956:

> There stood the palace; grey, as all things were grey in that hour and place, but solid and motionless, wall within wall, pillar and arch and architrave, acres of it, a labyrinthine beauty. As she had said, it was like no house ever seen in our land or age. Pinnacles and buttresses leaped up . . . unbelievably tall and slender, pointed and prickly as if stone were shooting out into branch and flower. (*TWHF,* 141)

One knows that she is describing Gothic architecture, but Gothic architecture as a Greek would see it, at first trying to fit it to Hellenic categories—"pillar and arch and architrave"—then admitting types of building possible for the Greeks but less characteristic—"pinnacle and buttress"—and finally carried away by natural imagery that conveys fundamental characteristics of Gothic architecture, its height and slenderness and similarity to trees, all rendered more intensely than one who was familiar with it would do.

For this shift from observing the strange with a familiar consciousness to a fascination with how consciousness may itself be strange, I can think of only one parallel in Lewis's writing before *Till We Have Faces,* and that is something written not perhaps very long before, and for a specific didactic end. It is from *Surprised by Joy:* "The very formula, '*Naus* means a ship,' is wrong. *Naus* and *ship* both mean a thing, they do not mean one another. Behind *Naus,* as behind *navis* or *naca,* we want to have a picture of a dark, slender mass with sail or oars, climbing the ridges, with no officious English word intruding" (*SJ,* 135). But although this presages the style of the two later novels, it has not quite achieved it. For the "dark, slender mass with sail or oars, climbing the ridges" might simply be the Greek, Roman, or Saxon ship as a present-day consciousness receives it. Lewis does not here distinguish this possibility from what the beautiful strangeness of the whole expression, its closeness to percept and remoteness from concept, also hints at, that one should imagine the ship in the figuration an ancient consciousness would give it. He remains in the scope of the Alexander-Lewis doctrine, for he may be saying simply that one should not allow contemplation of the word *ship* to distract one from contemplating the ancient ship. As a certain Elizabethan linguist remarks (I have heard) with as much insight as stupidity, "The Germans call bread *Brot*, the French call it *pain*, the Italians call it *pane*, and we call it *bread*. And we are right, because it is bread." We *are* right in a sense, because when we say bread there is no officious foreign word intruding between us and actual bread. Lewis would have us inhabit *naus* with this same simple conviction.

I wonder if Lewis ever did inhabit *naus* in that way, even though he clearly thought he did. He seldom or never conversed in a foreign language, let alone ancient Greek, and we are here involved in a subtler distinction of awareness than we could recognize by the need to look up a word in a dictionary. Here, as we have seen before, the incompatibility between enjoyment and contemplation depends on the strength or obsessiveness of the emotion we contemplate or on the degree to which we inhabit the language. Conceive yourself listening to a lecture in a foreign language, and though you may know the language with formal perfection, I think it probable that you will find Lewis's doctrine absolutely true. For if you try to examine the act of listening and understanding in relation to a language in which you are not native, you will probably, in examining what you have heard, have to cease listening. But in the language or languages where you inhabit the words or where for you the words are more transparent to the object they signify, you will lose some but not all of what is being said. Some of it will get through.

Now another way of saying what we have previously remarked on in Lewis's relation with his persona and his language is that in an immensely subtle sense he handles his own language as if it were foreign. But in *Till We Have Faces* and "After Ten Years," he does explicitly and at length what he only does implicitly and perhaps without fully understanding what he is doing in the phrase "dark, slender mass": he imagines an alien consciousness, and the paradoxical result is that he inhabits his native language more than ever before. In three ways, his language is more *immediate*. First, the person experiencing is, although fictional, highly specific, and in the formulation we earlier used from Barfield, Lewis is now offering, not "the sort of thing a man might say," but "what I—Yellowhead, Orual— say." Second, the experience is highly specific and in the formulation we earlier quoted, from Barfield using Coleridge, there is less sense of a conception's being substituted for an idea. The style is more translucent to the passing of time, presents concrete objects more abruptly. Third, Lewis and, following him, the reader inhabit the language more than in any earlier book of his. In brief, a greater sense of objects in themselves goes not, as Lewis would certainly have argued in his middle period, with the elimination of self-consciousness in an impersonal style, but with a greater awareness of the way a particular self experiences. In these novels, enjoyment and contemplation are not wholly distinguishable.

V. Image, Projection, and Object in Lewis's Last Writings

Implicit in the growing translucency of Lewis's use of words is a growing sense of the need to treat images of all kinds—and in particular our images of other people and of God—as necessary in general but provisional in any specific case. Both the truth and the difficulty of his middle-period understanding of consciousness are well given in *Beyond Personality* when he compares the self to a telescope in that "the instrument through which you see God is your whole self" (*MC*, 130). That is why, as he says, horrible nations have horrible gods. He thought in consequence that it was his duty to build up a good self as a telescope through which to see God, to build it up out of the materials of the Christian tradition which he had accepted. What he did not sufficiently take into account was that the self he built up in this manner was a persona, not the "he" that was choosing the materials and doing the building up. There was built up an artificiality in his relation with himself which lasted twenty years. (Contrast the sense in *Reflections on the Psalms*, written in 1957, of the need to allow Christ "to rebuild in us the defaced image of Himself.")[36] Moreover, the distinction between enjoyment and contemplation enabled him to underestimate what the image of the telescope ought to have stressed and what in the period of his "New Look" he had overestimated, the risk that much or all of what one sees through the telescope of oneself is (to change the metaphor slightly) projection.

The doctrine that the existence of a desire proves the possibility that the desire can be satisfied remained important to him all his life. Of course he guarded against thinking, as he put it in "The Weight of Glory" in June 1941, that "a man's physical hunger [proves] that that

36. Lewis, *Reflections on the Psalms* (London: Geoffrey Bles, 1958), 114.

man will get any bread. . . . But surely a man's hunger does prove that he comes of a race which repairs its body by eating and inhabits a world where eatable substances exist."[37] And about a month after the journey to Whipsnade in 1931, he suggested to his brother that the longing for a "'vague something' . . . which rouses desires that no finite object even pretends to satisfy" could supply what the ontological argument for the existence of God, the argument that the most perfect being must exist, requires: "not a mere abstract definition, but a real imaginative perception of goodness and beauty beyond" human resources (*Letters,* 144). As a guide, a suggestion pointing beyond the world that divides into facts, this line of thought is of great power. But as a means to understand or state anything about what the object of desire would be like, or indeed whether *object* is an appropriate word when talking about the relation of our world to the ineffable, it presumes too much the purity of our desires and recognizes too little our capacity for self-deception.

In *Surprised by Joy,* Lewis says that he knows by experience that this joy of longing "is not a disguise of sexual desire. . . . I learned this mistake to be a mistake by the simple, if discreditable, process of repeatedly making it. . . . One found pleasure; which immediately resulted in the discovery that pleasure (whether that pleasure or any other) was not what you had been looking for" (*SJ,* 160–61). Biographers have indulged in somewhat indecent and wholly irresoluble dispute about what kind of sexual satisfaction Lewis is speaking of. But even if Lewis had what he certainly had not by the time he wrote *Surprised by Joy,* a wholly satisfying and permanent marriage, I do not see that it would bear the weight of the argument. The heart of man is desperately deceitful, and as Lewis thought much more conspicuously in the last years of his life than before, it is particularly deceitful and utterly insatiable in its quest for idols, its imagination of objects to fit its desires.

In saying that Lewis thought this more conspicuously, I have in mind, first, "After Ten Years," which paradoxically and significantly he was planning just a month after the beginning of his marriage, in May 1956.[38] What we have of "After Ten Years" consists of several attempts (three principal ones) to tell how Menelaus, meeting Helen after the ten years' war at Troy, would find a middle-aged real woman where he expected a young idealized one. The fragments break off

37. Lewis, "The Weight of Glory," in *Transposition and Other Addresses* (London: Geoffrey Bles, 1949), 25.
38. See note 34 above.

where Menelaus is about to meet in Egypt his temptation, a false Helen who is exactly like the ideal Helen of his memory. The breaking off is curiously like the end of *Till We Have Faces*, where Orual is about to meet her god, but has the opposite meaning: Orual could not describe what is beyond her wishes, but Lewis breaks off his description of Menelaus's temptation just when the insistence that enjoyment and contemplation must remain separate renders one helpless before the projection that exactly matches one's desires—helpless to decide whether that image is true or false because one has ruled out looking at the source of projection.

Lewis tried to go on with "After Ten Years" after his wife died, but was unable to finish it. But I think it is really completed in *A Grief Observed* in the grievous dialectic by which he recognizes that his sorrow, his consciousness, is creating a false image of his dead wife, a projection, a toy, and goes beyond this state. Early in the book he repeats the argument about sexual experience and transcendent longings, but in a manner which increases its substance. In *Surprised by Joy* he had said that the fullness of erotic satisfaction showed how different a thing that was from the never-found satisfaction of Joy. In *A Grief Observed* he makes this a statement about a happy marriage and a belief shared by both husband and wife, and more crucially argues not from the disappointing nature of a satisfaction, but from a comparison of want with want. "We both knew we wanted something besides one another—quite a different kind of something, a quite different kind of want."[39] This swims against the tendency of the Lewis-Alexander doctrine, for he is looking not only at the object, real or hypothetical, but also at the wants as they existed in action: contemplating the normally enjoyed, considering the normally contemplated only as a want, even an absence.

In the years before his wife died, he had already been moving toward relating the longings of bereaved lovers to the compulsion on the bereaved "to try to believe, what we cannot yet feel." But it is always the case "that God is our true Beloved." In the closing passage of *The Four Loves* (completed June 1959) he goes on from this doctrine to ask if he has only been imagining that he loves God: "Is it a further delusion that even the imagining has at some moments made all other objects of desire—yes, even peace, even to have no more fears—look like broken toys and faded flowers? Perhaps. Perhaps, for

39. Lewis [N. W. Clerk, pseud.], *A Grief Observed* (London: Faber and Faber, 1961), 10.

many of us, all experience merely defines, so to speak, the shape of that gap where our love of God ought to be."[40]

Perhaps it was the awareness of his wife's approaching death that caused him to move towards this contemplation, this analysis of wants in themselves. It certainly seems that it was the actuality of her death that obliged him to continue this contemplation through *A Grief Observed*. Very soon he was aware of the "process that will make the H. I think of into a more and more imaginary woman," and he was fighting with "a ghastly sense of unreality, of speaking into a vacuum about a nonentity" when he prayed for her. From both image-making and separation he was delivered. "At the very moment when, so far, I mourned H. least, I remembered her best." And it seemed to him that it may be "the very intensity of the longing that . . . makes us feel we are staring into a vacuum when we think about our dead. . . . And so, perhaps, with God. . . . Perhaps your own reiterated cries deafen you to the voice you hoped to hear." In something of the spirit of the Alexander-Lewis doctrine, he presently remarks "that only a very little time ago I was greatly concerned about my memory of H. and how false it might become. For some reason—the merciful good sense of God is the only one I can think of—I have stopped bothering about that. And the remarkable thing is that since I stopped bothering about it, she seems to meet me everywhere."[41]

Reading the earlier pages of *A Grief Observed* suggests another answer, not at all incompatible with the mercy of God, for these deliverances from obsession. Because Lewis's relation with his dead wife was a powerful love, a glass which his passionate grief served only to distort, the introspection composing the book served as it would with a native language or any other translucent medium of consciousness. It clarified the relation and made his wife more visible.

This analysis and purgation of the relation with his wife comes to resemble the description of the relation between man and God in the fourteenth-century *Cloud of Unknowing*. Lewis attains a conviction of the reality of the relation, a conviction of the reality, personality, and activity of the object, and beyond these three qualities, a conviction of ignorance.

> All reality is iconoclastic. The earthly beloved, even in this life, incessantly triumphs over your mere idea of her. . . . But [her independent reality] is not now imaginable. In that respect H. and all the dead are like

40. Lewis, *The Four Loves* (London: Geoffrey Bles, 1960), 159–60.
41. Lewis, *Grief Observed*, 18, 21, 37, 38, 41–42.

God. In that respect loving her has become, in its measure, like loving
Him. In both cases I must stretch out the arms and hands of love—its
eyes cannot here be used—to the reality, through—across—all the
changeful phantasmagoria of my thoughts, passions, and imaginings.

Something about images logically follows:

> It doesn't matter that all the photographs of H. are bad. It doesn't mat-
> ter—not much—if my memory of her is imperfect. Images, whether on
> paper or in the mind, are not important for themselves. Merely links.
> Take a parallel from an infinitely higher sphere. Tomorrow morning a
> priest will give me a little round, thin, cold, tasteless wafer. Is it a disad-
> vantage—is it not in some ways an advantage—that it can't pretend the
> least *resemblance* to that with which it unites me?
>
> I need Christ, not something that resembles Him. I want H., not
> something that is like her. . . .
>
> . . . My idea of God is not a divine idea. It has to be shattered time
> after time. He shatters it Himself.[42]

What he says about images here applies to the form of the book in
which he says it—the abrupt paragraphs, the frequent questions to
himself, the short clauses, the paratactic sentences—all trying to
catch brief moments of awareness of his dead wife, of God, and of the
nature of his awareness, before the awareness changes, and maintaining, for those brief moments, an intense attention that, when they are
gathered together, appears unremitting. It is quite unlike his middle-
period style, although clearly prepared for in *Till We Have Faces* and
"After Ten Years." There may have been some element of literary
selection and arrangement. But the expression of love, grief, self-
questioning, and attention is direct and immediate, and an *I* is speaking, even though an *I* more disciplined and devoted than most of us.

His next step in thinking about images was a subtle doctrine
which I remember his giving under the title "A Toy, an Ikon and a
Work of Art" while sitting under a glowing green, blue, gold, and rose
reproduction of the most luminous and alive of icons, Rublyev's *Old
Testament Trinity*, in the House of St. Gregory and St. Macrina off
the Banbury Road in Oxford. A child's toy, he said, does not need
beauty or realism, because it is simply an object for the imagination to
focus on, and indeed the more it approximates to a piece of rag, the
freer the imagination can be. A work of art must have beauty or
realism because one's attention is focused entirely on it. But an icon,
an object made to be the means of worship, in a way resembles the

42. Lewis, *Grief Observed*, 52–53, 51–52.

child's toy, because the point of it is not to stop attention but to focus attention on something beyond it.

It is an illuminating doctrine, but I think plays down the aesthetic qualities which an icon needs to do its work, as in different ways Rublyev's picture and the style of A *Grief Observed* show. Peace and purity in line and color in the one, fragmentation and self-questioning in the other, work to direct the perceiver's mind. In *Letters to Malcolm*, Lewis repeats the doctrine but with two concessions, one briefly, one at length, which are enough to form the basis of a religious aesthetic. The briefly stated principle acknowledges the usefulness of "keeping one's eyes focused on something" (*Malcolm*, 110) as a help to concentration. He remarks that "the lines of a well designed church . . . have something of the same effect" though he apparently does not quite realize what a precise and demanding specification that is, for in a moment he speaks of "artistic merits" as a distraction (*Malcolm*, 111).

On mental images in prayer he yields far more, with a striking piece of introspection. He speaks of a "wave of images, thrown off like a spray from the prayer, all momentary, all correcting, refining, 'inter-animating' one another, and giving a kind of spiritual body to the unimaginable"; they are "contradicting one another (in logic) as the crowded metaphors of a swift poet may do. Fix on any one, and it goes dead" (*Malcolm*, 114, 113). This program not only for prayer but possibly for religious poetry turns out to be Neoplatonic. For Lewis picks up the childhood memory he used to illustrate the consciousness of the bear in *That Hideous Strength*, substituting the Platonic phrase "the terrible and the lovely" for the hypostatized emotions "a nameless delight or terror." He says that what those fugitive and fragmentary images mediate to him is "always something qualitative—more like an adjective than a noun. That, for me, gives it the impact of reality. For I think we respect nouns (and what we think they stand for) too much. All my deepest, and certainly all my earliest, experiences seem to be of sheer quality. The terrible and the lovely are older and solider than terrible and lovely things" (*Malcolm*, 113-14). The last sentence, as Lewis presently points out, is a way of describing Plato's theory of forms. And Platonically also he identifies God with His glory: "What He is (the quality) is no abstraction from Him" (*Malcolm*, 114).

Behind doctrines about images lie a philosophy of the universe and a philosophy of the self. Goodness or truth, he says in the next letter, are shafts of the glory as it strikes our will or our understanding; pleasures are shafts of the glory as it strikes "our senses and mood."

Just as "one can't see a familiar word in print as a merely visual pattern," so one should in adoration read a pleasure as God (*Malcolm,* 117). Then "one's mind runs back up the sunbeam to the sun" (*Malcolm,* 118).

The last sentence suggests that he has found a large modification to the Lewis-Alexander doctrine. For by *pleasures* he makes it clear that he means the concrete experience from which "Nature," or "the beauties of Nature," are abstractions and of which our consciousness appears to us to be an aspect. In Letter 15 he gives an elaborate picture of the relation of consciousness, the world, and God, in which his last statement of the Lewis-Alexander doctrine appears and is in a manner swallowed up:

> Here are the four walls of the room. And here am I. But both terms are merely the facade of impenetrable mysteries.
>
> The walls, they say, are matter. That is, as the physicists will try to tell me, something totally unimaginable. . . . If I could penetrate far enough into that mystery I should perhaps finally reach what is sheerly real.
>
> And what am I? The facade is what I call consciousness. I am at least conscious of the colour of those walls. I am not, in the same way, or to the same degree, conscious of what I call my thoughts: for if I try to examine what happens when I am thinking, it stops happening. (*Malcolm,* 104–5)

The doctrine might appear unchanged: but Lewis in fact goes on to describe the variety of the contents of the unconscious, to add "depths of time too: All my past; my ancestral past; perhaps my pre-human past"; and again to say, "Here again, if I could dive deeply enough, I might again reach at the bottom that which simply is" (*Malcolm,* 105).

He retains, certainly, the Lewis-Alexander doubt about the validity of "the very fallible activity called 'introspection'" as a means of reporting on the everyday, superficial self (*Malcolm,* 108); but he is in a much more fundamental way insisting on the contemplation of normally enjoyed consciousness when he says that "the moment of prayer is for me—or involves for me as its condition—the awareness, the re-awakened awareness, that this 'real world' and 'real self' are very far from being rock-bottom realities" (*Malcolm,* 108). And it is in being conscious of consciousness that he recognizes the presence of God when he describes the theological awareness behind this form of prayer: "The present operation of God 'in here,' as the ground of my own being, and God 'in there,' as the ground of the matter that surrounds me, and God embracing and uniting both in the daily miracle of finite consciousness" (*Malcolm,* 106).

It is not surprising that having now welcomed, for this particular purpose of contemplative prayer, the turning back of consciousness on itself, he should welcome also that sense of the fragility and dispensableness of the conscious self and of "the depth and variety" of what underlies it, which in his middle period he seemed to eschew as the pathological product of a diseased and corrosive breaking of the proper structure of the self. He stresses that "what I call 'myself' . . . is also a dramatic construction" which depends for its existence on "the real and unknown I" that is responsible even for making "mistakes about the imagined me. And in prayer this real I struggles to speak, for once, from his real being, and to address, for once, not the other actors, but—what shall I call Him? The Author . . . ? The Producer . . . ? Or the Audience . . . ?" (*Malcolm*, 108).

In his sense of the total dependence of creature on creator, Lewis's final position slightly resembles the near-pantheism of the period when he thought introspection legitimate in destroying "the object Me." Possibly the admirable poem on prayer which he uses in Letter 13 but says comes from "an old notebook" (*Malcolm*, 92) might come from that period:

> And thus you neither need reply
> Nor can; thus, while we seem
> Two talkers, thou art One forever, and I
> No dreamer, but thy dream.[43]

Nor perhaps is it quite fortuitous, when he writes in the same letter of "the point of junction, so to call it, between Creator and creature," to be reminded of his feeling, at the end of that period, a melting beginning in his back.

But he no longer displays any trace of pantheism: he is perfectly clear that his relation with God is one of being created, and certain of the existence of a created I. It may be a consequence of his coming near at last to Barfield's position on consciousness that he now appeals to Barfield's *Saving the Appearances* for the two maxims that relate Creator and creature: "On the one hand, the man who does not regard God as other than himself cannot be said to have a religion at all. On the other hand, if I think God other than myself in the same way in which my fellow-men, and objects in general, are other than myself, I am beginning to make Him an idol" (*Malcolm*, 93). It is on the second maxim that, in his last writings, Lewis has moved. The slight sense of fixity not only in his relations to his persona but also in

---

43. *Malcolm*, 93; "are" emended to "art" as in *Poems*, 123.

his awareness of God—the possible accusation of projection—is altogether gone. He no longer needs in this state to invoke "Obstinacy in Belief." Rather, because he is certain that "the prayer preceding all prayers is, 'May it be the real I who speaks. May it be the real Thou that I speak to,'" and because he is humbly certain that the levels from which we pray are infinitely various, he is equally certain that only God can draw forth the depths in us, and that He works constantly as iconoclast: "Every idea of Him we form, He must in mercy shatter" (*Malcolm*, 109).

The only defect of *Letters to Malcolm* is stylistic. The letter form, which enabled him to write what had begun ten years earlier as a rather dull academic work on prayer, does successfully embody the necessary tentativeness of what he now thinks, and he achieves an inaggressiveness previously foreign to him. But he certainly never achieves the Trahernian splendor of his dreamed-of archangelical letters, nor the unremitting intensity of A *Grief Observed*. Possibly the negative nature of his ideas on religious art is still working. But I think rather that there is in the book both the clairvoyant wisdom and the peaceful lack of vigor of a man approaching death. One of the finest passages is that in which he aspires to a still more profound quietness:

> Doesn't the mere fact of putting something into words of itself involve an exaggeration? Prose words, I mean. Only poetry can speak low enough to catch the faint murmur of the mind, the "litel winde, unethe hit might be lesse." The other day I tried to describe to you a very minimal experience—the tiny wisps of adoration with which (sometimes) I salute my pleasures. But I now see that putting it down in black and white made it sound far bigger than it really is. The truth is, I haven't any language weak enough to depict the weakness of my spiritual life. If I weakened it enough it would cease to be language at all. (*Malcolm*, 144)

The confession of failure creates its own success, and oddly enough the self-accusation, which would have been justly directed against countless passages of his middle period, is only barely valid for the passage about reading pleasures as God's glory from which I have already quoted. There is a certain resemblance in the prose of *Letters to Malcolm* to the poetry of a writer whom in his middle period Lewis would only confess to liking unawares: T. S. Eliot.

They had been indeed antitypes. Both engaged in a long struggle over consciousness of self, both had been converts to Christianity but by opposite routes. Lewis had thought the only possible alternative to Christianity was Hinduism, and for Eliot it was Buddhism—a contrast exactly consonant with Eliot's choosing a way of negation in relation to God and a ruthless self-anatomizing in relation to self and consciousness, while Lewis followed a way of affirmation of images in relation both to self and to God. Lewis had been capable, as his brother reports, of breaking off a "superb" reading of Eliot's poetry in 1947 with the declaration that it was "bilge."[44] Yet that this was only the consequence of the beliefs involved in his middle-period persona, and that he had the roots of a sympathy with that poetry, is shown, I think, by his praise in A *Preface to Paradise Lost* of the "penitential qualities" of Eliot's "best work" (*Preface*, 133) and his declaration, also in 1942, that the method of *Hamlet* is close to Eliot's own method in poetry.[45]

The convergence with Eliot in *Letters to Malcolm* happens partly because Lewis is there engaging with the burdens of consciousness. "One's mind runs back up the sunbeam to the sun" is a little like "The roses / Had the look of flowers that are looked at" in "Burnt Norton"; the sense of "All my past; my ancestral past; perhaps my pre-human past" recalls "The backward look behind the assurance / Of recorded history" in "The Dry Salvages"; the idea that the time sense of heaven may be something like the thickness of time "whenever we learn to attend to more than one thing at once" is the same as Eliot's "concentration / Without elimination" as a figure for mystical experience ("Burnt Norton"). But their common devotion to the incarnation and the incarnate Lord has also brought them together. There is a real likeness in the image for the presence of eternity in time with which Eliot ends "Little Gidding," "And the fire and the rose are one," and the image with which Lewis sums up his sense of the relations of God and man in prayer: "This situation itself, is, at every moment, a possible theophany. Here is the holy ground; the Bush is burning now" (*Malcolm*, 109).[46]

44. Green and Hooper, *C. S. Lewis*, 157.

45. Lewis, "Hamlet: The Prince or the Poem?" in *Selected Literary Essays*, ed. Walter Hooper (Cambridge: Cambridge University Press, 1969), 102.

46. See Eliot, *The Complete Poems and Plays* (New York: Harcourt Brace, 1952), 118, 133, 119, 145.

II. Narrative

IT MUST BE ADMITTED *that the art of Story as I see it is a very difficult one. What its central difficulty is I have clearly hinted when I complained that in* The War of the Worlds *the idea that really matters becomes lost or blunted as the story gets under way. I must now add that there is a perpetual danger of this happening in all stories. To be stories at all they must be series of events: but it must be understood that this series—the* plot, *as we call it—is only really a net whereby to catch something else. The real theme may be, and perhaps usually is, something that has no sequence in it, something other than a process and much more like a state or quality. . . . In life and art both, as it seems to me, we are always trying to catch in our net of successive moments something that is not successive.*

"On Stories"

Theology in Stories:
C. S. Lewis and
the Narrative Quality
of Experience

Gilbert Meilaender

At the outset of *The Voyage of the "Dawn Treader,"* Lucy, Edmund, and Eustace have been whisked magically off into Narnia and are now sailing with King Caspian and his crew on a quest. Caspian is seeking some lost lords of Narnia as well as the end of the world ("the utter East"). They have many adventures—some merely strange, others dangerous. The adventure which concerns us comes when they arrive at the island of the Dufflepuds. These strange creatures (who have one large foot on which they hop about and who are not particularly intelligent) have, for reasons we need not concern ourselves with, been made invisible. In order to become visible again they need a young girl to go into the Magician's house, up to the second floor, and find the proper spell in the Magician's book. And they are determined not to permit Caspian's party to leave their island until Lucy consents to undertake this task.

Since it seems they have little choice—battling invisible antagonists is rather hard to do—Lucy agrees to brave the frightening house. She finds the book and begins turning pages looking for the spell. As she does so, however, she becomes engrossed in the various spells she finds there and reads large portions of the book. At one point she finds a spell "for the refreshment of the spirit" (*VDT*, 144).

It turns out to be "more like a story than a spell." She begins to read, and "before she had read to the bottom of the page she had forgotten that she was reading at all. She was living in the story as if it were real" (*VDT*, 144). When she finishes it, she feels that it is the

---

This essay originally appeared in *Word and World* 1 (1981): 222–29.

loveliest story she has ever heard and wishes she could have gone on reading it for ten years.

She decides that she will, at least, read the story again but discovers that the pages will not turn backwards. "'Oh, what a shame!' said Lucy. 'I did so want to read it again. Well, at least, I must remember it.'" But she finds, unfortunately, that she cannot really remember the plot of the story. It all begins to fade in her memory. "And she never could remember; and ever since that day what Lucy means by a good story is a story which reminds her of the forgotten story in the Magician's Book" (*VDT*, 144).

I

We will not, I think, fully understand the wide appeal of Lewis's writings until we think carefully about the importance of stories for communicating Christian belief. Lewis often depicts the whole of life in terms of the Christian story of creation, fall, incarnation, redemption, and resurrection.[1] Beyond that, however, Lewis has, I believe, a strong sense of what Stephen Crites has called "the narrative quality of experience."[2] The very nature of human existence—conceived in Christian terms—is best understood within narrative.

Anyone who has read very far in Lewis will have encountered his characteristic theme of "romantic longing," or *Sehnsucht*. It is, in many ways, Lewis's restatement of the Augustinian theme of the restless heart. We are, as Lewis says, always trying to capture something, trying to "get *in*." We want to ride time, not be ridden by it, "to cure that always aching wound . . . which mere succession and mutability inflict on us."[3] The human being is, we may say, both finite and free: a bodily creature living in space and time, yet desiring to transcend such finite limitations and rest in God.

The crucial question, of course, is whether such a creature is an absurdity or whether this desired fulfillment is attainable. If fulfillment of the longing integral to our being is impossible, then we really

1. I have developed this theme in more detail in *The Taste for the Other: The Social and Ethical Thought of C. S. Lewis* (Grand Rapids, Mich.: Eerdmans, 1978).

2. Crites, "The Narrative Quality of Experience," *Journal of the American Academy of Religion* 39 (1971): 291–311.

3. Lewis, "The Weight of Glory," in *Transposition and Other Addresses* (London: Geoffrey Bles, 1949), 30–31; Lewis, *Reflections on the Psalms* (London: Geoffrey Bles, 1958), 138. To fully develop Lewis's views we would have to note his belief that, apart from sin, our experience of the tension between our freedom and our finitude is not painful (see Meilaender, *The Taste for the Other*, 170–72).

are absurd creatures, and we would be better simply to acknowledge the search as futile and endless, to vow with Faust never to say to any moment, "Stay a while, you are so lovely." Lewis is concerned with this question, concerned to know whether finite creatures such as we are can find any spell which offers genuine "refreshment of the spirit"—lasting refreshment of which we cannot be deprived by the corrosive powers of time.

The spell, if there is one, is not available in abstract, theoretical reasoning. Built into our thinking is a kind of frustration: a gap always exists between experiencing a thing and thinking about that thing. In thinking "about" anything we abstract ourselves from it, begin to separate it into its parts, and lose it as an object of contemplation. That is, while thinking about it we are cut off from experiencing it. A man cannot, as Lewis points out, experience loving a woman if he is busy thinking about his technique (*SJ*, 206).

Lewis searches, therefore, for some other way, some means other than abstract thought to find the "refreshment of the spirit" for which human beings seem to be made. One way to such refreshment, a way which always attracted Lewis, lies in myth. In his somewhat stipulative definition, myth is extraliterary. The fact that it must be communicated in words is almost accidental, for it is not so much a narration as it is a permanent object of contemplation—more like a thing than a story. That is to say, in myth we experience something timeless. Experiencing a myth is more like tasting than thinking, concrete rather than abstract. Yet it is also very different from other tastings, for it seems to bring experience not of some isolated tidbit of life which passes away but of what has timeless, universal significance.[4]

We can, of course, also think "about" the universal and in that way move beyond isolated particulars of life. But this gives no *experience* of what is timeless, no experience of anything which may satisfy the longing of the human spirit to transcend the constraints of our finite condition. Instead, thinking about what is universal and timeless—which simultaneously cuts us off from experiencing it—is merely one more testimony to thought's built-in frustration. Myth provides, if only for a moment, what we desire: to break through to some great truth in which the heart can rest and which can give coherence to the isolated particulars of life. It offers what no other experience can, an

---

4. See Lewis, *Experiment*, chap. 5; and "Myth Became Fact" (1944), in *God in the Dock: Essays on Theology and Ethics*, ed. Walter Hooper (Grand Rapids, Mich.: Eerdmans, 1970), 63–67.

actual tasting of a reality which transcends our finite existence. It brings us briefly into a world more real than our own, so real that any talk "about" it would have to be metaphorical.

However, myth offers no permanent peace for the quarrel between the two sides of our nature—our freedom and finitude. For a brief moment finitude is transcended, we are free of temporal constraints, and the transcendent is comfortingly passive. But the truth we are given in myth is not really a truth to live by in our here and now, for we live as creatures both free *and* finite. Because this is the case, Lewis looks elsewhere, away from myth to story, to find that "refreshment of the spirit" we desire. Although story cannot in any single moment of experience overcome the tension between finitude and freedom in the human being as completely as can myth, it points toward a more lasting peace, a peace we can live.

Lewis discusses the genre in his essay "On Stories." We can begin at the literary level of his ideas about story and move toward the theological. The story is, Lewis thinks, different from the novel, which concerns itself with delineation of character, criticism of social conditions, and so forth. The story is not merely, as some think, a vehicle of excitement and danger—anxious tension and then relief when the moment of danger passes. Lewis suggests that, at least for some readers, something more is going on when they read a story: a sense of atmosphere is conveyed; we feel that we have come close to experiencing a certain state or quality.

At the same time, there is frustration or tension in the structure of story, a frustration which story never fully overcomes. For a story is a net with which we try to catch something else, something timeless, something more like a state or quality—a grand idea like homecoming, or reunion with a loved one, or the simple idea of otherness. The tension arises because the story is also narrative, involving temporal succession and plot. A story must involve a series of events; it must move on. But the thing we are seeking is timeless. What we really seek to take hold of can never last in a story, and the storyteller is, therefore, doomed to frustration. The medium, the story, is inherently temporal; yet the storyteller is trying to catch something which is not really a process at all—what Lewis calls "theme" ("OnS," 103). The art of the storyteller is to break through the mere succession of particular experiences and to catch theme by means of plot.

What Lewis describes in his essay "On Stories" is essentially Lucy's experience on the island of the Dufflepuds. The story is a spell which brings "refreshment of the spirit." It brings one close to, if not directly into contact with, something entirely beyond time. But this all fades and is soon gone; for story is narrative. The spirit is both refreshed and frustrated because it has temporarily been drawn out of the constraints which time places upon us and yet has been so drawn by a literary form which is itself inherently temporal. Thus story—more than myth—unites the temporal and eternal as intimately as plot and theme.

II

This is Lewis's literary theory. Near the end of his essay "On Stories," however, Lewis makes a comment which carries us beyond literary considerations alone. "Shall I be thought whimsical," he writes, "if, in conclusion, I suggest that this internal tension in the heart of every story between the theme and the plot constitutes, after all, its chief resemblance to life?" Life, Lewis suggests, is frustrating in the same way a story is: "We grasp at a state and find only a succession of events in which the state is never quite embodied" ("OnS," 105). The author of a story uses the net of temporal plot to try to catch a timeless theme. Life is the same sort of net, amenable to being understood within the narrative genre: a net of successive experiences seeking to catch something which is not temporal at all. Lewis's literary theory and his belief that the human heart is restless until it rests in God meet here.

What I have described might *almost* be said to be Lewis's metaphysic. Certain human experiences take us beyond—or almost beyond—the finite boundaries of life. But they never last; they pass us by and are gone. Still, they are clues, if we will follow them. How do we do so? Not by constructing a completely explanatory theory which will itself attempt to be a timeless product, for our theories do not participate in the timelessness which we momentarily experience. The theorist is also a pilgrim; the theorist's own life has a narrative quality. As Stephen Crites has put it, every moment of experience is itself in tension, for memory and anticipation are the tension of every moment of experience.[5] Past and future, memory and anticipation, are themselves present. Hence, the present moment is "tensed." Tensed and therefore filled with tension. As long as we remain within history we cannot escape that. We are limited to the present, yet in that very present both memory and anticipation serve as signals of transcendence.

Crites suggests that only narrative can contain the full temporality

5. Crites, "The Narrative Quality of Experience," 301–3.

of our experience within a unity of form. And Lewis, I believe, is suggesting something similar. The human creature, made for fellowship with God, can touch the Eternal but cannot (within history) rest in it. Our experience is inherently narrative, relentlessly temporal. We are given no rest; the story moves on. Hence, the creature who is made to rest in God is in this life best understood as a pilgrim whose world is depicted in terms of the Christian story. This may explain why stories are sometimes the most adequate form for conveying the "feel" of human existence.

Most particularly, it is in stories that the quality—the feel—of creatureliness may be most adequately conveyed. Lewis himself suggests on one occasion that "if God does exist, He is related to the universe more as an author is related to a play than as one object in the universe is related to another."[6] By way of illustration, Lewis suggests that we think of looking for Shakespeare in his plays. In one sense, Shakespeare is present at every moment in every play, but not in the same way that Hamlet or King Lear is present. Yet we would not fully understand the plays if we did not understand them in relation to Shakespeare, as the product of his creative genius.

Even more important, narrative is the form which does justice to the experience of creatures who are embodied spirits. Crites has stressed the point that story does not isolate body and mind. Lewis, likewise, seems to suggest that the narrative genre is most appropriate for creatures who are finite yet free. By trying to catch in its net what is not temporal at all, story recognizes that we are made to transcend our present condition. At the same time, story is not just this grasping after a transcendent theme. Its bodily structure, plot, always moves on. It is relentlessly temporal, just as historical life is. Because story gives no lasting rest, we may try to escape its limitations. Lewis thinks we ought not. He suggests that being a pilgrim involves a willingness to accept the temporality of human experience, a willingness to understand ourselves in terms of narrative structure and to accept the tension of the "tensed present."

In his essay on the narrative quality of experience, Crites describes two ways in which we may try to escape the temporality of our existence and find a rest in some false infinite of our own making. A reader of Lewis's *The Pilgrim's Regress* will recognize a striking similarity to the Northern and Southern ways which the pilgrim John must avoid as he travels the road. On the one hand, Crites believes,

6. Lewis, "The Seeing Eye" (1963), in *Christian Reflections*, ed. Walter Hooper (London: Geoffrey Bles, 1967), 168.

we may try to escape from narrative by abstraction. We may seek refuge in some theory which pretends to be timeless. Abstraction has an intellectual character, isolating mind from body. This is Lewis's North, where all is arid, austere, bodiless, and finally sterile. The other attempted escape which Crites depicts is that of constriction: narrowing our attention to dissociated immediacies and disconnected particulars. In this case one assumes that feeling and sensation are irreducible in our experience. We accept our finite condition as the whole meaning of life and purchase timelessness by giving up the quest for the universal. We focus on the present, ignoring memory and anticipation, and do not see that particular experience calls us out beyond itself. This way is all body. It is Lewis's "South"—where the pilgrim can find himself present at an orgy.

The first way is content to talk "about" the universal but gives up the quest to experience it. The second refuses to notice how particular experience calls us away from itself toward something which transcends all particularity. Lewis's pilgrim, an embodied spirit, is to eschew both ways of escape. His is to be a "feeling intellect."[7] Lewis says in his preface to *The Pilgrim's Regress* that we were "made to be neither cerebral men nor visceral men, but Men"—things both rational and animal, creatures who are embodied and ensouled.[8] We can neither abstract from the temporal flow of our experience nor reduce it to immediate experience without ignoring something important in our nature.

III

If up to this point I have managed to convey my message at all successfully, its irony must certainly be clear; for in rather abstract fashion I have been suggesting that such abstract argument cannot convey a quality like creatureliness successfully. This raises, quite naturally, a problem for the theorist, in particular the theologian. If the quality of our experience through time is narrative, no theory— itself an abstraction from experience—can fully capture the truth of

7. The phrase "feeling intellect" is the subtitle of Corbin Carnell's *Bright Shadow of Reality: C. S. Lewis and the Feeling Intellect* (Grand Rapids, Mich.: Eerdmans, 1974). Lewis would have known the phrase from Wordsworth (*The Prelude* 14.226) or from Charles Williams (*Taliessin through Logres* [London: Oxford University Press, 1938], 55–56; *The Region of the Summer Stars* [London: Nicholson and Watson, 1944], 14). Cf. Lewis, *Arthurian Torso* (London: Oxford University Press, 1948), 161, 103.

8. Lewis, Preface to *The Pilgrim's Regress*, rev. ed. (London: Geoffrey Bles, 1943), 13.

reality. There may be occasions when abstraction is important and necessary; nevertheless, it is no accident that Lewis writes stories instead of a *Summa*. The story is, on his account, the form most true to our experience. Its form makes clear that we grasp after what is not fully given.

There are certain features of our experience, essential to serious discussion of the Christian life, which cannot be adequately conveyed by theological treatment, however careful and precise. Thus, for example, Christians have commonly wanted to say that our commitment to God must be freely and willingly given. Yet at the same time, they have wanted to say that we are of ourselves incapable of making this commitment, that it must be "worked in us" by God's grace. By abstracting, isolating, and emphasizing the divine activity, one ends up with irresistible grace, election of some to condemnation, and the suspicion that it is something of a sham to speak about our free and willing commitment. By abstracting, isolating, and emphasizing our own free commitment, one ends up with Pelagianism, having made grace superfluous. If one constructs instead, however, a narrative of one's own commitment (as Lewis does, for example, in *Surprised by Joy*), it may make good sense to say *both* "I might not have made this commitment which I now freely and willingly make" *and* "I could not have so committed myself had I not been drawn by God, and it is really his doing." That is what believers are likely to say in telling the story of how grace has abounded in their own commitment.

Within the narrative it seems to make sense to speak this way. Lewis writes in similar terms of the Oedipus story, in which, despite his efforts to avoid it, Oedipus kills his father and marries his mother: "We have just had set before our imagination something that has always baffled the intellect: we have *seen* how destiny and free will can be combined, even how free will is the *modus operandi* of destiny. The story does what no theorem can quite do. . . . It sets before us an image of what reality may well be like at some more central region" ("OnS," 101). To take an example from the history of Christian thought, there are, I think, few who would deny that St. Augustine's *Confessions* offers a more compelling picture of the relation of creature and Creator and conveys better the paradox of a freely given commitment, elicited solely by God's grace, than even the best of his more abstract treatises on the grace of Christ and on the predestination of the saints. However important and necessary those treatises are in certain contexts, they cannot convey the quality, the feel, of creatureliness in the way the *Confessions* do.

But the treatises *are* still necessary in certain contexts. The theologian's task is not superfluous. In one of his brief essays, Lewis distinguishes nicely between ordinary language, scientific language, and poetic language. He gives these illustrations of each: "(1) It was very cold (2) There were 13 degrees of frost (3) 'Ah, bitter chill it was! The owl, for all his feathers was a-cold; The hare limped trembling through the frozen grass, And silent was the flock in woolly fold: Numb'd were the Beadsman's fingers'" ("Lang," 129). Theological language tries to bring to religion the technical precision of scientific language. It is an attempt to provide what scientific language offers in different contexts—a precise test which can end dispute. It is language, as Lewis says, on which we can take action ("Lang," 130). We can, for example, use it to guard against mistaken understandings of our beliefs. But this is not the language the believer naturally speaks, for such language cannot convey the quality of religious belief and experience. Believers, when questioned, are usually more likely to tell their story.

My theme is by now becoming familiar: abstraction, however important, means a loss of immediacy—a loss, for example, of the sense of what it feels like to be a creature. To see this theme in Lewis's writings is to begin to understand the wide appeal those writings continue to demonstrate. He appeals far less to theoretical argument than many of his readers (and critics) have imagined. Rather, he tells stories which expand the imagination and give one a world within which to live for a time. Like Lucy, the reader can almost forget he is reading a story at all and can be "living in the story as if it were real." Lewis offers not abstract propositions for belief but the quality, the feel, of living in the world narrated by the biblical story. In stories we do not have to divide our treatment into separate *loci*—to talk first about the creature, then God (or the reverse, on which distinction a good many theological arguments can be constructed). Instead, we are permitted to see God and the creature as they really are—in a narrative in which it makes little sense to think of human beings abstracted from either time and history or from the God-relation.

We may grant that there will still be something dissatisfying about this. The relentlessly temporal character of human life will tempt us to try to make our peace by separating theme and plot, dividing the feeling intellect into its parts. We may seek to view ourselves as all body, finding significance only in isolated present experiences and perhaps regarding the longing for something more as an absurdity. Or we may seek to view ourselves as all intellect, all free, self-transcending person—as, in effect, one like God. But when we take either of these ways, we are not talking about human beings, creatures known properly only when known in relation to God, made for a destiny they cannot at present fully experience. The point is not, in the first instance, a religious one for Lewis. It is simply a claim about what rings true to our experience of what it means to be human. Of course, it leads on to a religious claim. If we understand ourselves as creatures, we will recognize the narrative quality of our experience and may perhaps find a way to make peace with it.

IV

How make that peace between the two sides of our nature? Like Lewis, who was always something of a Platonist, one might be drawn to myth, that permanent object of contemplation which, he believed, brings us into contact with a "more real" world. In myth one might transcend the limits of thought and "taste" the universal. However, this is a solution which temporarily eclipses but does not bridge the gap between time and eternity. We fall back from the mythic universal into our finitude and have no truth to live by *there*. We want and need more, or so Lewis thinks.

> In life and art both, as it seems to me, we are always trying to catch in our net of successive moments something that is not successive. Whether in real life there is any doctor who can teach us how to do it, so that at last either the meshes will become fine enough to hold the bird, or we be so changed that we can throw our nets away and follow the bird to its own country, is not a question for this essay. ("OnS," 105)

Elsewhere, however, Lewis takes up the question and suggests that incarnation—for him the central turning point in the Christian story—surpasses even myth.[9] The Christian story affirms that in one human being that other and more real world has entered our history and we need not transcend our finitude in order to find that more real world. The universal is particularized, located in time and space. The author has written himself into the play. As Augustine found the Word made flesh in the gospel but not in the Platonists, so Lewis has turned here from myth to story and found the story which promises to satisfy the longing of the restless heart while acknowledging, even affirming, the relentless temporality of a pilgrim existence.

9. Lewis, "Myth Became Fact," 66.

Orual's Story and the Art of Retelling: A Study of *Till We Have Faces*

Mara E. Donaldson

C. S. Lewis's first ambition was to be a poet, but he made his creative mark as a first-rate teller of stories.[1] He even credits one story, George MacDonald's *Phantastes*, with having "baptized" his imagination when he read it at sixteen (*SJ*, 171). What Lewis thought about story, especially about good stories, those which "baptize" the imagination, is scattered throughout his essays on particular works (*Paradise Lost*, for example), authors (Chaucer, Spenser, among others), and genres (epic, science fiction, fantasy). The essays are diverse and fragmented; they give us clues to the puzzle but hardly a complete picture. Even *An Experiment in Criticism*, Lewis's most suggestive work for a theory of story, is not about what makes a good book, but about what makes a good reader.

Lewis's greatest contribution to our understanding of stories may best be understood to have been not a theory of story, but his stories themselves. In particular, Lewis's last novel, *Till We Have Faces*, is itself explicitly a story about the nature and importance of story. Thus, it provides an excellent starting point for understanding Lewis's more implicit theory of story, the subject of this essay.

In the first section of the essay, I concentrate on the narrative structure of the novel by looking at three separate but related "stories" in the text. Each "story" has a distinctive plot and temporality which, I argue, is crucial to the meaning of the novel as a whole. The second section turns to what Lewis wrote about story in his critical works, concentrating on the distinction he made between story as

1. Walter Hooper discusses Lewis's early ambitions to be a poet in his preface to Lewis, *Selected Literary Essays*, ed. Walter Hooper (Cambridge: Cambridge University Press, 1969), vii–xvi.

Logos (something said) and story as Poiema (something made). However bold Lewis may have been in making metaphysical claims about
the Logos of a story, his literary-critical theory of Poiema lacked an
adequate way to account for the very complexities of narrative plot
and temporality which structure *Till We Have Faces*. To address this
need, the third section employs Paul Ricoeur's work on narrative time
to clarify Lewis's discussion of narrative as "something made." The
result is an understanding of the interaction of Logos and Poiema in
Till We Have Faces to produce a narrative capable of "baptizing" the
imagination.

I

Subtitled "A Myth Retold," *Till We Have Faces* tells and retells
Apuleius's Cupid and Psyche myth from the point of view of Orual,
the main character of Lewis's novel. Lewis had been fascinated with
Apuleius's version of the myth since his undergraduate days (before
his conversion to Christianity) and had abandoned two earlier versions in verse. In 1955, the year he married Joy Davidman and eight
years before his death, the proper form—narrative—came to him.[2]
The "telling" and "retelling" of Apuleius's story is central to the
"form" that Lewis's novel takes.

I have written elsewhere on the importance of metaphor in *Till
We Have Faces*. Here I am interested not in metaphor but in what
Stephen Crites has called "the narrative quality of experience."[3] The
presence of temporality, of plot, in narrative distinguishes it from
metaphor. Both narrative and plot are terms of considerable debate in
current literary theory, but I am using the terms in a straightforward
way.[4] I agree with Scholes and Kellogg that *narrative* is "a literary work

2. Lewis spoke of his long interest in Apuleius in the preface to the British edition
of *Till We Have Faces*, which was omitted from the American publication: "This reinterpretation of an old story has lived in the author's mind, thickening and hardening
with the years, ever since he was an undergraduate. That way, he could be said to have
worked at it most of his life. Recently, what seemed to be the right form presented itself
and themes suddenly interlocked: the straight tale of barbarism, the mind of an ugly
woman, dark idolatry and pale enlightenment at war with each other and with vision,
and the havoc which a vocation, or even a faith, works on human life" (*TWHF* [1]).
3. See my *Holy Places Are Dark Places: C. S. Lewis and Paul Ricoeur on Narrative
Transformation* (Lanham, Md.: University Press of America, 1988), 63–83; Crites, "The
Narrative Quality of Experience," *Journal of the American Academy of Religion* 39
(1971): 291–311.
4. See, for example, W. J. T. Mitchell, ed., *On Narrative* (Chicago: University of
Chicago Press, 1981), vii–x; Peter Brooks, *Reading for the Plot: Design and Intention in*

... distinguished by two characteristics: the presence of a story and a story-teller."[5] The whole of *Till We Have Faces* is a narrative, or in Lewis's terms simply "story," but as we shall see, it is made up of separate stories. By *plot* I mean the principal way of organizing a story, or narrative, by temporally ordering the story's action. To speak of plot, therefore, is to speak of temporal modes in a story.

Part 1 of *Till We Have Faces* appears to be easy to summarize because it has a chronological, linear arrangement. Part 2 of *Till We Have Faces* is not clearly linear and thus summarizing the plot is extremely difficult. Most critics begin their discussion of the novel with a plot summary, not attending to this dramatic shift in temporality from the outset of Part 1 to Part 2.[6] Whereas Part 1 indeed begins with a linear, emplotted telling of the story, it proceeds to retell that story in less and less linear fashion. By the beginning of Part 2 the shift is complete, from what Ricoeur calls "episodic time," or temporality understood as linear sequence, to what he calls "configurational" time, or time understood as nonlinear signification. This shift can also be understood, to use Mircea Eliade's well-known distinction, as the shift from "profane" time to "sacred" time.[7] Part 1 progresses from a "profane" telling of the story to an increasingly "sacred" telling of the story. Part 2 takes place almost entirely in "sacred" time.

There are three separate, but interwoven, stories in Part 1 of *Till We Have Faces:* (a) Orual's, (b) Psyche's, and (c) the priest of Issur's. Each is a telling of Apuleius's story. Yet each has a distinctive plot and temporality. Orual's story is first, though her actual telling of it occurs chronologically after Psyche's and the priest of Issur's. She writes at the end of her life, concerned with setting the record straight. Her story is the seemingly straightforward recollection of her life. The

---

Narrative (New York: Alfred A. Knopf, 1984), 3–23; and Nathan A. Scott, "The Rediscovery of Story in Recent Theology and the Refusal of Story in Recent Literature," in *Arts/Literature/Religion: Life on the Borders*, ed. Robert Detweiler, JAAR Thematic Studies 49.2 (1983): 139–55.

5. Robert Scholes and Robert Kellogg, *The Nature of Narrative* (Oxford: Oxford University Press, 1966), 4.

6. See, for example, Peter J. Schakel, *Reason and Imagination in C. S. Lewis: A Study of "Till We Have Faces"* (Grand Rapids, Mich.: Eerdmans, 1984), 9–86; Margaret Patterson Hannay, *C. S. Lewis* (New York: Frederick Ungar, 1981), 113–28; Clyde S. Kilby, *The Christian World of C. S. Lewis* (Grand Rapids, Mich.: Eerdmans, 1964), 52–64.

7. Ricoeur, "Narrative Time," in *On Narrative*, 165–86; Eliade, *The Sacred and The Profane: The Nature of Religion* (1957), trans. Willard R. Trask (New York: Harcourt Brace, 1959), 68–113.

plot of her story centers on her love for and loss of her beloved sister, Psyche, also called Istra.

(a) Orual was the eldest daughter of King Trom, ruler of Glome. The patron goddess of Glome was Ungit, a fertility goddess like Aphrodite. Orual was born a woman and ugly, two accidents her father cannot forgive. So she turned for love and joy to the Fox, the Greek slave her father bought to teach her, and to Psyche, her step-sister, whose mother died giving birth to Psyche. For a time the Fox, Orual, and Psyche lived an idyllic existence. When plagues and fam-ine threatened Glome, however, the chief priest of Ungit demanded a sacrifice, and Psyche was chosen by lot. Psyche was sacrificed to the god of the Grey Mountain. But when Orual went to the mountain to bring back Psyche's body, she found Psyche alive and well.

(b) Psyche then told Orual what had happened (*TWHF,* 114–38). She told Orual of having been drugged and taken to the mountain and tied to the sacred tree. She had been left alone. Cattle came, the weather changed, and then Psyche saw the god of the wind, the West-wind himself. The West-wind pulled her from the iron girdle and carried her to a House where she was invited by invisible voices to enter. In the evening, the Bridegroom came; he came only in the darkness and she was forbidden to look upon him.

The plot of Psyche's story concerns her experience of what Ru-dolf Otto called the "numinous."[8] Her experience of the divine as "holy" other, who was both hidden in darkness and revealed in that same darkness, broke the linear temporality of Orual's story and radically disrupted Psyche's own life. Her story marked the culmina-tion of her life, a life she had earlier told Orual was characterized by "longing."[9] Thus, there was a "timeless quality" to the story she told Orual.

The experience of the divine which Psyche recounted to her was utterly alien to Orual. Orual did not believe Psyche's telling of the

---

8. Otto, *The Idea of the Holy* (1920), trans. J. W. Harvey (London: Oxford Univer-sity Press, 1923). Lewis discussed the "numinous" in *The Problem of Pain* (London: Geoffrey Bles, 1940), 4–11.

9. Psyche expressed this longing to Orual just before being taken to the mountain: "The sweetest thing in all my life has been the longing—to reach the Mountain, to find the place where all the beauty came from" (*TWHF,* 83). Lewis calls this longing *Sehn-sucht,* which he said characterized much of his own religious search (see *SJ,* 22–24). For a discussion of *Sehnsucht* in *Till We Have Faces* and in other works of Lewis, see Schakel, *Reason and Imagination,* 30–34; and Corbin Scott Carnell, *Bright Shadow of Reality: C. S. Lewis and the Feeling Intellect* (Grand Rapids, Mich.: Eerdmans, 1974), 13–29, 110–15.

story. Although Orual could see that Psyche looked well fed and was radiantly happy, she could not taste the wine and honeycakes which Psyche offered her. More significantly, she could not see the palace Psyche showed her. Instead of believing or accepting Psyche's story, Orual decided that her sister was mad and forced her to disobey the god. Psyche was sent into exile, and Orual was forced to live without her (*TWHF*, 182–83).

Having lost Psyche, Orual became Queen of Glome and hid her grief as she hid her face. Her chief counselors were the Fox and Bardia, her father's captain of guards. At the end of her life, after the Fox died, and after a long and progressive reign as Queen, she decided to visit other lands. The third story in *Till We Have Faces*, Part 1 (*TWHF*, 250–56) came from this visit. It was the story of the priest of Issur, who told the "sacred" story of Istra, a new, young goddess.

(c) According to the priest's story, Istra was the youngest and most beautiful princess in the world. Her beauty angered Talapal, a goddess (like Ungit), who demanded Istra's sacrifice to a brute on a mountain. Talapal's son, Ialim, rescued Istra and visited her at night in holy darkness. Istra's sisters visited her at the palace and, after seeing the good fortune of her sister, they became jealous of her. They plotted against her and caused her downfall. In the story, when Istra completed the labors Talapal gave her, she was reunited with Ialim and became a goddess.

There was something familiar and something strange about the priest's story to Orual. She recognized the plot as the story of Psyche, but she disagreed with the details in the priest's version: "I've heard your story told otherwise, old man. . . . I think the sister—or the sisters—might have more to say for themselves than you know" (*TWHF*, 256). Thus, the reader of *Till We Have Faces* discovers at the end of Part 1 that Orual had written her story both to respond to versions of the story she could not believe (Psyche's) or accept (the priest's) and to defend her own conception of the events. Orual's version (a), which is Part 1 of the novel, is an effort to go behind the stories of Psyche and the priest and tell the "true" story.

In Part 2, Orual set out to "mend" her book because the past which she had written down was not the past that she thought she "had (all these years) been remembering" (*TWHF*, 263). She remembered, for example, hearing from the eunuch Tarin of the loneliness of her sister, Redival (*TWHF*, 265), whom she had portrayed in her book as a vain and spiteful person. Because she must be truthful, Orual revises her book. In addition to remembering events, such as Tarin's visit, which she had not recorded in her book, Orual begins to reinterpret the events she did record, particularly her relationships with key people in her life, such as Bardia (*TWHF*, 268–78) and especially Psyche. She compared her writing to the task of sorting seeds: "It was a labour of sifting and sorting, separating motive from motive and both from pretext; and this same sorting went on every night in my dreams, but in a changed fashion" (*TWHF*, 266).

Orual's external narrative breaks down further in Part 2, making the plot increasingly difficult to summarize. And when linear time breaks down in Part 2, the reader of *Till We Have Faces* is forced to shift attention from a concern with plot and sequence of events to a concern with character development. Orual begins to question the motives behind the events and the significance of the events them-selves. The reinterpretation of her life transforms Orual's under-standing of herself and her understanding of the gods.

The breakdown in linear temporality is illustrated, for example, in Orual's dream of having to fetch water for the goddess, Ungit. The bowl Orual carried to collect water for Ungit becomes her book, and she is taken to a court where she reads and rereads it: "I would have read it for ever, quick as I could, starting the first word again almost before the last was out of my mouth, if the judge had not stopped me" (*TWHF*, 303–4). Here, Orual herself becomes reader. When she fin-ished reading, she was asked if she had been answered. She replied: "The complaint was the answer. To have heard myself making it was to be answered. . . . I saw well why the gods do not speak to us openly, nor let us answer. Till that word can be dug out of us, why should they hear the babble that we think we mean? How can they meet us face to face till we have faces?" (*TWHF*, 305).

She ended her book (and *Till We Have Faces*) with a hymn of praise: "I know now, Lord, why you utter no answer. You are yourself the answer. Before your face questions die away. What other answer would suffice? Only words, words; to be led out to battle against other words. Long did I hate you, long did I fear you. I might—" (*TWHF*, 319–20). She dies in mid sentence.

Orual's rewriting of her book deconstructs her previous writing (*TWHF*, 263), and along with it her identity and her understanding of the gods. As a result, she can, at the end, like Psyche earlier, experi-ence the numinous. Each of the tellings of the story in *Till We Have Faces* is, not insignificantly, a retelling of Apuleius's Cupid and Psyche myth. Such an act of writing and rewriting is, in fact, crucial to Orual's conversion. For neither Orual's understanding of herself nor her understanding of the gods is directly accessible to her; both are mediated by her story, the story-within-the-story.

This first section of the essay has concentrated on the narrative structure of *Till We Have Faces* and on the changing temporal modes of the various stories within the narrative. I have argued that the structure and temporal modes of *Till We Have Faces* are critical to the process of conversion which is the subject of the novel. The centrality of stories in this narrative—written, deconstructed and rewritten—attests to the power of narrative to transform a life.

II

Till We Have Faces, however, does more than exemplify the way in which narrative "baptizes a life." It also provides a starting point for and guide to understanding Lewis's implicit theory of story. We are now prepared to turn to Lewis's literary critical works on story to see the ways in which *Till We Have Faces* clarifies and extends his theoretical comments. I will argue that, on the one hand, *Till We Have Faces* intentionally employs narrative for its particular kind of meaning, what Lewis calls Logos. By highlighting temporality and plot, on the other hand, the novel extends and strengthens Lewis's discussion of narrative, as not only a particular sort of "made thing" but as a peculiar "activity of making," what Lewis calls Poiema.

Lewis's theory of story plays through his literary critical works like a theme with many variations. It runs through his academic works on the classics, *The Allegory of Love* and *A Preface to Paradise Lost*. It is heard in Lewis's essays on popular literary genres, like "On Stories" and "Sometimes Fairy Stories May Say Best What's to Be Said." It sounds clearly in theoretical books like *The Personal Heresy: A Controversy*, an attack against the cult of personality in literary criticism, and in essays such as "Christianity and Literature," a meditation on the relationship between authors and their works. And it is played out in *An Experiment in Criticism*, a discussion of good readers which anticipates more recent interest in reader-response criticism.[10]

Throughout these essays several themes recur: story as something said and something made, the work as pointing to something else rather than being a new creation, the relationship between authors

10. For an excellent introduction to reader-response criticism, see Jane P. Tompkins, ed., *Reader-Response Criticism: From Formalism to Post-Structuralism* (Baltimore: Johns Hopkins University Press, 1980), ix–xxvi. Lewis's *An Experiment in Criticism* will be of interest to reader-response critics. He reverses the criteria for judging "good" books (*Experiment*, 1–4, 104–5). Instead of determining the value of a book by what critics say or by literary fashion, Lewis argues for a theory of reading by which a book is "received" rather than "used" (*Experiment*, 88–90, 19–26).

and books, and the relationship between good books and good reading—the kind of enjoyment a good book provides and the kind of genres which are most likely to provide such enjoyment. Among these many themes, the first, that a story is both something said and something made, is foundational. Understanding this distinction is critical to understanding what a story is. As Lewis says in *A Preface to Paradise Lost*, "The first qualification for judging any piece of workmanship from a corkscrew to a cathedral is to know *what* it is. . . . The first thing is to understand the object before you: as long as you think the corkscrew was meant for opening tins or the cathedral for entertaining tourists you can say nothing to the purpose about them" (*Preface*, 1). Stories, like poems, "can be considered in two ways—as what the poet has to say, and as a *thing* which he *makes*" (*Preface*, 2). Lewis develops this distinction between a story as something said and something made in *An Experiment in Criticism*:

> A work of art can be considered in two lights. It both *means* and *is*. It is both *Logos* (something said) and *Poiema* (something made). As Logos it tells a story, or expresses an emotion, or exhorts or pleads or describes or rebukes or excites laughter. As Poiema, by its aural beauties and also by the balance and contrast and the unified multiplicity of its successive parts, it is an *objet d'art*, a thing shaped so as to give great satisfaction. (*Experiment*, 132)

For Lewis, the original impulse for a story is not "the mass of experience, thought, and the like, inside the poet" (*Preface*, 2). To say so, Lewis came to see, is to commit what he called "the personal heresy." Rather, the story's original impulse is the author's effort to have the story mean something, and thus to imitate the ideal form. Logos is an invitation. "Literature as Logos is a series of windows, even of doors" (*Experiment*, 138). In this process of *meaning* for Lewis, the author's (or reader's) personality is of little importance.

Literature as Logos, as something which *means*, "admits us to experiences other than our own" (*Experiment*, 139). Orual's book became for her something which she did not intend—an invitation. Indeed, Lewis might have been thinking about Orual's book when he wrote the following: "Literary experience heals the wound, without undermining the privilege, of individuality. . . . In reading great literature I become a thousand men and yet remain myself. Like the night sky in the Greek poem, I see with a myriad eyes, but it is still I who see. Here, as in worship, in love, in moral action, and in knowing, I transcend myself; and am never more myself than when I do"

(*Experiment,* 140–41). According to Lewis, therefore, neither the author's creative vision nor the work itself is truly "original."

In Lewis's understanding of Logos, his Platonism clearly shows. Logos is like Plato's concept of Form. To claim, however, that there are pre-existing Forms to which the author responds is for Lewis not merely to engage in a sort of Platonic philosophy; it is to make a fundamentally theological claim. He discusses the nature of such claims in "Christianity and Literature," in which he proposes a distinctive Christian aesthetics. Here Lewis attacks the commonly held position in his day that the best literature is "creative," "original," "innovative," "self-expression." By contrast the Christian writer "reflects," "imitates," "mirrors" Divine Realities. The New Testament is the model for the Christian writer:

> In the New Testament the art of life itself is an art of imitation: can we, believing this, believe that literature, which must derive from real life, is to aim at being "creative," "original," and "spontaneous." "Originality" in the New Testament is quite plainly the prerogative of God alone; even within the triune being of God it seems to be confined to the Father. The duty and happiness of every other being is placed in being derivative, in reflecting like a mirror.[11]

The author is free, for example, to use Apuleius as a "source" for the story of *Till We Have Faces.* As Lewis says in the "Note" at the end of the American edition of the novel: "Apuleius was of course a man of genius: but in relation to my work he is a 'source,' not an 'influence' nor a 'model.'" That is to say, just as Robert Graves has pointed out that Apuleius, though the first to record the myth, was not the originator of the Cupid and Psyche story, by extension Lewis will not be the last or final person to tell it.[12] Lewis retells Apuleius, mirrors him, just as Apuleius's story was derivative, a retelling of a more original story.

If story must be understood as Logos, as something said whose meaning occurs as a telling and retelling, it must also be understood as Poiema, as something made. For unless it becomes incarnate in a particular work, Logos is unrealized: "It is only by being also a *Poiema* that a Logos becomes a literary *art* at all" (*Experiment,* 135–36; my

11. Lewis, "Christianity and Literature" (1939), in *Christian Reflections,* ed. Walter Hooper (London: Geoffrey Bles, 1967), 6.

12. Lewis, *Till We Have Faces: A Myth Retold* (New York: Harcourt Brace, 1956), 313; Graves, Introduction to *The Transformations of Lucius, Otherwise Known as The Golden Ass* by Lucius Apuleius, trans. Robert Graves (New York: Farrar, Strauss and Young, 1951), xix.

italics). When Lewis wrote the Narnia stories, for example, he came to see that the fairy tale, with "its brevity, its severe restraints on description, its flexible traditionalism, its inflexible hostility to all analysis, digression, reflections and 'gas,'" was the best form for books which "began with images; a faun carrying an umbrella, a queen on a sledge, a magnificent lion."[13]

In speaking of the beginning of his own stories, Lewis emphasized the relationship between Logos and Poiema: "In the Author's mind there bubbles up every now and then the material for a story. For me it invariably begins with mental pictures. This ferment leads to nothing unless it is accompanied with the longing for a Form: verse or prose, short story, novel, play or what not. When these two things click you have the Author's impulse complete."[14] Lewis finally wrote *Till We Have Faces* when the proper "form" came to him. The fact that he abandoned two earlier versions, a play and a long poem, and chose instead "narrative" suggests the importance of the particular form of *Till We Have Faces*.

Poiema refers to the "shape," "pattern," or "design" of the work itself. In terms of the present essay, Poiema refers to "the making of plots" and thus, at least implicitly, points towards the role of temporality. Poiema is "like 'doing exercises' under an expert's direction or taking part in a choric dance invented by a good choreographer." As in exercising or choreography, timing is crucial: "If the Poiema, or the exercises, or the dance is devised by a master, the rests and movements, the quickenings and slowings, the easier and the more arduous passages, will come exactly as we need them" (*Experiment*, 134). In the enjoyment of the Poiema "we entertain various imaginations, imagined feelings, and thoughts *in an order, and at a tempo*, prescribed by the poet" (*Experiment*, 133; my italics).

Lewis's comments about temporality remain, however, merely suggestive. In "On Stories," for example, he speaks of the internal tension in story, as in life, between theme and plot, but his explanation leaves unclear why linear temporality gets in the way of the theme: "We grasp at a state and find only a succession of events in which the state is never quite embodied" ("OnS," 105). Lewis recognized the importance of sequence to plot, but he also recognized the importance of something else: "To be stories at all they must be series

13. Lewis, "Sometimes Fairy Stories May Say Best What's to Be Said" (1956), in *Of Other Worlds: Essays and Stories*, ed. Walter Hooper (London: Geoffrey Bles, 1966), 36–37, 36.

14. Lewis, "Sometimes Fairy Stories," 35.

of events: but it must be understood that this series—the *plot*, as we call it—is only really a net whereby to catch something else. The real theme may be, and perhaps usually is, something that has no sequence in it" ("OnS," 103). In his discussion of Logos, Lewis is clearer about the "something else" of narrative, but he does not see that the lack of sequentiality has anything necessarily to do with the Poiema, the "net whereby to catch something else."

Yet as we have seen above, the disruption of linear temporality is critical to the "making" of *Till We Have Faces*. Here is one instance where an author's practice moves beyond his theory. To tease out the theoretical implications of the rupture of temporality in *Till We Have Faces*, we turn in the final section of the essay to Paul Ricoeur's work on narrative time. Ricoeur's work names and develops what is present but unrealized in Lewis's theory of Poiema.

III

Although Ricoeur's philosophy may seem to Lewis scholars an unexpected detour, his criticism clarifies Lewis's discussion of Poiema by highlighting the critical role temporality plays in narrative plot. Just as Logos remains unrealized until it is embodied by Poiema, temporality remains an abstraction unless it is embodied in narrative. As Ricoeur says in *Time and Narrative:* "Time becomes human time to the extent that it is organized after the manner of a narrative." Likewise, narrative only becomes what Lewis called a "net whereby to catch something else" (Logos, something meaningful) when, according to Ricoeur, "it portrays the features of temporal experience."[15] Thus, narrative and temporality are reciprocally related.[16]

Of the formal characteristics of narrative—plot, setting, tone, character—Ricoeur privileges plot as the most significant for understanding the reciprocal relationship between narrative and temporality. If narrative is, in the broad sense for Ricoeur, "the organization of the events,"[17] what Aristotle calls *mythos*, then "plot" refers specifically to the process by which the events become intelligible wholes, what Aristotle calls mimesis. To emphasize the active, productive character of plot, Ricoeur speaks of "emplotment" rather than plot.

Episode and configuration are two characteristics of the activity of

---

15. Ricoeur, *Time and Narrative*, trans. Kathleen McLaughlin and David Pellauer, 3 vols. (Chicago: University of Chicago Press, 1984–1988), 1:3.
16. Ricoeur ("Narrative Time," 165) advances an argument for such reciprocity.
17. Ricoeur, *Time and Narrative*, 1:36.

mimesis, or emplotment, which Ricoeur emphasizes in his discussion of narrative time. On the one hand, the episodic character of plot is what we understand as ordinary time; it is linear—composed of beginnings, middles, and ends. The episodic dimension of emplotment is most significant at the outset of Part 1 of *Till We Have Faces* and becomes less significant as the story progresses. The episodic character of emplotment is important because it allows us to follow a story from beginning to end.

On the other hand, the configurational character of emplotment is not linear; it is the creative activity of "eliciting a pattern from a succession." It takes over as the dominant function of emplotment in Part 2 of *Till We Have Faces*. The configurational character is important because it allows us to make "significant wholes out of scattered events."[18] Both episode and configuration are part, in various proportions, of every narrative plot. But for Ricoeur, configuration is the more significant and productive of the two.

Configuration is significant because it challenges our ordinary acceptance of time as linear sequence and because it ties the rupture of linear temporality directly to the production of meaning. We assume that temporality means chronological sequence. Narrative plot, however, is not just about the chronological sequence of beginnings, middles, and ends. It is also about making meanings out of events, and about the importance of particular events in a sequence. Using Lewis's terms to describe the position of Ricoeur, Logos (the meaning of a story) is itself dependent upon the temporality of Poiema (now understood as emplotment).

We can now see how Ricoeur's discussion of episode and configuration helps clarify the Poiema, or "pattern," of *Till We Have Faces*. As we discussed above, *Till We Have Faces* is structured by the interplay of three stories. Each is shaped by a particular plot and temporal ordering. Thus, Orual sets out to go behind the "false" story of the priest of Issur to write the "true" story. Her plot is linear and historical. Her case will be persuasive if she gets the facts in the proper order.

On the other hand, Psyche seeks to persuade her sister of the existence and benevolence of the gods, not on the basis of historical evidence, but on personal experience. She tells of her direct experience of the divine. The plot of her story has more to do with feelings than with facts; what counts is the fact that the god comes to her nightly in holy darkness. And it is nightly that time is suspended.

18. Ricoeur, "Narrative Time," 174.

In telling of the new goddess Istra, the priest of Issur is concerned with the ritual character of the plot of the sacred story. The priest's telling coincides with the seasonal cycles of worship: "In spring, and all summer, she is a goddess. Then when harvest comes we bring a lamp into the temple in the night and the god flies away. Then we veil her. And all winter she is wandering and suffering" (*TWHF*, 255–56). Linear temporality becomes ritual reenactment. Thus, even in Part 1, which is primarily episodic in character, linearity does not mean the same thing in each of the stories.

Part 2 of *Till We Have Faces* is also a retelling, but instead of a linear plot structure, temporality breaks down altogether in Orual's own story. The remaking of her book (Part 1) has less and less to do with an interest in chronological sequence and more and more to do with the significance of her most important relationships—with Bardia, for example, and especially with Psyche. The shift from the episodic dimension of plot to the configurational dimension of plot is graphically demonstrated in the structure of the novel by the breakdown of linearity from Part 1, the story-within-the-story, to Part 2. We do not "follow" the events in Part 2 in the same way we follow them in Part 1. What matters is how Orual makes sense out of what happens to her, not the order in which they occur.

As Orual reinterprets her past and rewrites her story, she understands herself and the gods differently. Her initial self-understanding, as wronged lover, and her understanding of the gods, as deceitful and unjust, are deconstructed in the act of writing and rewriting her story. As she realizes that her love for Psyche was possessive, she accepts herself, accepts the "face" that allows her to meet the gods, and accepts their grace. Neither identity nor faith is directly accessible to her. Only in narrative does Orual discover both. And only in the rupture of linear temporality does this narrative plot, as Poiema, become Logos, "a net whereby to catch something else."

IV

Given theology's recent interest in narrative, a renewed interest both in Lewis's stories themselves and in his criticism is not surprising.[19] I have argued that *Till We Have Faces* is itself a story about the nature and importance of story. As such, it is significant because it clarifies and extends Lewis's literary critical works on narrative.

Beyond the story itself, I have concentrated on two aspects of

19. See especially Scott, "Rediscovery of Story."

Lewis's theory: story as Logos, as something said, and story as Poiema, as something made. As a narrative of conversion, of the transformation of faith and identity, *Till We Have Faces* exemplifies Lewis's understanding of Logos. Lewis's discussion of Poiema, however, argues that the proper form, narrative, is crucial to *Till We Have Faces*. But it cannot by itself explain *why* such a narrative structure is crucial. Ricoeur's theory of narrative time has helped us to understand the importance of temporality to Poiema, the reason that narrative plot is crucial for a novel about personal and religious transformation. Yet if Ricoeur's discussion highlights the potential of certain narratives as Poiema to "baptize" a life, his discussion of narrative time does nothing to help us understand the *nature* of the transformation which Orual undergoes in *Till We Have Faces*.

For Lewis, Poiema, the *form* of the story as narrative, is part of what constitutes the story but not all. Lewis's Orual is converted to a new vision of being. Despite the potential limitations of his Platonism, Lewis's category of Logos enables him at least to raise both the issue of the world which the text as Poiema opens up to Orual and the question of narrative truth. The world which the text as Poiema opens up for Orual becomes, through narrative, Logos, where the possibility of new being is appropriated. Orual transcends herself, yet is never more herself than when she does.

If story, as Poiema, must be supplemented by a theory of temporality in order to explain the *how* of narrative transformation, a theory of story as Logos is needed in order to describe the *what* of narrative transformation. Thus, *Till We Have Faces*, as both Logos and Poiema, attests to the contributions a renewed reading of Lewis may still have to offer to those who would understand those narratives which "baptize the imagination."

Bent Language in *Perelandra*: The Storyteller's Temptation

Donald E. Glover

In all of Lewis's fiction, there is a sense of the value he placed on the truth of fiction, its ability to convey to those who read valuable meaning through pleasant instruction. Many have written on the significance of story as one of Lewis's tools for revealing truth, basing their commentary on the role which myth plays in his work as it recaptures essential truths. Nowhere is this important feature of his literary method more evident than in *Perelandra* where at every turn we are confronted with examples of concern over how the story is told, the effect it will have on the listener, the importance of language in telling story, and the dangerous power which stories have to expand knowledge and thus if wrongly used to distort truth and destroy meaning and life.

Lewis regarded storytelling as a divine act permitted to fall into the hands of humans for their pleasure and edification. Like Tolkien, he saw it as a subcreative act but with fewer of the restrictions Tolkien placed upon the human creator.[1] Lewis was less inhibited in his storytelling, a trait which annoyed Tolkien and brought him to regard Lewis as too creative a borrower, perhaps accounting for his jealousy of Lewis's achievement in the Chronicles of Narnia.[2] Lewis did enjoy writing, worked quickly, revised little, was a clever creator of stories which have enthralled nearly every reader who has discovered them. His storytelling is not limited to children's tales but extends to the space trilogy and beyond into works of Christian apology.

Often the action of storytelling becomes the focus of a work and the symbolic center of meaning, as in *Till We Have Faces,* where

1. See my *C. S. Lewis: The Art of Enchantment* (Athens: Ohio University Press, 1981), 30–33; and J. R. R. Tolkien, "On Fairy-Stories," in *Essays Presented to Charles Williams,* ed. C. S. Lewis (London: Oxford University Press, 1947), 67–68.
2. Humphrey Carpenter, *The Inklings: C. S. Lewis, J. R. R. Tolkien, Charles Williams, and Their Friends* (London: George Allen and Unwin, 1978), 224.

Orual "tells" us in her own words what has troubled her throughout her long and difficult life. Her manner of narration, the language, movement of plot, characterization of Bardia and Redival all contribute to our understanding of her dilemma: Who am I? What is my true story? Why is no one listening to me? Other characters in Lewis novels tell us about themselves in stories which vary in style but reveal the truth that the character is often unable at first to understand. Emeth in *The Last Battle* and Jadis in *The Magician's Nephew* are opposing but appropriate examples.

Stories are meant to reveal the truth, to uncover that which lies hidden, but they can be mistold or twisted in both language and plot so that they in fact distort or change the truth and lead the reader to quite wrong conclusions. *The Screwtape Letters* offers a fine example of what the Lord of Lies can do to transmute parables into lessons in religious seduction. Thus, built into the act of telling a tale is the potential danger of misdirection, misstatement, and intentional falsehood. It must have been an area of concern for Lewis, who in constructing *Perelandra* as he did made it clear to readers that one must be on guard against the temptation of either ego or an agenda creeping in and destroying the delicate balance between the known truth and how we tell it.

Perelandra offers one of the best examples of Lewis's conscious concern with the pitfalls of his own art form. We begin with the frame of the story placed firmly in the hands of Lewis, the fictional character who tells us where Ransom has been and introduces us to the story within the story. Obviously this device is a clever way of giving verisimilitude to an essentially extraterrestrial story; it also contains many points of thematic and symbolic interest linked to the main plot. Lewis the narrator suffers increasingly from the fear that he is going mad on his journey to Ransom's isolated home. He cannot account rationally for the feelings of dread he experiences. His language is expressive of confusion and disorientation, particularly uncharacteristic of one with Lewis's training and education. Without losing control of the story, he loses control of his rational faculties and begins to doubt Ransom's intentions, suspecting himself and Ransom to be dupes drawn into a plot and story created by some infernal, Wellsian bogeyman.

His telling of this short trip is powerful in evoking fear, self-doubt, anger, and finally chilling relief in accepting that *eldila* exist and that he is safely in the presence of what he sincerely tried to disbelieve. Ransom's story of a visit to Malacandra Lewis has found hard to swallow, but his disbelief diminishes before the feelings of being haunted and harried and the effect of Ransom's name spoken by the *eldil.* So we begin with a telling of Lewis's story, Ransom's earlier tale lying behind the opening chapter and both stories leading to Ransom's first-person account of his journey and the events on Perelandra.

There is a lesson for the reader before we ever get to the main story: at our most rational (like Lewis the narrator), we are loth to accept what cannot be demonstrated by scientifically verifiable means. Trust in the veracity of someone's story may go far toward persuading belief, but self-doubt can destroy such belief and replace it with monstrous possibilities. Lewis, as narrator, moves from disbelief in his own sanity to disbelief in Ransom's tale and, with the appearance of the *eldil,* to acceptance of the undeniable reality of life beyond Earth. His story in microcosm presents the dilemma of Ransom on Perelandra and of the reader approaching the novel: What is truth and how is it told? How will we know whether what is told is truth or only a "story"?

As Ransom begins his tale, there is no question of its reality. The narrative framework has provided us sufficient proof. Beyond that, Lewis the author is careful to make Ransom as philologist certify that the experiences on the planet were "too *definite* for language" (*Per,* 35). English is too slow a language to give adequate expression to the beauty and intensity of the landscape and sensations experienced in this new world. This will be a new and nearly inexpressible tale, like the tastes of the planetary fruit, "something unheard of among men, out of all reckoning, beyond all covenant" (*Per,* 47). In other words, Lewis will be able to tell a new and unique story; it was his challenge each time he attempted to incarnate mythic material into the literature of science fiction and fantasy.

As he becomes acclimated to the new world, Ransom describes his experience in much the same way Lewis the narrator describes his approach to the darkened house, as if it were a dream. Here, however, the sensation is pleasant though awesome as Ransom thinks he might be "enacting a myth" (*Per,* 52). There is great beauty in the author's description of the sea, and his talent for catching the reader up in a character's perceptions and feelings is strongly displayed. But the plot has not really begun to unfold. Ransom recognizes that he has a role to play in someone's story, but like all characters in authors' minds, he is not the first to know what the role will entail. He is like the reader waiting for the author to let him in on the story line. So, like Lewis the narrator and the reader of the novel, Ransom awaits the unfolding of events. We see here the analogy of novelist to God as speaker of the Word and author of the great story which informs so much of the reference to story in the Chronicles of Narnia.

Before Ransom makes contact with other creatures on the planet, he enacts story at the most basic level by explaining what is seen and experienced, bringing truth to life. Much of the appeal of this section of the novel rests on Lewis's skill at convincing us of the look and feel of the ocean and islands, the plant and animal forms, the sensations of an unexplored world. We believe what we read because it seems so convincingly real, and we have no reason to doubt Ransom. At this point, Ransom introduces a question about narrative which controls much of the thematic development of story as temptation that surfaces later. Is repetition of experienced pleasures, like slowing or rerunning a film in order to delay the conclusion of pleasure, the root of human evil? No two stories are the same, Lewis often says. To attempt to recreate an effect by repetition is pointless at best and dangerous when its goal is mere pleasure. Much later he will meditate on Un-man's satanic desire to make the Green Lady repeat the story of Eve by inviting her to play the role of tragic queen. We also remember Un-man's nauseating repetition of "Ransom" and "Nothing."

The narrative of Ransom's quest becomes an example of the storyteller's search for both theme and the appropriate form ("net") to clothe it in so that it conveys meaning to the reader ("OnS," 103). His search brings him quickly into contact with the nonverbal dragon and then with the listener/storyteller Green Lady. Their initial meeting recounts with humor the confusion which untutored sensation encounters when confronted with the unknown. Ransom and the Green Lady confuse what they see and laugh at their mistake. The narrative describes the confusion but is not confused itself, and we are reminded of how perception (narrative) is corrected by testing through experience. This theme is elaborated at length in Ransom's conversations with the Lady.

Lewis uses the somewhat awkward technique of having two tales told at once: Ransom instructing the Lady and the reader, and Maleldil silently "making the Lady older." The story Maleldil tells may be one which Ransom knows already, that of the Old and New Testament accounts of the creation, temptation, and fall, and of the incarnation, sacrifice, and resurrection. That story reveals its truth to her inner ear, or soul. Ransom's story must take the more difficult external path of trial and error, exploring what the Lady knows and translating into human terms concepts which Maleldil apparently does not explain to her.

Story now becomes the focal point for thematic development as

Ransom and Un-man vie in a tale-telling contest for the Lady's soul and the future of the planet. Before Weston appears, Ransom and the Lady explore the nature of consciousness and self-awareness using narrative process as analogue. As the Lady first discovers herself, she describes the experience as "stepping out of life into the Alongside and looking at oneself living as if one were not alive" (*Per*, 67). She expresses here the artifice of story, its potential for revelation, and its essentially fictitious character. She demonstrates its glory and its vulnerability to distortion, the two qualities which Un-man will use to seduce her and to which she will, given the chance, succumb.

Ransom's conversation with the Lady prefigures the Un-man/Lady/Ransom debate which follows. They first discuss rather than debate the story of our history, and Ransom experiences as startling an insight as she when she "makes him older" by saying "Among times there is a time that turns a corner and everything this side of it is new. Times do not go backward" (*Per*, 69). Ransom conceives of history as concluded, a finished story. His experience now offers the opportunity to rewrite history through a new creation, a new tale, one which he records for us and one in which he has a reluctant but significant part to play. He is a knowledgeable character in the story, the Lady an ingénue, although rapidly becoming sophisticated. Ransom, increasingly aware of his role in educating his pupil and conscious of her superiority, succeeds in introducing her to the concepts of free will and responsibility for choice—gaiety and gravity, delight and terror—and to the idea of death.

Storytelling has become serious, cosmic business. What the narrator records here is concurrently what he is making at the moment. We forget that our receipt of the tale is long after the fact. We feel present, included, and attentive to the intellectual tension which suspends other physical action and scenic description in favor of debate. In many ways, we are like the Lady as she attends to Un-man's stories. The story moves inward to become a narrative description of a game of words and wits with the future of innocence and beauty as the prize. Lewis reduces and then concentrates his focus on the basic confrontation between straight and bent language.

Before Weston splashes down, Ransom has already been reduced from teacher to advisor in anticipation of the unequal role he will soon play in counteracting Un-man's lies. Although the idea that there can be two kinds of bidding (story) coming from one source has surfaced, the Lady elects to wait for the King's judgment, admitting the possibility of contradiction into her previously single-plot narrative of life. Un-man will capitalize upon her uncertainty, suggesting

that story was created to permit the exploration of countless possibilities. Lewis would approve this means of gaining knowledge but
not the ends which Un-man proposes. Dressed as the great explorer
Livingston, Weston now enters with his story, "a dream begotten by
the hatred of death upon the fear of true immortality, fondled in
secret by thousands of ignorant men and hundreds who are not
ignorant" (*Per*, 92).

Weston's relationship to the Bent Oyarsa parallels that of the Lady
to Maleldil and Ransom to the Lady, Maleldil, and the Oyéresu.
Lewis underscores the significance of story as a tool for spreading
both truth and lies by permitting us to witness Weston on the verge of
capitulation to and submergence in untruth. Now fluent in Old Solar
and strangely altered in appearance, Weston, still in possession of his
own voice and mind, tells of his conversion to what he terms true
understanding of emergent evolution and to belief in blind, inarticulate purposiveness, or pure spirit. When Ransom challenges Weston
to produce proof, he reveals, in a chilling reversal of the Lady being
"made older," that he is being guided: "Things coming into my head.
I'm being prepared all the time. Being made a fit receptacle for it"
(*Per*, 107).

Thus the major characters are all "readers" of stories told them by
others. What distinguishes the true from the false? Lewis suggests the
ultimate choice is left to the reader either to accept without question,
wanting to believe what is being told, or more thoughtfully to question, investigate, test against the known and experienced and then
choose to believe or not. For the still naive Lady and the human and
limited Ransom, the task becomes a daunting and difficult one.
Weston has already chosen sides not on the basis of the truth of what
he hears but on the power he believes it will convey to him. Calling
himself the Universe, he sells his humanity for an illusion, assisted in
his destruction by pride in "his" knowledge and will. He has chosen,
like Eve, to play a role in an unreliable story that has no place for his
individuality. It is the oldest and most bent story of human folly.

As Un-man, Weston poses a formidable opponent in the narrative
competition for the Lady's soul. He brings all the skill at bending
language of the Dark Oyarsa. Lewis may have found the writing of
Screwtape's letters an arduous task, but there is a sense in his building of the Perelandrian debate that he relished calling up his skills as
an academic debater to draft this part of the novel. He makes Ransom
and the reader painfully aware of how skillfully Un-man twists language to change meaning and undermine logic. Although Ransom is
more aware of his own role in this story, he is no better prepared by

that knowledge to counteract the temptation to storytelling and false mythmaking which Un-man will offer the Lady.

Lewis believed that the glory of fiction is its ability to release us from one reality into the countless possibilities of others (*Experiment*, 137–38). It is just this quality that the Lady is tempted to see as the proof of her arrival at independence and adulthood. Story is, Un-man says, "for mirth and wonder and wisdom" (*Per*, 117). The earlier temptation was to walk alongside oneself as the Lady observed herself doing in her first talks with Ransom, but now it is to live wholly in that fictional world of "what might be and talking and making things out there . . . alongside the world" (*Per*, 118; Lewis's ellipsis). Un-man: "Might not that be one of the reasons why you are forbidden to do it [stay on the fixed land]—so that you may have a Might Be to think about, to make Story about as we call it?" (*Per*, 118).

The choice between the parallel realms of Story and of Life becomes the primary issue in the ensuing argument. Un-man argues for the primacy of fiction over fact. The Lady will enact her role in her own mind as story, creating her own role, creating herself in her own image or that of the fictitious characters of the past. In doing so she will neglect her place and role in life, the one made for her by the creator of truth and reality, not the creator of illusion and appearance. This temptation is that of the "sweet poison of the false infinite" (*Per*, 92) to which Weston has succumbed.

The Lady resists, readily telling about her potential children and the King, but finding no pleasure in making a story which uncreates her universe, turning the sky black and the water unfit to drink. The words "make" and "seem" appear frequently in the dialogue here, indicating as they come together in Un-man's urgings the sophistry of making appearance or desire into more than fictional reality. To tell a story is to make it seem to be so. But the Lady is more seasoned now, and her response reveals a nice logic: to play at what seems or might be is like fruit with no taste or words without meaning. Playing with language with no more purpose than speculating on the impossible is both childish and inane.

Failing to convince her of what is now possible, the enemy shifts tactics to offer story as the way to foresee what might distantly be, the "as if" which Lewis uses so effectively in the Chronicles of Narnia. Here, however, the projection which story offers supports the demonic claim used in the original Eden temptation—that knowledge is the only way to freedom. The Lady is urged to speculate about the reasons for the prohibition of the fixed lands and to wonder if she is being invited to explore her own will and walk out of it. The sharp

clash which follows between truth and falsehood involves the re-
counting of the Genesis story and the resulting Fall and recovery
through Christ's coming. Un-man's logic is impeccable, and Ransom
only recovers his lead when he insists that Satan tell his story: "Tell
her of *your* joys, and of what profit you had when you made Maleldil
and death acquainted" (*Per*, 138). The whole story, which Un-man
refuses to tell, would give the Lady fuller knowledge of Maleldil's plan
and of the truth obscured by the selective "truths" he gives her.

Ransom's meditation during the Lady's sleep focuses, as does Un-
man's later definition of life on the surface and at the core, on the
essential emptiness of knowledge for its own sake. Ransom sees that
true stories are so from the center to the outermost limit; perverted,
they are nothing at the core, "a black puerility, an aimless empty
spitefulness" (*Per*, 141). Stories that offer to bring power and control
are in fact what Weston has bought and sold his soul to obtain. For
such a person as the dying Weston all that remains is the memory of
the rind, desirable in view of horrors at the core like the fears that the
narrator Lewis experienced in the opening moments of the novel.

When the debate resumes, the pace increases as Ransom recounts
the many tales used to seduce the Lady's ego through sentiment,
offering her the examples of noble sacrificial women, tragic queens.
More subtle now, having failed to attract the Lady to willful disobedience, the enemy uses the narrative tools of characterization, analogy, and allusion to stir her imaginative soul to sacrifice. She will be
invited to become a new type of Christ figure, saving her descendants
by her noble disobedience. Her reward will be that of a *felix culpa*. In
The Great Divorce, Lewis examines the flaw in such thinking as he
dissects the motives of the mother "who gives up everything" for her
son and the wife who "sacrifices her life" to build up that of her
husband.[3] As Ransom watches, almost helpless in the face of Un-
man's eloquent persuasion, we perceive the contest narrowing to
focus on a basic aesthetic issue. Is story meant only to please or does it
have a duty to perform?

From the beginning, the Lady has resisted separation from the
will of Maleldil, often expressed in the image of "walking alongside"
or out of the path which she has instinctively known. Imaginative
fiction offers the door or "sluice" to a seeming reality which might or
might not exist. Fiction is not law. Its value rests, as Lewis often said,
on how it is received and used.[4] Neither good nor evil in itself, it

---

3. Lewis, *The Great Divorce* (London: Geoffrey Bles, 1946), 82–85, 77–81.
4. Cf. *Experiment*, 19.

permits interpretation and invites further speculation as its originality and imaginative appeal draw the reader further up and further in. The problem here, as well as in all of Lewis's imaginative works, is what to put our faith in. We obey the law for sound and practical reasons. We believe in fictions because they seem reasonable, and by their beauty and artistic force they compel belief.

We see, as does Ransom, the Lady being drawn toward her own destruction by the appeal to self-admiration. She is being asked to see herself standing outside of herself, essentially separated from her true center so that eventually she will become like Weston or the Dwarf and his Tragedian in *The Great Divorce* (97–105), no longer whole, more a fictional creation of her own powerful imagination than Maleldil's creature. What Ransom fears above all else as he watches her encounter herself in a mirror, is her love of her own soul. Still troubled by the division of her being into two parts, the Lady argues that since she is walking alongside herself, she needs to know what the other part looks like, and looking, she is trapped by the beauty and potentiality of what she sees reflected. She is no longer the ingénue; now she is the actress on the stage caught up in the pleasure of reenacting Eve's role.

The mirror image serves an important function here by reminding us of the mimetic quality of story as it represents life. Lewis believed that story was another way of catching the truths of our spiritual existence which were otherwise incommunicable. Music and art act in the same fashion. Only direct revelation to individuals and peoples by unspoken means or as recorded in the Bible is a more reliable form of divine communication to humans. So myth and story are echoes or hints of higher, deeper mysteries, echoes of the truth we know best by faith. Nevertheless, Aristotle and Plato warn of the arts' unreliability in telling the whole truth. The Lady looks in the mirror, and she mistakes appearance for reality, having been led to accept story in place of faith.

So Ransom cannot tell any story to change the course of events he sees unfolding before him. Only action will correct the inevitable conclusion of a tale gone awry. Lewis understood the power of fiction to convince. Orual's conviction of her complaint controls the tension in her story to within moments of the end. Once the narrative mistakes fiction for truth, it is nearly impossible to correct its course. At this point in the narrative, Lewis offers his corrective for false fictions: apply to the original creator, read the original story, look for your designated role, and step back into yourself, trusting that you will both know what to do and have the ability and strength to do it.

Ransom, like Weston and the Lady, has been playing a role. He was brought to do some task, wonders what that task is, mistakes his role as that of angelic advocate for the uninstructed Lady, and resuming his senses accepts his diminished position as executioner of Un-man. Fiction becomes true when it accords with patterns and universal imperatives which operate on and through humanity but beyond its unaided capacity to know.

Ransom accepts his role as representative of Maleldil and the responsibility for doing what he can and what must be done, not for himself but for mankind. His action saves Perelandra, and he thus participates in the perpetuation of the Cosmic Dance of which all humankind is a part. How far he has grown from Weston when they debated before the Oyarsa of Malacandra in *Out of the Silent Planet* (152–58) strikes the reader in their last verbal encounter when Weston is briefly released to tell his final, pitiful tale. Ironically, as Ransom is absorbed into Maleldil's purpose, he grows a more human and sound character; Weston's absorption reduces him to a caricature and then a pathetic dummy. Weston's nihilism, his relegation of real and unreal, true and false, to the rind or surface of life, presents Lewis with the opportunity to attack the then growing view of literature as the recorder of an existentialist and absurd view of reality. For even Weston with all his bravado retreats from that position, asking Ransom for salvation.

There are two more significant references to story in the anticlimactic conclusion of this novel. While Ransom waits in the underwater cave for day to break, he recites all the old tales he can remember, the great heroic epics prominent among them. They beguile his time and give him a hold on reality. They restore faith in an unseen and now far distant reality, reinforcing Lewis's claim that imperfect though they may be, they carry truth and power in their lines. Later when Ransom listens to the stories of the Oyéresu and the King, he understands that "The Muse is a real thing. . . . Our mythology is based on a solider reality than we dream: but it is also at an almost infinite distance from that base" (*Per*, 231–32).

More compelling than Ransom's recognition of the actuality of truth in myth is his brief comment on meeting the King for the first time, that where likeness exists and is greatest, there is the least possible chance for mistake. Story must look for likeness in order not to mistake the false for the real. There will be tale-tellers whose purpose is to please by artifice or clever craft. Others may have personal agendas they wish to circulate by incorporating them within an old story, using our familiarity with the original to lure us to bent meanings or conclusions. There are finally those who knowingly distort language, bend it to fit their aims with no remorse for wrenching meaning from language or significance from structure, thinking only to twist and warp both art and reality. The writer's responsibility, with such a potent tool as fiction in hand, is to keep the meaning clear and focused on the models which have carried truth through the ages. Though Lewis could brilliantly reveal how fiction and language could be bent, he did not succumb to the temptation himself. His consciousness of the disastrous results of such a choice must have been before him each time he began a new story.

C. S. Lewis
and the Tradition
of Visionary Romance
John D. Haigh

For too long the criticism of fiction, in all its variety, has been dominated by a realist outlook adapted to, and in large measure derived from, the modern novel born in the eighteenth century. In this essay I argue that Lewis's theory and practice of fiction can only be understood and appreciated when they are disentangled from the modern novel and the realist criticism which accompanies it. We need to think, and speak, in terms of the romance, an older form than the novel, yet one with perennial appeal and value. The primacy it gives to narrative, often decried as primitive, and the scope it allows to the marvelous enable it the better to convey a vision of our essential being and its spiritual context. Lewis's distinctive theorizing on the romance, his advocacy of particular romances, and his own practice of the form provide a unified body of work which has an interest and importance yet to be fully recognized.

From the first, Lewis sharply distinguished the romance from the novel. The romance was his native element; the novel, at best, an acquired taste. His mother had enjoyed Tolstoy, and his father Trollope, but Lewis's tastes were "incurably romantic" (*SJ*, 12-14). His childhood favorites included the fantasies of Edith Nesbit, the "scientifiction" of H. G. Wells, and, supremely, the Norse myths (*SJ*, chap. 1-5). From 1914 onwards the topic of "romance versus novel" became a talking point with his new friend, Arthur Greeves, who shared his enthusiasm for *Myths of the Norsemen* but also enjoyed the "classic English novelists." Greeves led Lewis to read and appreciate "all the best Waverleys, all the Brontës, and all the Jane Austens," but he also introduced him to William Morris's *The Well at the World's End*, which reinforced his taste for the prose romance (*SJ*, 125, 145, 155).

Lewis's ensuing letters to Greeves further document his rooted preference for poetry and romance over the novel, part of his wider preference for past literature over modern. Reading the *Iliad* with Kirkpatrick, he finds that Homer's lines "strike a chord in one's mind that no modern literature approaches." In a flippant mood he warns "Galahad" (Greeves) against becoming "stodgy" through reading only Trollope, Goldsmith, and Austen, and acknowledging the opposite danger in his own absorption in "lyrics and fairy tales" he admits, "but I find it so hard to start a fresh novel." After extolling *Arcadia*, he refers to "a foolish modern novel which I read at one sitting—. . . really most of them are pretty sickly with their everlasting problems." In contrast, there comes in March 1916 his momentous discovery of George MacDonald's *Phantastes*, the "Faerie Romance" which, he was to claim later, converted or baptized his imagination (*SJ*, 171). On the eve of his eighteenth birthday he extols *Beowulf* and Malory and reminds Arthur that "nearly all your reading is confined to about 150 years of one particular country" (i.e., to the period of the English novel's dominance), and with a characteristic emphasis he commends the older literature because it opens up "a different world."[1]

When his correspondence with Greeves revives in 1930, his views on fiction are more sophisticated but basically unchanged. He notes that George MacDonald's "only real form is the symbolical fantasy like *Phantastes* or *Lilith*," but he "sometimes has to *disguise* it as ordinary Victorian fiction." Isolating elements of "pure vision" in MacDonald's *Wilfred Cumbermede* and his own narrative poem *Dymer*, he asks: "Don't you get the feeling of something waiting there and slowly being recovered in fragments by different human minds according to their abilities, and partially spoiled in each writer by the admixture of his own mere individual invention?" This is very like Tolkien's comment on his own stories: "always I had the sense of recording what was already 'there,' somewhere: not of 'inventing.'"[2]

A reading of Tolstoy's *War and Peace* causes Lewis to reappraise his view that novels are a "*dangerous* form," encouraging "narrative lust" at the expense of finer literary pleasures (an accusation more often leveled at the romance!), but his preference for the romance is unchanged. Apropos of *A Winter's Tale* he finds that, for him, the value of plays and novels depends on the moments when, by whatever means, they succeed in "expressing the great *myths*." He and Tolkien were agreed, he reports, "that for what *we* meant by romance there

1. Lewis, *They Stand Together: The Letters of C. S. Lewis to Arthur Greeves (1914–1963)*, ed. Walter Hooper (London: Collins, 1979), 50, 95, 115–16, 92, 143.

2. Lewis, *They Stand Together*, 388; Tolkien, *The Letters of J. R. R. Tolkien*, ed. Humphrey Carpenter (London: George Allen & Unwin, 1981), 145.

must be at least the hint of another world—one must 'hear the horns of elfland.'"[3]

What Lewis and Tolkien valued, however, was out of step with the literary climate in the immediate postwar decades. The neoromantic poetry of the war years had faded and the revived poetic drama was to be short-lived. Working-class novels and plays came to the fore. The most influential critic of fiction was F. R. Leavis, who in *The Great Tradition* (1948) extolled the line running from Jane Austen through George Eliot and Henry James to Joseph Conrad and D. H. Lawrence. Though his views on the novel were criticized as too stringent and selective, Leavis reflected the prevalent realist outlook. His rigorist, exclusive stance on literature, along with his claims for the unique value of literary criticism, distinguished him sharply from Lewis, who had observed in 1939 that "the Christian will take literature a little less seriously than the cultured Pagan. . . . The unbeliever is always apt to make a kind of religion of his aesthetic experiences."[4] Later, in *An Experiment in Criticism* (1961), Lewis dealt directly with Leavis and his followers in a critique of what he called "the Vigilant school of critics," to whom "criticism is a form of social and ethical hygiene" (*Experiment*, 124). Lewis's book was a plea for literary tolerance and, among other things, a defence of the perennial element of the marvelous in literature.

Leavis himself professed an aversion to theoretic statements, but the sort of literary "realism" which he exemplified is aptly defined by Cecil Jenkins as "the tacit assumption that a human life is most truthfully presented in terms of the individual's milieu, of the particularity of social situation and historical circumstance."[5] Leavis added to this a burning moral fervor, well expressed in a quotation from Lawrence that prefaces *The Great Tradition*: "One has to be so terribly religious, to be an artist." He came closest to a manifesto in the claim that his select novelists are superior "in terms of the human awareness they promote; awareness of the possibilities of life."[6] Leavis made the word "life" work very hard, yet it tended to exclude the spiritual dimension central to Lewis. As for his particular judgments, it is not surprising that in a book where Dickens was found to want

3. Lewis, *They Stand Together*, 409–10, 420, 452.

4. Lewis, "Christianity and Literature" (1939), in *Christian Reflections*, ed. Walter Hooper (London: Geoffrey Bles, 1967), 10.

5. Jenkins, "Realism and the Novel Form," in *The Monster in the Mirror: Studies in Nineteenth-Century Realism*, ed. D. A. Williams (London: Oxford University Press, 1978), 5–6.

6. Leavis, *The Great Tradition* (London: Chatto and Windus, 1948), 2.

"form" and Flaubert "life" there was no space for consideration of "minor" fiction, but one may guess what Leavis might have made of Lewis's romances by his dismissive reference, in a footnote, to "the practitioners of the fantastic *conte* (or pseudo-moral fable) with its empty pretence of significance."[7]

Even among the Inklings themselves, the novelist and poet John Wain, a former pupil of Lewis's, was sharply dismissive of his fiction and of his advocacy of the romance. In his autobiography, *Sprightly Running*, he recalled an argument with Lewis some fourteen years earlier. Exasperated by Lewis's tendency "to push any author, from Spenser to Rider Haggard, who could be called a romancer," he maintained that "a writer's task . . . was to lay bare the human heart," and this could not be done if he were continually taking refuge in the spinning "of fanciful webs." Wain found "manifestly absurd" Lewis's retort that "the romancer, who invents a whole world, is worshipping God more effectively than the mere realist who analyses that which lies about him." In an essay of 1964, he extolled Lewis's scholarly works at the expense of the "popular and demagogic," referred in passing to Lewis's "novels" as "simply bad," and deplored "a telltale interest in science fiction, which is usually a reliable sign of imaginative bankruptcy."[8] The use of the realist term "novels" is significant.

Yet Wain is an undoubted admirer of Lewis, and in a more recent article he distinguishes "romancers" and "realists" more objectively. He sees Lewis as having a pre-1914 mentality and sensibility, laboring "always to achieve better understanding of that side of literature which concerns itself with the waking dream." On realistic literature Lewis's comments, he says, were no more than common sense, "yet he could expound Spenser or William Morris or George MacDonald; he could find what there was to say for Rider Haggard or Tolkien; he could move with ease from Malory and Chrétien de Troyes to Charles Williams." The list of authors is revealing, and reference to "waking dream" is particularly apt. Finally, Wain notes that Lewis regarded literature as less "serious" than religion, whilst "to a humanist like Leavis or myself, great literature will inevitably come to occupy something like the place of a body of scripture—a record of what mankind has found worth living and dying for."[9]

---

7. Leavis, *The Great Tradition*, 2 n. 2.

8. Wain, *Sprightly Running: Part of an Autobiography* (London: Macmillan, 1962), 182; "A Great Clerke" (1964), in *C. S. Lewis at the Breakfast Table and Other Reminiscences*, ed. James T. Como (New York: Macmillan, 1979), 74.

9. Wain, "C. S. Lewis," *The American Scholar* 50 (1980–1981): 75, 79.

The dismissal of the romance by Leavis and Wain and their eleva-
tion of the realistic novel expressed a bias in British criticism going
back at least as far as Henry James. In his essay "The Art of Fiction"
James argued against any subdivision of fiction, finding the attempt
to distinguish "the novel of character and the novel of incident . . . as
little to the point as the equally celebrated distinction between the
novel and the romance—to answer as little to any reality." R. L.
Stevenson, whose fiction had a strong romance element, replied to
James in "A Humble Remonstrance," arguing for the recognition of
three main classes: the "novel of adventure," the "novel of character,"
and the "dramatic novel."[10] In the ensuing friendly correspondence,
James's elaborate courtesy sometimes failed to conceal his unease
with Stevenson's kind of fiction.

James shared the nineteenth-century emphasis on "character"
and "characterization" at the expense of story, plot, or narrative, an
emphasis that early twentieth-century criticism retained. For instance,
the widely admired novelist E. M. Forster wrote of "story" as a resid-
ual, if inescapable, evil: "Yes—oh dear yes—the novel tells a story. . . .
That is the highest factor common to all novels, and I wish that it was
not so, that it could be something different—melody, or the perception of the truth, not this low atavistic form."[11] Why story is less
capable than, say, characterization of communicating "something
different" is not made clear. For "low" and "atavistic" why not "popular" and "perennial"? Yet Forster's distaste for "story" was widespread.

Both James and Forster are inclined to use the term "novel" as a
synonym for "prose fiction." This is unfortunate, since it obscures
the value of "novel" as a term to denote the kind of fiction stemming
from Fielding and Richardson. Moreover, in British criticism if not in
American, "novel" always evokes realist expectations. Those British
critics who, like John Wain, refer to Lewis's romances as "novels"
generally dislike them. It is true that in the last twenty years the prose
romance, and the fantasy elements in fiction, have been more appreciated, but in Lewis's time British critics generally relegated them to
minor status. The romance, if recognized, was often regarded as
inferior to the novel; or, it was argued, a change in our socioeconomic

10. James, "The Art of Fiction" (1884), in *Henry James and Robert Louis Stevenson: A Record of Friendship and Criticism*, ed. Janet A. Smith (London: Rupert Hart-
Davis, 1948), 69–70; Stevenson, "A Humble Remonstrance" (1884), in *Henry James and
Robert Louis Stevenson*, 93.
11. Forster, *Aspects of the Novel* (London: E. Arnold, 1927), 41.

structure since the early eighteenth century rendered all subsequent romances reactionary, escapist, or merely popular. In his own criticism Lewis would have none of this.

At the heart of Lewis's criticism and theoretical statements on the romance are "story" and "fantasy." In his essay "On Stories" Lewis complains that story has been generally neglected by critics. He notes three exceptions: Aristotle's *Poetics*, which puts story (or plot) in the center of Greek tragedy; Boccaccio's allegorical theory of story in the ancient myths; and Jung's doctrine of archetypes. Nevertheless, Lewis claims, "those forms in which everything else is there for the sake of the story have been given little serious attention" ("OnS," 90). Yet for the Inklings, as he reveals elsewhere, "the problems of narrative as such . . . were constantly before our minds."[12]

For Lewis, the appeal of story lies not in the excitement, or suspense, of its dangers—what he calls "the alternate tension and appeasement of imagined anxiety"—but in the way that "different kinds of danger strike different chords from the imagination." It is the "qualitative difference" of these imaginative chords that counts ("OnS," 93, 94). His copious examples draw on Homer, Poe, De La Mare, Masefield, Tolkien, E. R. Eddison, H. G. Wells, Rider Haggard, and David Lindsay. We are reminded of Lewis's strong visualizing power and the tendency of his own stories to originate in imaginative "pictures."[13]

A question arises here. Are "danger" or even "imagined anxieties" the sole ingredients of story? The emphasis seems excessive, but I think that attention to any effective romance will show how regularly Lewis's "alternate tension and appeasement" occurs. However these imaginative chords are evoked, they are clearly responsible, cumulatively, for that creation of a distinctive "otherworld," which is an important part of Lewis's conception of the romance. Of James Fenimore Cooper's Leather-Stocking Tales, which he enjoyed as a boy, Lewis writes: "The 'Redskinnery' was what really mattered. . . . For I wanted not the momentary suspense but *that whole world to which it belonged*—the snow and the snow-shoes, beavers and canoes, war-paths and wigwams, and Hiawatha names" ("OnS," 91; my italics). The way that imaginative chords compose an "otherworld" with

12. Lewis, Preface to *Essays Presented to Charles Williams*, ed. C. S. Lewis (London: Oxford University Press, 1947), v.

13. See Lewis, "It All Began with a Picture . . ." (1960), in *Of Other Worlds: Essays and Stories*, ed. Walter Hooper (London: Geoffrey Bles, 1966), 42; and "Sometimes Fairy Stories May Say Best What's to Be Said" (1956), in *Of Other Worlds*, 36.

its unique, complex quality is central to the visionary romance. Lewis finds it in the "Northernness" of Norse myth (*SJ*, 74, 77) and the "extra-terrestrial" note in the opening of *The War of the Worlds* ("OnS," 97). In his own fiction one thinks of Malacandra—remote, archaic, austere, masculine—and then of Perelandra—sunward, youthful, pleasurable, feminine. In the Chronicles of Narnia, each story provides a succession of complex "sensations": *The Silver Chair* has the jewelled brightness of Cair Paravel, the fine, fresh loneliness of Puddleglum's marshes, the sad sepulchral atmosphere of Underland, and the fiery brilliance of the Land of Bism; *The Magician's Nephew* has the rich, warm silence of the Wood between the Worlds, the lurid light of the realm of Charn, and the tingling magic of the creation song of Narnia.

In the evocation of imaginative "sensations," Lewis admits, there is a sense in which the romance cannot compete with poetry, but not all readers respond to poetry, and in one respect romance comes "where poetry will never come." The tension between theme and plot in the story, in one sense its weakness, brings it closer to real life, for in life, too, "we are always trying to catch in our net of successive moments something that is not successive" ("OnS," 105).

His lecture notes on *The Faerie Queene* develop these views on narrative. Here, the distinctive chords are called "images," but the musical analogy recurs and is extended. "A story of this kind," he says, "is in a way more like a symphony than a novel." He allows that these "images" may relate to Jung's archetypes, but insists that "it is always the symphonic treatment of the images that counts, the combination that makes out of them a poetic whole."[14] This statement is the key to a proper appreciation of romances, and especially of those of Lewis and Tolkien.

It becomes apparent that in Lewis's discussion of story two elements are held in tension. On the one hand, we have the element discussed above—what Lewis variously calls "sensations," "qualities," "intuitions," "chords," or "images"—each term suggesting the timeless. On the other hand, we have the "symphonic treatment"—what he calls in the essay "On Stories" the "series of events," the narrative "net" which stresses the inescapable temporal dimension. (One is reminded of the "paradigmatic" and "syntagmatic" dimensions of linguistic analysis.)[15] "On Stories" dwells on the first element, Lewis

14. Lewis, *Spenser's Images of Life*, ed. Alastair Fowler (Cambridge: Cambridge University Press, 1967), 116, 117.
15. For a valuable discussion of metaphor and metonymy relevant to this point,

going so far as to say that the "series of events . . . the *plot*, as we call it—is only really a net whereby to catch something else . . . something that has no sequence in it, something other than a process and much more like a state or quality" ("OnS," 103). In *Spenser's Images of Life*, he ultimately emphasizes the second element, claiming that "in Romance it is precisely the outward story that expresses inward life," a view close to Northrop Frye's description of romance as "a verbal imitation of ritual or symbolic human action."[16]

Lewis's views on fantasy are set out in *An Experiment in Criticism*. Lewis maintains that "as a literary term a fantasy means any narrative that deals with impossibles and preternaturals," and we may take this statement as affording a useful preliminary definition of the romance itself. His examples include *The Ancient Mariner, Gulliver's Travels, The Wind in the Willows, The Witch of Atlas,* and Apuleius's *Metamorphoses*. He first seeks to disinfect such stories from the senses of "fantasy" as that term is used pejoratively either for "Delusion" or for what he calls "Morbid Castle-building." He then seeks to turn the tables on those who find fantasy "escapist." Many writers provide, and many readers seek, material "which enables them to enjoy love or wealth vicariously," through the characters. Such readers seek "a general ordinariness" in the story which allows their daydream to be "in principle, realisable." Any hint of the admittedly impossible ruins their pleasure. Wish-fulfillment, or escapism, is shown to coexist with "a certain superficial realism" (*Experiment*, 50, 51, 53, 55, 56).

He seeks to further clarify his use of "fantasy" by juxtaposition with "realism" and "realistic." "Realism of Presentation" is marked by "sharply observed or sharply imagined detail," found as often in marvelous as in everyday stories. "Realism of content" is found in fiction "when it is probable or 'true to life.'" It is possible to have works, such as Constant's *Adolphe* and Racine's plays, in which "realism of content" is abundant while "realism of presentation" is minimal: "The two realisms are quite independent. You can get that of presentation without that of content, as in medieval romance: or that of content without that of presentation, as in French (and some Greek) tragedy; or both together, as in *War and Peace*; or neither, as in the *Furioso* or *Rasselas* or *Candide*." He claims that masterpieces can be produced in any of these four modes, but "the dominant taste at

---

see David Lodge, *The Modes of Modern Writing: Metaphor, Metonymy and the Typology of Modern Literature* (London: E. Arnold, 1979).

16. Lewis, *Spenser's Images of Life*, 124; Frye, *The Secular Scripture: A Study of the Structure of Romance* (Cambridge, Mass.: Harvard University Press, 1976), 55.

present demands realism of content." This has led, he says, to "the widespread neglect or disparagement of the romantic, the idyllic, and the fantastic, and the readiness to stigmatise instances of these as 'escapism'" (*Experiment*, 57, 59, 60). Lewis's literary examples, here and elsewhere, are always revealing. They show how wide his tastes were, despite a limited interest in post-1914 literature. In addition, as is the case with Eliot and other writers, the works he chooses are often those which have helped him in his own writing, which form the context and literary heritage out of which he worked. To that context I now turn.

The widest context is that of the epic poem: in general because, as Clara Reeve long ago remarked, "epic poetry is the parent of romance";[17] in particular because Lewis's early aspiration, as shown in *Dymer* and in his letters, was to be a major poet, and because the epic was at the apex of his literary hierarchy. One notes his youthful appetite for Homer and his deep feeling for Virgil. *Beowulf* was in his blood, Dante was a revered master, and *The Faerie Queene* was a lifelong companion. His enthusiasm for the Italian romantic epic shows the breadth of his taste. He defended *Paradise Lost*. Finally, he admired the epic vision of Shelley's *Prometheus Unbound*, a dramatic poem he placed with Dante and Milton.[18] It is, then, from the epic rather than the novel that Lewis's fiction derives its sweeping narratives, its symbolic journeys and quests, its vistas of time and space, its descents and ascents, its infernal and elysian episodes, its searches for identity, its crucial choices and eucatastrophes.[19]

Next comes the medieval and later prose romance. His early reading and his work on *The Allegory of Love* had made him completely at home with its origins, forms, and potential, while the heroic "matter" of Arthur and of Charlemagne was familiar to him in all its rich ramifications. It is true that much of this material has a limited role in Lewis's fiction. After *The Pilgrim's Regress*, which revives Bunyan's blend of chivalric adventure and Christian theology, its influence is mostly to be found in the Chronicles of Narnia, where, for instance,

17. Reeve, *The Progress of Romance* (1785), quoted in Gillian Beer, *The Romance* (London: Methuen, 1970), 7. Eighteenth-century views on the relation of epic, romance, and novel are quoted and discussed in Miriam Allott, *Novelists on the Novel* (London: Routledge and Kegan Paul, 1959), 3–20, 41–58.

18. See Lewis, *The Allegory of Love: A Study in Medieval Tradition* (Oxford: Clarendon Press, 1936), 297–304; and "Shelley, Dryden, and Mr. Eliot" (1939), in *Selected Literary Essays*, ed. Walter Hooper (Cambridge: Cambridge University Press, 1969), 203–8.

19. For more on Tolkien's term "Eucatastrophe," see discussion on p. 197 below.

the clear bright colors of Cair Paravel recall the brilliant descriptive passages of *Sir Gawain and the Green Knight,* while such knightly figures as Rilian and Reepicheep stem from Malory.

Yet the immediate, most important context is that of romances by certain more recent authors who constitute a distinctive Lewis lineage and contribute, variously, to his forms, matter, and vision. All three were provided by William Morris and George MacDonald, the dominant influences, as a glance at the index of *They Stand Together* will suggest. No reader of Lewis will have missed his often-confessed debt to MacDonald's mythopoeic romances, especially *Phantastes,* the "Curdie" books, and *Lilith.* Less well explored is the influence of Morris's late prose romances, which Lewis called "the real crown of his work."[20] *The Well at the World's End* and *The Water of the Wondrous Isles* were part of his imaginative furniture. So were such mythic romances of Rider Haggard as *She.* In the literature of our own century two "minor" genres captured his interest. Science fiction offered him H. G. Wells's *The Time Machine* and *The First Men in the Moon,* David Lindsay's *Voyage to Arcturus,* and Olaf Stapledon's *Last and First Men.* They suggested forms and themes and presented powerful visions. Their alien ideologies were provocative. The children's book, also, gave welcome scope to the fantasy denied to the novel. Kenneth Grahame's *The Wind in the Willows* appealed to his sense of fellowship and his feeling for the "numinous" element in Nature. Edith Nesbit's *The Amulet* opened his eyes to the "dark backward and abysm of time" (cited in *SJ,* 21).

If our concern were Lewis's spiritual debts, G. K. Chesterton and Charles Williams would figure at this point, but their fiction is too novelistic to be relevant to discussion of the romance. Instead we arrive at a third Christian, J. R. R. Tolkien, Lewis's distinguished coheir to the whole romance tradition. As Lewis wrote to Greeves, "he also grew up on W. Morris and George MacDonald," and both Lewis and Tolkien himself are clear on the sort of fiction that Tolkien wrote. In his reviews of *The Lord of the Rings,* Lewis refers to the work as "heroic romance" and later commends "the very high architectural quality of the romance," that is to say its complex narrative structure, while Tolkien himself wrote to a correspondent, "My work is *not* a 'novel,' but an 'heroic romance' a much older and quite different variety of literature."[21]

20. Lewis, "William Morris" (1939), in *Selected Literary Essays,* 226.
21. Lewis, *They Stand Together,* 449; Lewis, "Tolkien's *The Lord of the Rings*"

In disengaging Lewis's fiction from the modern realistic novel and establishing it as a variety of the prose romance, my evidence has thus far been largely external. A fuller study of the particular works would seek to establish from internal evidence that they do, in fact, share the features and qualities of the romance tradition. General features and qualities of romance are captured by the Ulster poet Louis MacNeice in *Varieties of Parable*. MacNeice believes that "a fairy story, at least of the classical folk variety, is a much more solid affair than the average naturalistic novel, whose roots go little deeper than a gossip column."[22] He links Spenser and Bunyan to Kafka, Beckett, Pinter, and Golding, thus demonstrating that "dream," "fantasy," "myth," and "parable" are not confined to past life and literature, but are perennial and valuable.

In his fourth chapter, on the Victorians, MacNeice discusses MacDonald, Kingsley, and Carroll, and discerns the following elements in what he calls "parable" writing:

1. The "creation of a special world," true "to the inner life of man rather than to his life in an objective context"
2. a spiritual or mystical element
3. concern with the "problem of identity"
4. concern with theme, leading to a "very strong storyline" with Everyman as hero
5. a kinship to dreams, suggesting a latent content
6. "a poetic rather than a documentary procedure"
7. the importance of formal elements
8. a world view[23]

Each of these eight points appears in, and would provide fruitful headings for a discussion of, Lewis's fiction and that of his "masters," MacDonald and Morris.

In *The Secular Scripture: A Study of the Structure of Romance*, Northrop Frye treats the form in depth. In his preamble, he refers to a particular tradition of prose romance in which "William Morris is to me the most interesting figure," and notes the recent success of Tolkien. "The guardians of taste and learning," he declares, have generally disapproved of the romance. His aim is "to bring it into the area of literary criticism" since, he believes, it is "central to literature as a whole."[24]

(1954, 1955), in *On Stories and Other Essays on Literature*, ed. Walter Hooper (London: Collins, 1982), 83, 87; Tolkien, *Letters*, 414.

22. MacNeice, *Varieties of Parable* (Cambridge: Cambridge University Press, 1965), 7.

23. MacNeice, *Varieties of Parable*, 76–79.

24. Frye, *The Secular Scripture*, 4, 23, 26, 31.

His lengthy analysis of the romance has much in common with MacNeice. The romance is "sensational" and "episodic" and has "action on two levels" with "a *vertical* perspective." Its characterization is "polarized," and often "hierarchical," as in *The Tempest* and *The Faerie Queene*. We find a contrast between the "waking" and the "dreaming" worlds, which are both taken seriously. Reality is often associated with a search for identity, often exhibiting "a cyclical movement of descent into a night world and a return to the idyllic world, or to some symbol of it like a marriage." (*Perelandra* and *The Silver Chair* at once spring to mind.) Narrative, especially in the romance, is "essentially a verbal imitation of ritual or symbolic human action."[25]

Two key features of romance fiction deserve more detailed attention, its use of "otherworlds" and of the quest. Most of the several types of invented "otherworlds" typical of romance appear in one or another of Lewis's works.

First, there is the allegorical landscape of such romances as *Le Roman de la Rose*, representing "inner space," or the individual psyche. Thus in works like *The Pilgrim's Regress*, where the protagonist or his superego appears, an elaborated "world" takes in the current social and intellectual scene. Second, the landscape, or world, may be symbolic, evoking an infernal or celestial realm, as in Lewis's *The Great Divorce*, with its insubstantial Greytown and its contrasting heavenly landscape—bright, diamond-hard, dynamic. Third, romances located in the material world may appeal to our sense of wonder by choosing remote settings. Rider Haggard's *She* places its long-lived heroine in "darkest Africa." Lewis sends Ransom to Perelandra, a version of the planet Venus. Fourth, the imagined world may be set in the future. When its imagined society lies in the near future, as in Morris's *News from Nowhere*, Huxley's *Brave New World*, and Orwell's *Nineteen Eighty-Four*, the manner is often novelistic and the purpose social or political. Where the remote future is envisaged, as in the later scenes of Wells's *The Time Machine* and Stapledon's *Last and First Men*, Lewis distinguishes an "Eschatological" type.[26] Fifth, the imagined world may lie in a quite different space-time framework from our own, as in Stapledon's *Star-Maker* or Lewis's Narnia stories.

In these last three types, the need to move from our world to the invented world gives scope for imaginative transitions. The technical

25. Frye, *The Secular Scripture*, 47, 49, 52, 53–54, 55.
26. Lewis, "On Science Fiction," in *Of Other Worlds*, 65–67.

means (Wells's Cavorite or Lewis's Weston Rays), though sometimes intriguing, are less significant than the gradual approach of some new and strange experience. Some transitions are made through "doorways": Nesbit's Egyptian scarab (*The Amulet*), MacDonald's antique mirror (*Lilith*), and Lewis's wardrobe, picture frame, garden gate, or railway accident.

A sixth type of imagined world is a "version" of Earth history, as in the several versions of a chivalric past to be found in the numerous retellings of the Arthurian legend. Morris's late prose romances portray a purely Germanic medieval England, where Norman elements and the Christian Church are either absent or marginal. Lewis notes the exclusion of Christian mysticism, Aristotelian philosophy, and courtly love.[27] Tolkien's Middle-earth offers a more thoroughgoing alternative to the known history of northwest Europe. While his world is self-contained—he spoke of it as "a Frameless Picture"—its links with European ethnic and linguistic history are vital to its appeal, as Tolkien pointed out and as Tom Shippey so splendidly documents.[28] Lewis's own *Till We Have Faces*, with its picture of a barbaric society on the northern fringe of ancient Greece, is an example of this type.

Yet any scheme of classification fails to cope with the rich complexities of the best romances. This is particularly true of a final category, identified by Lewis, in which "the marvellous is in the grain of the whole work. We are, throughout, in another world." This "mythopoeic" kind of story was the kind that Lewis liked best. His examples include *The Faerie Queene*, *The Ancient Mariner*, MacDonald's *Phantastes* and *Lilith*, Eddison's *The Worm Ouroboros*, David Lindsay's *Voyage to Arcturus*, and Mervyn Peake's *Titus Groan*. "I am not sure," he writes, "that anyone has satisfactorily explained the keen, lasting, and solemn pleasure which such stories can give." Primarily, as he notes earlier, "it is their wonder, or beauty, or suggestiveness that matter."[29]

Two contrasting examples may serve to illustrate Lewis's own gift for conveying this "solemn pleasure," the distinctive qualities of the marvelous, especially in the mythopoeic story. Writing of *Arcturus*, that harsh, disturbing vision, he chooses to emphasize Lindsay's mythopoeic gift:

27. See Lewis, "William Morris," 223.
28. Tolkien, *Letters*, 412; see also 283, 409n. Shippey refers to the Shire and Middle-Earth as "calques" (*The Road to Middle-Earth* [London: George Allen and Unwin, 1982], 77–78).
29. Lewis, "On Science Fiction," 70, 71, 69.

He builds whole worlds of imagery and passion, any one of which would have served another writer for a whole book, only to pull each of them to pieces and pour scorn on it. The physical dangers, which are plentiful, here count for nothing: it is we ourselves and the author who walk through a world of spiritual dangers which makes them seem trivial. There is no recipe for writing of this kind. But part of the secret is that the author (like Kafka) is recording a lived dialectic. His Tormance is a region of the spirit. . . . To construct plausible and moving "other worlds" you must draw on the only real "other world" we know, that of the spirit. ("OnS," 98)

Elsewhere, dealing with MacDonald's more congenial romances, he observes that "the meaning, the suggestion, the radiance, is incarnate in the whole story," and thus describes his initial, deep response to the imaginative world of *Phantastes*: "I was only aware that if this new world was strange, it was also homely and humble; that if this was a dream, it was a dream in which one at least felt strangely vigilant; that the whole book had about it a sort of cool, morning innocence, and also, quite unmistakably, a certain quality of Death, *good* Death."[30] He saw this story as having converted, or baptized, his imagination. Such literary appreciations demonstrate that among modern critics few, if any, have rivaled Lewis in his ability to analyze and convey the appeal of particular stories or, indeed, shared his conviction of the importance and significance of story itself.

A second important, recurring feature of the romance is the perennial theme of the quest. Deeply rooted in our psyche, it is a controlling factor in the narrative structures and imaginative impact of many romances. It is a theme close to Lewis's spiritual and imaginative development, one which figures in his literary criticism and is given varied and pervasive expression in his own fiction. W. H. Auden, in his essay "The Quest Hero," describes the quest story as "one of the oldest, hardiest, and most popular of all literary genres," finding that it expresses our sense of continual inward change and "of having continually to make a choice between given alternatives."[31] The quest is peculiarly congenial to Lewis, since choice is crucially important in all of his fiction and theology. One recalls, for instance, Ransom agonizing over his next move in the dark night of Perelandra, or Puddleglum and the two children debating whether to release the

30. Lewis, Preface to *George MacDonald: An Anthology*, ed. C. S. Lewis (London: Geoffrey Bles, 1946), 21.

31. Auden, "The Quest Hero" (1962), in *Tolkien and the Critics*, ed. Neil D. Isaacs and Rose A. Zimbardo (Notre Dame: Notre Dame University Press, 1968), 42.

Prince from his silver chair. In his preface to *The Great Divorce,* a work which echoes with the word "choice," Lewis expresses the theme in the journey metaphor basic to the quest. We are living, he says, "in a world where every road, after a few miles, forks into two, and each of those into two again, and at each fork you must make a decision."[32]

Auden identifies six elements essential to the quest. They may be summarized as 1) a precious object/person to be found, 2) a journey to find it, 3) a hero possessing the right qualities, 4) tests, 5) "guardians" of the object who may be enemies, and 6) helpers having special powers to assist the hero. He links these elements to our inward life, our sense of irreversible change, our own uniqueness and the conflicts within us.[33] This analysis could be illustrated at every point from Lewis's fiction, but Auden's illustration is given in an appreciative account of Tolkien's *The Lord of the Rings.*

In their own allusions to the quest form, both Tolkien and Lewis stress the journey element. Tolkien, grateful for the praise in an earlier review by Auden but wary of his psychological interpretation, says simply: "To a story-teller a journey is a marvellous device. It provides a strong thread on which a multitude of things that he has in mind may be strung to make a new thing, various, unpredictable, and yet coherent. My chief reason for using this form was simply technical."[34] Lewis, in *The Allegory of Love,* had praised the journey, in a fashion closer to Auden's, as the most effective narrative device to represent inner conflict:

> The journey has its ups and downs, its pleasant resting-places enjoyed for a night and then abandoned, its unexpected meetings, its rumours of dangers ahead, and, above all, the sense of its goal, at first far distant and dimly heard of, but growing nearer at every turn of the road. Now this represents far more truly than any combat in a *champ clos* the perennial strangeness, the adventurousness, and the sinuous forward movement of the inner life.[35]

This appreciative picture of the journey's appeal fits Lewis's favorite romances to perfection, from *Phantastes* and *The Well at the World's End* to *The Lord of the Rings.* It also warmly evokes his own questers and their varied journeys: John seeking his "island," Ransom on his way to Meldilorn, Jane and Mark on their separate routes to salvation

32. Lewis, *The Great Divorce: A Dream* (London: Geoffrey Bles, 1946), 7.
33. Auden, "Quest Hero," 44–45.
34. Tolkien, *Letters,* 239.
35. Lewis, *Allegory of Love,* 69.

and reunion, Shasta on his ride to Narnia, Orual on her more inward travels to self-knowledge.

Of particular power in these journeys is the anticipatory approach to the sought-for objective, that "sense of its goal." He admired this element in Rider Haggard's *She,* in Satan's approach to Eden (*Paradise Lost,* Book 4), and in Act Two of Shelley's *Prometheus Unbound.*[36] In his own stories it is marvelously conveyed in Ransom's gradual climb from his ordeal in the dark caverns to the wonders of the Holy Mountain (*Per,* chap. 14–16), and in the final ecstatic stages of the Narnians' voyage to the Utter East (*VDT,* chap. 13–16).

This culmination of the quest story in an affirmative phase of discovery, illumination, or consummation is characteristic of romance as a whole. The best term for it is provided by Tolkien in his celebrated essay "On Fairy Stories," where after discussing the elements of Fantasy, Recovery, and Escape, he speaks of an element of Consolation. This culminates, he says, in "the Consolation of the Happy Ending," for which he coins the useful term "Eucatastrophe," a counterpart to the catastrophe of dramatic tragedy.[37] Eucatastrophe, as Tolkien eloquently develops the concept, is eminently suited to the climax of what I have called the visionary romance, accommodating as it does some variety of tone and feeling. The close of Tolkien's *The Lord of the Rings,* for example, contains elements of loss within its notes of victory, reunion, and continuing life. Lewis's more buoyant imagination submerges the darker notes of his narrative patterns in what may be called the "triumph of joy." To generalize, we may say that whereas the catastrophe of dramatic tragedy brings death and waste, attended by pity, admiration, and a sense of grandeur, the Eucatastrophe of the visionary romance, particularly in its Christian practitioners, brings rebirth and consummation, attended by joy, love, and a sense of glory.

The Eucatastrophe is a complex movement in which distinctive phases, or moments, may usually be perceived. The preparatory phase is expressed in the proverb that "the darkest hour is before the dawn." There is some vision of darkness, descent to the depths, or disciplinary ordeal. The forces of evil impose a sense of isolation, or alienation, to which the protagonist (and his company, if any) variously respond, sometimes by heroic defiance, sometimes by a self-

36. For Lewis on Haggard, see "High and Low Brows" (1939), in *Selected Literary Essays,* 268; for Lewis on Milton, *Preface,* 47–50; and for Lewis on Shelley, "Shelley, Dryden," 207.

37. Tolkien, "On Fairy-Stories," in *Essays Presented to Charles Williams,* 81.

despairing commitment to divine grace. Then comes the reversal of fortune. Evil overreaches itself, and a countercurrent of good, which has been lost sight of for a time, overrules it.

Some kind of triumphant revelation follows, often quite complex in its unfolding. We move from destructive fear to creative hope, from isolation to fellowship, from alienation to communion. As in the fairy story, this usually turns on recovery and reunion, but in addition there is some vision, or actual "translation," which lifts the characters onto a higher plane. Typically there follows an ordered grouping, a triumphal procession, a participation in the Great Dance until in the final profusion of images, we catch a vision of what Lewis called "the real universe, the divine, magical, terrifying and ecstatic reality in which we all live."[38]

Lewis concedes at the close of "On Stories" that story rarely achieves a perfect fusion of theme and plot. Yet, he suggests, "this internal tension in the heart of every story between the theme and the plot constitutes, after all, its chief resemblance to life." For, he concludes, "in life and art both, as it seems to me, we are always trying to catch in our net of successive moments something that is not successive" ("OnS," 105). Here Lewis voices the Christian conviction on the relation of time and eternity that runs through Eliot's *Four Quartets* and is given definitive expression in the fifteenth chapter of 1 Corinthians. Yet the limitations of story do not preclude memorable moments in which the visionary romance succeeds in illuminating our inner being and its divine context. At these moments the romance enters regions of experience which are normally closed to the mundane patterns of the realistic novel, even when characters within the novel attempt to *voice* such experience. At these moments a realist criticism, based on the novel, is at a loss, especially if it rests on an implicit naturalism. It may be that the spiritual insights of the visionary romance call for a responsive element in the reader. As Paulina says in the statue scene of *The Winter's Tale* (5.3.94–95), the most Christian of Shakespeare's dramatic romances, "It is required / You do awake your faith." Or it may be that in the imaginative response which they awake, these moments become a preparation for the evangel, as happened to Lewis with *Phantastes*. This was certainly the conviction of Chesterton, of Tolkien, and of Lewis himself. Be that as it may, Lewis's theory and practice of the romance constitute, at the level of literature and beyond, a notable achievement.

38. Lewis, Preface to *George MacDonald*, 21.

Myth or Allegory?
Archetype and Transcendence
in the Fiction of
C. S. Lewis

Paul Piehler

I sometimes find myself bothered by the recollection that in Lewis's Oxford it was fashionable to say things like "Of course his academic work is quite brilliant, but why on earth does he waste everyone's time with all this religious stuff?" Since I was at that time enough of a hireling of Giant Zeitgeist to make that kind of remark myself without even having taken the trouble to read any of his religious writings, apologetic or fictional, I welcome the opportunity to recant for such shallow timeserving.

Nor can I be accused of attempting to revive a dead issue. The horse is alive and could stand some more flogging. A few years ago, a famous student of Lewis's who was a successful candidate for that Oxford Professorship of Poetry denied to Lewis, in the course of a handsome tribute to Lewis's greatness as a scholar, inserted the comment, "Setting aside his novels, which I take it are simply bad— he developed in later years a telltale interest in science fiction, which is usually a reliable sign of imaginative bankruptcy."[1]

John Wain's casual phrasing here would seem to imply that his views are so widely accepted among intelligent people that any actual argument to justify his contumely would be quite superfluous. Nonetheless, my own reading of Lewis's work leads me to quite opposite conclusions: in respect of Lewis's quite central interests in allegory and myth, his fictional works have been undervalued, and his scholarship has been in some respects overvalued. And since all discussions of allegory tend to involve reference to at least two levels of

---

1. John Wain, "A Great Clerke," in *C. S. Lewis at the Breakfast Table and Other Reminiscences*, ed. James T. Como (New York: Macmillan, 1979), 74.

reality, and thus to become somewhat complex, I shall, for the sake of clarity, summarize my conclusions in the form of four propositions:

First, Lewis's most famous scholarly work suffers from a strange critical flaw. The writer of *The Allegory of Love* never quite produced a sustainable definition of allegory.

Second, the problem of definition arises from a failure to make a necessary distinction between two diametrically opposed forms of the genre, the allegory of vision and the allegory of demystification.

Third, the outcome of this failure to resolve what is in fact a quite ancient critical dilemma is reflected not only in inconsistency in his theoretical position, but also in a constriction of scope in his own attempt at an allegory of demystification, *The Pilgrim's Regress.*

Fourth and most important, Lewis's readings in medieval visionary allegory inspired not only his academic scholarship but his literary imagination and are powerfully reflected in the structures and imagery of his own fiction.

As a scholar C. S. Lewis is deservedly most famous for *The Allegory of Love.* Although it appeared relatively early in his career, it was never equalled, in scope or authority, by any of his later works, brilliantly successful as they have been. Yet, paradoxically enough, Lewis himself had a surprisingly low opinion of allegory, as opposed to what he saw as the alternate or rival mode of symbolism. He writes, for example, "There is nothing 'mystical' or mysterious about medieval allegory; the poets know quite clearly what they are about and are well aware that the figures which they present to us are fictions. Symbolism is a mode of thought, but allegory is a mode of expression." Thus, for Lewis "the allegorist leaves the given—his own passions—to talk of that which is confessedly less real, which is a fiction." He does not see himself as "reaching after some transcendental reality which the forms of discursive thought cannot contain." The symbolist, on the contrary, "leaves the given to find that which is more real."[2] Allegory then would seem to be no more than a way of dressing up prettily what the poet and presumably his audience already know, so that if he wishes to explore and communicate new or transcendent truths he must have recourse to symbolism.

If this is all there is to allegory, it would hardly be worth discussing as anything more than a deservedly obsolete literary device, in no way relevant to the understanding of Lewis's fiction. But when we turn from his theories of allegory to actual interpretations, we discover

2. Lewis, *The Allegory of Love: A Study in Medieval Tradition* (Oxford: Clarendon Press, 1936), 48, 45, 47, 45.

hints that it may well be more important than his theoretical discussions imply. Considering *The Romance of the Rose,* for instance, he warns us not to be misled by modern allegory into thinking that "in turning to Guillaume de Lorris we are retreating from the real world into a shadowy world of abstractions." Nor do allegory and symbolism, or at least myth, seem so far apart in his elucidation of Lord Mirth's park in the same work:

> But, of course, its classical and erotic models only partially account for it. Deeper than these lies the world-wide dream of the happy garden—the island of the Hesperides, the earthly paradise, Tirnanogue. The machinery of allegory may always, if we please, be regarded as a system of conduit pipes which thus tap the deep, unfailing sources of poetry in the mind of the folk and convey their refreshment to lips which could not otherwise have found it.[3]

Lewis's sharp theoretical distinction between allegory and symbolism is by no means original with him but goes back as far as the critical writings of Coleridge, who doubtless based his views on the relatively trivial allegories of eighteenth-century classicism, as opposed to the new symbolism characteristic of Romantic poetry.

But we shall not need to explore any further the well-known but all too misleading distinction Lewis made between allegory and symbolism, for it goes nowhere unless it is applied to actual allegorical texts. And then it will turn out that the relationship between the two is almost the exact opposite of what the theory would lead us to expect. At all events Lewis makes no use of this distinction in his actual analysis of medieval allegories.

Nonetheless a useful theoretical division of this type can be made—even given practical application to actual allegories—but in rather different terms. While the majority of medieval allegories, as we shall see, do consistently reach after myth, archetype, and transcendence, there is another type equal in antiquity (if not in dignity) to the main tradition, a type which specifically and deliberately turns away from the evocation of spiritual realities. In fact this feature is its chief *raison d'être.* Let us take a look at this poor cousin, for she has an important role to play, and let us name her the allegory of demystification.

The great example of this secondary type is Prudentius's fourth-century Christian poem of the wars of the Virtues and Vices, the *Psychomachia.* These battles within the soul were depicted in terms of gory but repetitive clashes between ponderous, all too vociferous,

3. Lewis, *Allegory of Love,* 115, 119-20.

allegorized warriors, modeled on the battle descriptions of Vergilian or Statian epic. Today, for most readers, these epic combats seem quite repugnant when they are not simply boring. And most notably the persons and locales are totally deficient in the numinous or archetypal aura characteristic of true visionary allegory. Nonetheless, the *Psychomachia* was an immensely popular work for over a thousand years and the subject of innumerable imitations, as well as sculptural and mural illustrations.[4]

What, then, accounts for the intense and long-lived popularity of the work? The reason is not hard to find if we look at the kind of "psychoanalysis" that preceded Prudentius's work. Prior to the knock-'em-down style battles between Anger and Patience, Lust and Modesty, hacking each other about in their greaves and corslets, we find earlier heroes assaulted by infinitely more sinister powers. One sees them at work in Aeschylus's *Oresteia,* in the form of the Furies—they whom the Greeks, in their anxiety to speak inoffensively of such dread avengers of crimes and sin, named the Eumenides, the "Kindly Ones."

Thus, when the early Christian reader of Prudentius woke up in the small hours quivering in the cold sweat of some nightmare encounter with the Eumenides or Hecate, the sinister queen of darkness, he could take comfort from this new psychology. Prudentius had replaced such mysterious and terrifying beings with figures like *Cultura Veterum Deorum,* "Cult of the Ancient Gods," a scarcely intimidating daytime warrior who is ruthlessly smashed down by a single barehanded blow from the redoubtable Lady Fides.

This allegorical procedure, tedious as it sounds today, was extremely significant in an age when mankind desperately needed a method of coping with the negative forces that assault and overwhelm the reason. Thus Prudentius's allegorical procedures effected a separation between the sin itself, the punishment of the sin, and the supernatural terror which bonded these fears together, constituting an act of psychological analysis and demystification fundamental to the control of these dark irruptions from the underworld.

The spirit and style of Prudentius's *Psychomachia* survived the

4. See the introduction to P. Lavarenne's edition (Paris, 1933), and Adolf Katzenellenbogen, *Allegories of the Virtues and Vices in Mediaeval Art* (London: Studies of the Warburg Institute, X, 1939). More generally, see also my *The Visionary Landscape: A Study in Medieval Allegory* (Montreal: McGill University Press, 1971), 27–30, as well as the interesting new approach to the allegory of the poem in Carolynn van Dyck's *The Fiction of Truth: Studies of Meaning in Narrative and Dramatic Allegory* (Ithaca, NY: Cornell University Press, 1985).

iconoclasm of the Reformation, which put an end to the old style of numinous visionary allegory. It prevailed in the tepid rationalistic allegorizations of the eighteenth century and was thus indirectly influential in forming Coleridge's and Lewis's low opinion of allegory as a genre.[5]

Moreover, when we turn to Lewis's *The Pilgrim's Regress*, the only work he explicitly acknowledged as allegory, we find it to be largely composed in the limited psychomachia style, but written for an age when the urgency of such apotropaic demystification had long passed. It fits very well the definition of allegory Lewis made in a letter of 1958, where it is described as "a composition . . . in wh. immaterial realities are represented by feigned physical objects" (*Letters*, 283). In terms of this definition, *The Pilgrim's Regress* is a highly successful, indeed brilliant, work. Every character or scene encountered by the hero constitutes an ingenious representation of such assorted "immaterial realities" as Virtue, the Spirit of the Age, the Heroic Ideal, Philosophical Idealism, Mother Church, the Sin of Lust, and, finally, Death itself—all designed to constitute a convincing semi-autobiographical account, in allegorical terms, of Lewis's own intellectual and psychological journey from childhood credulity, through many phases of skepticism or apostasy, to genuine religious conversion.

Of course, there is something not quite satisfactory about *The Pilgrim's Regress*, and doubtless it merits no more than its relatively minor place in the Lewis canon. Why? Lewis himself gave us some indication of the problem in his preface to the second edition of 1943, where he clarifies, among other things, his system of psychological geography. North, for example, stands for excessive rigidity of thought, emotion, and belief, and South for excessive laxity. However, he goes on to confess, "But it remains true that wherever the symbols are best, the key is least adequate. For when allegory is at its best, it approaches myth, which must be grasped with the imagination, not with the intellect."[6] But in fact the intellectual significance of the allegory is at once so precise and so obscure that Lewis was prompted to emulate the editors of the original *Pilgrim's Progress* by putting explanatory "running heads" at the top of each page.

5. See my "Visions and Revisions: C. S. Lewis's Contribution to a Theory of Allegory," in *The Taste of the Pineapple: Essays on C. S. Lewis as Rhetorician, Literary Critic, and Creative Writer*, ed. Bruce L. Edwards (Bowling Green, Ohio: Popular Press, 1988), 86–88.

6. Lewis, *The Pilgrim's Regress. An Allegorical Apology for Christianity, Reason and Romanticism*, rev. ed. (London: Geoffrey Bles, 1943), 13.

The point is a crucial one. Compared to his later fiction, *The Pilgrim's Regress* is remarkable for its high proportion of "feigned physical objects" intellectually translatable into "immaterial realities" and equivalently for its low degree of that elusive but infinitely attractive "mythic" quality, which appeals primarily to the imagination and constantly challenges while constantly eluding cogent translation into intellectual terms.

The Pilgrim's Regress, therefore, works very well as an allegory of demystification, indeed as an allegory satirical of contemporary intellectual life, as its hero, John, visits the various schools of heresy or worldliness north or south of the true road. But it lacks a transcendent dimension. Unlike the true visionary allegory that inspired his later fiction, but faithful to the limited, reductionistic tendency of the psychomachia tradition, *The Pilgrim's Regress* does not, for instance, grant us more than the briefest glimpse of the landlord's castle on the other side of the stream of death. The work seems best defended as a legitimate but preliminary intellectual reconnaissance to discover and mark out the best routes to the place of transcendence.

Lewis does not seem to have changed his theoretical position on allegory, though in his later writings we find the role he previously attributed to symbolism being taken over by myth. In a letter to Peter Milward written in 1956, he says: "My view wd. be that a good myth (i.e. a story out of which ever varying meanings will grow for different readers and in different ages) is a higher thing than an allegory (into which *one* meaning has been put). Into an allegory a man can put only what he already knows; in a myth he puts what he does not yet know and cd. not come by in any other way" (*Letters,* 271). The weakness of this rather shaky polarity between allegory on the one hand and symbolism or myth on the other becomes clearer when we take a closer look at the way in which allegory actually functions in the Middle Ages. At the same time we shall see how Lewis's own fiction is itself largely based on the themes and structures of medieval allegory.

Confusion often arises concerning the term "allegory" because the word can refer either to a certain method of writing or to a complete work written in this allegorical style—in other words, to a mode of writing or to a genre. In *The Pilgrim's Regress* it is easy to miss the distinction, for it both functions as an allegory in the sense of genre and is written in the *mode* of allegory throughout. Indeed, the very thoroughness with which Lewis infused allegory of mode into his allegory of genre turns out to be its major limitation.

This odd situation in which allegory fails, it seems, by remaining too faithful to its own definition makes a good case for changing either the genre or the definition. Fortunately, the second, less drastic solution is available to us. If we turn our attention to great medieval visionary allegories which Lewis revived for the modern imagination, we find they contain a much higher proportion of myth than is perceptible in *The Pilgrim's Regress*. Moreover, the distinction between mythic and allegorical creation turns out to be not at all so hard and fast as it was to become in later centuries.

At the outset of *The Divine Comedy*, the type and pattern of all visionary allegories, the reader finds himself in the most famous of allegorical landscapes, Dante's *selva oscura*. With respect to this dark and fearsome forest, it would be much more difficult than in *The Pilgrim's Regress* to distinguish the specific roles of the literary forms, the myth, allegory, and symbolism that underlie and shape its imagery. In Dante's experience of mortal terror when he comes to realize he has lost his way in the wilderness, the surface allegorical significance of wandering from the true path merges seamlessly into the traditional mythic adventure of the dreadful encounter with the dark forest and its monsters experienced by almost every mythic hero from Gilgamesh to Frodo. Long before Dante, classical philosophers had made an allegorical identification of the forest with chaos—that is, matter in that unthinkable, fearful condition before it receives the imprint of form.[7] But such different levels of meaning are distinguishable only through the prisms of analysis. It would surely be inappropriate to Dante's intention (and to a proper experience of the poem) if we were to become overly conscious of these distinct elements as we read the text, whereas in reading *The Pilgrim's Regress* we should on the contrary be missing an essential part of the experience if we failed to remain alert to the separate but parallel lines along which story and interpretation are progressing. Indeed, the "running heads" are there to prompt the forgetful.

There is nothing precisely equivalent to Dante's dark wood in Lewis's fiction. But if we think about the way in which the experience of the wood prepares us for the reading of Dante's adventures in the afterworlds, the structural function of the wood if you like, then we can find many equivalences. As Dante and Lewis would be sufficiently aware, their readers will almost inevitably come to these works in a "normal" state of mind—that is, they will be clenched firmly in the grip of the prevailing, rarely questioned assumption that everyday experience gives us all we know or need to know of the true reality of things. How then to break the spell of this existential inertia? What

7. Piehler, *Visionary Landscape*, 75–77.

happens in the dark wood is what one might term a "disorientation experience," a disturbance of the normal postulates of everyday life sufficiently severe and sustained to cause the hero and, through him, ourselves (insofar as we participate imaginatively in the experience) to doubt the coherence of our familiar world as a sole or sufficient reality.

Such experiences of disorientation seem an essential preliminary to acceptance of the very different postulates of visionary realities shortly to be revealed to the hero. They occur, moreover, in just about every serious medieval vision. Not surprisingly, there is nothing similar at the opening of *The Pilgrim's Regress*. On the other hand, Lewis's later fiction abounds in such allegorical motifs, despite the fact that, in his view, these works are in no way to be thought of as allegories. Writing of the Narnian stories in a letter dated as late as 1958, he describes them rather as "suppositions," distinguishing them from allegory as follows:

> Allegory and such supposals differ because they mix the real and the unreal in different ways. Bunyan's picture of Giant Despair does not start from supposal at all. It is not a supposition but a *fact* that despair can capture and imprison a human soul. What is unreal (fictional) is the giant, the castle, and the dungeon. The Incarnation of Christ in another world is mere supposal; but *granted* the supposition, He would really have been a physical object in that world as He was in Palestine and His death on the Stone Table would have been a physical event no less than his death on Calvary. (*Letters*, 283)

Important as this distinction is, it is nonetheless these fictional, "suppositional" works that resemble and indeed appear to be inspired by the visionary allegories Lewis became familiar with during his writing of *The Allegory of Love*. It is in these that we find, for example, the preliminary disorientation experiences we have already identified. Thus, the first of the Narnian histories opens with young Lucy exploring the mysterious wardrobe, which she discovers would on occasion transform its dark recesses into the enticing, if somewhat menacing entrance, to a Narnian forest. In *The Magician's Nephew*, the "wood between the worlds" functions as a similar though rather more complex "locale of disorientation." In later stories, where the children are more accustomed to the Narnian reality (as, presumably, are most of Lewis's readers), we find fewer of these disorientation experiences, though in *The Voyage of the "Dawn Treader"* the shock of being plunged into the great ocean swells of the Narnian seas in the opening scene acts as a requisite and effective preliminary disorientation for benefit of the obnoxiously skeptical Eustace.

In the case of the planetary trilogy, Ransom's experiences upon arriving on Malacandra constitute a powerful and unusual disorientation experience, as he strives to make conceptual sense of the dizzyingly elongated vegetation, the near perpendicular mountains, and the grotesquely distorted appearance of the terrifying *sorns*—all baffling to his system of perceptions, nurtured on earthy Thulcandran landscapes. At the opening of *Perelandra*, on the other hand, we encounter a quite brilliant use of a contrary technique, the familiar made strange, when Lewis takes what should have been a tranquil evening stroll from the railway station to Ransom's cottage and transforms the gentle south-country scenery, in some uncanny fashion, into a landscape of nightmare.

Nonetheless, no instance of this disorientation experience compares with the intensity of confusion and terror experienced in the shifting, chaotic landscape of Dante's dark wood. Dante was of course reporting a more massive account of an otherworld experience than anything attempted by Lewis—or anyone else for that matter. None of Lewis's heroes is ever depicted as being in the intensity of spiritual peril Dante experiences at the start of his visionary journey, and the disorientations in the novels are appropriately milder experiences.

The most important of the allegorical motifs Lewis has in common with Dante is the earthly paradise. Almost every major work treated in *The Allegory of Love* embodies a striking instance of this motif, usually in a position of great importance in the story. Its occurrence in myth is equally pervasive, and, as in the case of all such major archetypes, when medieval allegory took over the motif, it acquired not only a Christian dimension but a greatly enhanced rational or explanatory element that nonetheless leaves the original power of the myth intact.

So far as Lewis's own fiction is concerned, the focal image of the earthly paradise similarly constitutes a focal point of almost all his work. But there is a striking difference in the nature of the paradise archetype as opposed to that of the dark wood. The disorientation and subsequent panic consequent upon getting lost in a forest are quite comprehensible experiences. But to the rational mind, it must seem hardly credible that anyone has ever encountered in normal waking experience an earthly paradise of the type that appears so frequently in the myths and allegories of every culture. These paradises, moreover, appear not as the setting for incidental adventure but as the ultimate goal of a sustained heroic quest, frequently comprising an underworld journey, the ascent of a sacred mountain, and the penetration of some formidable protective wall or similar barrier. Dante himself has to descend to the very lowest circles of hell and then make the painful ascent of Mount Purgatory before reaching the portals of the earthly paradise. And these, he tells us, have to be entered through a wall of flame so fierce that he would have leaped into molten glass to cool himself (*Purgatorio,* 27.7–51).

Thus *The Divine Comedy* and other medieval allegories had a primary role in supplying motif and inspiration for such Lewisian paradises as Meldilorn in Malacandra, the holy mountain of Perelandra, the country of heaven in *The Great Divorce,* the Narnian garden of Aslan, and the palace of Psyche in *Till We Have Faces.* Significantly, however, in *The Pilgrim's Regress* the hero never attains more than a brief and obscure vision of paradise, though his whole journey is inspired by his longing to find the source of the "sweet desire" that has haunted his life from his earliest childhood. This omission is characteristic of a work whose images tend to represent one-dimensional, intellectualized versions of the ancient archetypal patterns we have been describing. But only *That Hideous Strength,* with its grim, back to "the silent planet" theme, lacks a paradise. Its sacred grove, Bragdon Wood, at once eerie *selva oscura* and proto-paradise, is desecrated by man's malice, greed, or indifference, and is finally destroyed in an apocalyptic cataclysm. This act of destruction echoes, perhaps, Milton's rationale for God's iconoclastic obliteration of the earthly paradise in *Paradise Lost:* "To teach thee," as Michael puts it to Adam, "that God attributes to place / No sanctity, if none be thither brought / By Men who there frequent, or therein dwell" (11.836–38).

Curiously enough, the sources Lewis specifically acknowledged were all relatively modern. One might instance William Morris's heart-stirring but ultimately inconclusive paradise quests, the eerily unpredictable wanderings of George MacDonald's heroes (who do, however, finally attain the land of heart's desire rather than merely go in quest for it), and the brilliantly imagined wanderings of Maskull on Tormance in David Lindsay's *Voyage to Arcturus* (perhaps the most profound, surely the most provocative antiparadise romance ever written). One could also trace lesser debts to the early Yeats, to H. G. Wells, even to E. M. Forster perhaps. But apparently Lewis never alluded directly to his major debts to the medieval paradise visions as sources of inspiration.

What is the psychological significance of this paradise archetype, which, by definition, can never be encountered in normal experience? In terms of the psychology of landscape, man has dwelt, since the dawn of what we think of as human consciousness, in tense polarity between the settlement or city he has constructed and the other landscape, against and in defiance of which the city has been built—the wilderness, the unknown outerness. Since that dawn, man's energies have been persistently and in the main successfully directed to extending the area of the city at the expense of the wilderness, both in geographical and in concomitant psychological terms.

But consider the paradox underlying this expansion of the city: the more successful it is, the more diminished the power of the wilderness and the less, therefore, the energizing stimulus of this tension on the peoples who have pushed the wilderness back too far. Finally, today, the wilderness survives at all only as the result of the extraordinary efforts of such groups as the Sierra Club. Or in specifically psychological terms, the city is the very manifestation and representation of man's capacity for reason and order, while the wilderness manifests deep and awesome *potentiality*—in modern terms, the subconscious. Again, normal consciousness is totally dependent on a healthy balance between these mighty opposites, city and wilderness, reason and the subconscious.

But for the romantic, the lover of myth and allegory, the admirer of Lewis's fiction, this is hardly the whole story. From the intuition, that faculty of man which preeminently mediates between reason and subconscious, comes the message, the "Sweet Desire," from that land beyond the dark forest where the tension between the mighty opposites of city and wilderness is finally resolved and transcended. For this garden is the place where one may find the aching awesome beauty of the wilderness ordered and harmonized, walled and protected by the rationality we associate with the city. Psychologically, therefore, in this place reason and the subconscious are finally reconciled, the psyche reintegrated, and perfected.

Thus, as we might expect, if we look at the medieval allegories that embody this motif, we find that in such works as Bernardus's *Cosomographia,* John of Hanville's *Architrenius,* Dante's *Purgatorio,* Chaucer's *Parliament of Fowls,* Spenser's "Mutability Cantos," the garden is the place where the intellectual and emotional problems raised by the work find their solution, as intellect, emotion, and intuition achieve a harmony transcending all other expectations of happiness.

But in an age where commercial and political spokesmen tend to encourage expectation of instant gratification of desires, we can hardly avoid the question of why the hero has to endure such long, arduous, and quite frequently terrifying experiences on his wilderness journey before reaching his goal. Psychologically, however, these preliminary ordeals seem essential. In the first place, the ordeal of disorientation, the dark wood experience, purges the hero of what one might call the epistemological parochialism of his city, his tendency to think of the reality conventions of his civilization as prevailing in the universe as a whole.

In this way he becomes attuned to function in a region where external forms and inner realities have a startlingly close relationship, as compared to the city where the divisive analytical consciousness keeps the connections between mental and physical events to a minimum. Once this is achieved, the qualities of rationality and mental stability he has acquired in the city will be tested against the horrors and seductions manifesting out of the untamed forces of the subconscious. Thus, the final experience of paradise will synthesize and transcend both civic and wilderness elements of his existence. For each of these powerfully opposed forces must be fully manifested and reconciled within him before the external goal of paradise can become an inner reality.

The rationality of the city will not be sufficient in itself, however, for there will come to him on his journey spiritual beings who will bestow upon him the advice without which his journey could not be made nor his experiences comprehended. These spiritual beings may take such forms as gods, angels, or revered ancestors. In medieval allegory they frequently appear as personifications but by no means resemble the rather pallid figures of modern allegory. With all the dignity of their poetic ancestors, the gods of classical Rome, or the Platonic ideas from which they derive philosophically, they are usually so numinously awesome that the hero is liable to lose consciousness at the mere sight of their manifestation, suffering the kind of perturbation that Lewis reports of his own—one presumes fictional—account of his meeting with the Malacandrian Oyarsa in the opening chapter of *Perelandra*. He will also frequently have to discriminate against the advice or seductions of spiritual powers that would lure him from the true way. Finally, even after attaining paradise itself, there will be illuminating dialogue with the benevolent powers of that place, so that the experience may be comprehended intellectually as well as emotionally and the fullest possible integration of the faculties of the soul be attained.

But how is it that the rational wisdom of our great civilizations is so strangely inadequate that the hero has to undertake such an appalling journey to remedy its defects? For an answer we can turn to the greatest paradise myth, which describes the precise opposite of the psychic integration we have been discussing—the history of psychic disintegration and loss of paradise we find related in the book of Genesis. The consequence of eating the fruit of the forbidden tree is that one gains knowledge of good and evil only as separate entities that wage war against each other in endless patterns of polarity. No longer in that paradisal serenity where thought, will, and action remain in their original perfection, we form the habit of judging all events as internal or external, better or worse, active or passive, progressive or conservative, or whatever criteria one chooses.

The resulting mental fluctuations produce the transient fragmented hopes and anxieties, the cycle of malaise and satisfaction which the turns of Fortune's Wheel constantly inflict upon us. In terms of Lewis's *Perelandra,* this is the fate of those who allow themselves to fall into the state of separation from Maleldil that the Unman urges upon Tinidril, in the Perelandran version of the temptation of Eve (*Per,* chap. 8–10). In this way, the story of the Fall provides an explanation in mythic terms of how the hero gets into the world of turbulent relativities which in the end must make it impossible to find interests or purposes in human existence other than the long journey back to absolute life.

What about the biographical implications in all of this? We are all familiar with the astonishing scope of Lewis's mental activity, ranging from ruthless rationalistic polemics to the most intense of searches for suprarational transcendence. Owen Barfield, speaking of *The Great Divorce* as "itself a kind of myth," commented, "In that book, as perhaps not quite in any other, this ever diverse pair—atomically rational Lewis and mythopoeic Lewis—I will not say unite, but they do at least join hands."[8]

Lewis has himself evidently trodden the way of the archetypal hero, enduring, as he has, a life in constant tension between these mighty opposites, as the romantic artist always participates in the aesthetic worlds he creates. Out of respect for Lewis's views on the "personal heresy," however, I shall say no more than that, when it comes to his own book, the author is really no more than a special type of reader.

After his experiment with "pure" allegory of demystification in *The Pilgrim's Regress,* Lewis achieved a remarkable degree of success in reviving the medieval visionary form and, like the medieval allegorist, in inviting his readers not merely to play the role of noncom-

---

8. Barfield, "Some Reflections on *The Great Divorce* of C. S. Lewis," *Mythlore* 4, no. 1 (1976): 7.

mitted observers but to be themselves participants in a healing of the soul. In this respect Lewis's work might be described in terms of the intentions that Dante attributed to his own *Comedy* to remove those living this life from the state of misery and to bring them to the state of felicity (*Epistolae*, 10.15). It is for this reason as much as any other, I believe, that Lewis's books not only enjoy extraordinary and still increasing worldwide popularity but also engender in their readers a curious kind of loyalty, a sense of commitment to they know not quite what—even if at the same time provoking the profoundest misgivings among those who do not share such hopes of transcendent routes to human perfection.

The view I am putting forward here is that Lewis's contributions to the theory and practice of allegorical writing cannot be regarded as limited to *The Allegory of Love* and a few passing remarks in letters and prefaces. Although his study of allegory clearly ranks among the major scholarly works of the century in its field, its most significant achievement is its description and interpretation of actual medieval allegories, interpretation which, ironically enough, is far more advanced in its implied theoretical basis than the explicit theory the book puts forward. But Lewis's most important contribution to the history of allegory goes beyond either his theorizing or his specific interpretations. It is to be seen in his fictional work, where one may experience and enjoy an extraordinary revival of what is arguably the greatest collective achievement in literary history, the visionary allegory of the Middle Ages as a mode of psychic integration and healing of soul.

C. S. Lewis's Ransom Stories and Their Eighteenth-Century Ancestry

Jared C. Lobdell

Having not long ago published a short study of J. R. R. Tolkien's *The Lord of the Rings*, I have now returned my attention to the "trilogy" that first led me to Numenor, C. S. Lewis's Ransom stories. I put the word "trilogy" in quotation marks for two reasons. First, I am in fact considering all four, or rather three and a fraction, Ransom stories: *Out of the Silent Planet, The Dark Tower, Perelandra,* and *That Hideous Strength.* Second, these three or four books are related, for the most part, only by the presence of Elwin Ransom. And even Elwin Ransom changes from being John Ronald Tolkien (or perhaps Owen Barfield) in *Out of the Silent Planet* to being Charles Williams in *That Hideous Strength.* The interplanetary novels (not counting *The Dark Tower*) are a trilogy in the sense that *Tom Sawyer, Huckleberry Finn,* and *Tom Sawyer, Detective* are a trilogy, or *The Three Musketeers, The Vicomte de Bragelonne,* and *Twenty Years After.* They are three novels tied together by the presence of one character in all three, with one of his two antagonists in the first book appearing as the antagonist in the second and the other as an antagonist in the third. But whether they play a single theme or center on a single concept—as the Greek *trilogia* did—is at best problematical. They, like Tolkien's *The Lord of the Rings,* are *sui generis,* though the *genus* is a very different one. If in defining that *genus* we inquire not into the literary sources and analogues of the Ransom stories, ranging as they do from H. G. Wells back to Milton and beyond, but into the quality of mind and the *kind* of book being written—into what Lewis called the "plot" and the "state or quality" or "theme" captured by the plot ("OnS," 103)—we shall see that Lewis's trilogy is close kin to works from the ages of Johnson and of Swift.

That C. S. Lewis himself brings Dr. Johnson strongly to mind has often been remarked, yet, curiously, the resemblance as a possible avenue for a critical appreciation of the Ransom stories has not. But the Ransom stories are in part novels of intellect or ideas and are thus in a sense eighteenth-century creations. Of those for whom it seems strange to call eighteenth-century works like *Tom Jones, Robinson Crusoe, Pamela, Rasselas, Gulliver's Travels, Jonathan Wild* (to take an odd six) novels of intellect or ideas, I would ask, what else are they? Their characters, though drawn to life (or from life), are abstractions. Squire Western may be based on someone in Fielding's experience— so also may Squire Allworthy—but one cannot deny the element of abstraction or even of allegory. Robinson Crusoe is far more Every-man on a desert isle than Alexander Selkirk on his (quite specific) island. The characters are certainly not cardboard, but in many cases they are figures in a pageant. It is a pageant of inns and stagecoaches, maidens and lovers, captains and rogues, not (as it might have been earlier) of gods and emperors, knights and great ladies; but it is a pageant nonetheless, and presented (nearly always) with a moral intent. *Jonathan Wild*, which is, in Truman Capote's phrase, a novel of fact, asks but never answers a question about the morality of English law enforcement. In that it is certainly a novel of ideas. As for *Tom Jones*, although what one retains after reading and rereading (if my own experience can be used here) is the picture—the pageant—of eighteenth-century England, it has nonetheless always seemed to me that what is played out in that pageant is precisely "The Education of Tom Jones." Fielding and Defoe (in his study of civilized man and natural man) qualify as novelists of ideas. So, obviously, does Swift— indeed, though Lewis has told us that *A Voyage to Arcturus* taught him the proper use of science fiction, one wonders if the same lesson was not taught him earlier by *A Voyage to Lilliput*.

Fielding, Defoe, and Swift—and Lewis like them—also are examples of "Englishness" as described in Sir Nikolaus Pevsner's *The Englishness of English Art.*[1] "Englishness," according to Pevsner, involves the belief that art exists to preach and that the best preaching comes from the detailed observation of daily life. It is characterized as well by use of the background for gilding and illumination, in sheer joy of description, while the pageant of life goes on in the foreground.

Lewis denied that didactic purpose is part of his work. He has written that his stories begin, not with a moral, but with a vision, a picture. For *Out of the Silent Planet* that picture was of the Antrim Hills of his boyhood—the highland and lowland contrast that finds its fullest expression in the *harandra* and *handramit* of Malacandra. For

---

1. Pevsner, *The Englishness of English Art* (London: Architectural Press, 1956).

Perelandra the picture (although it may have some of its origins, obscurely, in the *Book of the Secrets of Enoch*) was from a child's mispronunciation of "Laboratory" (la bor a t'ry) as "bubble-tree": "the delightful word seemed to suggest the thing."[2] I would guess that the picture of origin for *The Dark Tower* comes from Tolkien's "On Fairy-Stories," which refers to "a time-telescope focused on one spot."[3] Nevertheless, I maintain that Lewis's art is English in the particular way in which Pevsner uses the word, that his art exists to preach. The mode of the preaching is the detailed observation of the minutiae of daily life. Lewis excels at the description, the visual imagination, the gilding, the illumination, the background detail—in short, the second part of Englishness. And he is very good at portraying moral pageant through this description—the first part of Englishness.

The "realization" of the Malacandrian world is tied to Ransom's absorption into and acceptance of Malacandrian life, including the underpinnings of that life. Lewis is extraordinarily good at this sort of thing—that is, at making Ransom's presence on this other world convincing—and his techniques are reminiscent not so much of H. G. Wells or David Lindsay as of Defoe and Swift. Partly, of course, this is the result of Ransom's being on Malacandra for a considerable length of time: thus, when Lewis records that it "was with a kind of stupefaction each morning that he found himself neither arriving in, nor escaping from, but simply living on, Malacandra" (*OSP*, 73), we are much more in Swift's "I had now been two Years in this Country; and, about the Beginning of the third, *Glumdalclitch* and I attended the King and Queen in Progress to the South Coast of the Kingdom. I was carried as usual in my Travelling-Box . . . ," than in Lindsay's world.[4] The key phrase in the passage from Swift is "as usual" and the key in Lewis's description is "simply living"; after all, as we have noted, it is the description of the detailed minutiae of daily life that provides the mechanism for the "sermon" of English art.

Intermixed with the description is the set of philosophical conversations which, as with Swift, are the central part (or, perhaps, the formal cause) of the book. Indeed, it is just after Ransom realizes that he is "simply living" on Malacandra that he begins his discoveries in Malacandrian knowledge. Later on, in *Perelandra*, Lewis would suc-

2. Letter to me, 22 October 1963.
3. Tolkien, "On Fairy-Stories," in *Essays Presented to Charles Williams*, ed. C. S. Lewis (London: Oxford University Press, 1947), 75.
4. Jonathan Swift, *Gulliver's Travels* (1726), ed. Herbert Davis, rev. ed. (Oxford: Basil Blackwell, 1959), 139.

cessfully convert philosophy into the Great Dance, but here he is much more in the world of his predecessors. There are some indications that his earliest attempts at (adult) fiction were a kind of cross between a Socratic dialogue and *Tristram Shandy*. Whatever this hybrid may have been like (it has not, so far as I know, survived), it is certain that the business of philosophy was, in Lewis's mind, very much mixed in with the business of fiction.

In fact, all through *Out of the Silent Planet*, passages of detailed description (or "realization") alternate with passages of philosophical inquiry and conversation. It is far from accidental that "things do not always happen as a man would expect. The moment of his arrival in an unknown world found Ransom wholly absorbed in a philosophical speculation" (*OSP*, 45). Similarly, chapter 12 is a conversation between Ransom and Hyoi; chapter 13 is the history of the *hnakra* hunt and Hyoi's death; chapter 14 is partly travel and partly internal dialogue (thus repeating the pattern for the voyage to Malacandra); chapter 15 is mostly conversation with Augray; and so on. For an author who once attacked the "scrappiness" of the chapters in *Tristram Shandy*,[5] these are doubtless short and scrappy chapters indeed, but what is more to the point, the plot (if that is the word) is carried on by the philosophy. In fact, to the degree that Chad Walsh is right and this is the reeducation of the fearful pilgrim, the philosophy could almost be said to *be* the plot.[6]

In that context the climactic episodes of Ransom's sojourn need to be considered, in part because they (more or less ideally) illustrate the intermixture that makes up *Out of the Silent Planet*, and in part because they seem sometimes to have been misunderstood. These are in chapters 17 through 20: the arrival at Meldilorn (including the meeting with the *pfifltrigg*), the meeting with the Oyarsa, the arrival of Weston and Devine (with Weston's "performance"), and the conversation of Weston and the Oyarsa. This last in particular has been attacked on what I take to be incorrect (though far from frivolous) grounds, but all four need to be placed in proper context. One might say in proper eighteenth-century context.

Let me begin by taking the objection commonly made to Weston's "conversation" with the Oyarsa—that the whole affair is low comedy,

---

5. Lewis, *They Stand Together: The Letters of C. S. Lewis to Arthur Greeves (1914–1963)*, ed. Walter Hooper (London: Collins, 1979), 197.

6. Walsh, "The Reeducation of the Fearful Pilgrim," in *The Longing for a Form: Essays on the Fiction of C. S. Lewis*, ed. Peter J. Schakel (Kent, Ohio: Kent State University Press, 1977), 64–72.

even slapstick, inconsonant with the dignity of whatever proper role the critic is envisioning for Lewis (or for Ransom). But this is very like the kind of attack levied against Swift on *Gulliver* and indeed levied against Swift generally. What the critics are missing is the fact that *Out of the Silent Planet* and the rest of the Ransom stories are no more realistic fiction than Swift's *Gulliver* or Johnson's *Rasselas* or even Defoe's *Crusoe* are realistic fiction. They are *told* realistically, to be sure. There is an accumulation of "realistic" details. But listen for a moment to Gulliver's departure from the Land of the Houyhnhnms, and reflect on the question whether Swift or Lewis is painting in strokes of broader comedy (and, at least in passing, on the question whether there is not an obvious connection between the language of the Houyhnhnms, with its persistent initial *h*, and the similar language of the *hrossa*):

> I was forced to wait above an Hour for the Tide, and then observing the Wind very fortunately bearing towards the Island, to which I intended to steer my Course, I took a second Leave of my Master: But as I was going to prostrate myself to kiss his Hoof, he did me the Honour to raise it gently to my Mouth. I am not ignorant how much I have been censured for mentioning this last Particular. Detractors are pleased to think it improbable, that so illustrious a Person should descend to give so great a Mark of Distinction to a Creature so inferior as I.[7]

Perhaps we should expand the question: not only is the comedy broader, but is the satire more savage in Swift or in Lewis? And perhaps, recalling that Gulliver's canoe is made from the skins of the Yahoos, even these questions are mild.

The vision of Meldilorn is in some ways very much the vision of the earthly paradise, though it is on a world other than the earth. But it is a "classic" vision, which I take to be very much an eighteenth-century phenomenon: "He had not looked for anything quite so classic, so virginal, as this bright grove—lying so still, so secret, in its coloured valley, soaring with inimitable grace so many hundred feet into the wintry sunlight. . . . Sweet and faint the thin fragrance of the giant blooms came up to him" (*OSP*, 118–19). Then (and already the description suggests the "prospects" of the eighteenth-century garden) comes the gradual learning that, like the formal garden, this is an *achieved* paradise. The *pfifltrigg*, with his bag-wig (or its appearance), is rather like an eighteenth-century version of a nineteenth-century craftsman: "rather like one of Arthur Rackham's dwarfs . . . and

7. Swift, *Gulliver's Travels*, 282.

rather like a little, old taxidermist whom Ransom knew in London"
(*OSP*, 127). He is both artist and artisan, in a way more common in
past centuries than in ours.

The decorations (so to speak) that surround the "trial" itself are, of
course, medieval: "He might, when the time came, be pleading his
cause before thousands or before millions: rank behind rank about
him, and rank above rank over his head, the creatures that had never
yet seen man and whom man could not see, were waiting for his trial
to begin" (*OSP*, 134). The resemblance to the ranks of heaven in the
medieval cathedral comes to mind. But the function of the trial,
within the pattern or structure of the book, is from quite a different
tradition. Here we have, I believe, an author conscious of himself as
an author more than as a redactor; here we have (so to speak) Fielding
revealing the truth of Tom Jones's parentage, thus putting an end to
his adventures, or Gay sending the King's pardon to Macheath. The
sword that has apparently been hanging over the protagonist's head
from the outset (or very nearly the outset) is neatly whisked away—
indeed, it was never there at all.

The arrival of Weston and Devine, with Ransom's seeing "the
human form with almost Malacandrian eyes" (*OSP*, 141), is essentially a Swiftian exercise. When Gulliver returns from Brobdingnag,
he sees his surroundings with Brobdingnagian eyes: "My Wife ran
out to embrace me, but I stooped lower than her Knees, thinking she
could otherwise never be able to reach my Mouth. My Daughter
kneeled to ask my Blessing, but I could not see her till she arose;
having been so long used to stand with my Head and Eyes erect to
above Sixty Foot."[8] And from this we pass into the comedy of Weston's conversation and the trip back to Thulcandra, a "conclusion, in
which nothing is concluded."

Those six words are the title of the final chapter of Dr. Johnson's
The History of Rasselas, Prince of Abyssinia, with which, despite
obvious surface dissimilarities, *Out of the Silent Planet* has much in
common. Not only are they much of a length, but the structures are
remarkably like, both being travels intermixed with philosophy, the
story being more in the philosophy than in the travels. Since a guided
tour of *Rasselas* would be out of place here, let me instead quote one
of the book's more recent editors. "We read *Rasselas* for the solidity of
its wisdom . . . and the verbal force and skill with which that wisdom
is pressed home, out of our realization that the author is concerned
with fundamentals rather than incidentals . . . and for its humour."

8. Swift, *Gulliver's Travels,* 149.

He goes on to remark that "Johnson's thought is drawn by the horses of instruction rather than the tigers of wrath, to use Blake's distinction" and to quote John Wain's characterization of *Rasselas* as putting "one in mind of a dragonfly—a purposeful and powerful body moving on wings of gauze."[9] All of which describes *Out of the Silent Planet*.

At the end of his pilgrimage, Ransom returns to Thulcandra, walks (possibly naked but I have never been sure) into a pub, and orders "A pint of bitter, please" (*OSP*, 172), thus echoing (probably unconsciously) Johnson's stanzas in which he asks of the "Hermit hoar, in solemn cell," the question "Where is bliss? and which the way?" and receives the answer "Come, my lad, and drink some beer."[10] Even if the precise echoing is unconscious, Lewis's own Johnsonian character comes out in the conclusion. Or perhaps "conclusion" is the wrong word, since there remains chapter 22, in which Lewis the author comes out from the wings, and the Postscript in which Ransom criticizes Lewis's auctorial effort and provides a brief first-person reminiscence of Malacandra. This is all, I believe, more within the eighteenth-century tradition than within the modern.

In *Perelandra* Lewis carries this technique about as far as he can, and I will look therefore at the completed second volume before looking at the uncompleted one, to which Father Hooper has given the title *The Dark Tower*. *Perelandra* pushes the form of the eighteenth-century novel so hard as to come up with a genuinely new thing. The "differentness" has been recognized by recent critics, but the eighteenth-century origins have not, which has led to a curious feature in the criticism. One of the best of recent books of Lewis criticism notes that in *Perelandra* Lewis has turned to a mechanism more supernatural and less scientific than in *Out of the Silent Planet* and finds this linked with the novel's differences in tone.[11] That the "machine" in *Perelandra* is less mechanical may indeed be tied to the greater theological content of the book, but I doubt it is very much

9. D. J. Enright, ed., "Introduction" to *The History of Rasselas, Prince of Abissinia* (Harmondsworth: Penguin, 1976), 9, 11, 12; Enright quotes Wain, *Samuel Johnson* (New York: Viking, 1974), 214.

10. Johnson, *The Complete English Poems*, ed. J. D. Fleeman (New Haven: Yale University Press, 1982), 132.

11. Donald E. Glover, *C. S. Lewis: The Art of Enchantment* (Athens: Ohio University Press, 1981), 95; I do not recall, however, that he quotes Lewis's own statement that he was wiser when he sent Ransom to Perelandra by angelic power than when he sent him to Malacandra in a spaceship (Lewis, "On Science Fiction," in *Of Other Worlds: Essays and Stories*, ed. Walter Hooper [London: Geoffrey Bles, 1966], 69).

tied to differences in tone; they are essentially the differences between the mythic Mars and the mythic Venus. Whatever it is tied to,
the tie is more complex than the critic's relatively simple statement
would suggest. After all, before we examine Lewis's answer to a particular auctorial problem, we should certainly know what the problem is and should probably know in what tradition he approached it.

The problem, on one quite obvious level, is what to do with
Ransom now that we have him back from Mars—to which the obvi-
ous answer is, we send him to Venus. (Just so might Swift, having
Gulliver back from the land of the Lilliputians in the South Pacific,
decide he should send him to the land of the Brobdingnagians in the
North Pacific.) On another nearly as obvious level, the problem is
how to have Ransom, who has been given a special revelation on
Malacandra, make use of that revelation in fulfilling God's saving
purposes. Had Lewis finished the time fragment generally known as
The Dark Tower, this would, I believe, have been what it was "about,"
and I can reconstruct roughly the theological line I think it would
have taken. The title I envision is *An Exchange in Time,* and the word
"exchange" should not merely recall Charles Williams but give a
strong indication of what Ransom's function might have been. Of
course he did not finish it, and instead of answering the question
"What do we do with Ransom now that he has traveled in space?" he
answered (as we have noted) the question "What do we do with
Ransom now that we have him back from Mars?" The form of the
question demands the answer—the Gulliverian answer.

We are set then with Ransom as, in some way, a mediator, a type of
Christ or at the very least a servant of Maleldil, and we are set that he
will be going to Venus (or rather, to Perelandra, since we have already
been introduced to that name in *Out of the Silent Planet* [102] and we
already have a man whose name is Ransom, not—for example—
Unwin, or something else less suitable). Is he then to have, on Perelandra, a series of adventures interspersed with philosophical conversation, where a pageant is played out across an heraldic *but detailed* landscape? Just so.

But something happened in the writing: the description of Perelandra ran riot. The pictures with which Lewis's writing "all began"
came tumbling over one another in such profusion that they could
not fully be brought into the story. The background and the heraldry
threatened to overwhelm the pageant (the travels) and the philosophic story. The visions of landscape cease to exist for the sake of the
story; instead they begin to have a life (perhaps it is a Jungian life) of
their own. They are what make *Perelandra* memorable, but they are

not what make it go. They are not even there to adorn the tale. They are fully subordinated neither to the character of this hero nor to the demands of the story. (Admittedly they illustrate his view of mythology, but it is highly unlikely that was their design.)

Something else also happened in the writing. The "conversations" became a battle—not with humor, as in Weston's "conversation" with the Oyarsa of Malacandra, but in deadly earnest, and not for the sake of the reader, with the author coming onstage at the end, but for the sake of the whole world. Since theology (as I have elsewhere argued)[12] begets mythopoeia, this may go some way toward explaining the descriptive mythological passages in *Perelandra*. What is more significant is that it forces Lewis to approach, if not transcend, the bounds confining his predecessors, and thus to make the final "conversation" visual and operatic both. It is important to recognize that this final "conversation," the Great Dance, is not unearthly and neither, indeed, is the rest of *Perelandra*. Lewis's Venus is drawn from earthly images. If there are new creatures, they are like those to be found in medieval bestiaries. If there are new landscapes, Lewis has given us their origin: "He opened his eyes and saw a strange heraldically coloured tree loaded with yellow fruits and silver leaves. Round the base of the indigo stem was coiled a small dragon covered with scales of red gold. He recognised the garden of the Hesperides at once" (*Per,* 49). Perelandra is, to be sure, mythological, but it is a well-established earthly mythology.

Yet this very mythology is what, along with the description, plays against the traditional form of *Perelandra*, the Swiftian or Johnsonian form. In *Out of the Silent Planet*, Swiftian form and Swiftian humor go together. Here, though occasional passages—the description of Weston's arrival on Perelandra, for example, or "Weston's" lecturing to Ransom after his arrival—and the leisure-time activities of the Unman have a Swiftian ring, the book is escaping its bounds.[13]

And as *Perelandra* escapes its bounds, it becomes, as we have said, a new thing, rather (though the parallel may seem forced) as Beckford's *Vathek* or even Walpole's *Castle of Otranto* became a new thing. Unlike Walpole's work, it has had no imitators; like it, it had an

12. See my *England and Always: Tolkien's World of the Rings* (Grand Rapids, Mich.: Eerdmans, 1981), 81–83.

13. My linking of Lewis's humor with Swift's, both here and earlier, is not purely idiosyncratic, as a comment by Derek Brewer makes clear: "He enormously enjoyed Swift's humour and thought his work fuller of real laughs than almost any other" ("The Tutor: A Portrait," in *C. S. Lewis at the Breakfast Table and Other Reminiscences*, ed. James T. Como [New York: Macmillan, 1979], 49).

immediate effect in the world of letters, from the 1948 *Atlantic Monthly* poem referring to "Sun of shadow and light / On a lost perelandran lane" to the paean in Marjorie Hope Nicolson's pioneering work on interplanetary voyages.[14] The effect shows the strength of *Perelandra,* and the lack of imitators testifies to its singularity.

Even *The Lord of the Rings, sui generis* at its publication, has had its imitators (far too many for my taste), but *Perelandra* has not. And if we look at it with the idea that it is science fiction cleared away and without our views of Tolkien or Charles Williams obscuring it, we can surely see why. Tolkien's book grew out of the Edwardian adventure story and Williams's out of the popular novel of the 1920s and early 1930s. Both of these are part of the immediate literary heritage of the twentieth century. Still more, both come from popular storytelling, and are thus ripe for imitation by popular storytellers (though, to be sure, only Madeleine L'Engle comes to mind as having followed in Williams's way). But Lewis, though he made himself into a storyteller, did not come by it naturally: the conversation, the scenery, the "realization" of different worlds (and these three not only in the Ransom stories, but in *Screwtape* and *The Great Divorce* and *The Pilgrim's Regress*) are his strong points. He could not see how to finish the time fragment; he set an overly schematic plot line for *That Hideous Strength*; he had trouble finishing his narrative poems; he eventually turned to "realizing" mythic stories in the Narnia books and in *Till We Have Faces,* in which, of course, he was learning from his medieval rather than his eighteenth-century predecessors.

In short, for a man who sang the beauties of "story" he had grave difficulties in producing one. This is not said in denigration. It was once said of Lewis that "he was a very good man, *to whom goodness did not come easily*"[15]—and equally he was, in the end, a very good storyteller, to whom storytelling did (or at least had) not come easily. About Lewis's juvenilia, the "Boxen" stories, Father Hooper has commented that "there is not the slightest bit of evidence on a single page of the juvenilia that the author had to labour to find 'filling' for his really good plots: the stories seem to write themselves."[16] Here, of course, he speaks as the expert and I from ignorance, but it does occur to me that a boy who entitles his juvenile creations *Boxen: or Scenes from Boxonian City Life,* or *The Life of Lord John Big of*

14. Daniel J. Berrigan, S. J., "Failure," *The Atlantic Monthly,* May 1948, 107; Nicolson, *Voyages to the Moon* (New York: Macmillan, 1948), 251–55.

15. Brewer, "The Tutor," 64.

16. Hooper, Preface to *Of Other Worlds,* vi.

Bigham, in 3 Volumes, has fairly definite models before him, from precisely the sort of books we would expect to find on his father's bookshelves. We should not be too far wrong if we traced the titles to such originals as, say, *The Life of Henry Lord Brougham, in Three Volumes* (I pick this from my own father's books), and though I cannot just now trace the origins of the *Boxen* subtitle, I am sure others can, and they will be found in some English or Irish three-decker of the earlier nineteenth century. But when we examine the Ransom stories *as stories* we must recognize that they are from a tradition we have largely left behind us, a heritage that, far from having squandered, we have put away in storage.

Let me turn now to what Lewis does when he is forced beyond the bounds. The best case is, as I have noted, the Great Dance, but this is far from the only case. In the early part of the book we are still by and large following the form of *Out of the Silent Planet*. Then, at a particular point (as with Jane Studdock at a particular corner of the garden in *That Hideous Strength*), the change comes: when the voice speaks to Ransom in the darkness, a voice revealing its reality by saying, "It is not for nothing that you are named Ransom" (*Per*, 168). We have moved from conversations with men or angels (the Oyéresu) to conversation with God. We have left the Augustan world and entered the Romantic. From this point on, we are in Lewis's vision of Paradise—or, to be fully accurate, of Hell, Purgatory, Paradise, and at last, in the Great Dance, of Heaven.

Ransom's words in chapter 3, "The reason why the thing can't be expressed is that it's too *definite* for language" (*Per*, 35), are a useful lead-in to the Great Dance and to the more purely visionary part of *Perelandra*. In the Great Dance,

> The voice that spoke next seemed to be that of Mars, but Ransom was not certain. And who spoke after that, he does not know at all. For in the conversation that followed—if it can be called a conversation—though he believes that he himself was sometimes the speaker, he never knew which words were his or another's, or even whether a man or an eldil was talking. The speeches followed one another—if, indeed, they did not all take place at the same time—like the parts of a music into which all five of them had entered as instruments or like a wind blowing through five trees that stand together on a hilltop. (*Per*, 246)

Later, a shift in Ransom's perception occurs:

> By a transition which he did not notice, it seemed that what had begun as speech was turned into sight, or into something that can be remembered only as if it were seeing. He thought he saw the Great Dance. It

seemed to be woven out of the intertwining undulation of many cords or bands of light, leaping over and under one another and mutually embraced in arabesques and flower-like subtleties. Each figure as he looked at it became the master-figure or focus of the whole spectacle, by means of which his eye disentangled all else and brought it into unity— only to be itself entangled when he looked to what he had taken for mere marginal decorations and found that there also the same hegemony was claimed, and the claim made good. . . . The whole solid figure of these enamoured and inter-inanimated circlings was suddenly revealed as the mere superficies of a far vaster pattern in four dimensions, and that figure as the boundary of yet others in other worlds: till suddenly as the movement grew yet swifter, the interweaving more ecstatic, the relevance of all to all yet more intense, as dimension was added to dimension and that part of him which could reason and remember was dropped farther and farther behind that part of him which saw, even then, at the very zenith of complexity, complexity was eaten up and faded . . . and a simplicity beyond all comprehension, ancient and young as spring, illimitable, pellucid, drew him with cords of infinite desire into its own stillness. (*Per*, 251–53)

I shall forbear further quotation, this being quite sufficient to demonstrate just how hard Lewis's substance is (so to speak) pressing against his form. (It also, by the way, demonstrates a certain Johnsonian Latinity in his style, which may or may not be relevant to our concerns.) I am not sure to what degree Lewis himself knew what was happening here, but we know that once he had "got Ransom to Venus and through his first conversation with the 'Eve' of that world; a difficult chapter," he realized what he was trying to do must "combine characteristics which the Fall has put poles apart" (*Letters*, 195). It is evident that he knew there would be difficulty in any literary expression of what he wanted to say, and given his concern at the time with the problems of literary form (as, specifically, in *A Preface to Paradise Lost*), I think it likely he knew perfectly well where the sticking point was.

The difficulty was real, and Lewis found a way to handle it, or his genius (in the old sense) found a way for him. This too is "realization," the imaginative reconstruction and filling out of what someone else's experience "must have been like," which is of course the quality Lewis particularly singled out for praise in Malory,[17] and which we have noted as characteristic of the "Englishness of English art." What I believe Lewis has done here is take descriptions, stories, of mystical

---

17. Lewis, "The English Prose *Morte*," in *Essays on Malory*, ed. J. A. W. Bennett (Oxford: Clarendon Press, 1963), 12–13.

experience and "realize" them—whose stories I do not know, but it is unlikely they come from the eighteenth century. Or perhaps they do. Perhaps the Great Dance is a "realization" of what things *must* be like if the plain and practical advice of, say, William Law is to be followed. To put the matter briefly, I am sure what Lewis has done but not what his original materials were.

I have toyed with the thought that the true analogue to the form of *Perelandra* is not to be found in the late eighteenth-century novels that pushed the form to its bounds, but in some nearly forgotten Romantic novels of the century after. But I think not. *Out of the Silent Planet* is classical; in *Perelandra* the romance pushes against the classical bounds, but the bounds are still there. It is not, I believe, accidental that when Ransom is on his first floating island, the simile Lewis uses is "looking down like Robinson Crusoe on field and forest to the shores in every direction" (*Per*, 45). Certainly Lewis must have had Crusoe in mind as he was writing.

The time fragment also is a "conversational" novel, or rather the beginnings of one, and we can make a stab at seeing what would have happened had Lewis continued it.[18] The names of the characters provide us with a pretty good idea of the story Lewis would have told: Scudamour will be a knight rescuing the true Camilla; Orfieu (Orpheus) will, by making a last-minute mistake, lose someone (to Othertime?); Ransom will be the ransom for the person lost—all of which suggests that the book, when finished, would have been sufficiently "theological" in its concerns.

But what kind—that is, what *genus*—of book would it have been, beyond the simple designation as a "conversational" novel? It would, I think, have been more like *Out of the Silent Planet* than like *Perelandra*. The heraldry would have been there, to be sure; some of it is. The curious medievalism of the "normal" life in the Othertime—the Dark Tower and the White Riders (very much the antithesis, one suspects, of Tolkien's Black Riders), the stone seats and the dais in the Tower, the lances of the Riders—suggests a kind of heraldry (and "Englishness") not far from that of *That Hideous Strength*. Moreover, the scientists of the Othertime, the jerkies, the Stingingman (monstrous perversion of the true unicorn), all have a considerable amount in common with the scientists, the dehumanized servants, and the Head of the N.I.C.E. One can easily imagine a "trilogy" in which the middle volume is not *Perelandra*, but (to take my conjectural title) *An*

18. For reasons to consider it Lewis's work, see "The Authorship of *The Dark Tower*" at the end of this essay.

Exchange in Time: Ransom first traveling in space, then in time, and then staying put. But none of this speculation fully answers the question we have set.

I think the book would have been more dry, perhaps more "rational" than *Perelandra,* in keeping with the picture that began it and with the "scientific" or (to bring back a 1920s word) "scientifictional" nature of the time-travel problem. From what we have, we can see that it would have alternated action and conversation, and we can surmise that the "dissolve" would have covered the action in "Othertime" between chapters 4 and 5. It is possible Lewis would have employed the same kind of parallelism between our time and Othertime that he subsequently used between Belbury and St Anne's in *That Hideous Strength,* though it may also be that reluctance to take on such a complex plot structure lay behind his putting the fragment aside. I would argue that he was prepared to write a "conversational" novel with more action than *Out of the Silent Planet,* but not yet (if ever) to write a novel of action.

In the time fragment, Lewis has introduced us to six characters (or seven if one counts Lewis himself), two of whom are known to have doubles in Othertime and three of whom (counting Lewis) seem unlikely to have any major part in the book. MacPhee presumably will play much the same part he plays in *That Hideous Strength.* In fact, it has been suggested that he is already, in the fragment we have, playing that role at far too great a length.[19] Lewis is there to record the action (though, I suppose, he might have a double, as Scudamour and Camilla do, and Orfieu may; Ransom presumably does not). The presence of Cyril Knellie may be merely portrayal of an academic "type" on a par with the portrayals of the Bracton Senior Common Room. Indeed, I detect a kind of academic pun in the fact that a man named Knellie is "nice in his eating," though I decline to believe he is there only for the sake of the pun. I hope he is not there only for the sake of providing us with an academic portrait (in the fragment he does contribute to the confusion that allows Scudamour's double to escape, but he is not necessary for that purpose). From time to time, of course, Lewis does introduce us to characters who then do very little—Grace Ironwood is an example—and it may be that would have been Knellie's fate.

In the end, I suppose, what produced the time-travel fragment was Lewis's disinclination to retravel the road he had traveled in *Out of*

---

19. Walter Hooper, "A Note on *The Dark Tower,*" in Lewis, *The Dark Tower and Other Stories,* ed. Walter Hooper (New York: Harcourt Brace Jovanovich, 1977), 97.

The Silent Planet, a disinclination which had come on him even as he finished that book and which was overcome only by the splendid pictures with which *Perelandra* began. Everything I have said here about *Perelandra* seems to suggest it is the odd man out in the Ransom books, and that the "trilogy" might have been better ordered had the fragment been finished as the middle volume. I think that is true, though *Perelandra* is certainly closer to being a great work than the fragment is likely to have been and though I am far from wanting to give it up. I suppose I have reread it thirty times or more. I have reread *The Dark Tower* twice.

Nevertheless, *Perelandra* has had one unfortunate effect. It has made it harder for readers coming on *That Hideous Strength* from its predecessors to accept the concluding volume on its own terms—harder than if they had come on it from reading our hypothetical *Exchange in Time.* The sensuousness of the descriptions, the realization of the mystic experience in the Great Dance, the feel of Perelandra and, I think, the beauty of holiness, all make it hard to come back to earth. They make it especially hard to come back to the earth of Bracton College and the N.I.C.E. And they certainly do not make it easy to receive and recognize the heraldry, the pageant, the gilding, and the "Englishness" which are in fact present in *That Hideous Strength.*

It is, Lewis says, a fairy tale: it begins in humdrum surroundings and at a time only vaguely designated, and goes from there to the "witches and ogres," or "pantomime animals" and "planetary angels," of Faerie (*THS,* 7). But not, in the case of the animals and angels, entirely of Faerie. Lewis may have come to inhabit that realm in the Narnian books (though Tolkien thought not),[20] but there is little or none of it in *That Hideous Strength,* and none at all in the other Ransom stories. This is not surprising. Lewis's roads lead to Heaven or Hell, but the road to Elfland, as we know from ballads—and from *The Queen of Drum* (*NP,* 129–75)—is the road between. Tolkien succeeded in combining Faerie with traditional Christian doctrine, but only in a pre-Christian world very far from the world of Elwin Ransom.

No, what we have in this "fairy tale" is not Faerie but myth, designed to bring to earth the pageantry of *Out of the Silent Planet* and *Perelandra.* In fact, there are two sets of myth, Williams's Arthur-

---

20. Humphrey Carpenter, *The Inklings: C. S. Lewis, J. R. R. Tolkien, Charles Williams, and Their Friends* (London: George Allen and Unwin, 1978), 223–24; but cf. Joe Christopher, "J. R. R. Tolkien, Narnian Exile," *Mythlore* 15, no. 1 (1988): 37–40.

iad and Tolkien's "mythology for England." They are not perhaps mixed entirely successfully, though the mixing (given the ingredients) probably is done as well as it could be. We should not on this account overlook the considerable strengths of the book. For one thing, there is (though it is overly schematic) a real plot, as complex as *Tom Jones* with other similarities as well: the young man and the young woman reunited at the end, both having learned virtue (and the woman having the easier part, as in *Tom Jones*). I make the comparison not because I think *That Hideous Strength* is Lewis's *Tom Jones* in the sense that *Out of the Silent Planet* may be his *Rasselas* or the two extraplanetary novels his *Gulliver*; to think that would be merely silly. I make it, rather, to emphasize the degree to which the English literary tradition, especially that of the eighteenth century, involves the teaching of virtue and to emphasize that a happy ending does not detract from a book's quality.

Indeed, if I were required to find a major English novel that provides an analogue for *That Hideous Strength*, I should be in trouble, because novels of ideas would not be "university" novels until the reformation of the universities in the nineteenth century. (This fact may help explain why eighteenth-century English novelists so frequently set even their "tutorial" novels in foreign countries.) We should probably look to see the ways in which eighteenth-century England expected ideas to be disseminated (besides on the tour), if we are to find any signs of an analogue to the university novel. Of course, *That Hideous Strength* is only partly a university novel, but it is in this part we might properly seek those signs.

It turns out we find a curious and transforming answer in this inquiry. Because the eighteenth-century universities were at their nadir as institutions of education, one of the chief institutions of education was made up of writers, most of whom used the novel as their chief instrument of education. One can see Professor Defoe of the economics faculty, Professor Swift in political science, Professor Fielding in sociology (and criminal justice), Professor Johnson (English and religion), Professor Walpole (art). Any conscientious eighteenth-century English novelist would be didactic, would be writing a novel of ideas, would in fact be writing a novel whose *personae* would quite properly discuss ideas because that was what the reader was looking for.

In one sense, then, any eighteenth-century novel is analogous to the university novel, which brings us to another strong point (in my view) of *That Hideous Strength*. It should be noted that the kinds of things one says to praise *That Hideous Strength* are the kinds of things one says to praise any old-fashioned novel. The characters are well-drawn ("realized" in our sense); the action follows logically (that is, the characters act "in character" and their action in character is the action of the book); the story is clearly told; the people are "real"; the book "overflows with life." My point is not that all of these are true all the time—there are certainly weak passages—but that this is the kind of statement whose degree of truth determines the book's success. Though it speaks with the tongues of men and of angels, it is rarely mythopoetic (Lewis once remarked that he was not very good at "Archangelese"—whether that is true or no, he, like Johnson, is showing us pictures of the "dogs he knows"); in fact, one of the difficulties Lewis's admirers seem to have is that the book remains resolutely earthbound until Ransom is ready to leave the earth.

To put it another way, the sudden transformation from "serious novel" to farce and vision (more or less simultaneously) leaves a considerable number of readers cold. The farce is, of course, well within the Swiftian tradition; what may be harder to recognize is that so also is the sudden vision. If we are unprepared, it is because we understand both "realism" and the function of the novel in ways different from the ways they were understood at least through Dickens. We expect (if subconsciously) that the fairy-tale mode will not obtain—that humdrum scenes will lead to further humdrum scenes, not to pantomime animals and planetary angels.

But do we then prefer the humdrum to the visionary? No, but we like to know where we stand. A mystery writer who introduces a coincidental solution to the mystery is not playing fair: he is instead changing the rules in mid-game. So here—or at least so we think here. That Lewis knew we might think so is shown by his initial warning in the Preface: "I have called this a fairy-tale in the hope that no one who dislikes fantasy may be misled by the first two chapters into reading further, and then complain of his disappointment" (*THS*, 7). He put that warning in its most easily understandable form, of course, much more understandable than if he had said, "I have called this an eighteenth-century English novel in the hope that no one who dislikes the intermixture of *didache*, comic characters, 'real life,' unreal estates, pageant, detailed observation, 'realization' (and so on) that characterizes the form may be misled." But I think the latter form would itself have been much less misleading.

The chief success of the Ransom books, then, comes when they combine Englishness in the medieval tradition—which Lewis studied and which is the origin of Pevsner's insight—with the later Englishness of the first great novelists. Those novelists themselves, looking at the Middle Ages as rude and Gothic, could not make that combination. Lewis could, and did.

The Authorship of *The Dark Tower*

I am aware that Kathryn Lindskoog thinks *The Dark Tower* is by a hand other than Lewis's.[21] It may be so, of course ("never say 'never'"), but it seems unlikely to me, on internal evidence. Professor Lewis was "a voracious and retentive reader,"[22] who was easily influenced by his models, and he did not settle into his recognized style until the early 1940s at the earliest. One of his letters to E. M. W. Tillyard in *The Personal Heresy*, as Owen Barfield has noted, is virtually pastiche.[23] If *The Dark Tower* is not so well written as other Lewis books, we might ask under whose influence it was written, and we should in any case note that he wrote himself into a corner and, failing to find a way out, simply stopped.

The point is not whether Gervase Mathew heard Lewis read the story or whether Lewis read it to the Inklings (being dissatisfied and not having a story that "went" anywhere, it would not be surprising if he read something else instead). The point is not whether the story is inferior to Lewis's other long fiction (it is, though not by much inferior to *The Pilgrim's Regress*). The point is not that the book shows a dark side of Lewis (the critics who argue this may be falling into the personal heresy—and in any case it is hard to see how it is darker than some of *The Pilgrim's Regress*). The point is simply that the book fits not only as a first attempt at following up *Out of the Silent Planet,* but as a first attempt at a middle work between *Out of the Silent Planet* and *That Hideous Strength.* I would note also that, although there are arid stretches and places where Lewis is still seeking his style, the best parts are too good and too "Ludovician" to be by another hand. I suppose my reaction to the view that the dull parts make it unlikely it was written by Lewis is that they make it even less likely it was written by a forger expert enough to do the good "Ludovician" parts. Even Homer nods, but a pseudo-Homer would try to nod in a recognizably Homeric way.

I suggest that the fundamental weakness of *The Dark Tower* lies in the attempt to combine the novel of ideas with allegory. The action is

21. Lindskoog, *The C. S. Lewis Hoax* (Portland, Ore.: Multnomah, 1988).
22. J. R. R. Tolkien in a letter to me of December 1963.
23. Barfield, Introduction to *Light on C. S. Lewis,* ed. Jocelyn Gibb (London: Geoffrey Bles, 1965), x.

stiff and strained because the plot is based on allegory, the transitions are awkward because they do not flow naturally with the story, and the talk is "talky" because ideas and allegory do not meld. Moreover, Lewis, with all his fascination with J. W. Dunne and the science of time, was not a scientist (nor was Dunne), and he is trying to imagine an "otherscience" for his "othertime." Stephen Hawking or Charles Sheffield might do it, but not, apparently, C. S. Lewis.

But this whole question of forgery seems to me rather a nuisance than a useful scholarly endeavor. I am constrained to consider it because it has recently become in certain circles a *cause célèbre*, but I had rather be otherwhere.[24]

24. George Sayer made the following comments in a lecture entitled "The C. S. Lewis I Remember," at Wheaton College, 11 October 1989: "I think the main charge, the charge about the *Dark Tower*, is nonsense. I think that's an inferior work . . . but I believe it is by Lewis. I think that for two reasons. Partly because I recognize the writing—I've seen a facsimile—as that of a certain period; and also because I remember his mentioning to me in conversation one or two of the ideas that are to be found in the book." See also John D. Rateliff, "The Kathryn Lindskoog Hoax: Screwtape Redux," *Mythlore* 15, no. 4 (1989): 53–56, which analyzes in detail the question of the authorship of *The Dark Tower*.

The Multiple Worlds
of the Narnia Stories

Michael Murrin

In the Narnia series C. S. Lewis developed an elaborate cosmological dialectic. Normally, this dialectic, this juxtaposing or contrasting of opposites which forces a two-way critical evaluation of both, depends on the interaction between two parallel worlds, that of Narnia and our own universe. At times, however, Lewis complicates this situation. He either adds more parallel worlds, as in *The Magician's Nephew*, or imagines a Platonic situation where one world mirrors a higher world, and that still another, as in *The Last Battle*. In fact, cosmological dialectic is central to the plots of these two books. Lewis wrote them last, with the rest of the series in mind, and they explain the origin and end of the Narnian cosmos. They also help to interpret the dialectic in the whole series.

This interplay between worlds suggests two interpretative possibilities which Lewis found in his sources. He used both the dialogues of Plato and the tradition of the art fairy tale, initiated by the German romantics, who distinguished the conscious creation of the individual artist from the folk fairy tale, an anonymous story told among the people. Lewis, while he accepted the distinction and wrote art fairy tales, really preferred Plato to the romantics. The analysis which follows will clarify the implications of this preference, mostly through the Narnia stories themselves, occasionally through Lewis's other works and those of his friend, Tolkien.

Interpretation of Lewis's dialectic requires first an understanding of its mechanics, in this case the various means by which he connects worlds. The children have four ways of transit between England and Narnia: by a door, by a picture, by a railroad station, and by rings which take them to the Wood between the Worlds. These ways open

This essay originally appeared in *VII: An Anglo-American Literary Review* 3 (1982): 93–112.

up several areas of interpretation, which, taken together, make up the basis for Lewis's dialectic.

Ways of Transit

I. The Door

The door is the normal mode of transit. We see its simple form in *Prince Caspian, The Voyage of the "Dawn Treader," The Silver Chair,* and *The Last Battle.* The children go through a door, directly from one world to another. *Prince Caspian* provides a dramatic example, where the children see two uprights and a crossbeam in empty space: "At one end of the glade Aslan had caused to be set up two stakes of wood, higher than a man's head and about three feet apart. A third, and lighter, piece of wood was bound across them at the top uniting them, so that the whole thing looked like a doorway from nowhere into nowhere" (188). When someone walked through the door, "Everyone's eyes were fixed on him. They saw the three pieces of wood, and through them the trees and grass and sky of Narnia. They saw the man between the doorposts: then, in one second, he had vanished utterly" (*PC*, 192).

In Narnia this door seems absurd. It does not lead into a room, is not even part of a building. Aslan explains why. It leads nowhere in Narnia because it leads out of Narnia altogether: "There were many chinks or chasms between worlds in old times, but they have grown rarer" (*PC*, 190). An interconnection between worlds must seem useless within a particular world or at least must serve another, humbler function, like the door of a wardrobe. As a mode between worlds, however, the door is wonderful. Onlookers watch the children walk between the uprights and vanish, while the children themselves see another universe. This wonder has an interpretative function and helps Lewis define his art within the tradition of the fairy tale.

In his essay "On Fairy-Stories," Tolkien uses the door as a metaphor when discussing the significance of moving from ordinary time into another temporal dimension, which we experience when we read fairy stories: "They open a door on Other Time, and if we pass through, though only for a moment, we stand outside our own time, outside Time itself, maybe." Tolkien attempts to convey this sense of the past at the outset of *The Hobbit:* "One morning long ago in the quiet of the world, when there was less noise and more green."[1] Lewis

---

1. J. R. R. Tolkien, "On Fairy-Stories," in *Essays Presented to Charles Williams,* ed. C. S. Lewis (London: Oxford University Press, 1947), 57; *The Hobbit; or There and Back Again* (London: George Allen and Unwin, 1937), 1.

uses the formula to begin *Prince Caspian.* He puts his child heroes in
a ruined castle, where they experience a sense of long ago. Next they
discover that this long ago is "Other Time," for they realize that they
once lived in the castle. There is a difference between Tolkien's and
Lewis's use, and this difference indicates how Lewis wishes to affect
his readers.

While Tolkien uses the door metaphorically to suggest our experience when we read a fairy tale, Lewis uses it literally, as part of his
plot. By doing so he distinguishes his stories from folk fairy tales. A
folk fairy tale frequently begins in fairyland; the characters are from
the outset participants in a world different from ours. Lewis, however, makes his characters part of our world and then has them pass
through a door into fairyland. He has taken Tolkien's metaphor, used
to explain folk fairy tales, and put it inside his own story so that the
characters enact within the tale the transformation which takes place
in *reading* a folk fairy tale. Moreover, he has made the door one of the
most wonderful things in stories where we expect gingerbread houses
and talking animals. With this additional marvel Lewis forces his
readers to reflect on his art, and it is this self-consciousness which
distinguishes the art from the folk fairy tale. Lewis looks to the
tradition of Ludwig Tieck and George MacDonald more than to that
of the brothers Grimm.

At the same time, the door serves a philosophical, Platonic function, for it points to the familiar ladder of imitation. In *The Lion, the
Witch and the Wardrobe,* the wardrobe door connects England and
Narnia because it is the last in a descending series. Its wood comes
from a tree in London that was planted from a Narnian seed, so above
this tree is a magical one in another world. Above that tree is still
another, the tree with silver apples which grows in the Narnian
paradise. In Platonic terms the first two trees are diminishing replicas
of this original one, and this Platonic notion of imitation helps to
interpret a familiar paradox in the Narnia books. For the children the
inside of the wardrobe is larger than the outside because it leads them
to Narnia, out of a closet into a new universe. Peter remarks: "I
suppose this whole country is in the wardrobe" (*LWW*, 56). He expresses in spatial terms a qualitative difference: Narnia is morally
superior to England. At this point the concern is only ethical. Peter is
not aware of the history of the wardrobe and does not think vertically.
It is in *The Last Battle* that Lewis dramatizes the ontology of Platonic
imitation.

Lewis indicates his ontological concern by a reevaluation of the
two scenes which we have just discussed and which he recapitulates:

the door in empty space and the wardrobe. The children first enter a stable and find inside it another world, so that, as with the wardrobe, they realize that the inside of the stable is larger than its outside. Next Lewis recalls the experience of *Prince Caspian,* for from within the stable door looks as if it stands alone in the open air. Tirian walks around this door, yet he sees historical Narnia through it (*LB,* 141–42). So far we have recapitulation, but the children next come upon an ontological puzzle. They eventually realize that the world inside the stable is another Narnia, with the same inhabitants and geographical contours. Moreover, this Narnia is physically larger than historical Narnia. Digory, the professor, draws the Platonic moral that historical Narnia is but a shadow of the real Narnia (*LB,* 169–71). The world within is more real than the historical world, and Lewis again expresses this superiority partially through a quantitative metaphor: distances are much greater in the inner world.

The children next discover an ontological series. They travel up to the Narnian garden of paradise only to repeat the previous experience. The inside is larger than the outside; the inside turns out to be Narnia; and this Narnia is larger than the previous Narnia. And here Lewis translates the Platonic ontological hierarchy into a literal ascent in the plot. The refrain which draws the children on is double: farther *up* and farther *in.* They climb a steep hill to get to paradise, then realize that they have in fact ascended a cliff, endlessly high. Next they see that the garden world is only the spur of a much higher mountain.

At the end of *The Last Battle,* the children see a mountainous terrain which recalls a familiar pattern, both vertical and geometric. Mountains surround Narnia in all three of its manifestations. Initially, there is Archenland to the south, the Giants' hills to the north, ice-covered mountains west, and far to the east, beyond the sea, the immeasurably high mountain which the children call Aslan's country. That country in turn suggests the Narnian paradise, for it has a cliff thousands of feet high. The landscape below is so far away that a viewer could not say whether he saw land or sea (*SC,* 21). In *The Last Battle* the children now perceive that mountains enclose their whole world (*LB,* 181). Aslan's country seems only one peak or plateau in a range, which has a peculiar feature. Though immeasurably high, the peaks lack a zone of snow and glaciers (*VDT,* 218; *LB,* 182). While this would be a scientific impossibility inside a world, these mountains make a circle outside the Narnian universe.

As they advance toward this range, the children see multiple worlds. England appears as a mountain range to the left, seen first, as mountains often are, as a brightly colored cloud. Then the children become aware of a new geometric pattern. They perceive that the peak which they call Aslan's country is the center, while the separate worlds are necks of land which become narrower and closer to each other, as the children approach the great peak (*LB*, 181–82). The new geometry presupposes a single high mountain, a center point to lower mountain ranges, which radiate from it as do spokes from the hub of a wheel.

The two views complement each other. From Narnia it looks as if mountains circle the world; from Aslan's country all the mountains radiate out. It is the same reality, but its appearance depends on where the children stand:

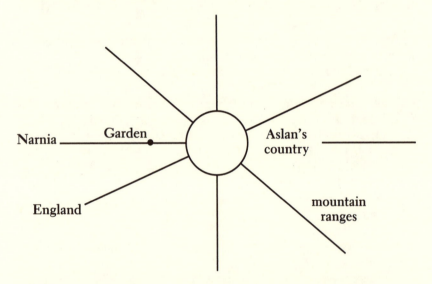

Wherever the children travel from Narnia, they eventually come to mountains, and so one would assume that mountains circle it. The children are misled by their perspective, for Narnia itself is a spoke in a wheel which is a mountain system. As we shall see, such shifts in points of view provide Lewis with narrative equivalents for the give-and-take of Socratic dialectic. This geometry explains why Aslan's country functions also as a cosmological crossroads. In *The Silver Chair* the children cross directly from England to Narnia and back again, passing each time through Aslan's country, the point where all the universes come together.

The closing sequence of *The Last Battle*, which we have just analyzed, likewise shows the way in which Lewis adapted Platonic dialectic to his plot. The children go through repeated experiences which gradually change their perception of reality. The view from Narnia, while correct, allows the false conclusion that Narnia is surrounded by mountains. Only when they are outside the world do the children perceive the actual pattern, and this geometrical diagram at the same time explains why they were both right and wrong earlier when they looked at the mountains from Narnia. Plato ranks geometry higher than sensible perception because it never lies. While we often make visual errors, guessing that a building is taller or nearer than it is, geometrical measurement indicates the truth. This movement upward requires a constant alteration and modification of judgment, even to a denial of what we see. Lewis takes what is a logical give-and-take in a Platonic dialogue and makes it into the episodes of his story. Finding more than one Narnia, the children must simultaneously see that one differs from another because it is better. Their adventures force them to think dialectically.

II. The Picture

The second mode of connection between worlds is the picture. Lewis uses the picture to begin The Voyage of the "Dawn Treader" (VDT, 11–16). A painting of a dragon-prowed ship reminds the Pevensey children of Narnia, and they get into a debate with Eustace, an unbeliever. Lucy praises the mimesis or realism of the picture: "I like it because the ship looks as if it was really moving. And the water looks as if it was really wet" (VDT, 13). The picture then proves her point, for it comes alive. The children see the Narnian world through its frame. A wind blows into the room, and water splashes them. Trying to pull the picture off the wall, Eustace finds himself standing instead on the picture frame. Terrified, he falls through and down, and a wave knocks the other children after him.

The picture serves two functions: like the door, it has a literary critical use, and philosophically it qualifies Lewis's Platonism. All artists have had to qualify Plato. In the Republic (10.596–98c) Socrates equates art with mere scene or shadow painting, two stages removed from reality. The idea of a couch, or the ontological universal, has its imitations in the couches which men make, and these in turn have their shadows in the paintings by artists, which are useless and confined to a single perspective. A man can walk around a couch made by a carpenter and see a real object from different perspectives. The viewer of a painting has only one view and sees only a phantasm or appearance. Artists traditionally answered this argument with the claim that they did not imitate things of this world but that they intimated through symbols a higher world of which our world is merely an imitation. Such an artist would imitate not the historical but one of the inner Narnias. Lewis, however, does not respond to Plato's argument in this fashion.

He accepts more of it than would a traditional artist. He agrees with Plato that art should reflect a phenomenal reality, for his picture imitates an object which really exists.[2] Moreover, the children value the painting for Platonic reasons, since it *reminds* them of Narnia (*VDT,* 12). At the same time, the painting does not represent a single view: the children see the ship from more than one perspective because it *moves.* The picture suddenly resembles a drama or a motion picture, and this ability to represent motion answers one of Socrates' criticisms. On the other hand, the children's judgment is provisional, since the picture turns out to be not a film but a window. Plato, Lewis, and Tolkien all reject the dramatic and cinematic, as well as the painterly. These writers share among themselves a preference for narrative, and Lewis closes his scene accordingly. The picture turns out to be neither a painting nor a film but an entry to the Narnian universe and the beginning of a written narrative.

Differences appear when we see why these writers prefer the narrative to the dramatic. Plato rejects art and drama because they confuse one's judgment. The painter deceives by imitating misleading appearances (*Republic,* 10.596–98c), and this deception affects drama because the painter does the stage sets (10.602–3b). The scene painter exploits the weakness of our visual perception, using distance to alter the apparent size of an object and making something appear hollow or convex. Narrative, of course, does not require stage sets and is, therefore, a superior art (*Republic,* 3.393–98b). Lewis and Tolkien, on the other hand, reject drama because it trivializes fantasy. Tolkien argues that fantastic painting tends to be morbid, and he belittles the witches in *Macbeth.* Lewis extends the critique to film, using as his example the film made from *King Solomon's Mines,* a romance which Lewis considers mythic.[3] While Lewis and Tolkien accept the Platonic judgment, their rationale for it is alien. The two defend fantasy, and in this defence they betray the influence of the German romantics.

Lewis, moreover, backs away from a hierarchical classification.

2. Lewis, "Christianity and Literature" (1939), in *Christian Reflections,* ed. Walter Hooper (London: Geoffrey Bles, 1967), 7; cited in Humphrey Carpenter, *The Inklings: C. S. Lewis, J. R. R. Tolkien, Charles Williams, and Their Friends* (London: George Allen and Unwin, 1978), 62–63.

3. Tolkien, "On Fairy-Stories," 68–69; Lewis, "OnS," 92.

Plato assumes a ladder of being, where one couch exists at a higher level than another. The older artists in the Platonic tradition make the same assumption. Narnia, however, while it is aesthetically and morally superior to England, exists at the same ontological level. The picture seems fanciful because another world naturally appears fantastic in ours. The situation fits Kathryn Lindskoog's remark about myth in Lewis: "The implication is that all elements of myth as we know them are shadows of a foreign reality."[4] Juxtaposition replaces the Platonic vertical ascent.

Lewis further distances himself from Plato when he uses the device a second time. This time it is a mirror rather than a picture, an analogy rather than an event. The children have gone through the stable door and are looking at the inner Narnia:

> It is as hard to explain how this sunlit land was different from the old Narnia as it would be to tell you how the fruits of that country taste. Perhaps you will get some idea of it if you think like this. You may have been in a room in which there was a window that looked out on a lovely bay of the sea or a green valley that wound away among mountains. And in the wall of that room opposite to the window there may have been a looking-glass. And as you turned away from the window you suddenly caught sight of that sea or that valley, all over again, in the looking-glass. And the sea in the mirror, or the valley in the mirror, were in one sense just the same as the real ones: yet at the same time they were somehow different—deeper, more wonderful, more like places in a story: in a story you have never heard but very much want to know. The difference between the old Narnia and the new Narnia was like that. The new one was a deeper country: every rock and flower and blade of grass looked as if it meant more. (*LB*, 171–72)

Lewis seems to reverse Plato and argue that the mirror image surpasses its object. He gives three reasons: the mirror scene is deeper, more wonderful, and more like a place in a story. This argument actually reaffirms basic Platonic positions, that art must reflect and that narrative art is the superior form. At the same time, the analogy seems more radical than the picture. A dragon-prowed ship is wonderful, but the mirror scene corresponds exactly to the landscape outside the window. The wonder presumably depends on Lewis's other two points, which are the ones he stresses—the mirror scene suggests a story and is deeper. Every blade of grass looks as if it *means* more.

4. Lindskoog, *The Lion of Judah in Never-Never Land* (Grand Rapids, Mich.: Eerdmans, 1973), 37.

This stress on meaning modifies Lewis's attacks on those who would allegorize his stories.[5] In fact, both Lewis and Tolkien maintain a complex attitude towards the mythic stories they write; they deny allegorical intent but allow for allegorical interpretation. Lewis expressed both when he first read Tolkien. He praised the reality in the background and the mystical value: "The essence of a myth being that it should have no taint of allegory to the maker and yet should *suggest* incipient allegories to the reader."[6] Both factors interrelate, for the mythic story needs a real background. In the analogy, the mirror reflects a real place. It seems wonderful to the viewer because he sees it as another world. For Tolkien, fairy stories are about a place, "the realm or state in which fairies have their being."[7] The author brings that other world to life through his plot. He does not manipulate symbols.

While the author strives to make this other world as lively and as realistic as possible, the reader generates meaning by wondering about this other place. What happens there? Does it obey the same laws? The frame suffices to make the mirrored landscape into another place. This sense of otherness creates depth. The mirrored scene seems deeper, though in reality there is only a surface. Yet the viewer does not merely project meaning on that surface. He stands between two worlds, his own and the one in the mirror or picture. His act of interpretation signals the interaction of the two.

Lewis derives this formula from MacDonald, but it originates with Tieck and the German romantics, who gave to their invented stories the equivalent of the depth we find in a folk fairy tale like "Snow White." They set two worlds parallel to each other, one that of fairy, the other our mundane world. The drama consists in their interaction. Heinrich Heine describes the result effectively, though in negative fashion, in *The Romantic School*, an essay attacking the German romantics as political conservatives and crypto-Catholics. Heine calls attention to scenes in *Der Blonde Eckbert* and *Runenberg*, where the hero feels a secret inwardness, a peculiar sympathy with nature, especially with plants and rocks. He thinks that the trees whisper his name. Everything breathes, everything listens, everything shivers in anticipation.[8] Such landscapes have depth, but not as vehicles for

---

5. Lewis, "Sometimes Fairy Stories May Say Best What's to Be Said" (1956), in *Of Other Worlds: Essays and Stories*, ed. Walter Hooper (London: Geoffrey Bles, 1966), 36.

6. Lewis, Letter to Tolkien, 7 December 1929, quoted in Carpenter, *Inklings*, 30.

7. Tolkien, "On Fairy-Stories," 42.

8. Heine, *Die Romantische Schule, Späte Lyrik*, Introduction by Susanne Teichgräber (Munich: Goldmann, 1964), 70, 15–17.

interpretation in the ordinary sense. The reader knows that the landscape itself is alive and thinking because the hero of the story is at the
place where two worlds meet. Heine connects this method to the medieval Grail story, which for a German means Wolfram von Eschen-
bach's *Parzival.* There the Grail world exists alongside and parallel to
the courtly world of Arthur, and the two occasionally cross. Heine contrasts this with classical art, which is an art of the limited, where Odysseus stands for Odysseus. The medieval is allegorical, and Heine argues
that this art originated in the gospel parables that frequently concern
the kingdom of heaven, which is not of this world but which impinges
on our own. This is an art of the unlimited. Such stories require interpretation not of symbols so much as of an existential situation. The
hero is caught between two or more worlds, which can make conflicting
demands on him and force him to choose. Tieck's heroes normally deny
the other world only to find that it has pursued them into ours.[9]

Lewis talks more simply than Heine. The analogy of the mirror
contrasts reality and story. The reflected world is more wonderful
because the objects seem to be in a story, one we would like to read.
By this explanation Lewis links the presence of other worlds to story,
and the mirror acquires potential significance through story. In this
sense the mirror and the picture go together. Both are mimetic—they
simply reflect. Both are spaces delimited by a frame, which signals
the story as much as the picture or reflection. Tolkien argues that "an
enchanted forest requires a margin, even an elaborate border."[10]
Fairy tales have formal beginnings and endings because story is endless. Such a frame indicates the unlimited, the consciousness that no
story ends, the sense of multiple worlds. In *The Last Battle,* it is also
the geography, the mountains which simultaneously enclose Narnia
and are separate universes.

The first two devices for interconnection allow for the following
inferences. Whether door or picture, they are self-reflexive. They
dramatize what happens every time we read such a tale, and they
draw attention to the genre, that of the art fairy tale. They thus are
the best places to gauge what Lewis is doing.

III. The Railroad Station

The third mode by which Lewis connects worlds is the railroad
station, which is used twice in the series. It appears first in *Prince*

9. See Tieck, *Der Blonde Eckbert, Der Runenberg, Die Elfen* (Stuttgart: Philipp
Reclam, 1965).
10. Tolkien, "On Fairy-Stories," 89 n. H.

Caspian, where the children are yanked out of a sleepy country station to their old castle in Narnia, Cair Paravel, and are returned to the station platform at the end of the story. In *The Last Battle,* a train crashes into a station platform and kills everyone.

Superficially the railroad station performs the same function as the door or picture. At a railroad station people meet, cross each other's routes, and travel in different directions. In *Prince Caspian,* for example, the boys and girls are about to take trains for different places. As such, the railroad station admirably suggests the crossing between worlds and anticipates the more elaborate Wood between the Worlds.

The station differs from the preceding modes in two ways. It does not draw attention to the literary art of the Narnia series, and it modifies the sense for multiple worlds. It is instead associated with separation and death. In *Prince Caspian,* Peter and Susan return to the country station, aware they can never go back to Narnia, and Susan later falls out of the system altogether, as she grows up and forgets about Narnia. She is excluded from the final reunion. On the second occasion all the heroes and heroines from our world die. Whereas the other modes intimate endless possibility, the crossing and recrossing between two or many worlds, this mode closes off possibilities by its association with irreversible actions and death.

IV. The Wood between the Worlds

The Wood between the Worlds is the last and most complicated of the modes and sums up all the others. Its geometry, which parallels that of Aslan's country, relates it to the doors; its pools, which reflect, recall the picture and the mirror; and its effects on people link it to the railroad station. We will start with the last, since it is the topic which we have just been discussing.

First of all the Wood causes forgetfulness:

> The strangest thing was that, almost before he had looked about him, Digory had half forgotten how he had come there. At any rate, he was certainly not thinking about Polly, or Uncle Andrew, or even his Mother. He was not in the least frightened, or excited, or curious. If anyone had asked him "Where did you come from?" he would probably have said, "I've always been here." That was what it felt like—as if one had always been in that place and never been bored although nothing had ever happened. As he said long afterwards, "It's not the sort of place where things happen." (*MN,* 32–33)

Digory has just arrived, yet he feels that he has always been there; Polly says the same immediately (*MN,* 33). Moreover, they are both sleepy, as Polly remarks: "This place is too quiet. It's so—so dreamy. You're almost asleep. If we once give in to it we shall just lie down and drowse for ever and ever" (MN, 34-35). The Wood, being an in-between place, exists outside history, of this or any other universe. In our daily lives we leave our historical concerns temporarily in sleep and finally in death. Perpetual sleep is between the two but is a normal metaphor for death. This is the danger which threatens Digory and Polly, if they stay in the Wood.

The Wood is connected to the door both as an interconnection and as the visualization of interconnections. The initial description makes clear the geometry:

> He was standing by the edge of a small pool—not more than ten feet from side to side—in a wood. The trees grew close together and were so leafy that he could get no glimpse of the sky. All the light was green light that came through the leaves: but there must have been a very strong sun overhead, for this green daylight was bright and warm. It was the quietest wood you could possibly imagine. There were no birds, no insects, no animals, and no wind. You could almost feel the trees grow-ing. The pool he had just got out of was not the only pool. There were dozens of others—a pool every few yards as far as his eyes could reach. You could almost feel the trees drinking the water up with their roots. This wood was very much alive. When he tried to describe it afterwards Digory always said, "It was a *rich* place. . . ." (MN, 31-32)

Each pool is the entrance to a separate universe. We get the following diagram, in which the points are pools:

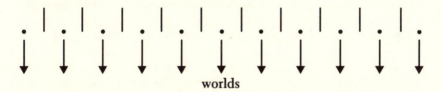

worlds

The geometry of Aslan's mountain had been that of the hub to the spokes in a wheel. Though consisting of mountain ranges, it made a pattern essentially horizontal. Here the emphasis is the same, since all the worlds lead to the Wood. The geometry differs the way a flat map does from a round globe. In both, all the longitudinal lines converge on the North Pole, which on a globe is a point like Aslan's mountain, on a flat map a line at the top, like the Wood between the Worlds. The two places, if they are not identical, must then relate closely to each other.

Lewis describes Aslan's country at the beginning of *The Silver Chair*, and the place does resemble the Wood between the Worlds (*SC*, 19–20). It is a forest of giant trees without undergrowth. All is silent; there is not even a wind. There are, however, differences in the two descriptions. In Aslan's country, brightly colored birds sing an advanced music, which the children do not quite catch at first. The sunshine is that of a summer's day, yet the wood is cool. These positive qualities suggest a paradise, while the Wood is more mysterious and labyrinthine. It has so many pools, and the trees are so close together that all light is filtered light (*MN*, 31). No birds and no music break the stillness. We must account for these differences.

Aslan's country is like paradise because it is eschatological. The good go there after death. The children find Caspian on the mountain just after they have witnessed his funeral in Narnia. The children themselves return there eventually after their railway accident. It is also the place where they will meet their parents, who lived and died in our world. The model for Aslan's country is the Earthly Paradise in Dante's *Purgatory* (Canto 28), from which Lewis borrows the notion of an immeasurably high mountain which has no frigid zone. On the top are old trees, flowers, and a stream. There is no wind, but Dante's Earthly Paradise has air motion produced by the turning of the heavens. Since Aslan's country is eschatological for all worlds, it can serve as a crossover point. One might then argue that the parallels between the Wood and Aslan's country are fortuitous, but this would not explain the similarities in the descriptions.

Lewis hints that the Wood between the Worlds might also have an eschatological dimension. He says that the tree roots drink up water from the pools (*MN*, 32). Are the pools worlds draining into the trees? Does the growth of the Wood correspond to the death of worlds? One pool dries up between visits.[11] Lewis gives no answers and does not develop the hint. He does emphasize, however, that the Wood, like Aslan's country, exists outside of time. He has Digory make the argument:

> I don't believe this wood is a world at all. I think it's just a sort of in-between place. . . .
> Think of our tunnel under the slates at home. It isn't a room in any of the houses. In a way, it isn't really part of any of the houses. But once you're in the tunnel you can go along it and come out into any of the houses in the row. Mightn't this wood be the same?—a place that isn't

11. For an opposite reading, see Evan K. Gibson, *C. S. Lewis, Spinner of Tales: A Guide to His Fiction* (Washington, D.C.: Christian University Press, 1980), 205–6.

in any of the worlds, but once you've found that place you can get into them all. . . .

That's why it is so quiet and sleepy here. Nothing ever happens here. Like at home. It's in the houses that people talk, and do things, and have meals. Nothing goes on in the in-between places. (*MN*, 37)

The Wood is a nowhere from which many "wheres" come. As such it is a simple magnification of the humdrum scene down in London. The two children live in adjacent row houses, and an attic tunnel under the roof connects all the houses in the row. The Wood then resembles Aslan's country both in its hinted eschatological dimension and in its relation to history.

Lewis, however, limits these parallels to the moral dimension. For this purpose he stresses the labyrinthine character of the Wood. Each pool and tree are alike, so the chances that someone might get lost are one hundred to one (*MN*, 39). The labyrinth is, of course, a popular modern image and brings Lewis close to fantasists working in different traditions—to Franz Kafka with his story of the imperial messenger, to Jorge Luis Borges and his libraries, to H. P. Lovecraft and the pulp gothic.[12] Lewis's own analogy is similar, and he includes a labyrinthine city in *The Magician's Nephew*. Digory and Polly come to the vast palace of Charn, empty of inhabitants, in a world about to dissolve (*MN*, 46). There is no end to the courtyards and halls of the palace, and the children never seem to get out. When they at last find the outer gate, they see that the city outside extends to the horizon (*MN*, 61). Lewis thus contrasts labyrinths, the dead urban environment of Charn, with the Wood, a rich place, intensely alive. The characters by their reactions support the contrast. In the Wood, Digory and Polly tend to forget about our world; the witch, however, can never remember the Wood (*MN*, 73). In Charn and London she is ten times more alive than the children (*MN*, 69), but in the Wood she is weak, pale, and dying, while the children have more strength than she (*MN*, 68). The witch fits the dead landscape, the children the living one. The image of the labyrinth thus creates a set of comparisons which in turn encourage an ethical analysis.

The Wood is an index of moral qualities, and it is this function

---

12. Kafka, "Eine kaiserliche Botschaft," in *Erzählungen*, ed. Max Brod, 3d ed. (New York: Schocken Books, 1957), 169–70; Borges, "La Biblioteca de Babel," in *Ficciones* (1956; reprint, Madrid and Buenos Aires: Alianza and Emecé, 1982), 85–95; Lovecraft, "The Dreams in the Witch House," *Weird Tales* 22 (1933): 86–111. Lovecraft assumes that the place between worlds must be labyrinthine and connects it to the angles and planes of the fourth dimension.

which relates it most fundamentally to Aslan's country. Its richness recalls the eschatological paradise, where the good live forever. In addition both places are quiet, removed from historical change. The Wood is also rich epistemologically, since it connects all the worlds. It has cosmological depth like Tieck's wood or the scene in the mirror, where everything is deeper. Besides eschatology, therefore, it recalls the literary critical problems which we discussed through Lewis's second mode, that of the picture and the mirror.

The pools reflect the green branches of the trees and look very deep. This is an optical illusion, since the water comes only to the children's ankles. Yet with the magic rings they can drop through to different universes. Lewis thus presents another variation on his second mode. The mirror was a simple reflection; it seemed deep but was merely a surface. The picture in *The Voyage of the "Dawn Treader"* was a mimetic representation of another world. The pools mirror nowhere or the in-between, and as long as they are taken only as pools, the sense of depth is illusory. Taken as doors, however, they lead to different universes.

The scene allows us to draw some inferences. Fantasy is not a series of symbols like those in the Apocalypse, but a plot with characters in action. Lewis began his essay "On Stories" with the complaint that few critics had concerned themselves with story ("OnS," 90). Fantasy must be mimetic, make a universe which the reader can enter, a world with its own set of laws. A hostile critic, on the other hand, could dismiss fantasy as a superficial art form. It does not reflect our world and has a bizarre cast of characters: children, witches, and talking animals. Lewis allows for this attitude through his images. The mirror and the pond lack depth, and the picture and the ponds reflect scenes which exist nowhere in our world. Depth comes instead from juxtaposition. The mere existence of another world requires the reader and often the hero to reevaluate his own at the same time as he tries to understand the new place. It is not a matter of interpretation but of dialectic.

We have yet to explain why the in-between place should be a quiet wood, why it should resemble the earthly paradise rather than a railroad station. Lewis may have drawn the image from Wilhelm Grimm, who used it when he introduced the second edition of the Grimm collection of fairy tales. Grimm was contrasting saga and fairy tale. Saga is historical—it joins the unusual, that which is far away in the past, to the everyday and the present. Fairy tale, on the other hand, does not belong to our historical world. It is a quiet place which knows no personal and family names or political areas, but belongs to the whole nation. Hänsel lacks a family name, and we never know whether his father lives in the Teutoburger Wald, the Black Forest, or any specific wood. The difference between saga and fairy tale is likewise shown in the characters. Saga has historical personages, while fairy tale has, in addition to royalty, characters closest to Nature, like millers and fishermen, characters who have no previous history. The whole cosmos, however, is animated. Stars give gifts, pixies live in streams, dwarves in the mountains.[13] These characteristics apply as well to Narnia. They are part of the personifications of Nature, when animals, plants, and stones talk. There is no *where* in ordinary fairy tale any more than in Nature, for it is outside history.

Now Narnia itself has a sketchy history, and the characters have personal names. The Wood between the Worlds points rather to the larger genre including both art and folk fairy tale, a quiet place outside our time. This is our basic sense of Narnia. Giants to the north build a palace which decays, and there is the urban, Arabic culture to the south, but in Narnia itself things do not change. There are no new societies, no growth and decay of civilizations, no complex political history. As the unicorn explains to Jill, thousands of years pass with no history (*LB*, 91). What historical crises occur relate to the earth children. The contrast is as much between our time and no time as it is between our time and their time.

Grimm's comparison, while it demonstrates how fairy tale differs from saga, does not indicate the fine differences which distinguish the art from the folk fairy tale, Narnia from "Snow White." Narnia has names and is a place, while folk fairy can dispense with both. Narnia has a sketchy history,[14] while "Snow White" assumes almost none. On the other hand, both forms are far away from the novel, and here Grimm's metaphor is appropriate and applies to both art and folk fairy tale. Compared to a novel of Stendhal, a Narnia story expresses an unhistorical and apolitical world and is hardly to be distinguished from "Snow White." The image of the wood shows what any fairy tale looks like from such a distance. The wood is beyond normal society with its farms and towns—the kind of setting presented in many nineteenth-century novels—and while the wood changes with the seasons, it ignores historical time.

13. Grimm, "Enleitung zur Zweiten Auflage der Kinder- und Hausmärchen," *Die Deutschen Romantiker*, ed. Gerhard Stenzel, 2 vols. (Salzburg: Bergland-Buch, 1954), 1:513–14.

14. Walter Hooper reproduces it in *Past Watchful Dragons* (New York: Collier Books, 1979), 41–44.

The Wood between the Worlds admirably sums up all the concerns which Lewis expresses through his other modes: the door, the picture, and the railroad station. Its pools express the double aspect of a fairy tale, considered as superficial mimesis or dialectically as an encounter with another world. The Wood is outside time and therefore has eschatological implications. Eschatology in turn always involves ethics. It is these concerns which set up the play of dialectic which characterizes the whole Narnia series.

The Dialectic

We have completed our survey of the interconnections between worlds. We can now discuss Lewis's dialectic, beginning with the question of time. In Narnia itself there is time but no change. While Lewis presents a whole planetary history from creation to apocalypse, focusing on temporary threats like those of the witch and the Calormenes, no radical change occurs in Narnia. Instead Lewis complicates his temporal sequence through the dialectic between worlds. The whole history of Narnia corresponds to a single life span on earth. It begins with the arrival of Digory and Polly and ends when the two die in a railway accident. An instant here, therefore, should equal a long time in Narnia. The basic adventure of *The Magician's Nephew*, for example, occurs in a moment, while people quarrel around a London taxi. In *The Silver Chair*, summer holidays in England correspond to the long life span of Caspian in Narnia, and Eustace on his return to Narnia finds his teenage friend now an old, dying man. The pattern, however, also works in reverse. While Tirian dozes briefly, tied to a tree, the children spend nearly a week in England, arranging their rescue expedition (*LB*, 51–52). The contrast of times depends, therefore, on the point of view, and as critics have noted, the two time sequences are irregular when juxtaposed.[15] One year here can equal three or 1303 Narnian years. This unevenness does not, however, change the basic formula: an instant here, whether in our world or Narnia, equals a long time in another world.

This formula may also explain the dreamlike apocalypse which the children watch in *The Last Battle:* "This part of the adventure was the only one which seemed rather like a dream at the time and rather hard to remember properly afterwards. Especially, one couldn't say how long it had taken. Sometimes it seemed to have lasted only a

15. See, for example, Gibson, *C. S. Lewis*, 158, or Hooper, *Past Watchful Dragons*, 39.

few minutes, but at others it felt as if it might have gone on for years" (*LB*, 154). The process presupposes a long time: stars fall, dragons and lizards scour Narnia and die. There is a flood, and the sun and moon are extinguished. The children sense this fact, yet at the same time they see the apocalypse as a speeded up sequence in a motion picture. They do so because they stand in inner Narnia, so a moment there would correspond to a long time in the outer or historical Narnia. The formula applies both to the interconnections of separate worlds and to the Platonic ontology of a particular world, where the historical cosmos mirrors a higher one.

In inner Narnia, the chronological sequences of ordinary time are simultaneous. It is early June, but fruits ripen on the trees (*LB*, 139). This simultaneity frequently marks a paradise, as it does in Milton, where the trees have blossom and fruit together.[16] Platonically, this simultaneity is a way to express the difference between the higher and lower world. Chronology applies only to the lower, phenomenal world. Lewis expresses the new situation both through the paradox of simultaneity and by the negation of time. He does the first here and the second in the Wood between the Worlds.

This dialectic with time sets up the following pattern:

man:	now		future
time:	linear	mixed	
here	there		there
change	no change		no change
England	historical Narnia		inner Narnia

Lewis presupposes our normal distinction between the outer and the inner man and adds the Christian eschatological dimension: man will exist after death. In the Narnia stories the pattern explains why a pool can also connect worlds. Its doubleness depends on the nature of the man who looks at the pool or goes through it to another universe. The "here" of the pattern indicates our external existence in this world, where we live in linear time and are in turn objects which others can walk around, like the doors in empty space. We can also be measured or destroyed. "There" or within our minds our sense of time relates in jagged fashion to external time. Minutes can seem forever. Within we can also experience multiple times simultaneously, and Lewis could argue that we occasionally go outside time altogether. The pattern

16. See *Paradise Lost* 4.147–49.

indicates the parameters of the dialectic which Lewis presents in the
Narnia stories. It was also for him a personal experience.

Lewis presupposes this dialectic in his autobiography. There he
talks of the split life which he began to live in school. There was the
outer life and his inner, imaginative one. The two did not interact but
went on side by side: "The two lives do not seem to influence each
other at all" (*SJ*, 79). Lewis carries this pattern over to his fairy tales.
The children go to school in England, their outer life, and have
wonderful adventures in Narnia, their inner life. The outsider, of
course, regards another's inner life as mere fantasy, hence Eustace's
limerick: "Some kids who played games about Narnia / Got gradually
balmier and balmier" (*VDT*, 13). Lewis says of his own experience: "I
could not help knowing that most other people, boys and grown-ups
alike, did not care for the books I read" (*SJ*, 102).

One world perceived in another normally appears as fantasy or
dream. We discussed it as fantasy when we analyzed Lewis's use of
pictures and mirrors. We have yet to talk about dream. In the Wood
between the Worlds, London seems a dream to the children (*MN*, 34).
The fact that Digory and Polly have both had the same dream starts
them recalling the truth. Lewis presents another version in *The Silver
Chair*. A conversation occurs in Aslan's country during which Caspian explains that, since he now lives on Aslan's mountain, he would
seem a ghost either in Narnia or in England (*SC*, 214). *The Last Battle*
has the most complicated dream sequence because we see the event
from both worlds. In Narnia, King Tirian dreams of our world, where
the children, Digory, and Polly are sitting together at a table (*LB*, 49).
At the same time, Tirian realizes that they perceive him as a ghost
(*LB*, 50). He tries to talk, but as is usual in dreams, he cannot say
anything.[17] Dreaming, then, expresses the perception of one world
by another, whether the first world is ontologically parallel, as Narnia
is to England, or ontologically higher and eschatological, as is Aslan's
country.

Dreaming stresses the confusion of times which runs throughout
Lewis's dialectical plots. Dreams occur very quickly, but they seem to
last a much longer time. And however jumbled, they imply a sequence of events, though not necessarily a plot. We must, however,
keep the analogy dialectical. It must work both ways, as it does when
Tirian dreams of England. Lewis earlier suggested a parallel situa-

17. Lewis may be imitating the séance in David Lindsay's *A Voyage to Arcturus*
(London: Methuen, 1920), which is first presented from the viewpoint of the onlooker
and then from that of the "ghost" (see 18–22, 121–23).

tion, when he tried to explain the *eldila* on Mars: "What we call firm things—flesh and earth—seem to [the *eldil*] thinner, and harder to see, than our light, and more like clouds, and nearly nothing. To us the *eldil* is a thin, half-real body that can go through walls and rocks; to himself he goes through them because he is solid and firm and they are like cloud."[18] The inner world of a mind is fantasy in the outer world of England. The reverse is also true. We have all had experiences where the daily external round of our lives suddenly seems dreamlike, less real than our mental life. For Plato the mental truth of arithmetic, $2 + 2 = 4$, never changes, while things in this phenomenal world do. New houses replace old, rivers change, and mountains rise and erode.

Dreaming, then, expresses the to-and-fro movement of the dialectic which becomes possible at those points where two worlds interact. Time becomes dislocated, and either world can appear dreamlike. Such moments also call into consciousness human nature as we outlined it in the previous diagram, for all man's powers and the realms in which he exists make simultaneous demands on him. These demands can lead to choice, even to action, and it is this ethical dimension which distinguishes Lewis's dialectic from that of other writers of the art fairy tale.

Why We Go Between

Lewis juxtaposes Narnia and England, and in Narnia itself, a world within and a world without. There are a limited number of ways to relate different worlds: we can choose one world over another, which is what Lewis and the Platonists do, or we can deny priority to any, the method of a Tieck and in the twentieth century of David Lindsay. We will consider examples of both ways.

David Lindsay much impressed Lewis with *Voyage to Arcturus* ("OnS," 97-98). In this story Lindsay multiplies moral systems and societies which live by different moral codes and thus cancel each other out. Maskull, the hero, visits societies ruled by altruism, the will to power, the Kantian categorical imperative, and Trinitarian mysticism. He ends up in the Tower of Muspel, the Nowhere which is Somewhere. Muspel is a place beyond good and evil because it is beyond willing. Maskull explains: "Muspel can't be willed for the

18. *OSP*, 107; cited by Richard Purtill, *Lord of the Elves and Eldils: Fantasy and Philosophy in C. S. Lewis and J. R. R. Tolkien* (Grand Rapids, Mich.: Zondervan, 1974), 157-58.

simple reason that Muspel does not concern the will. To will is a property of this world."[19] With this negative dialectic, Lindsay gives a new development to the art fairy tale. In *Runenberg*, Tieck had used romantic irony, where the reader distances himself from both worlds and remains superior to both. A century later, having read Schopenhauer and Nietzsche, Lindsay manifests a later stage in the German philosophical tradition.[20] For his hero all life choices are wrong. Both Lindsay and Lewis think philosophically, draw on the Germans, and develop their fantasies dialectically, but their ethical positions are far apart. Lewis establishes a moral hierarchy.

We can explore the other choice most simply through Plato. I will use the myth of the cave because Lewis does it in reverse fashion for *The Silver Chair*. The myth is an allegory of education and graphically demonstrates how painful learning must be for the student. The final part alone concerns us, once the hero has been dragged above ground. He takes five stages to adjust his eyes to daylight. First he looks at the shadows of things; second, at mirror images in water and shadows; third, directly at men and other objects; fourth, at the moon and stars in the night sky; and, finally, he glances hurriedly at the sun itself. He would conclude that the sun, though blinding to him, is the medium of vision, that by which we see everything else. Socrates allegorizes the myth. Our world, the upper world, stands for the intelligible world and our sun for the idea of the good, barely perceived but the intelligible cause of the just and the beautiful in things (*Republic*, 7.514–18). Lewis's equivalent would be the place between, which has no meaning because it is the place where meaning is generated. This place between is Aslan's country plus its shadow, the Wood between the Worlds. Either serves the function of Plato's sun. Such a place exists above historical worlds, which Lewis imagines as pools in a wood or as spurs of a central mountain. The thinking is Platonic, though the imagery is Dantesque.

The Platonic method has an ethical dimension which serves to distinguish it from the romantic. In Lewis when two things are juxtaposed, one is always better: the man and his shadow, the inner and the outer Narnia. We never doubt morally, as we do in Tieck or Lindsay. For Lewis morality is the same for all worlds, whatever the climate or society. Lewis makes this point theoretically in his prose

19. Lindsay, *Voyage to Arcturus*, 223.
20. J. B. Pick discusses Lindsay's debt to these two philosophers in J. B. Pick, Colin Wilson, and E. H. Visiak, *The Strange Genius of David Lindsay* (London: John Baker, 1970), 7–9.

tracts, where he argues that diverse ancient cultures shared the same moral standards. He presupposes the same moral norm for all the worlds of his Narnia series. Shasta, the hero of *The Horse and His Boy*, has an innate moral sense and is upset that he cannot love the man he erroneously thinks is his father.[21] All children, here or there, love their parents.

In such a dialectic, historical England and Narnia are places of moral testing. They are way stations through which Lucy and Eustace travel to the inner England or the inner Narnia, places where no good thing perishes (*LB*, 182). The witch provides a negative example. She chooses endless life in historical Narnia and seems much more alive in any historical world.[22] Conversely, she shrinks from the Wood between the Worlds and has no part in the inner Narnia. She exists at the rim of the wheel, as far as possible from the center. In this perspective she is not alive at all, and she creates dead environments: the empty ruin of Charn, the long winter in Narnia, the false Hades of *The Silver Chair*. At the beginning of Narnian time, she steals immortality and tempts the boy Digory with it. Yet she does not outlive Digory, whose death brings apocalypse to Narnia.

At the basis of this dialectic is the notion of joy which Lewis discusses in his autobiography. He defines it as the Platonic Eros, "an unsatisfied desire which is itself more desirable than any other satisfaction" (*SJ*, 23–24). "It is never a possession, always a desire for something longer ago or further away or still 'about to be'" (*SJ*, 78–79). In Narnia it is Shasta's desire to know what lies beyond the northern horizon.[23]

Lewis's dialectic helps to prolong this Eros or joy throughout the series. He diagrams the situation in an early fragment. A boy has just been out playing King Arthur and is going home: "It was the strangest systole and diastole—no sooner was home regained, than that other world of desert hills and distant, ominous castles enisled in haunted woods, rose up, clothed in its turn with all the alluring colours of the long-lost. And so one swung backwards and forwards. Each world was best just as you left it for the other."[24] In the Narnia stories the children similarly veer between breathless adventure in Narnia and

21. Gibson cites *The Abolition of Man* and *Mere Christianity* in support of universal moral standards (*C. S. Lewis*, 18). On *The Horse and His Boy*, see Gibson, *C. S. Lewis*, 148.

22. Lewis modeled her on the magician Simon in Charles Williams's *All Hallows' Eve* (London: Faber and Faber, 1945).

23. Gibson points this out in *C. S. Lewis* (148–49).

24. Cited in Hooper, *Past Watchful Dragons*, 25.

the safe humdrum of England. The systole and diastole between worlds makes both more desirable and can occur within an adventure. The children go to Harfang because they are tired of travel and want food and hot baths. This oscillation prolongs Eros throughout the series, delaying the final meeting beyond the worlds.

Lewis explains that the character of joy is determined by its object: "The form of the desired is in the desire" (*SJ*, 208). It is objective, a drive towards something outside the self. The good are travelers, not the witch.

For Lewis, to be beyond good and evil is to be above and *after* good and evil: to be after history, the area of moral choice. So he assimilates the modern tradition of dialectical fantasy to the older Christian and Platonic tradition. However, it is not Tieck's ironic suspension of commitment or its twentieth-century variations. Lewis instead looks to after-choice; he does not suspend it.

In summary this is what Lewis attempts through the interconnection of worlds. First, by his doorways and pictures he draws attention to the nature of his art. Second, by the juxtaposition of worlds, on either side of the door, he creates a narrative equivalent of a Platonic dialectic.

First, there are the self-reflexive images. The picture and the mirror indicate for Lewis the double nature of his own fairy tales. They can be seen as superficial, as mere fantasy, or they can be seen as profound art. They can be seen as mere fantasy because his fairy tales are not symbolic. They can be seen as profound because the reader finds a new world, parallel and additional to his own. Hence Lewis dramatizes the discontinuity between inner and outer time. The reader, however does not withdraw into his imagination. He instead begins a journey out of himself as well as out of his immediate environment. This journey is motivated by longing, by ideal scenes which he cannot help but desire. Historical Narnia is idealized but a world close enough to our own to stimulate this desire. It has time but no change. It is rich with life but a quiet place. It is quiet because evil, though present, is foreign to the place, something brought in from another world at the beginning of time. Next, by fine gradations Lewis leads beyond this ideal, shows it to be provisional, and ends his series with us outside both our own and his invented world. While an earlier Platonism might have led us out of the world by going within, Lewis phrases the new version: "I thus understood that in deepest solitude there is a road right out of the self" (*SJ*, 208).

Second, the juxtaposition of worlds creates dialectic, gives grit and guts to all these idealized pictures. Moral choice exists and is never ambiguous. Lewis thus answers Socrates' critique of mythology (*Republic*, 2.376e–78e). These stories do not create false standards in children but help establish our traditional morality. Eustace learns social responsibility in *The Voyage of the "Dawn Treader."* In particular Lewis stresses the effects of petty evil. A child's desire for candy, for example, leads to betrayal and the death of another. Furthermore, the dialectic creates a sense of discrimination. Things compared are often close to one another, a landscape outside and the same landscape in a mirror. The confusion between a true and a false lion brings apocalypse to Narnia. This constant juxtaposition creates a sense of meaning which does not depend on symbol. In fact, the dialectic prevents a straightforward interpretation of things. The Wood may be intensively alive, yet it threatens its visitors with death. Narnia may be a quiet place, but the children invariably have exciting adventures there. England, on the other hand, with its complex history and world wars, strikes them as humdrum. It is the juxtaposition and opposition of places and objects which stimulates thought. The reader and the heroes are between worlds and constantly sense that something extraordinary might happen because one world impinges on another.

Lewis differs from Plato in degree more than in kind. Plato uses myth to control dialectic but emphasizes the dialectic. Lewis stresses the myth but uses dialectic to preserve its value. The plot establishes the dialectic at the points between the worlds, where good and evil clash and where universes crisscross.

"Caught Up into the Larger Pattern": Images and Narrative Structures in C. S. Lewis's Fiction

Colin Manlove

In his essay "On Stories" Lewis makes, broadly, three points concerning narrative, all of them directed at the reader's experience and all of them concerning imaginative, rather than realistic, stories. First, he says that the excitement one derives from such narrative is for him not separable from the image that creates it. If he reads the story of *Jack the Giant-Killer* the excitement is not that simply of a man surmounting danger but of a man "surmounting *danger from giants*" ("OnS," 94). It is the particular source of the danger, not the danger by itself, that is for him thrilling. And stories, for him, exist to give such imaginative excitement.

Furthermore, when the source of the thrill is marvelous or mysterious, it is at its most potent. Lewis praises David Lindsay, author of *A Voyage to Arcturus* (1920), as "the first writer to discover what 'other planets' are really good for in fiction": "His Tormance is a region of the spirit. . . . No merely physical strangeness or merely spatial distance will realize that idea of otherness which is what we are always trying to grasp in a story about voyaging through space: you must go into another dimension. To construct plausible and moving 'other worlds' you must draw on the only real 'other world' we know, that of the spirit" ("OnS," 98). Lewis is making roughly the same point in his essay "On Science Fiction" when he says, "I took a hero once to Mars in a space-ship, but when I knew better I had angels convey him to Venus."[1]

Finally, Lewis says that when they work imaginative stories can capture for the reader in their action an elusive sense of their own quiddity—such as, say, giantness, otherness, or the desolation of

1. Lewis, "On Science Fiction," in *Of Other Worlds: Essays and Stories*, ed. Walter Hooper (London: Geoffrey Bles, 1966), 69.

space. The sequence of events, the plot, "is only really a net whereby to catch something else . . . something other than a process and much more like a state or quality" ("OnS," 103). At the end of the essay, Lewis seems to go a little further, suggesting that the quality so glancingly caught may be "news from another country," an image of our desire for Heaven:

> In life and art both, as it seems to me, we are always trying to catch in our net of successive moments something that is not successive. Whether in real life there is any doctor who can teach us how to do it, so that at last either the meshes will become fine enough to hold the bird, or we be so changed that we can throw our nets away and follow the bird to its own country, is not a question for this essay. But I think it is sometimes done—or very, very nearly done—in stories. ("OnS," 105)

Lewis's own fiction follows his first two precepts: it is full of moving and exciting images, and its settings are most usually the marvelous or supernatural. Indeed, Lewis puts the wonderful image first in the process of composition: "Everything began with images; a faun carrying an umbrella, a queen on a sledge, a magnificent lion." In another piece he wrote, "The starting point of . . . *Perelandra*, was my mental picture of the floating islands."[2] Whether his fiction succeeds in capturing the bird Lewis refers to is for each reader to say. But Lewis does elsewhere offer one other view of imaginative narrative, which is that what is myth in one world may be fact in some other, or that a story may prefigure truth, as did pagan anticipations of the story of Christ, such as the stories of Adonis, Osiris, or the vision in Virgil's Fourth Eclogue.[3] Here Lewis is talking about the whole sequence of the narrative coming true rather than containing a bird of truth in its lattice of invention. Not every story has the potency of myth, however, a potency which again can only be subjectively felt, not measured.[4] But we understand a central truth about Lewis when we grasp that he thought and felt "this" world to be no more or less real than the invented worlds of fantasy; such is the vision given at the close of *The Last Battle*. Considered from this point of view, his stories can be

2. Lewis, "Sometimes Fairy Stories May Say Best What's to Be Said" (1956), in *Of Other Worlds*, 36; Lewis, "Unreal Estates," in *Of Other Worlds*, 87.
3. See *Per*, 49, 168, and the story "Forms of Things Unknown," in *Of Other Worlds*, 119–26. On myth as prefiguration, see *PR*, 192–207, 219–20; *Mir*, 135–40, 161 n. 1, 191–92; *Reflections on the Psalms* (London: Geoffrey Bles, 1958), chap. 10–11; and "Myth Became Fact" (1944), in *God in the Dock: Essays on Theology and Ethics*, ed. Walter Hooper (Grand Rapids, Mich.: Eerdmans, 1970), 63–67.
4. For Lewis's criteria of myth itself, see *Experiment*, 43–44.

seen (as his protagonists often see them) as factual realizations or recreations of myths in our world—the myth of the Cyclops in the *sorns* of Mars, the story of the temptation of Eve in that of the Lady of Perelandra, the sacrifice of Christ in the death and resurrection of Aslan in *The Lion, the Witch and the Wardrobe*, the myth of Cupid and Psyche in *Till We Have Faces*. For Lewis the distinction between imaginative fiction and reality or truth is not final.

These are Lewis's views, and they show how important narrative is to him. These are not, however, subject to critical analysis: here it is a case of "each to his own"; we cannot decipher the precise literary equivalent of a joy. Nor does Lewis suggest that literary criteria are of much relevance in any case. For him a poor style can be finally irrelevant to the effect, as in the case of Lindsay's *A Voyage to Arcturus*, and very often a reader may "flood wretched material with suggestion" beyond its isolated means ("OnS," 102). Lewis even goes so far as to say that his reading of Kafka's *The Castle* added nothing to an account of the story he had been given in a conversation: "I had already received the myth, which was all that mattered."[5] In his own work Lewis is quite ready to interrupt his narratives, whether with explication (*The Pilgrim's Regress*), description and argument (*Out of the Silent Planet, Perelandra*), spiritual analysis (*That Hideous Strength*), interviews (*The Great Divorce*), or debate (*Till We Have Faces*). It is thus ironic to find him in an essay on the Narnia books saying he liked the form of the fairy tale because of "its brevity, its severe restraints on description, its flexible traditionalism, its inflexible hostility to all analysis, digression, reflections and 'gas.'"[6]

What we shall be doing here is considering other means by which Lewis's narratives work and the recurrent patterns of structure to be found in them. If we cannot talk about our own reaction to his stories, we can at least talk about the effect of the sequence of their experiences on his characters, and if we cannot describe the "magical birds" themselves, we can say how the techniques of the narratives put across Lewis's vision. For despite their apparent artlessness, techniques they certainly have.

One of the recurrent features of Lewis's stories is what may be called a method of dislocation. His characters are constantly having their assumptions about the world widened or reversed. In his first "novel," the allegorical work *The Pilgrim's Regress*, the protagonist,

5. Lewis, Preface to *George MacDonald: An Anthology*, ed. C. S. Lewis (London: Geoffrey Bles, 1946), 16.
6. Lewis, "Sometimes Fairy Stories," 36–37.

John, leaves his home and the bleak nearby mountain on which the seemingly harsh "Landlord" lives, to go westward in quest of the source of a vision of a happy island he has received. At his first experience of this island, "all the furniture of his mind was taken away" (PR, 18). Throughout the story he is continually giving different identifications to his experience of the island and having them removed. At the end of his journey, he finds that his search has brought him to a broad and impassable channel, on the other side of which is the very mountain from which he set out. His journey has proved not linear but circular, and his desire, which seemed to take him away from the Landlord, was actually directed towards him. To reach the source of his desire, John now has to travel home all the way he has come.

In *Out of the Silent Planet*, Ransom's quiet world of a vacation walking tour is upturned when he happens on a house at which two men are preparing a spaceship for a journey to Mars and he is forcibly taken there with them. His conceptions of normality are further overthrown as he is progressively exposed to the alien: first when he wakes on the spacecraft and is told that the planet he can see out of the window is not the Moon but the Earth, from which he is now 85,000 miles distant; and later, when on Mars he encounters the different intelligent races there and gradually finds his fear-based preconceptions about them becoming irrelevant. By the end of the story, he has become so well acquainted with the planet and its peoples and has been so long away from the men he came with that he cannot recognize them as men when they are brought before him (and, indeed, in a way these evil men Weston and Devine do remain the truly alien, the evil). During his experience even Ransom's notion of the vastness of space is altered as he sees it no longer as a cold vacuum but as a sea of life, in which little closed planets and his prisonlike spaceship swim.

In *Perelandra* Ransom's notion of reality is further undercut, to an extent and by means that deserve detailed attention. He has met alien beings on Mars and begun to understand that there is a supernatural fabric to life. On Venus he meets more than the alien: here he encounters the primally innocent. What is more, he meets it not in the strange shapes of the creatures of Mars, but in his own human form, even if green of skin. More still, it is not the man he first takes it to be, but a woman. The whole of *Perelandra* is full of dislocations that gradually open Ransom to an understanding of the truly "other." The planet is largely covered by an ocean of enormous waves, in which he is first deposited on his arrival. On this ocean float islands of matted vegetation that shape themselves to the changing waves beneath them and go where they will. Reality is plastic and constantly in motion: indeed, the prohibition that has been laid on this innocent Lady by Maleldil (God) is not to sleep on the solid or Fixed Land rooted to the planet (though such land may be briefly visited). Paradise is here no fixed location as Eden was on Earth, but the whole planet; and each island paradise is "dis-located" in the sense of being mobile. On the islands Ransom is continually being thrown over by the changing surface beneath him, and only gradually does he learn how to keep his footing. Further, every assumption he makes about the topography of an island is continually overset—for instance, when a wave beneath suddenly turns what he has perceived as a "valley" into a "ridge" (*Per*, 44, 56). He is constantly "thrown" psychologically by the Lady's innocence, which knows nothing of pain, sorrow, evil, or death and has no sense of self, of ownership, or of home.

Ransom is "thrown" further when Weston arrives and, after a long diatribe, calls the "force" of which he says he is the representative into him, falls in a fit, and does himself what seems to Ransom terrible physical harm; yet the next day he has disappeared, and Ransom is later to find him, apparently recovered, in conversation with the Lady. Furthermore, he is no longer Weston, but the Un-man, a devil in a human body. Even the character of his devilry is unexpected, being nothing savage or melodramatic, but an aimless, childish malignity. This Un-man tries to make the Lady break Maleldil's prohibition, while Ransom tries to show her the emptiness of its arguments. Then it produces a point that floors him. It says that if Eve had not fallen, men would never have experienced the colossal gift of Christ's redemption of them; out of the fall comes not evil but a better good. Ransom begins to lose the arguments. The arrangement on the planet seems unfair: the devil has appeared, but not God.

But then, in an interview with Maleldil (speaking in his mind at night), he is told that he is Maleldil's representative on the planet. Nor can he look to what may have happened in Eden to find his bearings and make comparisons: "Only the actual was real: and every actual situation was new" (*Per*, 166). He is further jolted with the information that if he does not save the Lady from the devil, Maleldil will have to redeem Venus too and by an act even greater and more unimaginable than that which took place on Earth. He realizes that he is being asked to fight the Un-man "physically," intervening with his fists. This he finds at first both terrifying and absurd. He is deadly afraid of the Un-man, and at the same time he feels that a physical intervention would be saving the Lady unfairly. But then he is pushed to a new awareness. He sees that a physical contest with the Un-man in reality comes down to one middle-aged, sedentary body against another, at least a case of equal odds. Maleldil tells him that his little categories of "mental" and "physical" are here unreal, that he has been combating the Un-man physically in the "mental" contest and will not cease to be arguing with it when he fights it. One other little category is also removed when Maleldil says to him, "It is not for nothing that you are named Ransom" (*Per*, 168). Ransom sees that his name, which seemed a mere "accident," was part of a great pattern in which he has from the beginning of time been set to play a central part. One further statement from Maleldil knocks the last prop from Ransom: "My name also is Ransom." He sees that he stands on this planet not as mere man but as Christ. "If he were not the ransom, Another would be"; a sense of enormous spiritual pressure and terror falls upon him. Yet a moment later he knows too that he has not been chosen for any particular merit in him, and that "it might as well be he as another" (*Per*, 171). The whole of Ransom's experience is felt by him "with a strange sense of 'fallings from him, vanishings'" (*Per*, 165), a series of dislocations, in which everything is more, less, or quite other than could ever have been conceived.

The rest of his story is partly an account of his development towards an understanding of the paradoxical, and thus dislocative, nature of truth, celebrated in a great hymn and vision—spoken and given to him at the end by the Oyéresu, or planetary guardians of Mars and Venus—in which he learns how in Maleldil all things are at once supremely important and superfluous, central and peripheral, how time is both serial and eternally copresent, how God is in the meanest grain as in the greatest *eldil*. This duality continues: Ransom may still be mere mortal at the end of this book, but he has also been translated beyond all knowing. The bleeding heel with which he returns to Earth is not more the mark of his approaching end than the signature of Maleldil that will bring him back to Perelandra and the blessed isle of Aphallin.

Other "dislocations" in Lewis's novels can be mentioned more briefly. In *That Hideous Strength*, many of the characters are "dislocated" in the sense of being taken out of their normal place. Mark and Jane Studdock separate, and he leaves his university job and goes to Belbury and the "important" researches of the scientific institute the N.I.C.E., only eventually to be shocked into awareness of the evil from which those so-called researches in fact emanate. Indeed, in the so-called "Objective Room" at Belbury, Mark experiences evil as a perverted displacement of reality (*THS*, chap. 14). Jane is shaken out of her sense of injured worth and false pride by the community of St. Anne's. The N.I.C.E. bend the town of Edgestow to their purposes, disturbing the peace of the university, displacing people and pulling down buildings. Merlin is awakened from his long sleep in Bragdon Wood. The great planetary intelligences, the Oyéresu, invade Earth. Speech is dislocated into nonsense at Belbury by magic means. In the end the ground literally opens up beneath Edgestow and it disappears. In *The Great Divorce* what seemed a capacious Hell turns out to be a barely perceptible crack in the soil of Heaven; Heaven itself is not the traditionally vague place, but is supremely solid, and heavy— it is Hell and its "ghosts" that are unreal beside it; what seem like free choices by the ghosts are in fact predetermined in eternity. In the Narnia books there is rather less in the way of dislocation, perhaps on the grounds that children, who form the main characters, are more adaptable and open to new experiences. They can accept the reality of a Narnia or an Aslan, or even the fact of their own deaths, without too great a sense of shock. Nevertheless, we have the theme of overset expectation in *The Lion, the Witch and the Wardrobe,* where Aslan destroys the old law by the very act of submitting to it in self-sacrifice for Edmund's sin and by rising from the dead by a deeper magic than the Witch who slays him knows. *Prince Caspian* opens with the children waiting at an English railway station to go back to school when suddenly they are whisked into Narnia. But unknown to them it is a Narnia hundreds of years beyond the time they were last there, and they do not at first recognize it. It takes them some time to discover that the overgrown ruin in which they find themselves first is in fact the remains of their old palace Cair Paravel. In *The Last Battle* the nature of reality is continually changing: Narnia shrivels down to a mere hut near Caldron Pool before being annihilated by Aslan; at the same time the hut becomes a doorway to a new Narnia, and to still more Narnias, "farther up and farther in." The children are told at the end by Aslan that the magic that brought them to Narnia this time was in fact their deaths in a railway crash, and they all journey further in, towards Aslan's country. The whole Narnia series, if read in published order, is dislocative to the reader, who learns nothing about Narnia's origins till the sixth book, *The Magician's Nephew,* only to see it destroyed in the next and final book. *Till We Have Faces* is a steady dislocation of the certainties of the central character, Orual. She finds that her complaint against the gods for taking Psyche from her and failing to give her a clear sight of Psyche's happiness with the god is its own answer. She learns that, in her pain and suppressed guilt at Psyche's loss, she has for years been helping Psyche with the tasks assigned to her by the god and that the god's statement, "You also shall be Psyche," has come to pass.

What is the purpose of such dislocations? Most simply they are there to stir the characters out of old assumptions into a wider awareness of reality. Lewis saw that as the effect of mythic narrative on the reader too:

> It goes beyond the expression of things we have already felt. It arouses in us sensations we have never had before, never anticipated having, as though we had broken out of our normal mode of consciousness and "possessed joys not promised to our birth." It gets under our skin, hits us at a level deeper than our thoughts or even our passions, troubles oldest certainties till all questions are re-opened, and in general shocks us more fully awake than we are for most of our lives.[7]

No one, in Lewis's view, is to be allowed to stay mentally and morally assured, for assurance is not the birthright of mortal man. But perhaps the key phrase is "out of": the characters in the fiction are to be taken *out of* their old selves. John leaves home. Ransom goes "out of the silent planet" of Earth. He is released from a coffin-shaped casket on Venus. The damned in *The Great Divorce* are asked to make the tiny step out of old habits of thought that will open to them all the joys of Heaven. Orual has to stop hiding from the truth, to take away the concealing veil; she finally goes out of herself in death.

Correspondingly, the stress in all Lewis's novels is on spiritual growth, from the education of Eustace in *The Voyage of the "Dawn Treader"* to the downward movement to moral bedrock of Mark Studdock or the unseen spiritual surgery carried out on Orual. Positions of stasis are on the whole condemned. The characters who move in *The Pilgrim's Regress*, Virtue and John, are in the right because their notion of "right" is continually being altered towards something better. Those who stay in one area only, such as the Clevers, Mr. Enlightenment, Neo-Angular, Mr. Broad, even Wisdom and History, either pervert or offer only a partial view of truth; on his journey back, John sees them for the dead things they really are. The same is often true in *The Voyage of the "Dawn Treader"* for those who stay on islands and the travelers who pass by. It is Ransom in *Out of the Silent Planet* who moves about on Mars, finding out about it, whereas Weston and Devine seem to have done virtually nothing;

7. Lewis, Preface to *George MacDonald*, 16–17.

and all the intelligent species of life on the planet make the pilgrimage to Meldilorn. In *Perelandra* fixity is the enemy: the Lady is forbidden to sleep on the Fixed Land, and the mobility of life on the sea provides a contrasting symbol. In *The Great Divorce* the journey to Heaven of the ghost has been tiny, as tiny as is the worth of their motives in going there. The real journey is to be made further into Heaven by any of them who can bring themselves to accept offered joy, but they do not, shrinking back always to the bus that brought them and to the stasis of their set responses. In *The Lion, the Witch and the Wardrobe,* the Witch has frozen Narnia in perpetual winter, and it is Aslan and the children who bring back spring, new life, and motion. Prince Rilian in *The Silver Chair* has to be released from an enchanted chair, and when he is, a whole underground world comes to life again. In *The Horse and His Boy,* the central characters must journey out of the slavery of the land of Calormen. Not all stasis is bad, however: the children should not have released the Witch from her statue form in *The Magician's Nephew,* for her existence is a threat to Narnia. It could be argued, however, that the wonder of Narnia itself might not have been brought into being had Aslan not needed a creative "answer" to the destruction of Charn caused by the Witch. In a way the very journeys and adventures that the stories describe are themselves images of growth. There are no "adventures" in *The Great Divorce* because the ghosts refuse to change.

So too, all enclosures are to be broken out of, from the room of the Steward or the prison of Mr. Enlightenment in *The Pilgrim's Regress* to the claustrophobic spaceship or even planets in Ransom's story, the narrow Hell of *The Great Divorce,* and the vortex of Orual's self, imaged in a descending series of chambers in *Till We Have Faces* (Part 2, chap. 2). Mark Studdock's inability to escape the walls and boundaries of Belbury, headquarters of the N.I.C.E. in *That Hideous Strength,* symbolizes his spiritual condition; St. Anne's by contrast seems virtually without walls or limits, especially during the description of the descent of the Oyéresu. When the devil takes over Weston in *Perelandra,* his personality becomes shut away in a deep hole inside what was once himself. Eustace in *The Voyage of the "Dawn Treader"* is locked in the body of a dragon as punishment, and Rilian in *The Silver Chair* is confined to an enchanted chair in an underground chamber. Uncle Andrew's behavior in *The Magician's Nephew* causes the animals to make a cage for him so that he may come to no harm—the cage representing his inability to come out of himself to see Narnia for what it is. (We recall too that Uncle Andrew is first found by the children in a hidden attic study and that he uses them to make journeys via his magic rings rather than go himself.) The enclosure that is the magic wardrobe in *The Lion, the Witch and the Wardrobe* is backless, opening on Narnia, and the children's castle of Cair Paravel is open to the sea that goes all the way to Aslan's Land, unlike the Witch's inland palace, shut between hills. The stable in *The Last Battle* opens on the whole universe.

One emphasis in Lewis's narratives is on meeting others. It is confinement to the self that distorts perspective, as we see with Rilian or Orual, or with the Earth cut off from the heavens. The salvation of the ghosts in *The Great Divorce* will be accomplished precisely by their being able truly to meet those celestial beings, their erstwhile friends and relations, who come to meet them. The narrator of this story, unlike the ghosts, is able to meet and have genuine exchange with someone, the risen self of George MacDonald. For Lewis, as he put it in the title to a chapter of *That Hideous Strength*, "real life is meeting." The only one of his characters who is largely alone is John in *The Pilgrim's Regress*. But even he ends in company with Virtue, and of course his objective is to meet his god. To some extent what is implied here is a kind of church, "where two or three are gathered together." Ransom's success on Mars is precisely his ability truly to go out of himself and meet the other races there, just as on Perelandra he meets the Lady, whereas the Un-man, who seeks to manipulate her, does not and never could. In *That Hideous Strength* the narrative at the "human" level revolves about the separation and eventual true coming together of Mark and Jane Studdock. In the Narnia books, the children have to act together or reform into doing so, and when they act aright have to do so by being at one with the indigenous Talking Animals of Narnia and with Aslan. In *Prince Caspian*, Caspian comes to meet all of Narnia; the journey of the ship in *The Voyage of the "Dawn Treader"* serves to bring all the islands visited into a measure of community; at the end of *The Last Battle*, all the characters from the various books come together for the final journey. In *Till We Have Faces* Orual learns that she is united with Psyche once more.

The journey out of self is of value both in itself and as a means of realizing or meeting the "other," the true nature of reality. That is the nature of Ransom's experience, and those of Jane and Mark Studdock in *That Hideous Strength*, and of Orual, who has for so long refused the god in *Till We Have Faces*. It is also the journey of John in *The Pilgrim's Regress*, who is searching for the source of his desire for the island-vision. For long he identifies it wrongly, whether with sex, romanticism, or beauty, or tries to deny it ascetically; but eventually he is brought to realize that it is an image sent to him from a divine source. The whole of his journey becomes the search for the "other," which turns out to have been at home, too. *The Voyage of the "Dawn Treader"* describes a journey in quest of Aslan's Land, towards progressively greater strangeness and otherness as we proceed, from magical island to mystical island and thence to a great lily-covered sea, at the end of which waits a sacramental lamb offering the children roast fish (as in John 21). In *The Horse and His Boy*, Shasta learns through his journey who he truly is—not Shasta, peasant boy of Calormen, but Cor, lost son of King Lune of Archenland—and as he approaches knowledge of who he is, so he meets and learns more of the nature of Aslan. Lewis said that stories were always a net for catching something else, some "otherness." Here we can see how the very act of making a narrative by going on a journey catches otherness for the hero too.

So too, the little province of the narrative is frequently broken down as we or the characters realize that it is part of some larger frame than could have been foreseen. This happens partly because the stories do not overtly refer to the Christian patterns they contain, so that the patterns are stumbled upon. Lewis said that his objective in the Narnia books was to get rid of "Sunday school associations" and steal past the "watchful dragons" of distaste for sermonizing, but he does more than this.[8] John in *The Pilgrim's Regress* seems at first a man in search of the land of his dreams; but the pattern of his journey gradually takes on the shape of a Christian's sufferings, and the image of the island with which he started, while still "real mythology," dwindles till it turns to the mountain from which he began. We and Ransom in *Out of the Silent Planet* are led to believe that he is to be sacrificed to a hostile Martian race, but the world of Mars proves to be infused with supernatural life whose purposes are far beyond such narrow categories. The pattern always becomes larger, until by the end of the story what seemed a mere space adventure à la Edgar Rice Burroughs has turned into the first act in a huge cosmic drama and the life of one planet becomes viewed as part of a great "celestial commonwealth" (*Per*, 231). This is taken a stage further in *Perelandra*, in which Ransom comes to realize that, far from being a little local matter that he has been sent to help in, his being on Perelandra to aid the Lady against the tempter has been planned from all eternity, that his name "Ransom" is no accident, and that he is called to play the part of a new Christ in both the salvation of a world and the frustration of the devil:

8. Lewis, "Sometimes Fairy Stories," 37.

The whole distinction between things accidental and things designed, like the distinction between fact and myth, was purely terrestrial. The pattern is so large that within the little frame of earthly experience there appear pieces of it between which we can see no connection, and other pieces between which we can. Hence we rightly, for our use, distinguish the accidental from the essential. But step outside that frame and the distinction drops down into the void, fluttering useless wings. He [Ransom] had been forced out of the frame, caught up into the larger pattern. (*Per*, 168)

The idea that what seem to us purely individual or local actions and choices are, in a larger view, predetermined is also presented in *The Great Divorce*, where what we and the narrator "Lewis" have for long accepted as willful and present acts of choice by the ghosts are shown to have been made since all eternity. The bottom, as it were, falls out of our world. In *The Lion, the Witch and the Wardrobe*, Narnia has been waiting for two Sons of Adam and two Daughters of Eve to come and liberate the land from perpetual winter and the power of the Witch. Only gradually do we realize that the four children, Peter, Lucy, Susan, and Edmund, who have apparently stumbled on this strange land through the back of an even stranger wardrobe, fulfill this prophecy and that the arrival of Aslan in Narnia at the same time is no coincidence. The children, whom we might dismiss—as readily as they themselves would—as "only children," play a much more central part than they or we suppose. Here again what might have seemed "only an adventure" becomes also a re-creation of the Christ story in Aslan's death and resurrection. Everything, while remaining itself, becomes more than itself. The same sort of revelation of deeper pattern is present in *The Silver Chair*, with its cyclic narrative of descent, release, and return; or in *The Horse and His Boy*, with its participation in the story of the journey out of slavery in Egypt to the Promised Land; or in *The Last Battle*, with its intimation of the end of all things described in the Book of Revelation.[9] In *Till We Have Faces*, a few family squabbles in the primitive realm of Glome turn out to be part of the Cupid and Psyche myth and that myth itself to be part of a still larger Christian reality; at the same time, in her spiritual suffer-

9. See Peter J. Schakel, *Reading with the Heart: The Way into Narnia* (Grand Rapids, Mich.: Eerdmans, 1979), 65–80. Cf. John Cox, "Epistemological Release in *The Silver Chair*," in *The Longing for a Form: Essays on the Fiction of C. S. Lewis*, ed. Peter J. Schakel (Kent, Ohio: Kent State University Press, 1977), 164–68. On *The Horse and His Boy*, see Schakel, *Reading with the Heart*, 81–84. On *The Last Battle*, cf. Charles A. Huttar, "C. S. Lewis's Narnia and the Grand Design," in *Longing for a Form*, 132–33.

ings Orual becomes part of a larger pattern as she has unknowingly been helping Psyche to carry out her tasks.

For Lewis fiction and reality, accident and design, are more closely entwined than we suppose. For him nothing is irrelevant, nothing too small. As the Oyéresu say of Maleldil at the end of *Perelandra*, the meanest grain of dust is as important to him, as central to the universe, as the greatest angel (*Per*, 249–50). Lewis's narrative structure here imitates what is for him the character of divine reality. A lamp-post in Narnia seems a purely fortuitous thing, and for long we do not know how it got there. Only in *The Magician's Nephew*, the sixth book published in the series, do we learn that it grew from the crosspiece of a lamp-post brought by the Witch to Narnia from Edwardian times and hurled by her at Aslan in a vain attempt to slay him. Out of the futile act has come something better though, because it is always the part of goodness to make a thing better than it seems: the lamp-post has grown from the fragment to provide a beacon for those entering or leaving Narnia through the strange wardrobe. As for the wardrobe itself, its magical properties turn out to be no mere accident either, for its wood originated in the tree grown from the apple that the child Digory picked for Aslan in the Narnian paradise. Lewis's vision of the equal "importance" of all things is close to that of his friend Charles Williams (who could see in bringing a glass of water to one's wife at night as "great" an act of love as Christ's sacrifice).[10] In throwing his pack over the locked gate at the beginning of *Out of the Silent Planet*, thereby committing himself to getting back home from work the son of an old lady he has just met, Ransom is performing as large an act as when he faces up to meeting a *sorn* or Oyarsa on Mars.[11] In lying to the other children that Lucy has only invented Narnia and the magic wardrobe in *The Lion, the Witch and the Wardrobe*, Edmund has in a real way committed a sin against light ("Lucy" = "lux" or "light"). One purpose of Lewis's writing books with child characters could be said to have been to show that no child or act is "mere"; the same purpose is served by the use of the mouse Reepicheep as hero. The ghosts in *The Great Divorce* have to make the tiniest of moves towards joy to be redeemed, yet that tiniest of moves must at the same time cross an immense spiritual chasm. (In Lewis's work it is the evil who say or make a thing less than it is, who say that John's desire for the island is only

10. Williams, *All Hallows' Eve* (London: Faber and Faber, 1945), 147.
11. See Thomas Howard, *The Achievement of C. S. Lewis: A Reading of His Fiction* (Wheaton, Ill.: Harold Shaw, 1980), 68–69.

lust or an illusion, or that Heaven is only a cheat, the sun a fiction, a god a brute.)[12]

In every hierarchy there is equality; in every center, a periphery (*Per*, 247-50). Lewis may sometimes organize his narratives in hierarchic sequence—as in Ransom's progress in *Out of the Silent Planet* from "ordinary" walk to extraordinary house to amazing journey and thence up a kind of ladder of alien being from *hross* to *sorn* to Oyarsa, or in the graded progress of *The Voyage of the "Dawn Treader"*—but in every such series there is a denial of series. Aslan appears throughout *The Voyage*, showing that he is no grand finale but is present equally in all places. Rather than a portrayal of hierarchy, even while that exists, Ransom's graded meetings in *Out of the Silent Planet* are an index to his fears of the unknown and the need to initiate him gradually: the shadowy *eldila* exist among the comfortable *hrossa*; and Oyarsa, though met by Ransom, reassuringly, in one place (Meldilorn), pervades—he discovers—the planet with his nature. *Perelandra* starts at once with angels, "black" and "white." *Perelandra* too, opens with a "hierarchy" which is reversed at the end: Ransom's first sight of Venus is of lines and shapes before his mind takes these in as waves; then he meets the vegetable (the islands and their trees), animals (the dragon), and finally human (the Lady); at the end the vision given to him by the Oyéresu turns all being back to a dancing pattern of lines and shapes.

Those of Lewis's narratives that are organized around a single center often prove to be about an evil. Action in *That Hideous Strength* revolves about Belbury and the N.I.C.E., who seek to draw all people to them, and at the center is the black archon of Hell. Here there is no journey outwards to all space or new worlds, but things have to come in to Earth, the prison planet of Satan, cut off from the celestial commonwealth. So too in *Till We Have Faces*, where the spiderlike Orual, Lewis's only "I" narrator, draws in all things to herself, including, by divine irony, her own regeneration. In *The Silver Chair* the children have to travel from Aslan's Land down to Narnia and beyond, and then into the depths of the earth to find the room and the chair in which the wicked Witch has Prince Rilian in servitude: the process imitates the draining of life the Witch causes, and as the children near her center in Underland the surroundings become progressively more dull and blurred—identity drops away. In others of Lewis's narratives, by contrast, what might have seemed an

---

12. Or who contend that "the *Tao* [is] . . . a mere natural product" (*Abol*, 40). The habit of reductionism is the central object of attack in the book.

act of central "importance" is made in another sense peripheral. Certainly the sacrifice of Aslan for Edmund is the "central" act in *The Lion, the Witch and the Wardrobe*, yet in a way this sacrifice was not part of the saving of Narnia itself, but only of Edmund for his purely local acts of treachery. Aslan's deed may permit the awakening of Narnia to go ahead, but it is not in itself part of that awakening. Similarly in *Perelandra*, by surrounding the story of the Lady and her temptation with accounts of Ransom's experience of Perelandra without reference to her, Lewis puts the whole matter of the averted fall in wider perspective. It is supremely important, it is a turning point in cosmic history, yet it is a very small thing, as small as Ransom too one-sidedly thinks it when he is far away on the vast wilds of the Perelandrian ocean: "What did these roarers with the yellow foam, and these strange people who lived in them, care whether two little creatures, now far away, lived or did not live on one particular rock?" (*Per*, 187). As the Oyéresu later say:

> In the plan of the Great Dance plans without number interlock, and each movement becomes in its season the breaking into flower of the whole design to which all else had been directed. Thus each is equally at the centre and none are there by being equals, but some by giving place and some by receiving it, the small things by their smallness and the great by their greatness, and all the patterns linked and looped together by the unions of a kneeling with a sceptred love. (*Per*, 250)

Evil makes self the sole center, and manipulates the world to serve it. Because of this desire to possess, it is often the evil who initiate the narratives in Lewis's books. They have all the plans and do all the initial choosing. Weston and Devine in *Out of the Silent Planet* aim to take a human sacrifice with them to Mars so that they can secure gold from the planet; if not for them, Ransom would never have got there and had his spiritually awakening experiences. On Perelandra it is the arrival of Weston and the tempting of the Lady by the Un-man that create a situation in which Ransom must do something. It is the N.I.C.E., propelled by the evil "Macrobes" in *That Hideous Strength*, who have all the purpose and cause all the disturbance at Edgestow—here again the good simply react. (It is interesting that when those at St. Anne's have, like the N.I.C.E., a plan to secure Merlin for their purposes, this plan fails, and Merlin comes to them of his "own" volition.) In *The Great Divorce* it is the damned who start every conversation with the celestial beings in *Heaven*. In *The Lion, the Witch and the Wardrobe*, the children arrive apparently at random and without purpose in Narnia, and it is the activities of the Witch that generate their own. The Ape Shift in *The Last Battle* begins the action by setting out to gain power for himself in Narnia through the use of a false Aslan to which the Narnians will subject themselves. The corrupt priest in *Till We Have Faces* begins the whole "story" by demanding that Psyche, of whose powers he is jealous, be given to the "Shadowbrute" on the mountain in sacrifice.

The "good," conversely, are often passive or suffering. On Mars Ransom is driven by circumstance or guided by the inhabitants; on Venus he is in the hands of the ever-changing ocean until his pursuit of the Un-man; in *That Hideous Strength*, ill, he is seated most of the time. In *The Lion, the Witch and the Wardrobe*, Aslan gives himself passively into the hand of the Witch so that she may slay him, yet through that extreme passivity of death he is to become supremely alive and active. In *Till We Have Faces*, Orual is operated on by "divine surgeons." Often the forces of good are helped by some greater power or destiny: the Oyéresu in *That Hideous Strength*, the preordained pattern behind *The Lion, the Witch and the Wardrobe*, Aslan in *The Horse and His Boy*. They have no wish to change things, indeed their object is to keep them as they are or were meant to be, independent of the self. John learns the true source of his island vision, outside himself. The Oyarsa of Mars ensures that its peoples remain free of the designs of Weston and Devine. Ransom helps to keep the Lady of Perelandra innocent and free of the Un-man. The disruptive potential of the N.I.C.E. in *That Hideous Strength* is destroyed. The perversions of Narnia by the Witch, the Telmarines, and Shift are reversed. In the end Orual gives back to Psyche the independence she has so long denied her.

For all their activity, none of the evil succeed in their plans. All end wretchedly, with good triumphant: Weston in the Un-man slain on Venus, Devine dead in the pit at Edgestow, the Black Archon driven back from his foothold on the world, the power of the Witch destroyed, the attempt of the priest to slay Psyche frustrated. Their schemes serve only to produce the very goodness they sought to deny. By killing Aslan, the Witch gives him more life; by creating a false Aslan, Shift brings back the true; by consigning Psyche to the Shadowbrute, the priest gives her in marriage to the god. By initiating actions which end in a victory for goodness, innocence, or God, Lewis dramatizes repeatedly in his narratives the fundamental Christian belief that out of every evil action comes some greater good.

We have looked at some of the techniques and strategies common to Lewis's narration. But now we can briefly consider the degree to which his narrative method changes or develops across his career. It can be said, for instance, that the earlier works tend to describe a journey, whether in search of an island or to Mars or Venus, while in the later ones we are more often in one place, whether Earth, Heaven, Narnia, or Glome (though there are exceptions within the Narnia books). The central figures in the earlier books, even while they meet others, are seen rather more in isolation (John on his pilgrimage or Ransom alone on Mars and Venus, for instance); but by *That Hideous Strength* Ransom has become head of a community, St. Anne's, and the spirits and ghosts come from groups in *The Great Divorce*. In the Narnia books, Narnia itself is a community and the children are always banded together, not only with themselves but with Narnians. In *Till We Have Faces*, though Orual may feel isolated, she still lives as part of a group as Queen of Glome; the Queen of Perelandra, on the other hand, had no subjects.

Other changes are to be seen between the bulk of Lewis's fiction and *Till We Have Faces*. The latter exhibits very little in the way of obvious narrative: Psyche is sent to sacrifice, Orual goes to see her and causes her exile by the god, then Orual's long and fairly uneventful reign as queen is described. There is no central concern with doing things in or to a world, no Ransom saving a Lady or Witch perverting a Narnia. In this story what is "happening" is invisible, as invisible as Orual makes the god's palace to herself; unknown to her, in her pain she is performing Psyche's tasks. The form of the story is an image of the inner nature of Orual. We have moved from an objective to a subjective view of reality, one we cannot take at face value. Ransom tried hard to convey what he saw of an innocent world largely beyond his grasp; Orual tries to cut herself off from facts which she (in part at least) knows only too well. Here we have a narrative that is continually introspective, with the character asking herself what was the true nature of her experience. The event itself is a mere datum—it is the way she interprets it in her mind and spirit that is central. The narrative is also retrospective because Orual is constantly looking backwards to her past dealings with Psyche and her concern throughout is with the past and what actually happened in it. This is a marked contrast with Lewis's other narratives, which have a forward movement: How will Ransom save the Lady? How will the Witch be overthrown? Will Mark Studdock arrive at the truth? Where will John's quest for his island take him? Furthermore, this last novel is centrally concerned with a relationship between two people and through that with God. Earlier novels dealt with actions of individual spiritual developments rather than with changing relations. Nearest is perhaps *That Hideous Strength*, in which Mark and

Jane Studdock can come together once more as man and wife at the end, but they have changed too much in isolation from one another to be able to do so.

One more difference in *Till We Have Faces* is that, so far as moral attitudes are concerned, Lewis dealt in his other fiction with what he himself called the Great Divorce, the total incompatibility between good and bad. There were no ambiguities or "half-way houses." Indeed, Lewis rejects Media Halfways and her brother Gus in *The Pilgrim's Regress*; one must opt either for the good or the evil. Mark Studdock chooses evil, and then good; Weston chooses to bring the dark force into himself, and Ransom to go with Maleldil; Edmund opts for the Witch and treachery, and then repents and becomes one with Aslan and the right. But Orual is a far more morally "mixed" character, with good and bad impulses growing up together. Even while she apparently chooses the bad course of blaming the god rather than herself for what happened to Psyche, her conscience or spirit continues to work in her unseen, until at the end all her protestations disintegrate, she sees herself for what she is, and she can repent and accept joy. The whole book refuses us certainties, even the certainty that Orual had done wrong. The god is both the "pagan" Cupid and somehow a participant in the Christian fabric of exchange and mercy, working "backwards" (if we may use such terms of acts in eternity) from Christ's life and death, in parallel with Orual's own "working backwards." At the end Orual finds how, when the god said to her, "You also shall be Psyche," he spoke the truth: her identity and that of Psyche, the ugly and the beautiful, have met together and exchanged natures. If Lewis's earlier fiction dealt often with the Great Divorce, this one could be said to celebrate a Great Marriage. The change it shows is not just one of fictional technique, but one involving some change of spirit on Lewis's part, a radically new understanding of the nature of human suffering and moral choice, and of the supernatural fabric of being in which they take place.[13]

Yet there is a sense too in which, for all this change, Lewis's fiction comes full circle, returning in this last book to the nature of the first book, *The Pilgrim's Regress*. Both novels are distinctive in Lewis's fiction in dealing with whole lives, from childhood to death; in other books we are concerned with more "local" adventures. The god on the mountain in *Till We Have Faces* is another version of the god on

13. See Gunnar Urang, *Shadows of Heaven: Religion and Fantasy in the Writing of C. S. Lewis, Charles Williams, and J. R. R. Tolkien* (London: SCM Press, 1971), 40–41, 49–50.

the mountain in *The Pilgrim's Regress,* and each is initially portrayed as harsh, ugly, or brutish, and rejected by the protagonist as such. *The Pilgrim's Regress* also deals with the inmost workings of the spirit of a single central figure, though in relation to an allegorical narrative of a journey. That book too was a psychomachia, in which the landscapes and characters met were in part extensions of the spirit of the central character. There too the issue was to discover or define the precise nature of a thing: John had to find out what he really desired when he longed for the island and whether it could be translated into some identifiable this-worldly pleasure. So too, Orual struggles to define, though in a more self-protective manner, exactly what happened between her and Psyche on the mountain and the dealings of the god with her.

Much of the rest of Lewis's fiction is concerned not so centrally with definition but with doing. In *The Pilgrim's Regress* and *Till We Have Faces,* Lewis deals most directly and continuously with the experience which led him to Christianity and largely kept him there, the experience of "joy" or *Sehnsucht*. One would not think joy was particularly present in the miseries of Orual in the latter book, but what she is doing throughout is refusing it, refusing the bliss of Psyche and her glorious experience, until in the end she is, in the words of the title of Lewis's autobiography, "surprised by joy." Indeed it is possible to see the two novels as forming a sort of diptych: *The Pilgrim's Regress* describing someone who too readily embraces the joy and misinterprets its source; *Till We Have Faces* portraying someone who resists the joy, even though presented with its source, and lives another kind of lie (through a sort of "negative way"). The first book deals with conversion relatively early in life, the last with a change almost at the end. It may be that in *Till We Have Faces,* which Lewis thought his best book, he is in some way depicting the removal of some deeper and more lasting recalcitrance in himself.[14]

A measure of circularity is also present within the narratives of Lewis's works. John in *The Pilgrim's Regress* ends at the mountain from which he set out. He has been to the end of the world to find the source of his desire and has seen it in that very place, from which he is divided by a channel and which he must retrace all his steps to reach. He has grown spiritually during the story, but the linear aspect of progress is ironically undercut by the course of his journey. Lewis's Ransom leaves and returns to Earth after his visits to Mars and Venus, as do the children in most of the Narnia books, and the ghosts

14. See Urang, *Shadows of Heaven*, 49–50.

return to Hell at the end of *The Great Divorce*. Ransom tells his story in *Perelandra* in a temporal loop—his return to Earth after his adventures is described before they are. The whole Narnia series could be said to have something of a circular form, beginning and ending with books that deal with spiritual matters concerning Narnia as a whole and having in the middle books concerned with more individual and local exploits—the adventures described in *The Voyage of the "Dawn Treader," The Silver Chair*, and *The Horse and His Boy*. And *Till We Have Faces* ends as it began, with Orual together with Psyche, if now in a transformed relationship. Here too there is narrative undercutting, since the version of events Orual gives us for most of the novel is overthrown by a new experience she has after she had finished it. If we like, we can assign such circularity to the character of fantasy, which frequently ends its stories where they began; or we can even, in some cases, say that their circularity imitates the perfection of the circle of Heaven. But we should also see such circularity, perhaps, as an ironic comment on the nature of spiritual growth in our mortal condition—no steady, linear advance to a distant goal and sometimes even a matter of running very hard to keep on the spot. Lewis, we may also recall, disliked "the fatal serialism of the modern imagination—the image of infinite unilinear progression which so haunts our minds" (*Abol*, 39). The same principle at work may make us hesitate before seeing the development of his fiction as a whole in evolutionary terms, towards greater profundity, sophistication, or subtlety of technique. Each of his works is good in its own way and in its own right, even while it may mark a stage in a development or process.

It is on this note of individuality that we can end, for perhaps the first and last striking feature of Lewis's fictions is the degree to which they change from work to work. We have considered his narratives as sequences and patterns, but these are embodied in images: Lewis considered both essential to the effect of story. After the allegory *The Pilgrim's Regress*, Lewis wrote stories of travel to other planets; then something of a novel of "real life" in *That Hideous Strength* and again in *Till We Have Faces*; then he gave us a vision of Hell and Heaven; then he composed what he saw as fairy tales for children. And each world is strikingly different, from the allegory-land of *The Pilgrim's Regress*, through Malacandra, Perelandra, "this" contemporary Earth, Hell, Heaven, Narnia, and Glome. It could almost be said of Lewis as his Oyéresu say of Maledil, "Never did He make two things the same; never did He utter one word twice. After earths, not better earths but beasts; after beasts, not better beasts but spirits. After a falling, not recovery but a new creation. Out of the new creation, not a third but the mode of change itself is changed for ever" (*Per*, 246–47).

But it is not only Lewis's belief that "all is new" that explains this variety. For him, all images are only shadows of the truth. If we cling to them, as we might, say, to Perelandra as an image of the desirable, we are mistaken. This is the meaning of John's experience in *The Pilgrim's Regress,* and it is a dialectic lived by Lewis himself on the road to conversion which he describes in *Surprised by Joy.* Here again, but in a larger mode, we find Lewis using a "technique," if so it may be called, of dislocation. By literally "dis-locating" us, throwing us into a new location as Ransom is thrown into the ocean of Perelandra after the "solid" world of Malacandra or even by showing the old fade, as Narnia is removed by Aslan, Lewis keeps us moving perhaps "farther up and farther in" through image after image until we may learn that

> the books or the music in which we thought the beauty was located will betray us if we trust to them; it was not *in* them, it only came *through* them, and what came through them was longing. These things . . . are good images of what we really desire; but if they are mistaken for the thing itself they turn into dumb idols, breaking the hearts of their worshippers. For they are not the thing itself; they are only the scent of a flower we have not found, the echo of a tune we have not heard, news from a country we have never yet visited.[15]

15. Lewis, "The Weight of Glory," in *Transposition and Other Addresses* (London: Geoffrey Bles, 1949), 24.

Perelandra Revisited
in the Light of
Modern Allegorical Theory
Marius Buning

It may seem hazardous to regard one of C. S. Lewis's finest fictions as allegorical, since the author himself explicitly disowns such a description in his brief preface to *Perelandra:* "All the human characters in this book are purely fictitious and *none of them allegorical*" (my italics). One is reminded of a similar strong denial by J. R. R. Tolkien about *The Lord of the Rings:* "It has *no* allegorical intentions, general, particular or topical, moral, religious or political."[1] C. S. Lewis endorsed this view when he wrote, "Tolkien's book is not an allegory—a form he dislikes" (*Letters,* 271). Such unambiguous authorial statements would seem to settle the matter, and any critical attempt still to call their work "allegorical" may run the risk of what Swift once called "*Scholiastick* Midwifry," in which the critics "deliver'd them of Meanings, that the Authors themselves, perhaps, never conceived."[2]

Yet there are, I think, several good reasons for looking at *Perelandra* as allegorical fiction. In the first place, on closer consideration Lewis's theory of allegory, as put forward in his *The Allegory of Love: A Study in Medieval Tradition* and in various stray comments in letters and prefaces, turns out to be less stable than is usually assumed since it is not without inner inconsistencies and contradictions. As I will show, his ambiguous attitude towards allegory and his innate preference for symbolism (and its cognates "sacramentalism" and "myth") are essentially Romantic, nineteenth-century views, in the tradition of Goethe and Coleridge.

Second, even a superficial glance at the reception of *Perelandra*

---

1. Quoted in Lin Carter, *Tolkien: A Look Behind "The Lord of the Rings"* (New York: Ballantine Books, 1969), 84.
2. Jonathan Swift, *A Tale of a Tub* (1704), ed. A. C. Guthkelch and D. Nichol Smith, 2d ed. (Oxford: Clarendon Press, 1958), 186.

demonstrates that almost all the critics have treated it as allegorical fiction, although nominally it is referred to as science fiction, or myth, or fantasy. This need not surprise us since, in a broad sense, all criticism is allegorical activity because it attaches ideas to the structure of poetic imagery and, according to Northrop Frye, translates into discursive and explicit language what was implicit in the poem. Or in modern semiotic parlance, criticism is a form of "secondary encoding."[3] Criticism tends to be all the more allegorical when dealing with fictions about other worlds that invite comparison with our own world and our cultural assumptions.

Finally, in the light of recent theories of allegory advanced by Edward Honig, Rosemond Tuve, Gay Clifford, Maureen Quilligan, and in particular Angus Fletcher in his seminal study *Allegory: The Theory of a Symbolic Mode*, we must conclude that allegory, far from being outmoded and inferior to symbolism, has become a privileged term in contemporary critical discourse. According to Paul de Man, "the prevalence of allegory always corresponds to the unveiling of an authentically temporal destiny"; for him "symbolism" and "allegory" are tropes or figures for language and thought, and for certain forms of blindness and insight.[4] In my analysis of *Perelandra*, I will draw freely on these modern theories, arguing that—*pace* Lewis's opinion (and Tolkien's)—allegory, both as a mode of thought and of figurative expression, is essential to this novel and to the way we read and respond to it.

The Allegory of Love is unquestionably Lewis's most important work of criticism.[5] It deals with the birth and growth of allegory from Prudentius to Spenser and in particular with medieval allegorical love poetry. To be more exact, Lewis writes about the kind of allegory or picture language which is concerned with man's inner struggle and

---

3. Frye, *Anatomy of Criticism: Four Essays* (Princeton: Princeton University Press, 1957), 89. On criticism as secondary encoding, see David Lodge, *Small World: An Academic Romance* (London: Secker and Warburg, 1984), 25.

4. Honig, *Dark Conceit: The Making of Allegory* (Evanston: Northwestern University Press, 1959); Tuve, *Allegorical Imagery: Some Medieval Books and Their Posterity* (Princeton: Princeton University Press, 1966); Clifford, *The Transformations of Allegory* (London: Routledge and Kegan Paul, 1974); Quilligan, *The Language of Allegory: Defining the Genre* (Ithaca: Cornell University Press, 1979); Fletcher, *Allegory: The Theory of a Symbolic Mode* (Ithaca, N.Y.: Cornell University Press, 1964); de Man, *Blindness and Insight: Essays in the Rhetoric of Contemporary Criticism* (1971), rev. ed. (London: Methuen, 1983), 206.

5. For the critical reception of *The Allegory of Love*, see Joe R. Christopher and Joan K. Ostling, *C. S. Lewis: An Annotated Checklist* (Kent, Ohio: Kent State University Press, 1974), 233–36.

manifests itself as a struggle between virtues and vices. Although some critics have later quarreled about some of its details, his description of the allegorical impulse and its realization in medieval Europe is likely to remain of permanent value. Indeed the book is as much about the allegory of love as about Lewis's reverence of allegory. Given the fact that it appeared at a time when neither the Middle Ages nor allegory itself were at all popular, his study has certainly contributed to the revaluation of allegory. One of its most perceptive comments is that "allegory, in some sense, belongs not to medieval man but to man, or even to mind, in general."[6] In a preface to the Oxford English Texts edition of Bunyan's *The Pilgrim's Progress* more than twenty years later, we find Lewis still vindicating allegory which "gives you one thing in terms of another. All depends on respecting the rights of the vehicle, in refusing to allow the least confusion between the vehicle and its freight." He deplores

> the pernicious habit of reading allegory as if it were a cryptogram to be translated; as if, having grasped what an image (as we say) "means," we threw the image away and thought of the ingredient in real life which it represents. But that method leads you continually out of the book back into the conception you started from and would have had without reading it. The right process is the exact reverse. We ought not to be thinking "This green valley, where the shepherd boy is singing, represents humility"; we ought to be discovering, as we read, that humility is like that green valley. *That way, moving always into the book, not out of it, from the concept to the image, enriches the concept.* And that is what allegory is for.[7]

Yet in *The Allegory of Love* he also professes in no uncertain terms his greater love for symbolism:

> This fundamental equivalence between the immaterial and the material may be used by the mind in two ways. . . . On the one hand you can start with an immaterial fact, such as the passions you actually experience, and can then invent *visibilia* to express them. If you are hesitating between an angry retort and a soft answer, you can express your state of mind by inventing a person called *Ira* with a torch and letting her contend with another invented person called *Patientia*. This is allegory. . . . But there is another way of using the equivalence, which is almost the opposite of allegory, and which I would call sacramentalism or sym-

6. Lewis, *The Allegory of Love: A Study in Medieval Tradition* (Oxford: Clarendon Press, 1936), 44.

7. Lewis, "The Vision of John Bunyan" (1962), in *Selected Literary Essays*, ed. Walter Hooper (Cambridge: Cambridge University Press, 1969), 148, 149; my italics.

bolism. If our passions, being immaterial, can be copied by material inventions, then it is possible that our material world in its turn is the copy of an invisible world. As the god Amor and his figurative garden are to the actual passions of men, so perhaps we ourselves and our "real" world are to something else. The attempt to read that something else through its sensible imitations, to see the archtype in the copy, is what I mean by symbolism or sacramentalism. . . . The difference between the two [allegory and symbolism] can hardly be exaggerated.

Furthermore, he writes that the poetry of symbolism does not find its greatest expression in the Middle Ages but in the Romantic period, a fact that is "significant of the profound difference that separates it from allegory." Arguing that there is nothing "mystical" or mysterious about medieval allegory, he concludes that "symbolism is a mode of thought, but allegory is a mode of expression."[8]

With only a few exceptions, Lewis's restrictive view of allegory and his unmistakable enthusiasm for symbolism or sacramentalism have gone unchallenged by the majority of his readers and critics. One of the first scholars to object to his theory on logical grounds was A. D. Nuttall, who pointed out that Lewis's notion of allegory is less systematic than it would appear on first sight. He distinguished a "proto-Lewis," for whom allegory is concerned with the less real, and a "deutero-Lewis," for whom the opposite seems to be true. The presence of the second Lewis can be spotted, for instance, in his discussion of Guillaume de Lorris's *Roman de la Rose*, when he finds that, at least in the first part of that long poem, the "'abstract' places and people" are, in fact, "presentations of actual life," whereas the "concrete" places and people in Chrétien de Troyes' *Lancelot* are not.[9]

To describe the allegorical figure as "less real" than the passions it represents and symbolism as "more real" is, however, question-begging; as Paul Piehler cautiously observed, the word "real" is a dangerous one.[10] In a similar vein, Louis MacNeice questioned the supposed dichotomy between allegory as a mode of expression and symbolism as a mode of thought, pointing out that this presupposes

8. Lewis, *Allegory of Love*, 44–45, 46, 48.

9. Nuttall, *Two Concepts of Allegory: A Study of Shakespeare's "The Tempest" and the Logic of Allegorical Expression* (New York: Barnes and Noble, 1967), 18–20; Lewis, *Allegory of Love*, 115.

10. Piehler, *The Visionary Landscape: A Study in Medieval Allegory* (London: Edward Arnold, 1971), 43. See also Lewis's discussion of the concept of the "real" in *Per*, 232.

the separation of form from content and suggests a delimitation between the two modes that cannot be maintained in actual practice.[11]

Moreover, the very concept of allegory is not a single one. Following Northrop Frye in this respect, we may distinguish a sliding scale of allegorical explicitness, ranging from the most allegorical to the least:[12]

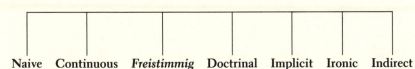

Naive   Continuous   *Freistimmig*   Doctrinal   Implicit   Ironic   Indirect

As is suggested by the term *freistimmig*, allegory is a contrapuntal technique of writing in which the relation between structurally significant imagery and examples and precepts varies a great deal. Lewis's *Perelandra* can be classified as a *freistimmige* or, as I would prefer to call it, a "free-style" allegory, with a penchant to "doctrinal" allegory, in which the relation between image or symbol and theme or idea is unsystematic and intermittent. We only read on the two levels simultaneously or point-to-point when we feel that the literal level is penetrated by metaphorical significance. As Rosemond Tuve has reminded us, there are always signposts in the text for such "double" readings, such as the authorial voice, explicit and implicit parallels between the *concretion,* or sensuous detail, and the *abstraction,* and genre conventions.[13]

There is enough evidence to suggest that Lewis entertained a narrow view of allegory. He is mainly concerned with "naive" and "continuous" allegory in which the relation between the two levels is predetermined and overly systematized, with little or no freedom for the reader to make up his or her own mind. This is the case, for instance, in Prudentius' *Psychomachia,* which Lewis takes to be the archetype of all allegories, and in his own *The Pilgrim's Regress,* subtitled "An Allegorical Apology for Christianity, Reason and Romanticism." Of the latter work it can only be said that it epitomizes naive, frigid, inferior allegory, with its tedious abstractions and bloodless personifications.

As for Lewis's preference for symbolism, it is not difficult to link it

11. MacNeice, *Varieties of Parable* (Cambridge: Cambridge University Press, 1965), 3–5. See also Graham Hough, *An Essay on Criticism* (London: Duckworth, 1966), 123–28.

12. Robert D. Denham, *Northrop Frye and Critical Method* (University Park: Pennsylvania State University Press, 1978), 38.

13. Tuve, *Allegorical Imagery,* 184–86, 391–92.

up with the general Romantic preference for symbolism over allegory. As I have argued elsewhere at length, there runs a clear line
from Goethe to Coleridge, who believed in a kind of *participation
mystique* of the symbol with the idea symbolized; to later nineteenth-
century Symbolist poetics, which hypostatized a mysterious relation
between—to use Saussurian terms—the word as *signifier* and the
object as *signified,* leading to a form of higher Truth; and finally to
the New Critics, who continued to believe in a natural alliance between the symbol and the transcendental.[14] The following quotation
from the Dutch historian Johan Huizinga illustrates to perfection the
Romantic belief in the unmediated vision:

> All realism, in the medieval sense, leads to anthropomorphism. Having
> attributed a real existence to an idea, the mind wants to see this idea
> alive, and can only effect this by personifying it. In this way allegory is
> born. It is not the same thing as symbolism. Symbolism expresses a mys-
> terious connection between two ideas, allegory gives a visible form to the
> conception of such a connection. Symbolism is a very profound func-
> tion of the mind, allegory is a superficial one. It aids symbolic thought to
> express itself, but endangers it at the same time by substituting a figure
> for a living idea. The force of the symbol is easily lost in the allegory. So
> allegory in itself implies from the outset normalizing, projecting on a
> surface, crystallizing.[15]

In the light of modern linguistics and semiotics, this overdeter-
mined, Romantic preference for the symbol as the privileged mode of
expression had to be demystified. We have become much more aware
of the arbitrary nature of the linguistic sign, its conventionality, and
the unstable relation between word and meaning. According to Paul
de Man, the symbolist view that language can express a unity between the representative and the semantic function is unacceptable,
since there is always a disjunction between experience and the expression of experience, between nature and language. Any claim that
the subject and the object can be fused in language is for him
"illusionary" and a "historical error," even a form of "self-induced
blindness." On the contrary, allegory is for him a privileged mode of
figural writing precisely because in it sign and meaning never coincide, since the sign always exists within a system of allegorical signs:

14. See my *T. F. Powys: A Modern Allegorist: The Companion Novels "Mr. Weston's
Good Wine" and "Unclay" in the Light of Modern Allegorical Theory* (Amsterdam:
Rodopi, 1986).

15. Huizinga, *The Waning of the Middle Ages* (1919), trans. F. Hopman (London:
Edward Arnold, 1924), 186.

Whereas the symbol postulates the possibility of an identity or an identification, allegory designates primarily a distance in relation to its own origin, and, renouncing the nostalgia and the desire to coincide, it establishes its language in the void of this temporal difference. In doing so it prevents the self from an illusionary identification with the non-self, which is now fully, though painfully, recognized as a non-self.[16]

In my linguistically oriented view, allegory is a form of polysemy, or multiple meaning, structured in such a way that the reader is encouraged to look constantly for further significance above and beyond the literal surface of the fiction. Both allegory and symbolism (including sacramentalism) are theme-dominated modes of symbolization which, although they are to be distinguished, cannot be considered mutually exclusive categories. Both are concerned with the metaphysical aspects of reality and the figurative expression thereof; both deal with the supposed relation between the material and the immaterial world, using images and symbols to express the supposed similarities and equivalences. What distinguishes the former is the more systematic and obsessive way in which the reader is made aware of this relation. In other words, all allegory entails symbolism and inasmuch as the latter becomes more highly patterned it tends towards allegory in a formal sense.

Although in Lewis's later criticism his preference for symbolism is replaced by a similar enthusiasm for the notion of myth, the same linguistic objections can be raised against it. In his praise of "myth" at the expense of allegory he is, it is true, in line with much modern criticism which, in its search for certain recurrent archetypal patterns and symbols, tends to attribute evaluative force to mythopoeic fiction. It would seem that the term "myth," when used in this way, is the heir of "symbol" in the older controversy over allegory and symbolism. Thus we find Lewis writing to Fr. Peter Milward in 1956 about *The Lord of the Rings*: "My view wd. be that a good myth (i.e. a story out of which ever varying meanings will grow for different readers and in different ages) is a higher thing than an allegory (into which *one* meaning has been put). Into an allegory a man can put only what he already knows; in a myth he puts what he does not yet know and cd. not come by in any other way" (*Letters*, 271). He praised Orwell's satiric allegory *Animal Farm* because it is a story that transcends its allegorical significance and becomes a full-fledged myth

16. De Man, *Blindness and Insight*, 141, 207.

that speaks for itself.[17] In his chapter "On Myth" he affirms that myth transcends the simpler expository or allegorical form and will continue to feel more important than all allegorical explanations showered upon it (*Experiment*, 44).

Although there is much to admire in this essay, particularly his emphasis on the nonmimetic nature of myth and its resistance to easy identification, one fails to see why some of the features attributed to myth are not equally applicable to such model allegories as Dante's *The Divine Comedy* or the anonymous medieval poem *Pearl*. The quality of the "numinous," for instance, defined as something of great moment that has been communicated (*Experiment*, 44), is surely present in them. Above all, the proclaimed open-endedness of myth, inviting interpretation, is equally applicable to the great allegories, as the history of Dante criticism shows. Both myth and allegory are also open-ended in that they are open to further narratives. *Perelandra* illustrates the point. It is itself part of a trilogy, with *Out of the Silent Planet* as precursor and *That Hideous Strength* as successor. Each of these fictions deals with the central myth of creation and with related myths, and each pivots on Ransom's adventures and experiences. Clearly, myth and allegory overlap in important ways since the latter is the narrative encapsulation of the former, and insofar as myth is verbal it is highly structured, as Lévi-Strauss's theory of the logic of "primitive thought" (*pensée sauvage*) has made clear.[18] Both mediate symbolically, though in different ways, between such irreconcilable oppositions as life/death, body/soul, male/female, good/evil; or in terms of the novel under discussion, the oppositions of accidental/designed, fact/myth, unreal/real, material/immaterial, and ephemeral/timeless.

Given that a literary recreation of mythic material is inevitably a conscious act, the likelihood of an allegorical treatment is increased, since allegory always echoes the language of a prior and potentially sacred text, usually the Bible or another authoritative text in which the sacred is articulated.[19] This is particularly the case with *Perelandra*, dedicated to some members of the Community of St. Mary the Virgin at Wantage. From the author's correspondence with Sister Penelope, his evangelical zest and his doctrinal bent become evident:

17. Lewis, "George Orwell" (1955), in *On Stories and Other Essays on Literature*, ed. Walter Hooper (London: Collins, 1982), 103.

18. Claude Lévi-Strauss, "The Structural Study of Myth," in *Structural Anthropology*, trans. Claire Jacobson and Brooke Grundfest Schoepf (New York: Basic Books, 1963), 206–31.

19. See Quilligan, *Language of Allegory*, 100.

I've got Ransom to Venus and through his first conversation with the "Eve" of that world; a difficult chapter. I hadn't realized till I came to write it all the *Ave-Eva* business. I may have embarked on the impossible. This woman has got to combine characteristics which the Fall has put poles apart—she's got to be in some ways like a Pagan goddess and in other ways like the Blessed Virgin. But, if one can get even a fraction of it into words, it is worth doing. (*Letters*, 195)

From the way the Green Lady is depicted in the novel, it becomes clear that her characterization depends considerably on Lewis's pre-existing dogmatic belief. It may even be concluded that his aim to present her as totally innocent and yet capable of falling is not quite successful for that very reason, but in any case Lewisian myth is not as open and polysemous as he would have his readers believe (see the letter to Milward quoted above). Nor can it be, in view of the strong belief expressed throughout his work that myth reflects essence or reality since it is a "real though unfocussed gleam of divine truth falling on human imagination" (*Mir*, 161, note 1). To the extent that myth is verbalized, language itself can convey spiritual truth through images and metaphors.[20] A brief examination of the many references to myth and comments on language will illustrate their thematic importance. In doing so I shall be using modern allegorical theory which, interestingly enough, also emphasizes the central concern of allegory with language and meaning.

According to Quilligan's *The Language of Allegory*, the latest study on the subject, allegory is a radically *linguistic* procedure (it is "hung up with words") that codifies the text and the reader's expectations of the text. Its focus is language and the production of meaning: "Allegorical narrative unfolds as a series of punning commentaries, related to one another on the most literal of verbal levels—the sounds of words." She insists on the literalness (letter-all-ness) of the allegorical text, which is a self-reflexive landscape of language, a radical form of punning or wordplay whose multiple meanings must be deciphered by the active reader. Allegory always contains a "threshold" image, emblem, or symbol in the form of some linguistic construct or wordplay which is subsequently commented upon by the narrative, so that an allegory is both a text and its own narrative

---

20. For Tolkien's similar view of myth as reflecting "a splintered fragment of the true light, the eternal truth that is with God," see Humphrey Carpenter, *Tolkien: A Biography* (London: George Allen and Unwin, 1977), 147. For a useful summary of Lewis's ideas on language, see William L. White, *The Image of Man in C. S. Lewis* (Nashville: Abingdon Press, 1969), chap. 2.

commentary on it. She amply illustrates her theory with convincing examples from writers as far apart as William Langland and Thomas Pynchon.[21] Although Lewis's fiction is nowhere mentioned (only his favorable comments on medieval allegories), it seems to me that her focus on language, particularly on wordplay and on polysemy, and her view of the allegorical narrative as action designed to comment on the verbal implications of the words describing the imaginary action are equally relevant to his work and will offer fresh insights into its profoundly allegorical nature.

No reader of *Perelandra* will deny that it is concerned with language in several important ways. In the creation of protagonist Elwin Ransom, a Cambridge philologist, the implied author's deep concern with language and meaning is given free play and at the same time made acceptable to the reader, who is asked imaginatively to share this interest. In my view the key passage of the novel is to be found in the description of the crucial moment when Ransom is called upon to act and face his antagonist, Weston, the devil incarnate. This scene may be called a "threshold" symbol, embedded in a sophisticated pun on his name. In the darkness he hears Maleldil's voice speaking to him: "It is not for nothing that you are named Ransom." This puzzling statement is followed by a lengthy reflection on Ransom's part and concluded by the pronouncement, "My name also is Ransom" (*Per,* 168). In this central passage two kinds of philology and language systems are contrasted: on the one hand, human philology and Tellurian language, in which the relation between words and things is accidental; and on the other, "divine" philology and the Old Solar language, in which the relation is essential, leading to a higher Truth, a form of knowledge about the unseen reality, "the larger pattern." The first viewpoint can be associated with Ferdinand de Saussure, the father of modern linguistics, for whom the relation between word (*signifier*) and thing (*the signified*) is arbitrary and conventional; the second is the novel's particular message—based on an *a priori* belief—which is further unfolded by Ransom's subsequent actions. This same contrast between "arbitrariness" and "naturalness," or between language as mediation and the unmediated vision based on the supposed fusion between the symbol and the idea symbolized, also underlies Lewis's famous distinction between allegory and symbolism that we discussed before.

The importance of language is further emphasized by the au-

21. Quilligan, *Language of Allegory,* 15, 22, 51–54. The notion of the "threshold image" is taken from Honig, *Dark Conceit,* 72.

thor's elaborate attempts to create a special kind of prelapsarian, otherworld language, which was "originally a common speech for all rational creatures" (*Per*, 26), but has now been lost in our own language because of the Fall and the subsequent confusion of tongues at Babel. Its register is, broadly speaking, religious, full of biblical and Miltonic phrases with their own highly peculiar sentence structure, as well as scientific—a kind of space language, full of compound words, like *Hlab-Eribol-ef-Cordi* for Perelandrian speech, or *Tor-Oyarsa-Perelendri* for Maleldil's viceroy on the floating island, or "the bent Oyarsa" for Satan's representative on Tellus, our earthly planet. In many cases the reader will be tempted to unravel this theological science fiction language in search of further significance. Sometimes one needs the author's interpretative comments in order to make sense out of words like *eldila* (footnoted on *Per*, 19), *hru* (blood), "Lur" (a river that is far hence), and *sorns* (white giants on Mars), or even extratextual explanations (given by Lewis himself for *Maleldil* [Jesus Christ], "the Old One" [the Father] and "the Bent One" [Satan]). It is not necessary to go deeply into the semantic ramifications of the "other-speak" here; suffice it to suggest that its presence in the text is a powerful linguistic means of exerting authorial control over the reader, intended to make him or her aware of its "higher semantics."

Capitalization is another linguistic device that is noticeable throughout the novel. In general it is used to identify a specific person, place, or thing as a proper noun, but in *Perelandra* it occurs so frequently and so idiosyncratically that the reader cannot fail to notice its potential for conveying semantic emphasis. Naturally, all nouns connected with the numinous Perelandra world are capitalized, but also terrestrial persons and things are singled out in this way: "the Earth," "waves of Atlantic Height," "the Sun," "a Breakdown," "Madness." We notice in particular the striking use of capitalized adjective plus capitalized noun, collocations, or sometimes capitalized adjective only ("he is what we would call Bad" or "it seemed Blasphemous"): "the Upward Path," "the Great Risk," "the Wounded World," "the Empirical Bogey."

This "foregrounding" of the figurative, metaphorical nature of language by means of capitalization can also be interpreted as a form of *personification*, a standard device in allegories of all kinds, intended to represent the inanimate in human terms. Many religious and (quasi-) mystical concepts are personified in this way: "the Third One" (the Holy Ghost), "the Prince of Darkness," "the Giant's Causeway," "the Great Dance," "stepping into the Alongside," meeting "Pleasure," "Real" and "Unreal," and of course the "Un-man." We

may conclude that the various linguistic markers—such as the ono-
mastic profusion, capitalization, and personification—are expressive,
rhetorical strategies to emphasize the polysemous nature of the text
and how it should be read.

The key passage referred to earlier also allows us to link up the
author's views on language with those on myth as ultimate reality, in
particular the distinction between myth and fact, and that between
myth and antimyth. We learn that for Ransom "the whole distinction
between things accidental and things designed, like the distinction
between fact and myth, was purely terrestrial" (*Per*, 163). Once on the
floating island, he feels that he is not just following an adventure but
"enacting a myth" (*Per*, 52). Although he is at times assaulted by doubt
(the "old suspicion") and has to fight off his enemy's disparaging view
of religious belief as a matter of "pure mythology," for him Perelandrian mythology is "based on a solider reality than we dream."
Earthly mythology, on the other hand, is but "gleams of celestial
strength and beauty falling on a jungle of filth and imbecility" (*Per*,
231–32). This Platonic view of myth being equal to Reality or Truth is
worked out further in a Socratic exchange on appearance and reality
between Ransom and the Oyarsa of Mars, hinging on the key word
"real":

> "But do I see you as you really are?" he asked.
> "Only Maleldil sees any creature as it really is," said Mars.
> "How do you see one another?" asked Ransom.
> "There are no holding places in your mind for an answer to that."
> "Am I then seeing only an appearance? Is it not real at all?"
> "You see only an appearance, small one. You have never seen more
> than an appearance of anything—not of Tellus, nor of a stone, nor of
> your own body. This appearance is as true as what you see of those."
> "But . . . there were those other appearances."
> "No. There was only the failure of appearance."
> "I don't understand," said Ransom. "Were all those other things—the
> wheels and the eyes—more real than this or less?"
> "There is no meaning in your question," said Mars. (*Per*, 232)

This argument about more or less "real" inevitably reminds us of *The
Allegory of Love*, where it occurs with reference to the distinction
between allegory and symbolism, as we saw; its repetition in a fictional work is indicative of Lewis's philosophical preoccupation with
the problem of ultimate reality, which transcends knowledge and
becomes a matter of belief.

Diametrically opposed to the old true myths is the false, modern
antimyth, called by Ransom mockingly "The Empirical Bogey": "the

great myth of our century with its gases and galaxies, its light years and evolutions, its nightmare perspectives of simple arithmetic in which everything that can possibly hold significance for the mind becomes the mere by-product of essential disorder" (*Per*, 188). This antimyth of humanistic evolution and scientific progress is embodied in the character of Weston, who is intended to personify "scientism": "the belief that the supreme moral end is the perpetuation of our own species, and that this is to be pursued even if, in the process of being fitted for survival, our species has to be stripped of all those things for which we value it—of pity, of happiness, and of freedom."[22] Serving "the Force" he worships, Weston is willing to falsify his experiments, and consequently he becomes the Un-man, the personification of evil bent on the destruction of mankind, reenacting the myth of Satan's rebellion against God, which led to his final downfall.

These two kinds of myth are symbolized by two kinds of language in the novel: the "unfallen" Perelandrian speech, full of fresh images and perceptions, and the Tellurian language, replete with clichés and abstractions, employed by Weston, particularly in the great temptation scenes. With Ransom's victory over his opponent, the supremacy of revelatory language over earthly speech is clearly established in the novel's last chapters, which can only be problematic for critics applying mimetic standards of characterization and action. If we are willing to accept *Perelandra* as a sophisticated treatment of an idiosyncratic, Christian view of language and meaning, these chapters are entirely convincing. In my view, they underpin the allegorical nature of the text as a whole.

At the same time it should be realized that the novel's claim regarding the relation of language and myth to truth and essence is far removed from contemporary, deconstructionist philosophy, which has called into question the very notion of "presence" through language. According to Jacques Derrida, for instance, there is no absolute meaning

> since no element can function as a sign without referring to another element which itself is not simply present. This interweaving results in each "element" . . . being constituted on the basis of the trace within it of the other elements in the chain or system. This interweaving, this textile, is the *text*. . . . Nothing, neither among the elements nor within

22. Lewis, "A Reply to Professor Haldane," in *Of Other Worlds: Essays and Stories*, ed. Walter Hooper (London: Geoffrey Bles, 1966), 77.

the system, is anywhere ever simply present or absent. There are only, everywhere, differences and traces of traces.[23]

As for the "trace," it is "not a presence but the simulacrum of a presence that dislocates itself, displaces itself, refers itself, it properly has no site—erasure belongs to its structure. . . . The paradox of such a structure, in the language of metaphysics, is an inversion of metaphysical concepts, which produces the following effect: the present becomes the sign of signs, the trace of a trace."[24] For him as for Paul de Man, presence reveals itself paradoxically as absence—of nature, of reality, of God, and of eternity. But for Ransom as for Lewis himself, Christianity was "myth become fact," and *Perelandra* is the impressive allegorical narrative of this doctrinal conviction.[25]

This conclusion can be underpinned with recent allegorical theory as well. The most intricately systematic and self-contained account of allegory is that of Angus Fletcher in *Allegory: The Theory of a Symbolic Mode.* I shall be using his allegorical model as a working hypothesis for describing and interpreting the allegorical mode of *Perelandra,* though here no more than a summary can be given. Fletcher's model offers not only the most comprehensive and satisfactory account but it has, moreover, the advantage over other theories that it is itself based on Coleridge's well-known description of allegory:

> We may then safely define allegorical writing as the employment of one set of agents and images with actions and accompaniments correspondent, so as to convey, while in disguise, either moral qualities or conceptions of the mind that are not in themselves objects of the senses, or other images, agents, actions, fortunes, and circumstances so that the difference is everywhere presented to the eye or imagination, while the likeness is suggested to the mind; and this connectedly, so that the parts combine to form a consistent whole.[26]

Although the terms have been elaborated and sometimes refined in

23. Derrida, *Positions* (1972), trans. Alan Bass (London: Athlone Press, 1981), 26.

24. Derrida, *Writing and Difference* (1977), trans. Alan Bass (London: Routledge and Kegan Paul, 1978), 24.

25. Lewis, "Myth Became Fact" (1944), in *God in the Dock: Essays on Theology and Ethics,* ed. Walter Hooper (Grand Rapids, Mich.: Eerdmans, 1970), 66–67.

26. Samuel Taylor Coleridge, *Miscellaneous Criticism,* ed. T. M. Raysor (Oxford: Clarendon Press, 1907), 30. See also ibid, 99; and "The Statesman's Manual," in *Lay Sermons,* vol. 6 of *The Collected Works of Samuel Taylor Coleridge,* ed. R. J. White (Princeton: Princeton University Press, 1972), 16–17.

the context of modern scholarship (comparative religion, anthropology, and psychoanalysis), the five distinctive elements in Coleridge's descriptive definition remain essentially intact. The key concepts of Fletcher's model are: "daemonic agency," "cosmic imagery," "symbolic action," "magical causation," and "ambivalence."

As for agency or characterization, a distinction is to be made between the "conceptual hero," who displays a relatively wide range of human behavior and is thematically complicated, and the "personified agents" with their minimal though adequate human and thematic range. The conceptual hero is capable of generating subcharacters who, as alter egos, represent and reveal aspects of himself or embody undeveloped facets of his personality. Allegorical agency is further characterized by daemonic possession exercised by powers potent for either good or evil and often at war with each other, causing characters to behave in a constricted, compulsive manner in accordance with the overall thematic design or central conception. This compartmentalization of function turns them into static images or iconographic emblems and transmutes agency into imagery.[27]

The novel's conceptual hero is unquestionably Elwin Ransom, who is sent to the unfallen or prelapsarian planet Venus by a higher spiritual force, Maleldil, to save original innocence. He is not only the most concrete and the most humanized but also the most central thematic character. He is endowed with several individualizing traits: he is inquisitive as well as sophisticated but at the same time not without some practical sense, as becomes clear from his careful preparations with regard to his will before his departure for Venus. Once on the planet he shows remarkable fortitude, though at times he is beset by fear and suffers from loneliness. After defeating the Unman, he remains humble in spite of the praise bestowed on him by Queen Tinidril and King Tor.

All the other characters are personified agents and therefore less concretely realized. They enact in personified form several virtues and vices—retained innocence and fallen pride in the cases of the Green Lady and the megalomaniac Weston. They are not only the principal subcharacters but at the same time Ransom's alter egos, who act either in support of him or in opposition to him. They can also be looked upon as symbolizing aspects of himself that must be either defended or resisted. Since personified agents possess a semblance of human personality only, there is no point in attempting to account for their behavior in quasi-realistic or psychological terms;

27. Fletcher, *Allegory*, 32–37, 87.

the criticism of the King, for instance, who is often accused of being pompous or "unfeeling" towards his wife, is entirely beside the point in allegory, which by definition flouts the criterion of realism. Of marginal thematic importance are the narrator and Doctor Humphrey, who function mainly on the levels of narration and plot; the fictional Lewis acts as an external focalizer, responsible for introducing Ransom to the reader and for the creation of atmosphere and suspense.

Daemonic possession can be seen at work in Ransom and Weston, who both act under compulsion; the former is activated by "the Voice" to save the Lady and in so doing save mankind, the latter is manipulated by "the Force," which misguides him and turns him into an Un-Man. In the course of the narrative, both the conceptual hero and the personified agents become increasingly abstract and emblematic, which is tantamount to saying that each character has become an image of an idea. Employing a variation on A. C. Bradley, we might conclude that in allegory character is imagery.[28]

Images are organized either on the principle of synecdoche (including ellipsis), which relates each image to an overall symbolic organization, or on the basis of metonymy, by substituting one name for another with possible thematic connotation. Every image is part of a "kosmos," or hierarchically ordered system of symbols, each with its own place and value within the system. Although images may appear to be disconnected from each other and thus distort the reader's perspective ("diagrammatic isolation"), they always link up and interact with the "cosmic image," or seminal metaphor, which is essentially ambivalent and open to inherently contradictory meanings. Denoting both the power hierarchy of a given universe and its microcosmic sign or ornament, kosmos is ultimately epideictic in character and belongs to the rhetoric of praise or blame. In classic allegory the kosmos, with its double sense, is affirmative and reflects an ideal order or system, whereas in modern allegory it tends to be ironic and unstable, and rejects any established order in favor of a private and often internalized universe.[29]

The cosmic image of the novel is Perelandra itself, the floating interplanetary island which we know as Venus. As an archetypal image, Venus may connote spiritual love, according to J. E. Cirlot.[30] In the novel it is also clearly associated with femininity since Ransom

28. Bradley, *Shakespearean Tragedy* (London: Macmillan, 1904), 7.

29. Fletcher, *Allegory*, 85, 108–9.

30. Cirlot, *A Dictionary of Symbols*, trans. Jack Sage (London: Routledge and Kegan Paul, 1962), 359.

is described as being "breast-fed by the planet Venus herself" (*Per*, 213). The principle of synecdoche allows us to link up the novel's major images and image clusters—such as the sea and its waves, greenness and other colors, nakedness, the cave, and the Great Dance—with the cosmic image of the island, which encapsulates the novel's central meaning in symbolic form.

It hardly needs emphasizing how important metonymy, in particular the process of name substitution, is in *Perelandra*. Earlier in this essay I drew attention to the key passage (*Per*, 168) in which Ransom's name figures prominently; his Christian name, Elwin, is glossed later in the novel as "friend of the eldila."[31] Weston's name is generally taken to be derived from "western," suggesting degenerated modern Western science as well as symbolizing death or the death wish. Most of the other proper names have been accounted for by the critics and occasionally by C. S. Lewis himself, who offers angel for *Eldil*, Christ for *Maleldil*, archangel for *Oyarsa*, and the Devil for the *Bent Eldil*.[32] In all cases it is more important for the reader to realize the signifying process inherent in these allegorical or "speaking" names than to establish an exact meaning for each name.

The kosmos, or power hierarchy, in this other-worldly universe where Ransom undergoes a spiritual rebirth (his "second infancy") is firmly established: at the top stands Maleldil, followed by the Oyarsas (archangels) and the *eldila* (angels), and the Green Lady with her kingly husband, representing the world's as yet unfallen first couple:

> Adam's kingly manner is the outward expression of his supernatural kingship of earth and his wisdom. . . . In considering his relations with Eve we must constantly remind ourselves of the greatness of both personages. Their life together is ceremonial—a minuet, where the modern reader looked for a romp. Until they are fallen and robbed of their original majesty, they hardly ever address each other simply by their names but by stately periphrases. (*Preface*, 115)

At the bottom of the hierarchy are the "bent Oyarsa" (Satan) and his helper Weston, who acts like a Mephistopheles in his master's service. It is a hierarchical order reminiscent of the medieval conception of the great Chain of Being (itself metaphorically invoked in the novel's last chapter), which Lewis has elsewhere described:

31. *Per*, 224. For possible connections with Tolkien, see Carpenter, *Tolkien*, 171.
32. Roger Lancelyn Green and Walter Hooper, *C. S. Lewis: A Biography* (London: Collins, 1974), 172.

According to this conception degrees of value are objectively present in the universe. Everything except God has some natural superior; everything except unformed matter has some natural inferior. The goodness, happiness, and dignity of every being consists in obeying its natural superior and ruling its natural inferiors. When it fails in either part of this twofold task we have disease or monstrosity in the scheme of things until the peccant being is either destroyed or corrected. (*Preface*, 72)

The novel as a whole can be seen as a highly skillful form of rhetoric in praise of the divine order that must be maintained and believed in.

In the light of Fletcher's model, *Perelandra* must be called a classic allegory (though written in this century) since its kosmos is affirmative throughout. This can be further illustrated by considering briefly the presence of prior texts or textual fragments or echoes which help to shape textual meaning. Not only do we find a dense web of references and allusions to the Bible (as is to be expected in a fiction that takes it as the most authoritative, sacred "pre-text" in the dual sense of that word),[33] but also to English literature (Herrick, Milton, Pope, Defoe, Blake, Lewis Carroll, H. G. Wells, David Lindsay, George MacDonald) and to the classics (Homer, Virgil), including mythology and history. Taken collectively these references and allusions tend to affirm rather than to contradict the truth and authority of their pre-texts, and by virtue of their figurative nature they support the novel's central metaphor and theme. They also turn out to be a powerful authorial means of exerting control over the reader in order to make him aware of the allegory of the text and of the text as allegory.

The plot is structured according to ritualistic necessity, as opposed to probability, and therefore, allegorical action differs basically from mimetic plot by always being symbolic in nature. This "symbolic action," according to Fletcher's model, tends towards one of two patterns: "progress" (the questing journey, either physical or spiritual) or "battle" (conflict ranging from physical violence to ideological warfare). These two forms of symbolic action, which often merge into each other within the same work, correspond to two forms of symbolic patterning, "parataxis" (coordination) and "hypotaxis" (subordination); they also correspond to two forms of overall symbolic rhythm with attendant emotional and hypnotic effects. These forms of syntactic and rhythmic patterning are also often conjoined within the single work. I take the liberty at this point to add to Fletcher's model another form of patterning, in this case on the narrative level,

33. Quilligan, *Language of Allegory*, 97–98.

where we find both *episodic narration,* which conforms to symbolic action as progress, and *expository narration,* which is related to the battle pattern. The constant alternation between these two patterns is typical of allegorical narrative.[34]

The dominant pattern of symbolic action is the battle, which is already introduced early in the novel in the attack of the dark *eldila* on the narrator "Lewis" while he is waiting in Ransom's dark cottage. Battle comprises several forms of fighting, both concrete and abstract. In a literal sense there is the actual fight between Ransom and Weston, described in vivid detail. There is also the spiritual fight between them: as symbolic representatives of God and Satan, they are involved in a *psychomachia,* or soul battle, fighting for the possession of the Green Lady's soul. Another form of battle is the verbal conflict, or debate, in the form of an exchange with a question-and-answer structure. There are several long theological disputations between the conceptual hero and his antagonist, as well as a number of discussions between Ransom and the Green Lady and between Ransom and the King about Perelandrian metaphysics. The battle pattern is echoed on the story level by a good many references to the two world wars.

The other fundamental pattern of symbolic action is the progress, or questing journey, characterized by a straight line of plot development which produces a daemonic effect because the allegorical agent can only move in one direction and stays bound on his quest. On the literal level this progress deals with Ransom's interplanetary voyage to Venus and his subsequent return to Tellus; in a spiritual sense the questing journey is concerned with the discovery of true Reality beyond language.

As befits allegorical action, the patterns of progress and battle often conjoin, which is equally true of their textual expressions in the shape of parataxis and hypotaxis. Although the style is mainly hypotactic, we find many examples of parataxis as well, particularly in the more ecstatic passages such as the descriptions of the lush richness of the Perelandrian landscape or the highly formalized rendering of the Great Dance in the last chapter. Analysis of the narrative structure reveals the predominance of exposition and commentary over straightforward narration, as can be expected from a theme-dominated mode of writing such as allegory.

Causality, the way plot events are connected through cause and effect, is based not on probability but on daemonically controlled

34. Fletcher, *Allegory,* 151–67.

magical force. Two aspects of this magical causation, or nonmimetic plausibility, are relevant to the aforementioned patterns of battle and progress. "Imitative magic" is the basis of causality when symmetry predominates and "contagious magic" when the underlying structure is ritualistic. The former—based on similarity—manifests itself in various types of "doubling" on the levels of plot (subplots, for instance) and agency (exemplified by character doubles). The latter—based on contiguity—can be seen at work in the magic invested in objects, names, and numbers. Once again, it must be remembered that the two forms of magic interpenetrate in most cases. The cure against magical contagion by which events and characters interact, infecting each other with various virtues and vices, is "symbolic isolation" in central places possessing magical powers for either good or evil—or, more often, for good and evil mingled. These centers of isolation function as zones of absolute reality where the supernatural and the natural meet.[35]

It is evident that magic, understood as supernatural agency that invests people, places, and objects with supernatural powers, is of prime importance in this novel, particularly when considered as a specimen of science fiction. Maleldil's control over Ransom and Satan's manipulation of Weston are characteristic examples of magical forces that determine the subsequent plot events and therefore require the reader's suspension of disbelief in magical causation. We find doubling not only on the level of plot, where the events on Perelandra, for instance, are foreshadowed in the opening chapters, but also when we extend this notion to include any type of doubling or symmetry of the characters and images as well, either through repetition or through contrast. Doubling is also inherent in the ritualistic and repetitive nature of the progress and battle patterns of allegorical action.

It should also be clear that magical causation acts as a form of authorial control over the reader at the same time; the implausible events, or *deus ex machina* acts, violate the reader's ordinary conception of time and place (including space) and force him to attend to the narrative's deeper meaning. The floating island of Perelandra can be seen as the principal instrument of symbolic isolation. Other examples of places under daemonic control by good and evil powers are Ransom's earthly cottage, the Fixed Land, the cave where Weston is finally defeated, the Valley of Life, and the transmortal mountains.

35. Fletcher, *Allegory*, 181–84, 195–96, 208–19.

These places can be seen as "symbols of the centre," in which mac-rocosmic meanings are enacted in concrete terms.[36]

Finally, theme or subject-matter in allegory is always dualistic in nature and involves a radical opposition between good and evil. This thematic dualism (love and hatred, ignorance and enlightenment, etc.) is expressed by an ordering of agency and imagery which is equally dualistic. "Ambivalence," or inner conflict (which is related to the concept of taboo), appears to lie at the heart of this dualism and is responsible for various thematic effects. "Emotive ambivalence" refers to the mixture of opposite feelings experienced by characters who are tempted by what is forbidden or, in a more intellectualized form, who experience a forbidden sense of doubt. "Philosophic am-bivalence" would seem to relate to the author's own ambivalent attitude to his work and manifests itself chiefly by means of irony and paradox, which add tension and calculated obscurity to the text and elicit an interpretative response from the reader.[37]

The thematic opposition between good and evil, God and Satan, Ransom and Weston permeates the novel's structure in all the aspects we have discussed so far. Further oppositional relationships or—to use structuralist terminology—"binary oppositions" of all kinds are to be found between Tellus and Perelandra, the Fixed Land and the floating island, body and soul, death and rebirth, damnation and salvation, and myth and fact. These polarities can be grouped to-gether horizontally ("syntagmatically") as well as vertically ("paradig-matically") to form clusters or parallel oppositions like Tellus-the Fixed Land-body-death-damnation-false myth versus Perelandra-the floating island-soul-rebirth-salvation fact.

But because of ambivalence, good and evil are not always so easy to distinguish, for sometimes they appear to merge even within a single character or image. Since temptation is at the heart of the novel, we are likely to find several examples of emotive ambivalence. The Green Lady, for instance, almost falls victim to Weston's sophis-ticated strategies of temptation at the end of chapter 10. A more intellectualized kind of ambivalence can be detected in Ransom himself, who is repeatedly confused by the seemingly logical argu-ments of his opponent, aptly called "the Tempter," and even momen-

36. See Mircea Eliade, *The Myth of the Eternal Return; or, Cosmos and History* (1949), trans. Willard R. Trask, Bollingen Series 46 (New York: Pantheon Books, 1954), 12–17; and Eliade, *The Sacred and the Profane: The Nature of Religion* (1957), trans. Willard R. Trask (New York: Harcourt Brace, 1959), 36–47.

37. Fletcher, *Allegory*, 224–29.

tarily questions Maleldil's divine providence. But, as befits affirmative allegory, the temptations are eventually resisted with a view to
the higher goal. It is therefore no surprise that the novel lacks philosophic ambivalence, since for its author the absolute truth of the
Christian conviction was not to be questioned. In this respect too,
Perelandra is decidedly not a modern allegory, a statement that accords with the conclusion reached earlier about the constructive nature of its intertextuality.

Although C. S. Lewis's intention is nowhere stated explicitly in
the novel, the reader can hardly be doubtful about its implicit intention: "What is hoped, of course, is that the reader will grasp the
similarity between the quality of the Perelandrian scenes and hap-
penings and the quality of Reality as understood by orthodox Christianity, in terms of God, Providence, angels and devils, the Incarnation, and the unity of all things in God's creative act."[38] It seems safe
to conclude, in conjunction with circumstantial evidence from C. S.
Lewis's letters and stray comments, that this authorial statement
comes close to his original intention. It can also be concluded that
allegory as a mode of thought, a way of perceiving ideas and phenomena in some concretely imagined form, and as a mode of figurative expression has proved eminently suitable for articulating such a
spiritual conviction in original fictional form.

---

38. Gunnar Urang, *Shadows of Heaven: Religion and Fantasy in the Writings of
C. S. Lewis, Charles Williams, and J. R. R. Tolkien* (Philadelphia: Pilgrim Press, 1971),
21.

Afterword
Owen Barfield

Merits apart, the outstanding feature of Lewis's *An Experiment in Criticism* was the novelty of its whole approach to the subject. Everyone had always been looking at different types of literature; why not try looking at different types of reader? It has occurred to me, as a result of reading the foregoing essays, that there is room for an experiment in what has come to be called "Lewis scholarship." Not quite so topsy-turvy no doubt, since what I am suggesting is a revised taxonomy rather than a reversed direction, but hardly less novel. Everyone, or nearly everyone, has treated the topic *C. S. Lewis* as approachable under four sharply divisible heads: (1) his Christian apologetics and the theology implicit in them; (2) his fiction and, less conspicuously, his poetry; (3) his literary criticism and scholarship; (4) his life and personality. Some have confined themselves to only one of these categories, others have dealt with more than one but in doing so have kept the division between them well to the fore. What I am suggesting is a different *threefold* classification, tabulable (if there is such a word) roughly as follows:
1. Theory (including philosophy, literature, and theology)
2. Art (including both fiction and poetry)
3. Psychography (his personal biography with the main emphasis on the history of his mind).

In this sort of domain and perhaps in the long run, it is true of *all* intellectual, as distinct from technological, activity that the value of distinguishing rather than dividing is that it makes possible a return towards *realized* unity by the process of cognizing particular relationships. Topical dissection has been replaced by functional discrimination. My impression is that, without consciously formulating it in my pedantic way, nearly all the contributors to this collection have worked with this threefold distinction at the back of their minds rather than the more obvious fourfold division—with the result that it is superior, I suspect, to any other collection that has so far appeared. I say "suspect," because I have long given up the attempt to read all, or even most, of what is written about Lewis.

299

To justify this contention by adequately illustrating it would take far too long. To illustrate it inadequately on the other hand entails an apparently invidious selection of one or two contributors from the others. Nevertheless, it may be better to risk that than to attempt the kind of careful survey of the whole that would be more appropriate to a review than to a brief epilogue gently closing a solid performance. If the title alone of Stephen Medcalf's essay, "Language and Self-Consciousness: The Making and Breaking of C. S. Lewis's Personae," seems to bear me out, that does not mean that others are not significant from the same point of view. In this case it is especially the relation between the first and third of my un-watertight compartments that is so fruitfully handled (though the second is by no means omitted from the survey), and this has enabled the importance for Lewis of his reliance on S. W. Alexander's enjoyment/contemplation dichotomy to be treated in the depth it deserves. In Paul Piehler's essay, by contrast, it is the complex of accord and discord between the first and second categories that predominates, in the context of a general discussion on allegory, symbol, and myth and the true relation between them.

Symbol and myth, and to a lesser extent allegory, were much more than mere literary tools for Lewis, and it is this that Colin Manlove emphasizes, concentrating on the relation between the second and third heads, and acutely observing, in doing so, that "the god in the mountain in *Till We Have Faces* is another version of the god on the mountain in *The Pilgrim's Regress*; and each is initially portrayed as harsh, ugly or brutish, and rejected by the protagonist as such."

One comes across many observations in this book that evoke the response not just of an acquiescent nod but of further reflection. This last is one of them, and I am tempted to air my own response to it before retiring behind the curtain. *The Pilgrim's Regress* does not mark the first appearance of that myth of the Monster-God in Lewis's literature and life. It is central to his early, and in my opinion underrated, poem *Dymer*. Moreover, in his preface to the 1950 edition of that poem he writes:

> I am told that the Persian poets draw a distinction between poetry which they have "found" and poetry which they have "brought": if you like, between the given and the invented, though they wisely refuse to identify this with the distinction between good and bad. Their terminology applies with unusual clarity to my poem. What I "found," what simply "came to me," was the story of a man who, on some mysterious bride, begets a monster: which monster, as soon as it has killed its father, becomes a god. This story arrived, complete, in my mind somewhere about

my seventeenth year. To the best of my knowledge I did not consciously or voluntarily invent it, nor was it, in the plain sense of that word, a dream. All I know about it is that there was a time when it was not there, and then presently a time when it was.

What may it signify that this violently symbolic myth was lurking somewhere in his makeup from near the beginning of his thinking life through to its end? I have no theory; nor presumably had Lewis himself, for he adds to the above account: "Every one may allegorise it or psychoanalyse it as he pleases: and if I did so myself my interpretations would have no more authority than anyone else's."[1] I do, however, suspect that an attentive awareness of it is one requisite for any well-willing attempt to be presently in touch with the true being of the man.

1. Lewis, *Narrative Poems*, ed. Walter Hooper (London: Geoffrey Bles, 1969), 3.

Contributors

OWEN BARFIELD was for many years a practicing solicitor in London and a regular contributor to the *New Statesman* and the *London Mercury*. He has spent periods in residence at Drew University, Brandeis University, and Hamilton College; he is now retired and lives in East Sussex, England. He is editor of Coleridge's *Philosophical Reflections* and the author of *History in English Words, Poetic Diction, Romanticism Comes of Age, Saving the Appearances, Worlds Apart, What Coleridge Thought,* and many articles.

MARIUS BUNING is on the faculty of the Free University of Amsterdam. He is the author of *T. F. Powys: A Modern Allegorist*.

MICHAEL A. COVINGTON is Associate Research Scientist in computational linguistics at the University of Georgia. He is the author of books and articles on the history of linguistics, computer programming, and astrophotography.

MARA E. DONALDSON, currently teaching in the Religion Department at Dickinson College, is author of *Holy Places are Dark Places: C. S. Lewis and Paul Ricoeur on Narrative Transformation*. She has published articles on biblical narrative and modern female heroes and is currently writing a book on Christian understandings of the problem of self-love.

VERLYN FLIEGER is Associate Professor of English at the University of Maryland at College Park, Maryland. She is the author of *Splintered Light: Logos and Language in Tolkien's World,* as well as articles on Owen Barfield, J. R. R. Tolkien, and E. R. Eddison.

DONALD E. GLOVER, Distinguished Professor of English at Mary Washington College in Fredericksburg, Virginia, is author of *C. S. Lewis: The Art of Enchantment*.

JOHN D. HAIGH is the author of an early Ph.D. dissertation on Lewis, "The Fiction of C. S. Lewis" (University of Leeds, 1962). A retired college lecturer, he now lives in Oxford and is a member of the Oxford C. S. Lewis Society.

CHARLES A. HUTTAR, Professor of English at Hope College, Holland, Michigan, is the editor of *Imagination and the Spirit* and the author of many essays on Lewis, Tolkien, and Charles Williams as well as numerous articles on sixteenth- and seventeenth-century British literature.

JARED LOBDELL is editor of *A Tolkien Compass* and author of *England and Always: Tolkien's World of the Rings.*

COLIN MANLOVE is Reader in English Literature at the University of Edinburgh. He is the author of *Modern Fantasy, Literature and Reality 1600–1800, The Gap in Shakespeare, The Impulse of Fantasy Literature, Science Fiction: Ten Explorations, C. S. Lewis: His Literary Achievement,* and *Critical Thinking: A Guide to Interpreting Literary Texts.*

STEPHEN MEDCALF, Reader in English in the School of European Studies, University of Sussex, Brighton, England, has written on the coincidence of myth and fact in Lewis's thought and contributed the description of Hugo Dyson to Humphrey Carpenter's *The Inklings.* He has also written essays on, among other topics, Virgil, Thomas Usk, G. K. Chesterton, P. G. Wodehouse, and T. S. Eliot, and a book on *William Golding.* He was editor and contributor to *The Later Middle Ages,* Glanville's *The Vanity of Dogmatizing,* and *Literary Education and Religious Values.*

GILBERT MEILAENDER, Professor of Religion at Oberlin College, Oberlin, Ohio, is author of *The Taste for the Other: The Social and Ethical Thought of C. S. Lewis, Friendship: A Study in Theological Ethics, The Theory and Practice of Virtue,* and *The Limits of Love.* He is on the Editorial Board of the *Journal of Religious Ethics.*

MICHAEL MURRIN is Professor of English, Comparative Literature, and Divinity at the University of Chicago. He has written *The Veil of Allegory* and *The Allegorical Epic.* He is currently working on a study of epic and warfare in the Renaissance.

PAUL TYNEGATE PIEHLER was a student of C. S. Lewis at Magdalen College, Oxford. Now Associate Professor of English at McGill University in Montreal, he has published *The Visionary Landscape: A Study in Medieval Allegory* and writes on various aspects of mythic and allegorical literature.

PETER J. SCHAKEL, Professor of English at Hope College, Holland, Michigan, is editor of *The Longing for a Form: Essays on the Fiction of C. S. Lewis* and author of *Reading with the Heart: The Way into Narnia* and *Reason and Imagination in C. S. Lewis* as well as a book and many articles on Jonathan Swift and verse satire in eighteenth-century England.

LYLE H. SMITH, JR., is Associate Professor of English at Biola University, La Mirada, California. He is the author of several articles on American, English, and Continental novelists and poets.

THOMAS WERGE, Professor of English at the University of Notre Dame, is coeditor of the journal *Religion and Literature* and author of *Thomas Shepard* and many essays on the theological dimensions of American narrative literature.

GREGORY WOLFE is Assistant Professor of English at Christendom College, Front Royal, Virginia. He is the editor of *The Intercollegiate Review* and the author of *After This Our Exile: Contemporary Literature and the Christian Imagination*. He founded the Oxford C. S. Lewis Society in 1981.

Permissions

Index

Adey, Lionel, 37n11
Aeschliman, Michael D., 66n11
Alexander, Samuel W., 116–18, 121, 123, 134, 135, 137, 141, 300
Allegory: medieval, 6, 200–209 *passim*, 212; of vision, 6, 201, 205–11, 284; of demystification, 6, 201–5, 211, 274, 278–79, 281; modern theories of, 7, 281–86, 290–98; in interpreting scripture, 85; in *Till We Have Faces*, 130; in Chronicles of Narnia, 119, 206, 240; and myth, 187, 204–5, 240, 277, 283–84, 288–90, 300; Lewis's contributions to, 199–201, 212, 277; and symbolism, 200–201, 277–84, 300; techniques and effects of, 205–10; in *Perelandra*, 290–98
Allott, Miriam, 190n17
Alston, William P., 40n17
Anscombe, G. E. M., 126, 127
Anselm, Saint, 127, 128, 130
Apuleius, Lucius, 130, 158, 165, 189
Aquinas, Saint Thomas, 62, 75, 83
Archetypes, 6, 103, 205–10, 211, 233–48, 254, 283, 295–96
Aristotle, 62, 75, 167, 179, 187
Arnold, Matthew, 127
Auden, W. H.: on quest, 195–96; mentioned, 91
Augustine, Saint, 62, 83, 148, 154, 156
Ayer, A. J., 40

Baker, Leo, 92n15, 93n17
Barfield, Owen: on metaphor, 3, 12, 24, 38, 59; influence on Lewis, 3, 24, 38, 43–57 *passim*, 62, 142; on semantic unity, 15–16, 45–46, 49, 54–55, 59, 67; on meaning change, 37–38; on original participation, 44–45; on figuration, 48, 51–52; on evolution of consciousness, 59–64; on *Out of the Silent Planet* and *Perelandra*, 73n17; on "The Birth of Language," 107–8; on pastiche in Lewis, 112–13, 119, 120, 129, 134, 135, 230; on "The Man Born Blind," 117; on myth in *The Great Divorce*, 211; as model for Ransom, 213

Beardsley, Monroe, 11
Beckett, Samuel, 133
Beckford, William, 221
Beowulf, 183, 190
Berdyaev, Nicolas, 79–80
Berggren, Douglas, 11, 13, 25, 27
Berkeley, George, 33–34
Berrigan, Daniel J., "Failure," 222
Beversluis, John, 76n1
Bible: as literature, 92, 165; Genesis, 73, 174, 177–78, 210–11; Exodus, 267; Joshua, 77; Psalms, 118; Apocrypha, 215; Gospels, 68, 77, 78, 128, 130, 174, 267; Acts, 73, 75; Revelation, 267; mentioned, 284, 294. *See also* Paradise; Paul, Saint
Black, Max, 3, 11, 13, 26, 27
Blake, William, 294
Boccaccio, Giovanni, 187
Bodle, Rhona M., 106n30
Bonhoeffer, Dietrich, 126
Boorstin, Daniel J., 78
Booth, Wayne, 11
Bradley, A. C., 292
Bréal, Michel, 29n1, 38
Brewer, Derek, 221n13, 222
Brooks, Peter, 158n4
Bultmann, Rudolf, 77, 78, 82
Buning, Marius, 7, 282n14
Bunyan, John, 190, 206, 279

Campbell, Jackson J., 30nn4,5
Carnell, Corbin, 153n7, 160n9
Carpenter, Humphrey: on myth and language, 44; on *Out of the Silent Planet*, 55; on Tolkien and Narnia, 171, 227n20; on myth, 285n20; on *eldil*, 293n31
Carroll, Lewis, 294
Cassirer, Ernst, 12
Chesterton, G. K., 83–84, 191, 198
Christopher, Joe R., 95n19, 227n20
Christophersen, Paul, 30n2
Cirlot, J. E., 292
City: as archetype, 209, 210
Clifford, Gay, 278
Cloud of Unknowing, The, 138

Images: power of, 4, 41, 76–85, 96, 106, 135, 256; in Lewis's fiction, 109–10, 127, 166, 187, 220, 233–48, 254, 257, 293; and Lewis's conversion, 110–12; and grief, 137–40

Imagination, 2, 4, 9, 14, 16, 46, 61, 63, 69, 73, 76, 82, 83–85, 99, 127, 157, 170

Incarnation, 3, 4, 65, 69, 70, 73, 76–77, 81–82, 83–85, 105, 107, 123, 206

Jakobson, Roman, 26, 27

James, Henry, 186

Jenkins, Cecil, 184

Johnson, Mark, 11, 24

Johnson, Samuel: compared to Lewis, 86, 213, 224, 229; *Rasselas,* 189, 214, 217, 218–19, 228; "Lines on Thomas Warton's Poems" quoted, 219; mentioned, 71n16

Johnson-Laird, P. N., 32n6

Jonas, Hans, 84–85

Journey, 195–97, 254, 262, 264–68, 272, 295

Joy. *See* Longing

Joyce, James, 75, 120–21, 124

Jung, C. G., 114, 187, 188, 220

Kafka, Franz, 195, 245, 258

Kant, Immanuel, 114, 251

Katzenellenbogen, Adolf, 202n4

Keats, John, 19, 115

Kellogg, Robert, 158–59

Kierkegaard, Søren, 121

Kilby, Clyde S., 159n6

Kirkpatrick, John, 92n14, 107n32

Lactantius, 77–78

Language: Lewis's ideas on, 2, 3, 9, 14–15, 29–41, 80, 97–107, 122; radically metaphorical, 12, 14–16, 24, 38, 45–46, 59, 80, 287; Lewis's categorization of, 19–20, 61, 98–101, 106, 155; primordial, 24, 50, 52, 53–54, 58, 75, 104, 286–87; invented, 42, 49, 50–56, 61, 67–68, 287; as theme in Lewis's poems and stories, 42–57, 58–75, 87, 92–94, 103–7, 286–90; decay of, 43, 45–46, 50, 55, 60, 64–65, 68, 73, 75, 93–94, 102, 105, 289; abuse of, 55–56, 104, 176, 177, 181; as human trait, 103–4, 107; failure of, 104, 106–7, 282; as symbol, 105; and style, 129, 131; native vs. foreign, 131–32; and allegory, 285–86. *See also* Metaphor; Semantics

Lavarenne, P., 202n4

Lawrence, D. H., 121, 184

Leavis, F. R., 184–85, 186

L'Engle, Madeleine, 222

Lewis, Albert, 1

Lewis, C. Day, 96n22

Lewis, C. S.: style, 4, 28, 54–55, 71n16, 115, 129, 131–35, 143, 172, 224, 231, 287–88; medieval influences on, 6, 120, 200, 218, 221, 222, 225, 241; conversion to Christianity, 44, 110–14, 118; and science fiction, 47, 50, 66, 157, 193–94, 214, 219, 222, 226, 256; as satirist, 54–56, 72, 86, 125, 216–17; as apologist, 74, 76–85, 126–27, 171, 199; views of modern poetry, 75, 94–97, 95nn19,20, 96n22, 143–44; desire to be a poet, 86, 157, 166, 190; poetry, prosody and sound in, 87–93, 95n19; on alliterative meter, 90–92; consciousness and persona in, 114–44; on style, 125; marriage, 129, 136, 158; as character in his fiction, 172, 210. *See also* Allegory; Dialectic; Fairy Tale; Fantasy; Images; Language; Longing; Metaphor; Myth; Plato; Romance; Story

—Poetic Works: "The Apologist's Evening Prayer," 104, 107; "The Birth of Language," 60, 73, 74, 89, 105, 106, 107–8; "A Cliché Came Out of Its Cage," 93; "A Confession," 94–97, 101, 103; "The Country of the Blind," 64–65, 71, 93–94, 102; *Dymer,* 86, 95n19, 104, 183, 190, 300–301; "The Ecstasy," 87n4; "Epigram 13," 104; "Footnote to All Prayers," 106; "The Last of the Wine," 93n18; *Launcelot,* 91n10, 92–93; "The Magician and the Dryad," 125; "Le Roi s'Amuse," 89n8, 104; "The Naked Seed," 107n32; *The Nameless Isle,* 86, 91; "Narnian Suite," 89–90; "No Beauty We Could Desire," 106–7; "On the Atomic Bomb," 87–88; "Pan's Purge," 89n8; "Pattern," 87nn4,5; "The Planets," 87, 91, 105n29; "Prayer," 107, 107n32, 142; *The Queen of Drum,* 95n19, 104, 105, 227; "Re-adjustment," 93; "The Saboteuse," 92n14; "The Small Man Orders His Wedding," 89n8; "Solomon," 88; *Spirits in Bondage,* 86n1; "The Turn of the Tide," 89n8; "Two Kinds of Memory," 89; "Vitrea Circe," 87n4; "Vowels and Sirens," 87n4; "Young King Cole," 87n4

—Prose Works:

Abolition of Man, The: and metaphor, 17–18, 60; and objectivity, 22, 102, 118,